2005 SUPPLEMENT

CASES AND MATERIALS

DOMESTIC RELATIONS

FIFTH EDITION

by

WALTER WADLINGTON
James Madison Professor of Law,
University of Virginia School of Law

RAYMOND C. O'BRIEN
Professor of Law
The Catholic University of America

NEW YORK, NEW YORK
FOUNDATION PRESS
2005

D1404258

© 2005 By FOUNDATION PRESS

       395 Hudson Street
       New York, NY 10014
       Phone Toll Free 1–877–888–1330
       Fax (212) 367–6799
       fdpress.com

Printed in the United States of America

SBN 1–58778–789–X

 TEXT IS PRINTED ON 10% POST CONSUMER RECYCLED PAPER

NOTE ON EDITING

   Some citations, footnotes and text have been omitted in order to keep
the materials at manageable size. Footnotes retain the original numbering
when there have been omissions. Citations to secondary authorities and
some "string citations" with brief explanatory notes that have been deleted
may not include indication of their omission. Ellipses, or bracketed explanations containing summaries of omitted material, indicate where other
text has been deleted. In some opinions you may find that specific pages
for a few reporter citations are missing. This reflects the recent nature of
the cases that are included and appeared in the version that was down-
loaded.

*

TABLE OF CONTENTS

V. MARITAL BREAKDOWN: RESOLVING THE FINANCIAL CONCERNS

C. Permanent Alimony and Maintenance

VI. PARENT AND CHILD: LEGAL AND BIOLOGICAL RELATIONSHIPS

B. Establishing Legal Parentage

VII. RAISING CHILDREN: COMPETING INTERESTS OF PARENT, CHILD AND STATE

A. The Interest in Assuring an Education

§ 6910. Parent or guardian may authorize care provider to consent

VIII. VYING FOR CUSTODY

A. Parent Versus Parent

§ 48-9-206. Allocation of custodial responsibility

§ 48-9-207. Allocation of significant decision-making responsibility

F. Problems of Enforcement

IX. PARENTAL RIGHTS TERMINATION AND ADOPTION

A. Severing Parental Rights Involuntarily

§ 383.50. Treatment of abandoned newborn infant

§ 383.51. Confidentiality; identification of parent leaving newborn infant at hospital, emergency medical services station, or fire station

B. Adoption

§ 9000. Petition for adoption; caption; contents; guardianship petition; order of adoption

TABLE OF CASES

Principal cases are in bold type. Non-principal cases are in roman type. References are to Pages.

2005 SUPPLEMENT

DOMESTIC RELATIONS

*

CHAPTER I

CHANGING CONCEPTS OF MARRIAGE AND FAMILY

A. FUNCTION VERSUS FORM IN "FAMILY" RELATIONSHIPS

Add the following opinion at the end of the NOTE *titled* Non–Marital Couples, Landlords and the First Amendment *at page 11.*

Catholic Charities of Sacramento Inc. v. Superior Court

Supreme Court of California, 2004.
32 Cal.4th 527, 10 Cal.Rptr.3d 283, 85 P.3d 67.

■ WERDEGAR, J.

In this case, we address a church-affiliated employer's constitutional challenges to the Women's Contraception Equity Act (WCEA), under which certain health and disability insurance contracts must cover prescription contraceptives. The plaintiff employer, which opposes contraceptives on religious grounds, claims the statute violates the establishment and free exercise clauses of the United States and California Constitutions. (U.S. Const., 1st Amend.; Cal. Const., art. I, § 4.) The lower courts rejected the employer's claims. We affirm. The Legislature enacted the WCEA in 1999 to eliminate gender discrimination in health care benefits and to improve access to prescription contraceptives. Evidence before the Legislature showed that women during their reproductive years spent as much as 68 percent more than men in out-of-pocket health care costs, due in large part to the cost of prescription contraceptives and the various costs of unintended pregnancies, including health risks, premature deliveries and increased neonatal care. Evidence also showed that, while most health maintenance organizations (HMO's) covered prescription contraceptives, not all preferred provider organization (PPO) and indemnity plans did. As a result, approximately 10 percent of commercially insured Californians did not have coverage for prescription contraceptives.

The Legislature chose to address these problems by regulating the terms of insurance contracts. The WCEA does not require any employer to offer coverage for prescription drugs. Under the WCEA, however, certain health and disability insurance plans that cover prescription drugs must cover prescription contraceptives. As an exception, the law permits a "religious employer" to request a policy that includes drug coverage but excludes coverage for "contraceptive methods that are contrary to the religious employer's religious tenets." Health and Safety Code section

1

1367.25 governs group health care service plan contracts;[3] Insurance Code section 10123.196 governs individual and group disability insurance policies.

Plaintiff Catholic Charities of Sacramento, Inc. (hereafter Catholic Charities) is a California nonprofit public benefit corporation. (See Corp.

3. Health and Safety Code section 1367.25 provides:

"(a) Every group health care service plan contract, except for a specialized health care service plan contract, that is issued, amended, renewed, or delivered on or after January 1, 2000, and every individual health care service plan contract that is amended, renewed, or delivered on or after January 1, 2000, except for a specialized health care contract, shall provide coverage for the following, under general terms and conditions applicable to all benefits:

"(1) A health care service plan contract that provides coverage for outpatient prescription drug benefits shall include coverage for a variety of federal Food and Drug Administration approved prescription contraceptive methods designated by the plan. In the event the patient's participating provider, acting within his or her scope of practice, determines that none of the methods designated by the plan is medically appropriate for the patient's medical or personal history, the plan shall also provide coverage for another federal Food and Drug Administration approved, medically appropriate prescription contraceptive method prescribed by the patient's provider.

"(2) Outpatient prescription benefits for an enrollee shall be the same for an enrollee's covered spouse and covered nonspouse dependents.

"(b) Notwithstanding any other provision of this section, a religious employer may request a health care service plan contract without coverage for federal Food and Drug Administration approved contraceptive methods that are contrary to the religious employer's religious tenets. If so requested, a health care service plan contract shall be provided without coverage for contraceptive methods.

"(1) For purposes of this section, a 'religious employer' is an entity for which each of the following is true:

"(A) The inculcation of religious values is the purpose of the entity.

"(B) The entity primarily employs persons who share the religious tenets of the entity.

"(C) The entity serves primarily persons who share the religious tenets of the entity.

"(D) The entity is a nonprofit organization as described in Section 6033(a)(2)(A)i or iii, of the Internal Revenue Code of 1986, as amended.

"(2) Every religious employer that invokes the exemption provided under this section shall provide written notice to prospective enrollees prior to enrollment with the plan, listing the contraceptive health care services the employer refuses to cover for religious reasons.

"(c) Nothing in this section shall be construed to exclude coverage for prescription contraceptive supplies ordered by a health care provider with prescriptive authority for reasons other than contraceptive purposes, such as decreasing the risk of ovarian cancer or eliminating symptoms of menopause, or for prescription contraception that is necessary to preserve the life or health of an enrollee.

"(d) Nothing in this section shall be construed to deny or restrict in any way the [D]epartment [of Managed Care's] authority to ensure plan compliance with this chapter when a plan provides coverage for prescription drugs. "(e) Nothing in this section shall be construed to require an individual or group health care services plan to cover experimental or investigational treatments."

Code, § 5110 et seq.) Although independently incorporated, Catholic Charities describes itself as "operated in connection with the Roman Catholic
Bishop of Sacramento" and as "an organ of the Roman Catholic Church."
The nonprofit corporation "offer[s] a multitude of social services and
private welfare programs to the general public, as part of the social justice
ministry of the Roman Catholic Church." These services and programs
include "providing immigrant resettlement programs, elder care, counseling, food, clothing and affordable housing for the poor and needy, housing
and vocational training of the developmentally disabled and the like."

Catholic Charities offers health insurance, including prescription drug
coverage, to its 183 full-time employees through group health care plans
underwritten by Blue Shield of California and Kaiser Permanente. Catholic
Charities does not, however, offer insurance for prescription contraceptives
because it considers itself obliged to follow the Roman Catholic Church's
religious teachings, because the Church considers contraception a sin, and
because Catholic Charities believes it cannot offer insurance for prescription contraceptives without improperly facilitating that sin.

As mentioned, the WCEA permits a "religious employer" to offer
prescription drug insurance without coverage for contraceptives that violate the employer's religious tenets. (Health & Saf.Code, § 1367.25, subd.
(b).) The act defines a "religious employer" as "an entity for which each of
the following is true: [¶] (A) The inculcation of religious values is the
purpose of the entity. [¶] (B) The entity primarily employs persons who
share the religious tenets of the entity. [¶] (C) The entity serves primarily
persons who share the religious tenets of the entity. [¶] (D) The entity is a
nonprofit organization as described in Section 6033(a)(2)(A)(I) or iii, of the
Internal Revenue Code of 1986, as amended." (*Ibid.*) The cited provisions
of the Internal Revenue Code exempt, from the obligation to file an annual
return, "churches, their integrated auxiliaries, and conventions or associa-
tions of churches" (26 U.S.C. § 6033(a)(2)(A)(I)) and "the exclusively
religious activities of any religious order" (*id.,* § 6033(a)(2)(A)(I) and (iii)).

Catholic Charities does not qualify as a "religious employer" under the
WCEA because it does not meet any of the definition's four criteria. (See
Health & Saf.Code, § 1367.25, subd. (b)(1)(A)–(D).) The organization candidly acknowledges this in its complaint, offering the following explanation:
"The corporate purpose of Catholic Charities is not the direct inculcation of
religious values. Rather, [its] purpose ... is to offer social services to the
general public that promote a just, compassionate society that supports the
dignity of individuals and families, to reduce the causes and results of
poverty, and to build healthy communities through social service programs
such as counseling, mental health and immigration services, low-income
housing, and supportive social services to the poor and vulnerable. Further,
Catholic Charities does not primarily employ persons who share its Roman
Catholic religious beliefs, but, rather, employs a diverse group of persons of
many religious backgrounds, all of whom share [its] Gospel-based commitment to promote a just, compassionate society that supports the dignity of
individuals and families. Moreover, Catholic Charities serves people of all

[handwritten margin note: Criteria to qualify as religious]

faith backgrounds, a significant majority of [whom] do not share [its] Roman Catholic faith. Finally, ... Catholic Charities, although an exempt organization under 26 U.S.C. § 501(c)(3), is not a nonprofit organization pursuant to [s]ection 6033(a)(2)(A)(I) or (iii) of the Internal Revenue Code of 1986. Consequently, ... Catholic Charities is not entitled ... to an exemption from the mandate imposed by [the WCEA]."

As mentioned, the WCEA implicitly permits any employer to avoid covering contraceptives by not offering coverage for prescription drugs. But this option, according to Catholic Charities, does not eliminate all conflict between the law and its religious beliefs. Catholic Charities feels obliged to offer prescription drug insurance to its employees under what it describes as the "Roman Catholic religious teaching" that "an employer has a moral obligation at all times to consider the well-being of its employees and to offer just wages and benefits in order to provide a dignified livelihood for the employee and his or her family."

Perceiving no option consistent with both its beliefs and the law, Catholic Charities filed this action seeking a declaratory judgment that the WCEA is unconstitutional and an injunction barring the law's enforcement. Defendants are the State of California, the Department of Managed Health Care and the Department of Insurance. Catholic Charities' challenges to the WCEA arise under the establishment and free exercise clauses of the United States and California Constitutions. (U.S. Const., 1st Amend.; Cal. Const., art. I, § 4.) The superior court, finding no reasonable likelihood that Catholic Charities would prevail on the merits, denied its motion for a preliminary injunction. Catholic Charities sought review of this ruling by petition for writ of mandate, which the Court of Appeal denied. We granted review of the Court of Appeal's decision.

Catholic Charities, in its brief to this court, asserts eight constitutional challenges to the WCEA. All refer to the religion clauses of the federal and state Constitutions. (U.S. Const., 1st Amend.; Cal. Const., art. I, § 4.) Catholic Charities begins with a set of three arguments to the effect that the WCEA impermissibly interferes with the autonomy of religious organizations. (See 10 Cal.Rptr.3d p. 294, 85 P.3d p. 76 et seq., *post.*) Next, Catholic Charities claims the WCEA impermissibly burdens its right of free exercise. As part of this claim, Catholic Charities offers four arguments for subjecting the WCEA to strict scrutiny, despite the United States Supreme Court's holding that the right of free exercise does not excuse compliance with neutral, generally applicable laws. (*Employment Div., Ore. Dept. of Human Res. v. Smith* (1990) 494 U.S. 872, 876–890, 110 S.Ct. 1595, 108 L.Ed.2d 876; see 10 Cal.Rptr.3d p. 299, 85 P.3d p. 81 et seq., *post.*) Finally, Catholic Charities contends the WCEA fails even the rational basis test. (See p. 315, 85 P.3d p. 94 et seq., *post.*)

A. Religious Autonomy

1. Interference with matters of religious doctrine and internal church governance

  ... Catholic Charities asserts that the Legislature, in enacting the WCEA, violated the rule of church property cases by interfering with matters of internal church governance and by rejecting the Catholic Church's decision that prescription contraceptives are sinful. These assertions are incorrect. This case does not implicate internal church governance; it implicates the relationship between a nonprofit public benefit corporation and its employees, most of whom do not belong to the Catholic Church. Only those who join a church impliedly consent to its religious governance on matters of faith and discipline. (*Watson, supra,* 13 Wall. 679, 80 U.S. 679, 729.) Certainly the WCEA conflicts with Catholic Charities' religious beliefs, but this does not mean the Legislature has decided a religious question. Congress has created, and the high court has resolved, similar conflicts between employment law and religious beliefs without deciding religious questions and without reference to the church property cases. (E.g., *Tony and Susan Alamo Foundation v. Sec'y of Labor* (1985) 471 U.S. 290, 303–306, 105 S.Ct. 1953, 85 L.Ed.2d 278 [religious organization must comply with federal minimum wage laws]; *United States v. Lee* (1982) 455 U.S. 252, 256–261, 102 S.Ct. 1051, 71 L.Ed.2d 127 [Amish employer must pay Social Security and unemployment taxes].) Neither does this case require us to decide any religious questions. Instead, we need only apply the usual rules for assessing whether state-imposed burdens on religious exercise are constitutional. (See *Church of Lukumi Babalu Aye, Inc. v. Hialeah* (1993) 508 U.S. 520, 531–533, 113 S.Ct. 2217, 124 L.Ed.2d 472; *Employment Div., Ore. Dept. of Human Res. v. Smith, supra,* 494 U.S. 872, 876–882, 110 S.Ct. 1595.) This we do below, in the context of Catholic Charities' separate claims under the free exercise clause. (See 10 Cal. Rptr.3d p. 299, 85 P.3d p. 81 et seq., *post.*)

. . .

2. Distinction between religious and secular activities

    Catholic Charities next argues that the First Amendment forbids the government to "premis[e] a religious institution's eligibility for an exemption from government regulation upon whether the activities of the institution are deemed by the government to be 'religious' or 'secular'...." The argument is directed against the four statutory criteria an employer must satisfy to claim exemption from the WCEA as a "religious employer." (Health & Saf.code, § 1367.25, subd. (b)(1)(A)–(D); see 10 Cal.Rptr.3d p. 292, 85 P.3d p. 75, *ante.*) The argument lacks merit.

    The exception to the WCEA accommodates religious exercise by relieving statutorily defined "religious employers" (Health & Saf.Code, § 1367.25, subd. (b)) of the burden of paying for contraceptive methods that violate their religious beliefs. The United States Supreme Court has long recognized that the alleviation of significant governmentally created burdens on religious exercise is a permissible legislative purpose that does not offend the establishment clause. (*Corporation of Presiding Bishop v. Amos* (1978) 483 U.S. 327, 334–335, 107 S.Ct. 2862, 97 L.Ed.2d 273; *Hobbie v. Unemployment Appeals Comm'n of Fla.* (1987) 480 U.S. 136, 144–145, 107 S.Ct. 1046, 94 L.Ed.2d 190; cf. *Employment Div., Ore. Dept. of Human Res. v. Smith, supra,* 494 U.S. 872, 890, 110 S.Ct. 1595.) Such legislative accommodations would be impossible as a practical matter if the government were, as Catholic Charities argues, forbidden to distinguish between the religious entities and activities that are entitled to accommodation and the secular entities and activities that are not. In fact, Congress and the state legislatures have drawn such distinctions for this purpose, and laws embodying such distinctions have passed constitutional muster. (E.g., *Corporation of Presiding Bishop v. Amos, supra,* 483 U.S. 327, 334–340, 107 S.Ct. 2862 [upholding statutory exemption of "religious" employers from liability for religious discrimination; 42 U.S.C. § 2000e–1(a)]; *East Bay Asian Local Development Corp. v. State of California* (2000) 24 Cal.4th 693, 704–718, 102 Cal.Rptr.2d 280, 13 P.3d 1122 [upholding state laws exempting "religiously affiliated" organizations from landmark preservation laws, Gov.Code, §§ 25373, subds. (c) & (d), 37361, subd. (c)].)

. . .

Our conclusion that the government may properly distinguish between secular and religious entities and activities for the purpose of accommodating religious exercise does not mean that any given statute purporting to draw such distinctions necessarily passes muster under the free exercise clause. "[A] law targeting religious beliefs as such is never permissible," and a court " 'must survey meticulously the circumstances of governmental categories to eliminate, as it were, religious gerrymanders.' " (*Church of Lukumi Babalu Aye, Inc. v. Hialeah, supra,* 508 U.S. 520, 533–534, 113 S.Ct. 2217, quoting *Walz v. Tax Commission* (1970) 397 U.S. 664, 696, 90 S.Ct. 1409, 25 L.Ed.2d 697 (conc. opn. of Harlan, J.).) We address below Catholic Charities' separate argument that the WCEA's definition of "religious employer" in fact embodies a legislative effort to target Catholic organizations for unfavorable treatment. (See 10 Cal.Rptr.3d p. 303, 85 P.3d p. 84 et seq., *post.*)

3.   Excessive entanglement

Catholic Charities contends that the WCEA's exemption for "religious employer[s]" (Health & Saf.Code, § 1367.25, subd. (b)) violates the establishment clause by mandating an entangling inquiry into the employer's religious purpose and into its employees' and clients' religious beliefs. The argument refers to the first three of the four statutory criteria for identifying a "religious employer," namely, whether "[t]he inculcation of religious values is the purpose of the entity" (*id.,* subd. (b)(1)(A)), whether "[t]he entity primarily employs persons who share the religious tenets of the entity" (*id.,* subd. (b)(1)(B)), and whether "[t]he entity serves primarily persons who share the religious tenets of the entity" (*id.,* subd. (b)(1)(C)). A law that fosters an excessive governmental entanglement with religion can for that reason violate the establishment clause. (*Lemon v. Kurtzman* (1971) 403 U.S. 602, 612–613, 91 S.Ct. 2105, 29 L.Ed.2d 745.)[6] Moreover,

6. The court in *Lemon v. Kurtzman, supra,* 403 U.S. 602, 91 S.Ct. 2105, 29 L.Ed.2d 745, "gleaned from [its prior] cases" three tests for determining whether a statute violates the establishment clause: "First, the statute must have a secular legislative purpose; second its principal or primary effect must be one that neither advances nor inhi-

recent judicial opinions have criticized rules and laws that invite official "trolling through a person's or institution's religious beliefs." (*Mitchell v. Helms* (2000) 530 U.S. 793, 828, 120 S.Ct. 2530, 147 L.Ed.2d 660 (plur. opn. of Thomas, J.); *University of Great Falls v. N.L.R.B.* (D.C.Cir.2002) 278 F.3d 1335, 1342–1348.)

The argument might have merit as applied to a hypothetical employer that sought to qualify under the WCEA's exemption for religious employers (Health & Saf.Code, § 1367.25, subd. (b)) but objected on establishment clause grounds to an entangling official effort to verify that its purpose was the inculcation of religious values, and that it primarily employed and served persons who shared its religious tenets. But Catholic Charities candidly alleges in its complaint that it does not qualify under the exemption because it does not satisfy any of the four criteria. More specifically, Catholic Charities concedes that its purpose is not the inculcation of religious values, that it does not primarily hire and serve Catholics, and that it does not fall within either of the relevant provisions of the Internal Revenue Code (26 U.S.C. § 6033(a)(2)(A)(I) and (iii), cited in Health & Saf.Code, § 1367.25, subd. (b)(1)(D)). Consequently, no entangling inquiry into Catholic Charities' purpose or beliefs, or the beliefs of its employees and clients, has occurred or is likely to occur. Therefore, even if in some other case the statute might require an entangling inquiry, in this case, as applied to Catholic Charities, the establishment clause offers no basis for holding the statute unconstitutional.

B. Free Exercise of Religion

Catholic Charities argues the WCEA violates the free exercise clauses of the federal and state Constitutions (U.S. Const., 1st Amend.; Cal. Const., art. I, § 4) by coercing the organization to violate its religious beliefs, in that the WCEA, by regulating the content of insurance policies, in effect requires employers who offer their workers insurance for prescription drugs to offer coverage for prescription contraceptives. Catholic Charities wishes to offer insurance, but may not facilitate the use of contraceptives without violating its religious beliefs.

. . .

The general rule affirmed in *Smith, supra,* 494 U.S. 872, 110 S.Ct. 1595, would at first glance appear to dispose of Catholic Charities' free exercise claim. The WCEA's requirements apply neutrally and generally to all employers, regardless of religious affiliation, except to those few who satisfy the statute's strict requirements for exemption on religious grounds. (Health & Saf.Code, § 1367.25, subd. (b).) The act also addresses a matter the state is free to regulate; it regulates the content of insurance policies for the purpose of eliminating a form of gender discrimination in health benefits. The act conflicts with Catholic Charities' religious beliefs only

---

bits religion . . .; finally, the statute must not foster 'an excessive governmental entanglement with religion.' " (*Id.,* at pp. 612–613, 91 S.Ct. 2105, quoting *Walz v. Tax Commission, supra,* 397 U.S. 664, 674, 90 S.Ct. 1409.)

incidentally, because those beliefs happen to make prescription contraceptives sinful. Accordingly, it appears Catholic Charities may successfully challenge the WCEA only by demonstrating an exception to the general rule.

. . .

2. Religious gerrymander

Our analysis does not end with the conclusion that the WCEA is facially neutral towards religion. The First Amendment requires more than facial neutrality. It protects against " 'subtle departures from neutrality' " and "governmental hostility which is masked as well as overt." (*Lukumi, supra,* 508 U.S. 520, 534, 113 S.Ct. 2217, quoting *Gillette v. United States, supra,* 401 U.S. 437, 452, 91 S.Ct. 828.) Thus, a court " 'must survey meticulously the circumstances of governmental categories to eliminate, as it were, religious gerrymanders.' " (*Ibid.,* quoting *Walz v. Tax Commission, supra,* 397 U.S. 664, 696, 90 S.Ct. 1409 (conc. opn. of Harlan, J.).) Catholic Charities argues the Legislature gerrymandered the WCEA to deny the benefit of the exemption to Catholic organizations. The law discriminates, Catholic Charities contends, both against the Catholic Church and against religious organizations of any denomination that engage in charitable work, as opposed to work that is purely spiritual or evangelical.

We find no merit in the argument that the WCEA discriminates against the Catholic Church. It was at the request of Catholic organizations that the Legislature added an exception permitting religious employers to deny coverage for "contraceptive methods that are contrary to the religious employer's religious tenets." (Health & Saf.Code, § 1367.25, subd. (b).) Because most religions do not object to prescription contraceptives, most religious employers are subject to the WCEA. The Legislature's decision to grant preferential treatment to religious employers who do object is justifiable as an accommodation of religious exercise under the principles discussed above. (*Amos, supra,* 483 U.S. 327, 334–335, 107 S.Ct. 2862.) That the exemption is not sufficiently broad to cover all organizations affiliated with the Catholic Church does not mean the exemption discriminates against the Catholic Church.[9]

. . .

---

9. Indeed, rather than discriminating against the Catholic Church, the WCEA can more plausibly be viewed as benefiting the Catholic Church in practical effect, since no other religious group opposed to prescription contraceptives has been identified. But the WCEA does not for this reason violate the establishment clause. A law intended not to discriminate among religions but to alleviate a governmentally created burden on religious exercise does not necessarily violate the establishment clause, even though only a single religion in need of accommodation has been identified, if the law is phrased neutrally, to allow for the possibility that other as-yet-unidentified religions in need of the same accommodation will be able to claim it. (See, e.g., *Kong v. Scully* (9th Cir.2003) 341 F.3d 1132; *Children's Health. Is A Legal Duty v. Min De Parle* (8th Cir.2000) 212 F.3d 1084; *Droz v. Commissioner of I.R.S.* (9th Cir.1995) 48 F.3d 1120.)

Catholic Charities' intent may be to argue that the WCEA discriminates against charitable social work *as a religious practice*. Such an argument would implicate "[t]he principle that government, in pursuit of legitimate interests, cannot in a selective manner impose burdens only on conduct motivated by religious belief. . . ." (*Lukumi, supra,* 508 U.S. 520, 543, 113 S.Ct. 2217.) Applying this principle, the high court in *Lukumi* held unconstitutional an ordinance that permitted the killing of animals for food or sport, but not in religious rituals. The ordinance had " 'every appearance of a prohibition that society is prepared to impose upon [Santeria worshippers] but not upon itself.' " (*Id.,* at p. 545, 113 S.Ct. 2217, quoting *The Florida Star v. B.J.F.* (1989) 491 U.S. 524, 542, 109 S.Ct. 2603, 105 L.Ed.2d 443.) The WCEA is not similar. If a religiously affiliated organization fails to qualify for exemption because its purpose is something other than the "inculcation of religious values" (Health & Saf.Code, § 1367. 25, subd. (b)(1)(A)), then the result is simply that the organization becomes subject to the same obligations that apply to all other employers. Because the WCEA applies to all nonreligious employers engaged in charitable social work, no argument can logically be made that the WCEA imposes a burden on charitable social work only when performed for religious reasons.

As additional support for its claim that the WCEA's purpose is to discriminate against the Catholic Church, Catholic Charities contends the Legislature drafted the "religious employer" exception (Health & Saf.Code, § 1367.25, subd. (b)) with the specific intention of excluding Catholic hospitals and social service agencies like Catholic Charities. Catholic Charities draws an analogy to *Lukumi, supra,* 508 U.S. 520, 540–542, 113 S.Ct. 2217, in which the high court considered specific statements by members of the Hialeah City Council as evidence that the ordinance prohibiting animal sacrifice was intended to suppress the Santeria religion. Catholic Charities' assertions about the legislative history of the WCEA do not justify a similar conclusion in this case.

According to Catholic Charities, the history of the WCEA suggests the Legislature intended the law to close a "Catholic gap" in insurance coverage for prescription contraceptives. The evidence does not support the contention. The phrase "Catholic gap" appears only in Catholic Charities' brief, not in the legislative history. Catholic Charities refers to the Senate testimony of a representative of Planned Parenthood, which opposed any exception for religious employers. Explaining that organization's position, the witness stated: "Primarily our intent was to close the gap in insurance coverage for contraception and prescription benefit plans. Our concern with granting an exemption is that that defeats the original purpose of the bill." The "gap" to which the witness apparently referred was the gap identified by a national consulting firm's 1999 study of health insurance for prescription contraceptives. This study, which received much attention in the Legislature, concluded that approximately 10 percent of commercially insured Californians did not already have insurance coverage for prescription contraceptives. The study identified this minority not as the employees of Catholic organizations, but as persons covered by PPO and indemnity plans. While most HMO's covered prescription contraceptives, not all PPO and indemnity plans did. Catholic Charities' assertion that the purpose of the WCEA was to close a "Catholic gap" rather than a statewide statistical gap in coverage has no apparent evidentiary support.[11]

Next, Catholic Charities argues the Legislature deliberately narrowed the statutory exception for "religious employer[s]" (Health & Saf.Code, § 1367.25, subd. (b)) to include as few Catholic organizations as possible and specifically to exclude Catholic hospitals and social service organizations. The legislative history does show that the bill's sponsors argued against a broader exception. The bill's Senate sponsor, for example, stated in a committee hearing that "the intention of the authors as it relates to creating a religious exemption may not be the same intentions of the religions themselves in wanting to be exempted. [¶] The intention of the religious exemption in both these bills is an intention to provide for exemption for what is religious activity. The more secular the activity gets, the less religiously based it is, and the more we believe that they should be required to cover prescription drug benefits for contraception." Catholic Charities describes this and similar statements as evidence that the Legislature targeted specific Catholic organizations for disadvantageous treatment. But we have already examined and rejected that argument. The law treats some Catholic organizations more favorably than all other employers by exempting them; nonexempt Catholic organizations are treated the same as all other employers.

. . .

4. California Constitution

Catholic Charities' final argument for applying strict scrutiny invokes the free exercise clause of the California Constitution. (Cal. Const., art. I, § 4.)[16] That clause, Catholic Charities contends, forbids the state to burden the practice of religion, even incidentally, through a neutral, generally applicable law, unless the law in question serves a compelling governmental interest and is narrowly tailored to achieve that interest. Catholic Charities asserts, in other words, that we must interpret the California Constitution the same way the United States Supreme Court interpreted the federal Constitution's free exercise clause in *Sherbert v. Ve[rner], supra,* 374 U.S. 398, 83 S.Ct. 1790.

---

11. Catholic Charities also argues that the Legislature acted out of antipathy and spite towards the Catholic Church. Through this argument, Catholic Charities seeks to compare the Legislature's consideration of the WCEA with the Hialeah City Council's decision (see *Lukumi, supra,* 508 U.S. 520, 113 S.Ct. 2217) to ban animal sacrifice as a way of suppressing the Santeria religion. In discussing the council's decision, the high court noted that Hialeah city officials had castigated Santeria as an "abomination to the Lord" and "the worship of demons," and

that a public crowd attending the city council's meeting had interrupted with jeers and taunts the President of the Santeria Church. (*Id.,* at p. 541, 113 S.Ct. 2217.) The legislative history of the WCEA discloses no comparable antipathy to the Catholic Church.

16. "Free exercise and enjoyment of religion without discrimination or preference are guaranteed. This liberty of conscience does not excuse acts that are licentious or inconsistent with the peace or safety of the State...." (Cal Const., art. I, § 4.)

What might be the proper standard of review for challenges to neutral, generally applicable laws under the state Constitution's free exercise clause is a question we left open in *Smith v. Fair Employment & Housing Com.* (1996) 12 Cal.4th 1143, 1177–1179, 51 Cal.Rptr.2d 700, 913 P.2d 909 (*Smith v. FEHC*). There we rejected, under both federal and state law, a landlord's religiously based claim to exemption from a fair housing statute prohibiting discrimination on the basis of marital status. (Gov.Code, § 12955, subd. (a).) Although the case arose after the high court's decision in *Smith, supra,* 494 U.S. 872, 110 S.Ct. 1595, we nevertheless applied strict scrutiny to the landlord's federal claim because the Religious Freedom Restoration Act required us to do so. (42 U.S.C. § 2000bb et seq., hereafter RFRA; see *Smith v. FEHC,* at pp. 1165–1167, 51 Cal.Rptr.2d 700, 913 P.2d 909.) We did not decide whether the landlord's claim under the state Constitution's free exercise clause required strict scrutiny. A plurality of three justices assumed for the sake of argument that it did, but declined to "address the scope and proper interpretation of California Constitution, article I, section 4." (*Smith v. FEHC,* at p. 1179, 51 Cal.Rptr.2d 700, 913 P.2d 909 (plur. opn. of Werdegar, J., George and Arabian, JJ., conc.).) "These important questions," the plurality wrote, "should await a case in which their resolution affects the outcome." (*Ibid.*) Justice Mosk's concurring opinion provided a fourth vote for the disposition. (*Id.,* at pp. 1179–1192, 51 Cal.Rptr.2d 700, 913 P.2d 909 (conc. opn. of Mosk, J.).)

No decision about the appropriate standard of review can be gleaned from the various separate opinions in *Smith v. FEHC, supra,* 12 Cal.4th 1143, 51 Cal.Rptr.2d 700, 913 P.2d 909. The subject of Justice Mosk's concurring opinion was his view that RFRA was unconstitutional; he did not address the state Constitution. (*Smith v. FEHC,* at pp. 1179–1192, 51 Cal.Rptr.2d 700, 913 P.2d 909 (conc. opn. of Mosk, J.).) Justice Kennard, who also wrote separately, would have held that the challenged law violated RFRA; she, too, did not address the state Constitution. (*Id.,* at pp. 1192–1218, 51 Cal.Rptr.2d 700, 913 P.2d 909 (conc. & dis. opn. of Kennard, J.).) Justice Baxter, who otherwise agreed with Justice Kennard, wrote separately to emphasize the point we now make, namely, that the court's various opinions left unsettled "the scope of protection of religious liberty under the free exercise clause of our state Constitution." (*Id.,* at p. 1250, 51 Cal.Rptr.2d 700, 913 P.2d 909 (conc. & dis. opn. of Baxter, J., with Lucas, C.J., conc.).)

The only published decision purporting to determine the standard of review for claims under the California Constitution's free exercise clause is *Brunson v. Department of Motor Vehicles* (1999) 72 Cal.App.4th 1251, 85 Cal.Rptr.2d 710. The Court of Appeal in *Brunson* rejected the contention that the plaintiffs' religious beliefs excused them from complying with a statutory duty (Veh.Code, §§ 1653.5, 12800, subd. (a)) to provide their Social Security numbers to the Department of Motor Vehicles when applying for drivers' licenses. The court interpreted *Smith v. FEHC, supra,* 12 Cal.4th 1143, 51 Cal.Rptr.2d 700, 913 P.2d 909, as mandating application of the rational basis test to the petitioners' claims under the state free exercise clause. (*Brunson v. Department of Motor Vehicles, supra,* at pp.

1255–1256, 85 Cal.Rptr.2d 710.) The court's reading of *Smith v. FEHC* was erroneous. As we have just explained, in *Smith v. FEHC* we left the question open. The Court of Appeal in the case before us, while acknowledging *Brunson,* examined the question independently and concluded that challenges under the state free exercise clause to neutral, generally applicable laws should be evaluated under the rational basis standard of *Smith, supra,* 494 U.S. 872, 110 S.Ct. 1595.

Certainly the high court's decision in *Smith, supra,* 494 U.S. 872, 110 S.Ct. 1595, does not control our interpretation of the state Constitution's free exercise clause. Neither does the decision in *Sherbert, supra,* 374 U.S. 398, 83 S.Ct. 1790. We have observed many times "that the meaning of the California Constitution article I, section 4 . . . is not dependent on the meaning of any provision of the federal Constitution. The state charter declares in so many words that '[r]ights guaranteed by this Constitution are not dependent on those guaranteed by the United States Constitution.' (Cal. Const., art. I, § 24.) 'Respect for our Constitution as 'a document of independent force' [citation] forbids us to abandon settled applications of its terms every time changes are announced in the interpretation of the federal charter.' " (*Smith v. FEHC, supra,* 12 Cal.4th 1143, 1177, 51 Cal.Rptr.2d 700, 913 P.2d 909, quoting *People v. Pettingill* (1978) 21 Cal.3d 231, 248, 145 Cal.Rptr. 861, 578 P.2d 108, and *People v. Brisendine* (1975) 13 Cal.3d 528, 549–550, 119 Cal.Rptr. 315, 531 P.2d 1099.) Thus, if a settled interpretation of the California Constitution's free exercise clause had existed before 1990, when the United States Supreme Court abandoned the *Sherbert* test, we would simply adhere to that interpretation, regardless of *Smith, supra,* 494 U.S. 872, 110 S.Ct. 1595.

However, no settled interpretation of the state Constitution's free exercise clause existed in 1990. Between the dates of *Sherbert [v. Verner], supra,* 374 U.S. 398, 83 S.Ct. 1790, and *Smith, supra,* 494 U.S. 872, 110 S.Ct. 1595, our own decisions assessing the constitutionality of neutral, generally applicable laws that incidentally burdened religious practices applied the federal and state free exercise clauses interchangeably, without ascribing any independent meaning to the state clause. (*Walker v. Superior Court* (1988) 47 Cal.3d 112, 138–141, 253 Cal.Rptr. 1, 763 P.2d 852; *Molko v. Holy Spirit Assn.* (1988) 46 Cal.3d 1092, 1112–1120, 252 Cal.Rptr. 122, 762 P.2d 46; In re Arias (1986) 42 Cal.3d 667, 692 & fn. 28, 230 Cal.Rptr. 505, 725 P.2d 664; *People v. Woody* (1964) 61 Cal.2d 716, 718, fn. 1, 40 Cal.Rptr. 69, 394 P.2d 813.) In decisions prior to *Sherbert,* we generally took an approach similar to the high court's decisions of the same era, declining to exempt religiously motivated conduct from neutral, generally applicable laws. We wrote, for example, that "a person is free to hold whatever belief his conscience dictates, but when he translates his belief into action he may be required to conform to reasonable regulations which are applicable to all persons and are designed to accomplish a permissible objective." (*Rescue Army v. Municipal Court* (1946) 28 Cal.2d 460, 470, 171 P.2d 8.) We also wrote that, "[i]f the applicability of government regulation turned on the religious motivation of activities, plausible motivations would multiply and in the end vitiate any regulation." (*Gospel Army v. City of Los*

Angeles (1945) 27 Cal.2d 232, 243, 163 P.2d 704; see also *Gabrielli v. Knickerbocker* (1938) 12 Cal.2d 85, 90–92, 82 P.2d 391 [declining to reinstate a pupil expelled from public school for refusing on religious grounds to salute the flag]; Ex parte Andrews (1861) 18 Cal. 678, 683–685, 1861 WL 941 [upholding a Sunday closing law].)

In view of this history, we may safely agree with the scholars who concluded in 1993, years after the high court decided *Smith, supra,* 494 U.S. 872, 110 S.Ct. 1595, that "[s]ection 4 has not so far played an independent role in free exercise claims." (Grodin et al., The Cal. State Constitution: A Reference Guide (1993) p. 44.)

In a case that truly required us to do so, we should not hesitate to exercise our responsibility and final authority to declare the scope and proper interpretation of the California Constitution's free exercise clause. (Cal. Const., art. I, § 4.) Here, however, we need not do so because Catholic Charities' challenge to the WCEA fails in any event. As we explain below, the statute passes strict scrutiny. A future case might lead us to choose the rule of *Sherbert, supra,* 374 U.S. 398, 83 S.Ct. 1790, the rule of *Smith, supra,* 494 U.S. 872, 110 S.Ct. 1595, or an as-yet unidentified rule that more precisely reflects the language and history of the California Constitution and our own understanding of its import. But "[t]hese important questions should await a case in which their resolution affects the outcome." (*Smith v. FEHC, supra,* 12 Cal.4th 1143, 1179, 51 Cal.Rptr.2d 700, 913 P.2d 909.)

We therefore review Catholic Charities' challenge to the WCEA under the free exercise clause of the California Constitution in the same way we might have reviewed a similar challenge under the federal Constitution after *Sherbert, supra,* 374 U.S. 398, 83 S.Ct. 1790, and before *Smith, supra,* 494 U.S. 872, 110 S.Ct. 1595. In other words, we apply strict scrutiny. Under that standard, a law could not be applied in a manner that substantially burdened a religious belief or practice unless the state showed that the law represented the least restrictive means of achieving a compelling interest or, in other words, was narrowly tailored. (See *Thomas v. Review Bd., Ind. Empl. Sec. Div.* (1981) 450 U.S. 707, 718, 101 S.Ct. 1425, 67 L.Ed.2d 624; *Sherbert, supra,* 374 U.S. 398, 403, 406, 407–408, 83 S.Ct. 1790.) For these purposes, a law substantially burdens a religious belief if it "conditions receipt of an important benefit upon conduct proscribed by a religious faith, or where it denies such a benefit because of conduct mandated by religious belief, thereby putting substantial pressure on an adherent to modify his behavior and to violate his beliefs...." (*Thomas v. Rev. Bd., Ind. Empl. Sec. Div., supra,* 450 U.S. 707, 717–718, 101 S.Ct. 1425.)

Applying this standard, we consider first whether the WCEA in fact burdens Catholic Charities' religious beliefs. We do not doubt Catholic Charities' assertion that to offer insurance coverage for prescription contraceptives to its employees would be religiously unacceptable. Catholic Charities adequately supports the assertion with the declaration of a Roman Catholic priest who serves as Executive Director of the Secretariat for

Doctrine and Pastoral Practices of the National Conference of Roman Catholic Bishops. Catholic Charities may, however, avoid this conflict with its religious beliefs simply by not offering coverage for prescription drugs. The WCEA applies only to employers who choose to offer insurance coverage for prescription drugs; it does not require any employer to offer such coverage.

. . . Congress and the courts have been sensitive to the needs flowing from the Free Exercise Clause, but every person cannot be shielded from all the burdens incident to exercising every aspect of the right to practice religious beliefs. When followers of a particular sect enter into commercial activity as a matter of choice, the limits they accept on their own conduct as a matter of conscience and faith are not to be superimposed on the statutory schemes which are binding on others in that activity. (*Ibid.;* cf. *Tony and Susan Alamo Foundation v. Sec'y of Labor, supra,* 471 U.S. 290, 303–306, 105 S.Ct. 1953 [religious organization must comply with federal minimum wage laws]; *Dole v. Shenandoah Baptist Church* (4th Cir.1990) 899 F.2d 1389, 1393–1400 [religious school must comply with federal law requiring equal pay for men and women].) We see no reason why a different rule should apply when a nonprofit corporation enters the general labor market.

Nor are any less restrictive (or more narrowly tailored) means readily available for achieving the state's interest in eliminating gender discrimination. Any broader exemption increases the number of women affected by discrimination in the provision of health care benefits. Catholic Charities argues the Legislature could more widely exempt employers from the WCEA without increasing the number of affected women by mandating public funding of prescription contraceptives for the employees of exempted employers. The Legislature included such a provision in an earlier version of the WCEA (Assem. Bill No. 1112 (1997–1998 Reg. Sess.)), which the Governor vetoed. But Catholic Charities points to no authority requiring the state to subsidize private religious practices. (Cf. *Lyng v. Northwest Indian Cemetery Prot. Assn., supra,* 485 U.S. 439, 447–453, 108 S.Ct. 1319 [government need not forgo road building or timber harvesting on its own property to avoid interference with Native American religious practices].)

Catholic Charities next argues the WCEA is underinclusive, and therefore not narrowly tailored, because it does not facilitate access to prescription contraceptives for "indigent women, unemployed women, stay-at-home mothers, women whose employers do not offer health insurance benefits, and women in part-time employment [who] do not qualify for health benefits." But this argument misconceives the principal purpose of the WCEA, which is not to facilitate access to contraceptives but to eliminate a form of gender discrimination in the provision of health benefits. The situations Catholic Charities identifies, in which no employer or insurer is providing health benefits, do not entail such discrimination.

Finally on this point, Catholic Charities argues the WCEA is not narrowly tailored because it is *overinclusive.* Catholic Charities justifies this surprising assertion by arguing that the law must be overinclusive if it applies to employers that do not discriminate on the basis of gender, and that Catholic Charities does not discriminate on that basis because it does not provide contraceptive coverage to women or to men (e.g., vasectomies). With this argument, however, Catholic Charities merely restates its disagreement with the Legislature's determination that the exclusion of prescription contraceptives from health care plans constitutes a form of gender discrimination. As we have already explained, the Legislature was entitled to reach that conclusion.

For these reasons, applying the strict scrutiny test of *Sherbert, supra,* 374 U.S. 398, 83 S.Ct. 1790, to Catholic Charities' claim against the WCEA under the free exercise clause of the state Constitution, we find the WCEA meets that test. We do not hold that the state free exercise clause requires courts to apply the *Sherbert* test to neutral, generally applicable laws that incidentally burden religious practice. Instead, as explained above, we leave that question for another day.

C. Rational Basis

Catholic Charities' final challenge to the WCEA is that it violates the rational basis test. More specifically, Catholic Charities argues the State has defined the exempt category of "religious employer" (Health & Saf. Code, § 1367.25, subd. (b)) with arbitrary criteria. "In effect," according to Catholic Charities, "the Legislature decided that any religious institution that employs individuals of other faiths or that ministers to persons of all faiths (or no faith)—in effect any 'missionary' church or church with social outreach—is not sufficiently 'religious' to qualify for exemption," and that these classifications are "wholly unrelated to any legitimate state interest."

The argument lacks merit. The WCEA's exemption for religious organizations, even if not applicable to Catholic Charities, rationally serves the legitimate interest of complying with the rule barring interference with the relationship between a church and its ministers, (See *ante,* 10 Cal.Rptr.3d at p. 296, 85 P.3d at p. 78 et seq.) Although the high court has not spoken on the subject, the lower federal courts have held that the constitutionally based ministerial exemption survives the decision in *Smith, supra,* 494 U.S. 872, 110 S.Ct. 1595.... Most organizations entitled to invoke the ministerial exemption will be involved in the "inculcation of religious values," which the first criterion requires. (Health & Saf.Code, § 1367.25, subd. (b)(1)(A).) many will also satisfy the WCEA's fourth exemption criterion, which requires that a religious employer qualify for federal tax exemption as a church, an integrated auxiliary of a church, a convention or association of churches, or a religious order. (See 26 U.S.C. § 6033(a)(2)(A)(I) and (iii), cited in Health & Saf.Code, § 1367.25, subd. (b)(1)(D).) If in any case the constitutionally required ministerial exception were broader than the statutory exemption, the former would of course take precedence.

The second criterion, to which Catholic Charities specifically objects as lacking a rational basis, requires that an employer "primarily employ [ ] persons who share the religious tenets of the entity." (Health & Saf.Code, § 1367.25, subd. (b)(1)(B).) This provision, in effect, accommodates religious employers more broadly than the ministerial exemption requires by extending the WCEA's exemption to employees who could not fall within the ministerial exemption. The provision has the legitimate, rational purpose of accommodating a state-imposed burden on religious exercise. (*Amos, supra,* 483 U.S. 327, 334–335, 107 S.Ct. 2862.)

The third criterion, to which Catholic Charities also objects, is problematic. To qualify under it, an employer must "serve[ ] primarily persons who share the religious tenets of the entity." (Health & Saf.Code, § 1367.25, subd. (b)(1)(C).) To imagine a legitimate purpose for such a requirement is difficult. Reading the provision literally, a hypothetical soup kitchen run entirely by the ministers of a church, which inculcates religious values to those who come to eat (thus satisfying the first, second, and fourth criteria), would lose its claim to an exemption from the WCEA if it chose to serve the hungry without discrimination instead of serving co-religionists only. The Legislature may wish to address this problem. Catholic Charities, however, cannot successfully challenge the WCEA on this ground because the organization concedes it does not qualify under any of the criteria for exemption, including the relatively objective terms of the federal tax statute cited in the fourth criterion. (Health & Saf.Code, § 1367.25, subd. (b)(1)(D).) Catholic Charities thus cannot qualify for exemption in any event.

The decision of the Court of Appeal is affirmed.

■ WE CONCUR: GEORGE, C.J., BAXTER, CHIN, and MORENO, JJ.

■ [The separate concurring opinion by KENNARD, J. and the dissenting opinion by BROWN, J. have been omitted.]

B. MAKING YOUR OWN DEAL: CONTRACTUAL ARRANGEMENTS AS AN ALTERNATIVE TO MARRIAGE

1. THE MARVIN TRILOGY

The State of California has adopted a comprehensive provision for establishing domestic partnerships; please replace the San Francisco Administrative Code at page 50 with the following:

CALIFORNIA FAMILY CODE (West 2004 and 2005 Cum. Supp.)

§ 297. Domestic partners and partnership; establishment

(a) Domestic partners are two adults who have chosen to share one another's lives in an intimate and committed relationship of mutual caring.

(b) A domestic partnership shall be established in California when both persons file a Declaration of Domestic Partnership with the Secretary of State pursuant to this division, and, at the time of filing, all of the following requirements are met:

(1) Both persons have a common residence.

(2) Neither person is married to someone else or is a member of another domestic partnership with someone else that has not been terminated, dissolved, or adjudged a nullity.

(3) The two persons are not related by blood in a way that would prevent them from being married to each other in this state.

(4) Both persons are at least 18 years of age.

(5) Either of the following:

(A) Both persons are members of the same sex.

(B) One or both of the persons meet the eligibility criteria under Title II of the Social Security Act as defined in 42 U.S.C. Section 402(a) for old-age insurance benefits or Title XVI of the Social Security Act as defined in 42 U.S.C. Section 1381 for aged individuals. Notwithstanding any other provision of this section, persons of opposite sexes may not constitute a domestic partnership unless one or both of the persons are over the age of 62.

(6) Both persons are capable of consenting to the domestic partnership.

(c) "Have a common residence" means that both domestic partners share the same residence. It is not necessary that the legal right to possess the common residence be in both of their names. Two people have a common residence even if one or both have additional residences. Domestic partners do not cease to have a common residence if one leaves the common residence but intends to return.

§ 297.5. Rights, protections and benefits; responsibilities; obligations and duties under law; date of registration as equivalent of date of marriage

(a) Registered domestic partners shall have the same rights, protections, and benefits, and shall be subject to the same responsibilities, obligations, and duties under law, whether they derive from statutes, administrative regulations, court rules, government policies, common law, or any other provisions or sources of law, as are granted to and imposed upon spouses.

(b) Former registered domestic partners shall have the same rights, protections, and benefits, and shall be subject to the same responsibilities, obligations, and duties under law, whether they derive from statutes, administrative regulations, court rules, government policies, common law, or any other provisions or sources of law, as are granted to and imposed upon former spouses.

(c) A surviving registered domestic partner, following the death of the other partner, shall have the same rights, protections, and benefits, and shall be subject to the same responsibilities, obligations, and duties under law, whether they derive from statutes, administrative regulations, court rules, government policies, common law, or any other provisions or sources of law, as are granted to and imposed upon a widow or a widower.

(d) The rights and obligations of registered domestic partners with respect to a child of either of them shall be the same as those of spouses. The rights and obligations of former or surviving registered domestic partners with respect to a child of either of them shall be the same as those of former or surviving spouses.

(e) To the extent that provisions of California law adopt, refer to, or rely upon, provisions of federal law in a way that otherwise would cause registered domestic partners to be treated differently than spouses, registered domestic partners shall be treated by California law as if federal law recognized a domestic partnership in the same manner as California law.

(f) Registered domestic partners shall have the same rights regarding nondiscrimination as those provided to spouses.

(g) Notwithstanding this section, in filing their state income tax returns, domestic partners shall use the same filing status as is used on their federal income tax returns, or that would have been used had they filed federal income tax returns. Earned income may not be treated as community property for state income tax purposes.

(h) No public agency in this state may discriminate against any person or couple on the ground that the person is a registered domestic partner rather than a spouse or that the couple are registered domestic partners rather than spouses, except that nothing in this section applies to modify eligibility for long-term care plans pursuant to Chapter 15 (commencing with Section 21660) of Part 3 of Division 5 of Title 2 of the Government Code.

(i) This act does not preclude any state or local agency from exercising its regulatory authority to implement statutes providing rights to, or imposing responsibilities upon, domestic partners.

(j) This section does not amend or modify any provision of the California Constitution or any provision of any statute that was adopted by initiative.

(k) This section does not amend or modify federal laws or the benefits, protections, and responsibilities provided by those laws.

(*l*) Where necessary to implement the rights of registered domestic partners under this act, gender-specific terms referring to spouses shall be construed to include domestic partners.

(m)(1) For purposes of the statutes, administrative regulations, court rules, government policies, common law, and any other provision or source of law governing the rights, protections, and benefits, and the responsibilities, obligations, and duties of registered domestic partners in this state, as effectuated by this section, with respect to community property, mutual responsibility for debts to third parties, the right in particular circumstances of either partner to seek financial support from the other following the dissolution of the partnership, and other rights and duties as between the partners concerning ownership of property, any reference to the date of a marriage shall be deemed to refer to the date of registration of a domestic partnership with the state.

(2) Notwithstanding paragraph (1), for domestic partnerships registered with the state before January 1, 2005, an agreement between the domestic partners that the partners intend to be governed by the requirements set forth in Sections 1600 to 1620, inclusive, and which complies with those sections, except for the agreement's effective date, shall be enforceable as provided by Sections 1600 to 1620, inclusive, if that agreement was fully executed and in force as of June 30, 2005.

§ 299. Termination of registered domestic partnership; filing of Notice of Termination of Domestic Partnership; conditions; effective date; setting aside termination; jurisdiction

(a) A registered domestic partnership may be terminated without filing a proceeding for dissolution of domestic partnership by the filing of a Notice of Termination of Domestic Partnership with the Secretary of State pursuant to this section, provided that all of the following conditions exist at the time of the filing:

(1) The Notice of Termination of Domestic Partnership is signed by both registered domestic partners.

(2) There are no children of the relationship of the parties born before or after registration of the domestic partnership or adopted by the parties after registration of the domestic partnership, and neither of the registered domestic partners, to their knowledge, is pregnant.

(3) The registered domestic partnership is not more than five years in duration.

(4) Neither party has any interest in real property wherever situated, with the exception of the lease of a residence occupied by either party which satisfies the following requirements:

(A) The lease does not include an option to purchase.

(B) The lease terminates within one year from the date of filing of the Notice of Termination of Domestic Partnership.

(5) There are no unpaid obligations in excess of the amount described in paragraph (6) of subdivision (a) of Section 2400, as adjusted by subdivision (b) of Section 2400, incurred by either or both of the parties after registration of the domestic partnership, excluding the amount of any unpaid obligation with respect to an automobile.

(6) The total fair market value of community property assets, excluding all encumbrances and automobiles, including any deferred compensation or retirement plan, is less than the amount described in paragraph (7) of subdivision (a) of Section 2400, as adjusted by subdivision (b) of Section 2400, and neither party has separate property assets, excluding all encumbrances and automobiles, in excess of that amount.

(7) The parties have executed an agreement setting forth the division of assets and the assumption of liabilities of the community property, and have executed any documents, title certificates, bills of sale, or other evidence of transfer necessary to effectuate the agreement.

(8) The parties waive any rights to support by the other domestic partner.

(9) The parties have read and understand a brochure prepared by the Secretary of State describing the requirements, nature, and effect of terminating a domestic partnership.

(10) Both parties desire that the domestic partnership be terminated.

(b) The registered domestic partnership shall be terminated effective six months after the date of filing of the Notice of Termination of Domestic Partnership with the Secretary of State pursuant to this section, provided that neither party has, before that date, filed with the Secretary of State a notice of revocation of the termination of domestic partnership, in the form and content as shall be prescribed by the Secretary of State, and sent to the other party a copy of the notice of revocation by first-class mail, postage prepaid, at the other party's last known address. The effect of termination of a domestic partnership pursuant to this section shall be the same as, and shall be treated for all purposes as, the entry of a judgment of dissolution of a domestic partnership.

(c) The termination of a domestic partnership pursuant to subdivision (b) does not prejudice nor bar the rights of either of the parties to institute an action in the superior court to set aside the termination for fraud, duress, mistake, or any other ground recognized at law or in equity. A court may set aside the termination of domestic partnership and declare the termination of the domestic partnership null and void upon proof that the parties did not meet the requirements of subdivision (a) at the time of the filing of the Notice of Termination of Domestic Partnership with the Secretary of State.

(d) The superior courts shall have jurisdiction over all proceedings relating to the dissolution of domestic partnerships, nullity of domestic partnerships, and legal separation of partners in a domestic partnership. The dissolution of a domestic partnership, nullity of a domestic partnership, and legal separation of partners in a domestic partnership shall follow the same procedures, and the partners shall possess the same rights, protections, and benefits, and be subject to the same responsibilities, obligations, and duties, as apply to the dissolution of marriage, nullity of marriage, and legal separation of spouses in a marriage, respectively, except as provided in subdivision (a), and except that, in accordance with the consent acknowledged by domestic partners in the Declaration of Domestic Partnership form, proceedings for dissolution, nullity, or legal separation of a domestic partnership registered in this state may be filed in the superior courts of this state even if neither domestic partner is a resident of, or maintains a domicile in, the state at the time the proceedings are filed.

§ 299.2. Recognizing same sex unions from another jurisdiction as a valid domestic partnership

A legal union of two persons of the same sex, other than a marriage, that was validly formed in another jurisdiction, and that is substantially equivalent to a domestic partnership as defined in this part, shall be recognized as a valid domestic partnership in this state regardless of whether it bears the name domestic partnership.

NOTES

Domestic partnership has increased in scope and practice, as the California legislation indicates. The statutes above went into effect on January 1, 2005. California now applies retroactive standing to a decedent's domestic partner in wrongful death cases, Bouley v. Long Beach Memorial Med. Ctr., 127 Cal.App.4th 601, 25 Cal.Rptr.3d 813 (2005), and concomitantly, there is no denial of equal protection in denying that same right to unmarried couples of the opposite sex. Opposite sex couples may not enter into domestic partnerships unless one of them is at least 62 years of age or eligible for age-based benefits under the Social Security Act. Ability of opposite sex couples to marry and their refusal to do so indicates a lack of commitment that the court found a rational reason for different treatment. Holguin v. Flores, 122 Cal.App.4th 428, 18 Cal.Rptr.3d 749 (2004). But in Montana the state constitution's equal protection clause demands that same-sex domestic partners be provided with health benefits at Montana University if the state provides such benefits to the declared common law spouses of heterosexual employees. Snetsinger v. Montana Univ. Sys., 325 Mont. 148, 104 P.3d 445 (2004).

Suggested Reading: **Grace Ganz Blumberg**, *Legal Recognition of Same–Sex Conjugal Relationships: The 2003 California Domestic Partner Rights and Responsibilities Act in Comparative Civil Rights and Family Law Perspectives*, **51 UCLA L. REV. 1555–1617 (2004); Margaret F. Brinig** *and* **Steven L. Nock**, *Mary Me, Bill: Should Cohabitation be the (Legal) Default Option?*, **64 LA. L. REV. 403–442 (2004); Ann Laquer Estin**, *Embracing Tradition: Pluralism in American Family Law*, **63 MD. L. REV. 540–604 (2004).**

D. MARRIAGE: THE STATE'S INTEREST

Following **Fisher v. Fisher***, please add to the* **NOTE** *at page 60:*

A Connecticut trial court has ruled that it did not have subject-matter jurisdiction to annul a same-sex marriage entered into in Massachusetts one year earlier. The court reasoned that it could decline jurisdiction because the public policy of Connecticut did not recognize civil unions or same-sex marriages. *Court Won't Annul Lesbians' Marriage Because It Finds It Was Never Valid*, 31 Fam. L. Rep. (BNA) 1243 (Apr. 5, 2005); *see also* Citizens for Equal Prot., Inc. v. Bruning, 290 F.Supp.2d 1004 (D. Neb. 2003). For the latest updates on same-sex marriage and related issues, see LAMBDA LEGAL, at http://www.lambdalegal.org (last visited Apr. 12, 2005). But a federal district court has ruled that the Defense of Marriage Act's provision that no state may be forced to recognize a same-sex marriage valid in another state is constitutional. Wilson v. Ake, 354 F.Supp.2d 1298 (M.D. Fla. 2005).

E.   REGULATING MARRIAGE AND OTHER INTIMATE RELATIONSHIPS: SOME CONSTITUTIONAL DIMENSIONS

Following Roe v. Wade, *please add at page 87:*

Stenberg v. Carhart

Supreme Court of the United States, 2000.
530 U.S. 914, 120 S.Ct. 2597, 147 L.Ed.2d 743.

■ JUSTICE BREYER delivered the opinion of the Court.

We again consider the right to an abortion. We understand the controversial nature of the problem. Millions of Americans believe that life begins at conception and consequently that an abortion is akin to causing the death of an innocent child; they recoil at the thought of a law that would permit it. Other millions fear that a law that forbids abortion would condemn many American women to lives that lack dignity, depriving them of equal liberty and leading those with least resources to undergo illegal abortions with the attendant risks of death and suffering. Taking account of these virtually irreconcilable points of view, aware that constitutional law must govern a society whose different members sincerely hold directly opposing views, and considering the matter in light of the Constitution's guarantees of fundamental individual liberty, this Court, in the course of a generation, has determined and then redetermined that the Constitution offers basic protection to the woman's right to choose. *Roe v. Wade,* 410 U.S. 113, 93 S.Ct. 705, 35 L.Ed.2d 147 (1973); *Planned Parenthood of Southeastern Pa. v. Casey,* 505 U.S. 833, 112 S.Ct. 2791, 120 L.Ed.2d 674 (1992). We shall not revisit those legal principles. Rather, we apply them to the circumstances of this case.

Three established principles determine the issue before us. We shall set them forth in the language of the joint opinion in *Casey.* First, before "viability . . . the woman has a right to choose to terminate her pregnancy." *Id.,* at 870, 112 S.Ct. 2791 (plurality opinion).

Second, "a law designed to further the State's interest in fetal life which imposes an undue burden on the woman's decision before fetal viability" is unconstitutional. *Id.,* at 877, 112 S.Ct. 2791. An "undue burden is . . . shorthand for the conclusion that a state regulation has the purpose or effect of placing a substantial obstacle in the path of a woman seeking an abortion of a nonviable fetus." *Ibid.*

Third, " 'subsequent to viability, the State in promoting its interest in the potentiality of human life may, if it chooses, regulate, and even proscribe, abortion except where it is necessary, in appropriate medical judgment, for the preservation of the life or health of the mother.' " *Id.,* at 879, 112 S.Ct. 2791 (quoting *Roe v. Wade, supra,* at 164–165, 93 S.Ct. 705).

We apply these principles to a Nebraska law banning "partial birth abortion." The statute reads as follows:

"No partial birth abortion shall be performed in this state, unless such procedure is necessary to save the life of the mother whose life is endangered by a physical disorder, physical illness, or physical injury, including a life-endangering physical condition caused by or arising from the pregnancy itself." Neb.Rev.Stat. Ann. § 28–328(1) (Supp. 1999).

The statute defines "partial birth abortion" as:

"an abortion procedure in which the person performing the abortion partially delivers vaginally a living unborn child before killing the unborn child and completing the delivery." § 28–326(9).

It further defines "partially delivers vaginally a living unborn child before killing the unborn child" to mean

"deliberately and intentionally delivering into the vagina a living unborn child, or a substantial portion thereof, for the purpose of performing a procedure that the person performing such procedure knows will kill the unborn child and does kill the unborn child." *Ibid.*

The law classifies violation of the statute as a "Class III felony" carrying a prison term of up to 20 years, and a fine of up to $25,000. §§ 28–328(2), 28–105. It also provides for the automatic revocation of a doctor's license to practice medicine in Nebraska. § 28–328(4).

We hold that this statute violates the Constitution.

Dr. Leroy Carhart is a Nebraska physician who performs abortions in a clinical setting. He brought this lawsuit in Federal District Court seeking a declaration that the Nebraska statute violates the Federal Constitution, and asking for an injunction forbidding its enforcement. After a trial on the merits, during which both sides presented several expert witnesses, the District Court held the statute unconstitutional. 11 F.Supp.2d 1099 (D.Neb. 1998). On appeal, the Eighth Circuit affirmed. 192 F.3d 1142 (1999); cf. *Hope Clinic v. Ryan,* 195 F.3d 857 (C.A.7 1999) (en banc) (considering a similar statute, but reaching a different legal conclusion). We granted certiorari to consider the matter.

B

Because Nebraska law seeks to ban one method of aborting a pregnancy, we must describe and then discuss several different abortion procedures. Considering the fact that those procedures seek to terminate a potential human life, our discussion may seem clinically cold or callous to some, perhaps horrifying to others. There is no alternative way, however, to acquaint the reader with the technical distinctions among different abortion methods and related factual matters, upon which the outcome of this case depends. For that reason, drawing upon the findings of the trial court, underlying testimony, and related medical texts, we shall describe the relevant methods of performing abortions in technical detail.

The evidence before the trial court, as supported or supplemented in the literature, indicates the following:

1.   About 90% of all abortions performed in the United States take place during the first trimester of pregnancy, before 12 weeks of gestational age. Centers for Disease Control and Prevention, Abortion Surveillance— United States, 1996, p. 41 (July 30, 1999) (hereinafter Abortion Surveillance). During the first trimester, the predominant abortion method is "vacuum aspiration," which involves insertion of a vacuum tube (cannula) into the uterus to evacuate the contents. Such an abortion is typically performed on an outpatient basis under local anesthesia. 11 F.Supp.2d, at 1102; Obstetrics: Normal & Problem Pregnancies 1253–1254 (S. Gabbe, J. Niebyl, & J. Simpson eds.3d ed.1996). Vacuum aspiration is considered particularly safe. The procedure's mortality rates for first trimester abortion are, for example, 5 to 10 times lower than those associated with carrying the fetus to term. Complication rates are also low. *Id.,* at 1251; Lawson et al., Abortion Mortality, United States, 1972 through 1987, 171 Am. J. Obstet. Gynecol. 1365, 1368 (1994); M. Paul et al., A Clinicians Guide to Medical and Surgical Abortion 108–109 (1999) (hereinafter Medical and Surgical Abortion). As the fetus grows in size, however, the vacuum aspiration method becomes increasingly difficult to use. 11 F.Supp.2d, at 1102–1103; Obstetrics: Normal & Problem Pregnancies, *supra,* at 1268.

2.   Approximately 10% of all abortions are performed during the second trimester of pregnancy (12 to 24 weeks). Abortion Surveillance 41. In the early 1970's, inducing labor through the injection of saline into the uterus was the predominant method of second trimester abortion. *Id.,* at 8; *Planned Parenthood of Central Mo. v. Danforth,* 428 U.S. 52, 76, 96 S.Ct. 2831, 49 L.Ed.2d 788 (1976). Today, however, the medical profession has switched from medical induction of labor to surgical procedures for most second trimester abortions. The most commonly used procedure is called "dilation and evacuation" (D & E). That procedure (together with a modified form of vacuum aspiration used in the early second trimester) accounts for about 95% of all abortions performed from 12 to 20 weeks of gestational age. Abortion Surveillance 41.

3.   D & E "refers generically to transcervical procedures performed at 13 weeks gestation or later." American Medical Association, Report of Board of Trustees on Late–Term Abortion, App. 490 (hereinafter AMA Report). The AMA Report, adopted by the District Court, describes the process as follows.

Between 13 and 15 weeks of gestation:

"D & E is similar to vacuum aspiration except that the cervix must be dilated more widely because surgical instruments are used to remove larger pieces of tissue. Osmotic dilators are usually used. Intravenous fluids and an analgesic or sedative may be administered. A local anesthetic such as a paracervical block may be administered, dilating agents, if used, are removed and instruments are inserted through the cervix into the uterus to removal fetal and placental tissue. Because fetal tissue is friable and easily broken, the fetus may not be removed intact. The walls of the uterus are scraped with a curette to ensure that no tissue remains." *Id.,* at 490–491.

After 15 weeks:

"Because the fetus is larger at this stage of gestation (particularly the head), and because bones are more rigid, dismemberment or other destructive procedures are more likely to be required than at earlier gestational ages to remove fetal and placental tissue." *Id.,* at 491.

After 20 weeks:

"Some physicians use intrafetal potassium chloride or digoxin to induce fetal demise prior to a late D & E (after 20 weeks), to facilitate evacuation." *Id.,* at 491–492.

There are variations in D & E operative strategy; compare *ibid.* with W. Hern, Abortion Practice 146–156 (1984), and Medical and Surgical Abortion 133–135. However, the common points are that D & E involves (1) dilation of the cervix; (2) removal of at least some fetal tissue using nonvacuum instruments; and (3) (after the 15th week) the potential need for instrumental disarticulation or dismemberment of the fetus or the collapse of fetal parts to facilitate evacuation from the uterus.

4.   When instrumental disarticulation incident to D & E is necessary, it typically occurs as the doctor pulls a portion of the fetus through the cervix into the birth canal. Dr. Carhart testified at trial as follows:

"Dr. Carhart: . . . 'The dismemberment occurs between the traction of . . . my instrument and the counter-traction of the internal os of the cervix. . . .

"Counsel: 'So the dismemberment occurs after you pulled a part of the fetus through the cervix, is that correct?

"Dr. Carhart: 'Exactly. Because you're using—The cervix has two strictures or two rings, the internal os and the external os . . . that's what's actually doing the dismembering. . . .

"Counsel: 'When we talked before or talked before about a D & E, that is not—where there is not intention to do it intact, do you, in that situation, dismember the fetus in utero first, then remove portions?

"Dr. Carhart: 'I don't think so. . . . I don't know of any way that one could go in and intentionally dismember the fetus in the uterus. . . . It takes something that restricts the motion of the fetus against what you're doing before you're going to get dismemberment.' " 11 F.Supp.2d, at 1104.

Dr. Carhart's specification of the location of fetal disarticulation is consistent with other sources. See Medical and Surgical Abortion 135; App. in Nos. 98–3245 and 98–3300(CA8), p. 683, (testimony of Dr. Phillip Stubblefield) ("Q: So you don't actually dismember the fetus in utero, then take the pieces out? A: No").

5.   The D & E procedure carries certain risks. The use of instruments within the uterus creates a danger of accidental perforation and damage to neighboring organs. Sharp fetal bone fragments create similar dangers. And fetal tissue accidentally left behind can cause infection and various other complications. See 11 F.Supp.2d, at 1110; Gynecologic, Obstetric, and Related Surgery 1045 (D. Nichols & D. Clarke–Pearson eds.2d ed.2000); F. Cunningham et al., Williams Obstetrics 598 (20th ed.1997). Nonetheless studies show that the risks of mortality and complication that accompany the D & E procedure between the 12th and 20th weeks of gestation are significantly lower than those accompanying induced labor procedures (the next safest midsecond trimester procedures). See Gynecologic, Obstetric, and Related Surgery, *supra,* at 1046; AMA Report, App. 495, 496; Medical and Surgical Abortion 139, 142; Lawson, 171 Am. J. Obstet. Gynecol., at 1368.

6.   At trial, Dr. Carhart and Dr. Stubblefield described a variation of the D & E procedure, which they referred to as an "intact D & E." See 11 F.Supp.2d, at 1105, 1111. Like other versions of the D & E technique, it begins with induced dilation of the cervix. The procedure then involves removing the fetus from the uterus through the cervix "intact," *i.e.,* in one pass, rather than in several passes. *Ibid.* It is used after 16 weeks at the earliest, as vacuum aspiration becomes ineffective and the fetal skull becomes too large to pass through the cervix. *Id.,* at 1105. The intact D & E proceeds in one of two ways, depending on the presentation of the fetus. If the fetus presents head first (a vertex presentation), the doctor collapses the skull; and the doctor then extracts the entire fetus through the cervix. If the fetus presents feet first (a breech presentation), the doctor pulls the fetal body through the cervix, collapses the skull, and extracts the fetus through the cervix. *Ibid.* The breech extraction version of the intact D & E is also known commonly as "dilation and extraction," or D & X. *Id.,* at 1112. In the late second trimester, vertex, breech, and traverse/compound (sideways) presentations occur in roughly similar proportions. Medical and Surgical Abortion 135; 11 F.Supp.2d, at 1108.

7.   The intact D & E procedure can also be found described in certain obstetric and abortion clinical textbooks, where two variations are recognized. The first, as just described, calls for the physician to adapt his method for extracting the intact fetus depending on fetal presentation. See Gynecologic, Obstetric, and Related Surgery, *supra,* at 1043; Medical and Surgical Abortion 136–137. This is the method used by Dr. Carhart. See 11 F.Supp.2d, at 1105. A slightly different version of the intact D & E procedure, associated with Dr. Martin Haskell, calls for conversion to a breech presentation in all cases. See Gynecologic, Obstetric, and Related

Surgery, *supra*, at 1043 (citing M. Haskell, Dilation and Extraction for Late Second Trimester Abortion (1992), in 139 Cong. Rec. 8605 (1993)).

8. The American College of Obstetricians and Gynecologists describes the D & X procedure in a manner corresponding to a breech-conversion intact D & E, including the following steps:

"1. deliberate dilatation of the cervix, usually over a sequence of days;

"2. instrumental conversion of the fetus to a footling breech;

"3. breech extraction of the body excepting the head; and

"4. partial evacuation of the intracranial contents of a living fetus to effect vaginal delivery of a dead but otherwise intact fetus." American College of Obstetricians and Gynecologists Executive Board, Statement on Intact Dilation and Extraction (Jan. 12, 1997) (hereinafter ACOG Statement), App. 599–560.

Despite the technical differences we have just described, intact D & E and D & X are sufficiently similar for us to use the terms interchangeably.

9. Dr. Carhart testified he attempts to use the intact D & E procedure during weeks 16 to 20 because (1) it reduces the dangers from sharp bone fragments passing through the cervix, (2) minimizes the number of instrument passes needed for extraction and lessens the likelihood of uterine perforations caused by those instruments, (3) reduces the likelihood of leaving infection-causing fetal and placental tissue in the uterus, and (4) could help to prevent potentially fatal absorption of fetal tissue into the maternal circulation. See 11 F.Supp.2d, at 1107. The District Court made no findings about the D & X procedure's overall safety. *Id.,* at 1126, n. 39. The District Court concluded, however, that "the evidence is both clear and convincing that Carhart's D & X procedure is superior to, and safer than, the ... other abortion procedures used during the relevant gestational period in the 10 to 20 cases a year that present to Dr. Carhart." *Id.,* at 1126.

10. The materials presented at trial referred to the potential benefits of the D & X procedure in circumstances involving nonviable fetuses, such as fetuses with abnormal fluid accumulation in the brain (hydrocephaly). See 11 F.Supp.2d, at 1107 (quoting AMA Report, App. 492 (" 'Intact D & X may be preferred by some physicians, particularly when the fetus has been diagnosed with hydrocephaly or other anomalies incompatible with life outside the womb' ")); see also Grimes, The Continuing Need for Late Abortions, 280 JAMA 747, 748 (Aug. 26, 1998) (D & X "may be especially useful in the presence of fetal anomalies, such as hydrocephalus," because its reduction of the cranium allows "a smaller diameter to pass through the cervix, thus reducing risk of cervical injury"). Others have emphasized its potential for women with prior uterine scars, or for women for whom induction of labor would be particularly dangerous. See *Women's Medical Professional Corp. v. Voinovich,* 911 F.Supp. 1051, 1067 (S.D.Ohio 1995); *Evans v. Kelley,* 977 F.Supp. 1283, 1296 (E.D.Mich.1997).

11.   There are no reliable data on the number of D & X abortions performed annually. Estimates have ranged between 640 and 5,000 per year. Compare Henshaw, Abortion Incidence and Services in the United States, 1995–1996, 30 Family Planning Perspectives 263, 268 (1998), with Joint Hearing on S. 6 and H.R. 929 before the Senate Committee on the Judiciary and the Subcommittee on the Constitution of the House Committee on the Judiciary, 105th Cong., 1st Sess., 46 (1997).

II

The question before us is whether Nebraska's statute, making criminal the performance of a "partial birth abortion," violates the Federal Constitution, as interpreted in *Planned Parenthood of Southeastern Pa. v. Casey,* 505 U.S. 833, 112 S.Ct. 2791, 120 L.Ed.2d 674 (1992), and *Roe v. Wade,* 410 U.S. 113, 93 S.Ct. 705, 35 L.Ed.2d 147 (1973). We conclude that it does for at least two independent reasons. First, the law lacks any exception " 'for the preservation of the . . . health of the mother.' " *Casey,* 505 U.S., at 879, 112 S.Ct. 2791 (plurality opinion). Second, it "imposes an undue burden on a woman's ability" to choose a D & E abortion, thereby unduly burdening the right to choose abortion itself. *Id.,* at 874, 112 S.Ct. 2791. We shall discuss each of these reasons in turn.

A

The *Casey* plurality opinion reiterated what the Court held in *Roe;* that " 'subsequent to viability, the State in promoting its interest in the potentiality of human life may, if it chooses, regulate, and even proscribe, abortion *except where it is necessary, in appropriate medical judgment, for the preservation of the life or health of the mother.*' " 505 U.S., at 879, 112 S.Ct. 2791 (quoting *Roe, supra,* at 164–165, 93 S.Ct. 705) (emphasis added).

The fact that Nebraska's law applies both previability and postviability aggravates the constitutional problem presented. The State's interest in regulating abortion previability is considerably weaker than postviability. See *Casey, supra,* at 870, 112 S.Ct. 2791. Since the law requires a health exception in order to validate even a postviability abortion regulation, it at a minimum requires the same in respect to previability regulation. See *Casey, supra,* at 880, 112 S.Ct. 2791 (majority opinion) (assuming need for health exception previability); see also *Harris v. McRae,* 448 U.S. 297, 316, 100 S.Ct. 2671, 65 L.Ed.2d 784 (1980).

. . .

1

Nebraska responds that the law does not require a health exception unless there is a need for such an exception. And here there is no such need, it says. It argues that "safe alternatives remain available" and "a ban on partial-birth abortion/D & X would create no risk to the health of women." Brief for Petitioners 29, 40. The problem for Nebraska is that the parties strongly contested this factual question in the trial court below; and the findings and evidence support Dr. Carhart. The State fails to demonstrate that banning D & X without a health exception may not create significant health risks for women, because the record shows that significant medical authority supports the proposition that in some circumstances, D & X would be the safest procedure.

[Relevant findings and evidence have been omitted.]

. . .

4

The upshot is a District Court finding that D & X significantly obviates health risks in certain circumstances, a highly plausible record-based explanation of why that might be so, a division of opinion among some medical experts over whether D & X is generally safer, and an absence of controlled medical studies that would help answer these medical questions. Given these medically related evidentiary circumstances, we believe the law requires a health exception.

The word "necessary" in *Casey's* phrase "necessary, in appropriate medical judgment, for the preservation of the life or health of the mother," 505 U.S., at 879, 112 S.Ct. 2791 (internal quotation marks omitted), cannot refer to an absolute necessity or to absolute proof. Medical treatments and procedures are often considered appropriate (or inappropriate) in light of estimated comparative health risks (and health benefits) in particular cases. Neither can that phrase require unanimity of medical opinion. Doctors often differ in their estimation of comparative health risks and appropriate treatment. And *Casey's* words "appropriate medical judgment" must embody the judicial need to tolerate responsible differences of medical opinion—differences of a sort that the American Medical Association and American College of Obstetricians and Gynecologists' statements together indicate are present here.

For another thing, the division of medical opinion about the matter at most means uncertainty, a factor that signals the presence of risk, not its absence. That division here involves highly qualified knowledgeable experts on both sides of the issue. Where a significant body of medical opinion believes a procedure may bring with it greater safety for some patients and explains the medical reasons supporting that view, we cannot say that the presence of a different view by itself proves the contrary. Rather, the uncertainty means a significant likelihood that those who believe that D & X is a safer abortion method in certain circumstances may turn out to be right. If so, then the absence of a health exception will place women at an unnecessary risk of tragic health consequences. If they are wrong, the exception will simply turn out to have been unnecessary.

In sum, Nebraska has not convinced us that a health exception is "never necessary to preserve the health of women." Reply Brief for Petitioners 4. Rather, a statute that altogether forbids D & X creates a significant health risk. The statute consequently must contain a health exception. This is not to say, as Justice THOMAS and Justice KENNEDY claim, that a State is prohibited from proscribing an abortion procedure whenever a particular physician deems the procedure preferable. By no means must a State grant physicians "unfettered discretion" in their selection of abortion methods. *Post,* at 2629 (KENNEDY, J., dissenting). But where substantial medical authority supports the proposition that banning a particular abortion procedure could endanger women's health, *Casey* requires the statute to include a health exception when the procedure is " 'necessary, in appropriate medical judgment, for the preservation of the life or health of the mother.' " 505 U.S., at 879, 112 S.Ct. 2791. Requiring such an exception in this case is no departure from *Casey,* but simply a straightforward application of its holding.

B

The Eighth Circuit found the Nebraska statute unconstitutional because, in *Casey's* words, it has the "effect of placing a substantial obstacle in the path of a woman seeking an abortion of a nonviable fetus." *Id.,* at 877, 112 S.Ct. 2791. It thereby places an "undue burden" upon a woman's right to terminate her pregnancy before viability. *Ibid.* Nebraska does not deny that the statute imposes an "undue burden" *if* it applies to the more commonly used D & E procedure as well as to D & X. And we agree with the Eighth Circuit that it does so apply.

Our earlier discussion of the D & E procedure, *supra,* at 2606–2607, shows that it falls within the statutory prohibition. The statute forbids "deliberately and intentionally delivering into the vagina a living unborn child, or a substantial portion thereof, for the purpose of performing a procedure that the person performing such procedure knows will kill the unborn child." Neb.Rev.Stat. Ann. § 28–326(9) (Supp.1999). We do not understand how one could distinguish, using this language, between D & E (where a foot or arm is drawn through the cervix) and D & X (where the body up to the head is drawn through the cervix). Evidence before the trial court makes clear that D & E will often involve a physician pulling a "substantial portion" of a still living fetus, say, an arm or leg, into the vagina prior to the death of the fetus. 11 F.Supp.2d, at 1128; *id.,* at 1128–1130. Indeed D & E involves dismemberment that commonly occurs only when the fetus meets resistance that restricts the motion of the fetus: "The dismemberment occurs between the traction of ... [the] instrument and the counter-traction of the internal os of the cervix." *Id.,* at 1128. And these events often do not occur until after a portion of a living fetus has been pulled into the vagina. *Id.,* at 1104; see also Medical and Surgical Abortion 135 ("During the mid-second trimester, separation of the fetal corpus may occur when the fetus is drawn into the lower uterine segment, where compression and traction against the endocervix facilitates disarticulation").

Even if the statute's basic aim is to ban D & X, its language makes clear that it also covers a much broader category of procedures. The language does not track the medical differences between D & E and D & X—though it would have been a simple matter, for example, to provide an exception for the performance of D & E and other abortion procedures. *E.g.,* Kan. Stat. Ann. § 65–6721(b)(1) (Supp.1999). Nor does the statute anywhere suggest that its application turns on whether a portion of the fetus' body is drawn into the vagina as part of a process to extract an intact fetus after collapsing the head as opposed to a process that would dismember the fetus. Thus, the dissenters' argument that the law was generally intended to bar D & X can be both correct and irrelevant. The relevant question is *not* whether the legislature wanted to ban D & X; it is whether the law was intended to apply *only* to D & X. The plain language covers both procedures. A rereading of this opinion, *supra,* at 2606–2608, as well as Justice THOMAS' dissent *post,* at 2637–2639, will make clear why we can find no difference, in terms of *this* statute, between the D & X procedure as described and the D & E procedure as it might be performed. (In particular, compare *post,* at 2637–2638, (THOMAS, J., dissenting), with *post,* at 2638–2640 (THOMAS, J., dissenting).) Both procedures can involve the introduction of a "substantial portion" of a still living fetus, through the cervix, into the vagina—the very feature of an abortion that leads Justice THOMAS to characterize such a procedure as involving "partial birth."

. . .

In sum, using this law some present prosecutors and future Attorneys General may choose to pursue physicians who use D & E procedures, the most commonly used method for performing previability second trimester abortions. All those who perform abortion procedures using that method must fear prosecution, conviction, and imprisonment. The result is an undue burden upon a woman's right to make an abortion decision. We must consequently find the statute unconstitutional.

The judgment of the Court of Appeals is

Affirmed.

■ JUSTICE STEVENS, with whom JUSTICE GINSBURG joins, concurring.

Although much ink is spilled today describing the gruesome nature of late-term abortion procedures, that rhetoric does not provide me a *reason* to believe that the procedure Nebraska here claims it seeks to ban is more brutal, more gruesome, or less respectful of "potential life" than the equally gruesome procedure Nebraska claims it still allows. Justice GINSBURG and Judge Posner have, I believe, correctly diagnosed the underlying reason for the enactment of this legislation—a reason that also explains much of the Court's rhetoric directed at an objective that extends well beyond the narrow issue that this case presents. The rhetoric is almost, but not quite, loud enough to obscure the quiet fact that during the past 27 years, the central holding of *Roe v. Wade,* 410 U.S. 113, 93 S.Ct. 705, 35 L.Ed.2d 147 (1973), has been endorsed by all but 4 of the 17 Justices who have addressed the issue. That holding—that the word "liberty" in the Fourteenth Amendment includes a woman's right to make this difficult and extremely personal decision—makes it impossible for me to understand how a State has any legitimate interest in requiring a doctor to follow any procedure other than the one that he or she reasonably believes will best protect the woman in her exercise of this constitutional liberty. But one need not even approach this view today to conclude that Nebraska's law must fall. For the notion that either of these two equally gruesome procedures performed at this late stage of gestation is more akin to infanticide than the other, or that the State furthers any legitimate interest by banning one but not the other, is simply irrational. See U.S. Const., Amdt. 14.

■ JUSTICE O'CONNOR, concurring.

The issue of abortion is one of the most contentious and controversial in contemporary American society. It presents extraordinarily difficult questions that, as the Court recognizes, involve "virtually irreconcilable points of view." *Ante,* at 2604. The specific question we face today is whether Nebraska's attempt to proscribe a particular method of abortion, commonly known as "partial birth abortion," is constitutional. For the reasons stated in the Court's opinion, I agree that Nebraska's statute cannot be reconciled with our decision in *Planned Parenthood of Southeastern Pa. v. Casey,* 505 U.S. 833, 112 S.Ct. 2791, 120 L.Ed.2d 674 (1992), and is therefore unconstitutional. I write separately to emphasize the following points.

First, the Nebraska statute is inconsistent with *Casey* because it lacks an exception for those instances when the banned procedure is necessary to preserve the health of the mother. See *id.,* at 879, 112 S.Ct. 2791 (plurality opinion). Importantly, Nebraska's own statutory scheme underscores this constitutional infirmity. As we held in *Casey,* prior to viability "the woman has a right to choose to terminate her pregnancy." *Id.,* at 870, 112 S.Ct. 2791. After the fetus has become viable, States may substantially regulate and even proscribe abortion, but any such regulation or proscription must contain an exception for instances " 'where it is necessary, in appropriate medical judgment, for the preservation of the life or health of the mother.' " *Id.,* at 879, 112 S.Ct. 2791 (quoting *Roe v. Wade,* 410 U.S. 113, 165, 93 S.Ct. 705, 35 L.Ed.2d 147 (1973)). Nebraska has recognized this constitutional limitation in its separate statute generally proscribing postviability abortions. See Neb.Rev.Stat. Ann. § 28–329 (Supp.1999). That statute provides that "[n]o abortion shall be performed after the time at which, in the sound medical judgment of the attending physician, the unborn child clearly appears to have reached viability, *except when necessary to preserve the life or health of the mother.*" *Ibid.* (emphasis added). Because even a postviability proscription of abortion would be invalid absent a health exception, Nebraska's ban on previability partial birth abortions, under the circumstances presented here, must include a health exception as well, since the State's interest in regulating abortions before viability is "considerably weaker" than after viability. *Ante,* at 2609. The statute at issue here, however, only excepts those procedures "necessary to save the life of the mother whose life is endangered by a physical disorder, physical illness, or physical injury." Neb.Rev.Stat. Ann. § 28–328(1) (Supp.1999). This lack of a health exception necessarily renders the statute unconstitutional.

If Nebraska's statute limited its application to the D & X procedure and included an exception for the life and health of the mother, the question presented would be quite different from the one we face today. As we held in *Casey,* an abortion regulation constitutes an undue burden if it "has the purpose or effect of placing a substantial obstacle in the path of a woman seeking an abortion of a nonviable fetus." 505 U.S., at 877, 112 S.Ct. 2791. If there were adequate alternative methods for a woman safely to obtain an abortion before viability, it is unlikely that prohibiting the D & X procedure alone would "amount in practical terms to a substantial obstacle to a woman seeking an abortion." *Id.,* at 884, 112 S.Ct. 2791. Thus, a ban on partial birth abortion that only proscribed the D & X method of abortion and that included an exception to preserve the life and health of the mother would be constitutional in my view.

Nebraska's statute, however, does not meet these criteria. It contains no exception for when the procedure, in appropriate medical judgment, is necessary to preserve the health of the mother; and it proscribes not only the D & X procedure but also the D & E procedure, the most commonly used method for previability second trimester abortions, thus making it an undue burden on a woman's right to terminate her pregnancy. For these reasons, I agree with the Court that Nebraska's law is unconstitutional.

■ JUSTICE GINSBURG, with whom JUSTICE STEVENS joins, concurring.

I write separately only to stress that amidst all the emotional uproar caused by an abortion case, we should not lose sight of the character of Nebraska's "partial birth abortion" law. As the Court observes, this law does not save any fetus from destruction, for it targets only "a *method* of performing abortion." *Ante,* at 2609. Nor does the statute seek to protect the lives or health of pregnant women. Moreover, as Justice STEVENS points out, *ante,* at 2617 (concurring opinion), the most common method of performing previability second trimester abortions is no less distressing or susceptible to gruesome description. Seventh Circuit Chief Judge Posner correspondingly observed, regarding similar bans in Wisconsin and Illinois, that the law prohibits the D & X procedure "not because the procedure kills the fetus, not because it risks worse complications for the woman than alternative procedures would do, not because it is a crueler or more painful or more disgusting method of terminating a pregnancy." *Hope Clinic v. Ryan,* 195 F.3d 857, 881 (C.A.7 1999) (dissenting opinion). Rather, Chief Judge Posner commented, the law prohibits the procedure because the state legislators seek to chip away at the private choice shielded by *Roe v. Wade,* 410 U.S. 113, 93 S.Ct. 705, 35 L.Ed.2d 147 (1973), even as modified by *Planned Parenthood of Southeastern Pa. v. Casey,* 505 U.S. 833, 112 S.Ct. 2791, 120 L.Ed.2d 674 (1992). 195 F.3d, at 880–882.

[The dissenting opinion of CHIEF JUSTICE REHNQUIST has been omitted.]

■ JUSTICE SCALIA, dissenting.

. . .

I have joined Justice THOMAS's dissent because I agree that today's decision is an "unprecedented expansio[n]" of our prior cases, *post,* at 2652, "is not mandated" by *Casey's* "undue-burden" test, *post,* at 2651, and can even be called (though this pushes me to the limit of my belief) "obviously irreconcilable with *Casey's* explication of what its undue-burden standard requires," *post,* at 2636. But I never put much stock in *Casey's* explication of the inexplicable. In the last analysis, my judgment that *Casey* does not support today's tragic result can be traced to the fact that what I consider to be an "undue burden" is different from what the majority considers to be an "undue burden"—a conclusion that cannot be demonstrated true or false by factual inquiry or legal reasoning. It is a value judgment, dependent upon how much one respects (or believes society ought to respect) the life of a partially delivered fetus, and how much one respects (or believes society ought to respect) the freedom of the woman who gave it life to kill it. Evidently, the five Justices in today's majority value the former less, or the latter more, (or both), than the four of us in dissent. Case closed. There is no cause for anyone who believes in *Casey* to feel betrayed by this outcome. It has been arrived at by precisely the process *Casey* promised—a democratic vote by nine lawyers, not on the question whether the text of the Constitution has anything to say about this subject (it obviously does not); nor even on the question (also appropriate for lawyers) whether the legal traditions of the American people would have sustained such a limitation upon abortion (they obviously would); but upon the pure policy question whether this limitation upon abortion is "undue"—*i.e.,* goes too far.

In my dissent in *Casey,* I wrote that the "undue burden" test made law by the joint opinion created a standard that was "as doubtful in application as it is unprincipled in origin," *Casey,* 505 U.S., at 985, 112 S.Ct. 2791; "hopelessly unworkable in practice," *id.,* at 986, 112 S.Ct. 2791; "ultimately standardless," *id.,* at 987, 112 S.Ct. 2791. Today's decision is the proof. As long as we are debating this issue of necessity for a health-of-the-mother exception on the basis of *Casey,* it is really quite impossible for us dissenters to contend that the majority is *wrong* on the law—any more than it could be said that one is *wrong in law* to support or oppose the death penalty, or to support or oppose mandatory minimum sentences. The most that we can honestly say is that we disagree with the majority on their policy-judgment-couched-as-law. And those who believe that a 5-to-4 vote on a policy matter by unelected lawyers should not overcome the judgment of 30 state legislatures have a problem, not with the *application* of *Casey,* but with its *existence. Casey* must be overruled.

While I am in an I-told-you-so mood, I must recall my bemusement, in *Casey,* at the majority opinion's expressed belief that *Roe v. Wade,* 410 U.S. 113, 93 S.Ct. 705, 35 L.Ed.2d 147 (1973), had "call[ed] the contending sides of a national controversy to end their national division by accepting a common mandate rooted in the Constitution," *Casey,* 505 U.S., at 867, 112 S.Ct. 2791, and that the decision in *Casey* would ratify that happy truce. It seemed to me, quite to the contrary, that "*Roe* fanned into life an issue that has inflamed our national politics in general, and has obscured with its smoke the selection of Justices to this Court in particular, ever since"; and that, "by keeping us in the abortion-umpiring business, it is the perpetuation of that disruption, rather than of any *Pax Roeana,* that the Court's new majority decrees." *Id.,* at 995–996, 112 S.Ct. 2791. Today's decision, that the Constitution of the United States prevents the prohibition of a horrible mode of abortion, will be greeted by a firestorm of criticism—as well it should. I cannot understand why those who *acknowledge* that, in the opening words of Justice O'CONNOR's concurrence, "[t]he issue of abortion is one of the most contentious and controversial in contemporary American society," *ante,* at 2617, persist in the belief that this Court, armed with neither constitutional text nor accepted tradition, can resolve that contention and controversy rather than be consumed by it. If only for the sake of its own preservation, the Court should return this matter to the people—where the Constitution, by its silence on the subject, left it—and let *them* decide, State by State, whether this practice should be allowed. *Casey* must be overruled.

■ Justice Kennedy, with whom The Chief Justice joins, dissenting.

For close to two decades after *Roe v. Wade,* 410 U.S. 113, 93 S.Ct. 705, 35 L.Ed.2d 147 (1973), the Court gave but slight weight to the interests of the separate States when their legislatures sought to address persisting concerns raised by the existence of a woman's right to elect an abortion in defined circumstances. When the Court reaffirmed the essential holding of *Roe,* a central premise was that the States retain a critical and legitimate role in legislating on the subject of abortion, as limited by the woman's right the Court restated and again guaranteed. *Planned Parenthood of Southeastern Pa. v. Casey,* 505 U.S. 833, 112 S.Ct. 2791, 120 L.Ed.2d 674 (1992). The political processes of the State are not to be foreclosed from enacting laws to promote the life of the unborn and to ensure respect for all human life and its potential. *Id.,* at 871, 112 S.Ct. 2791 (plurality opinion). The State's constitutional authority is a vital means for citizens to address these grave and serious issues, as they must if we are to progress in knowledge and understanding and in the attainment of some degree of consensus.

The Court's decision today, in my submission, repudiates this understanding by invalidating a statute advancing critical state interests, even though the law denies no woman the right to choose an abortion and places no undue burden upon the right. The legislation is well within the State's competence to enact. Having concluded Nebraska's law survives the scrutiny dictated by a proper understanding of *Casey,* I dissent from the judgment invalidating it.

. . .

Substantial evidence supports Nebraska's conclusion that its law denies no woman a safe abortion. The most to be said for the D & X is it may present an unquantified lower risk of complication for a particular patient but that other proven safe procedures remain available even for this patient. Under these circumstances, the Court is wrong to limit its inquiry to the relative physical safety of the two procedures, with the slightest potential difference requiring the invalidation of the law. As Justice O'CONNOR explained in an earlier case, the State may regulate based on matters beyond "what various medical organizations have to say about the *physical* safety of a particular procedure." *Akron v. Akron Center for ReproductiveHealth, Inc.,* 462 U.S. 416, 467, 103 S.Ct. 2481, 76 L.Ed.2d 687 (1983) (dissenting opinion). Where the difference in physical safety is, at best, marginal, the State may take into account the grave moral issues presented by a new abortion method. See *Casey,* 505 U.S., at 880, 112 S.Ct. 2791 (requiring a regulation to impose a "significant threat to the life or health of a woman" before its application would impose an undue burden (internal quotation marks omitted)). Dr. Carhart does not decide to use the D & X based on a conclusion that it is best for a particular woman. Unsubstantiated and generalized health differences which are, at best, marginal, do not amount to a substantial obstacle to the abortion right. *Id.,* at 874, 876, 112 S.Ct. 2791 (plurality opinion). It is also important to recognize that the D & X is effective only when the fetus is close to viable or, in fact, viable; thus the State is regulating the process at the point where its interest in life is nearing its peak.

. . .

The United States District Court in this case leaped to prevent the law from being enforced, granting an injunction before it was applied or interpreted by Nebraska. Cf. *Hill v. Colorado,* 530 U.S. 703, 120 S.Ct. 2480, 147 L.Ed.2d 597 (2000). In so doing, the court excluded from the abortion debate not just the Nebraska legislative branch but the State's executive and judiciary as well. The law was enjoined before the chief law enforcement officer of the State, its Attorney General, had any opportunity to interpret it. The federal court then ignored the representations made by that officer during this litigation. In like manner, Nebraska's courts will be given no opportunity to define the contours of the law, although by all indications those courts would give the statute a more narrow construction than the one so eagerly adopted by the Court today. *E.g., Stenberg v. Moore,* 258 Neb. 199, 206, 602 N.W.2d 465, 472 (1999). Thus the court denied each branch of Nebraska's government any role in the interpretation or enforcement of the statute. This cannot be what *Casey* meant when it said we would be more solicitous of state attempts to vindicate interests related to abortion. *Casey* did not assume this state of affairs.

IV

Ignoring substantial medical and ethical opinion, the Court substitutes its own judgment for the judgment of Nebraska and some 30 other States and sweeps the law away. The Court's holding stems from misunderstanding the record, misinterpretation of *Casey,* outright refusal to respect the law of a State, and statutory construction in conflict with settled rules. The decision nullifies a law expressing the will of the people of Nebraska that medical procedures must be governed by moral principles having their foundation in the intrinsic value of human life, including the life of the unborn. Through their law the people of Nebraska were forthright in confronting an issue of immense moral consequence. The State chose to forbid a procedure many decent and civilized people find so abhorrent as to be among the most serious of crimes against human life, while the State still protected the woman's autonomous right of choice as reaffirmed in *Casey*. The Court closes its eyes to these profound concerns.

From the decision, the reasoning, and the judgment, I dissent.

■ JUSTICE THOMAS, with whom THE CHIEF JUSTICE and JUSTICE SCALIA join, dissenting.

. . .

I

None of the opinions supporting the majority so much as mentions the large fraction standard, undoubtedly because the Nebraska statute easily survives it. I will assume, for the sake of discussion, that the category of women whose conduct Nebraska's partial birth abortion statute might affect includes any woman who wishes to obtain a safe abortion after 16 weeks' gestation. I will also assume (although I doubt it is true) that, of these women, every one would be willing to use the partial birth abortion procedure if so advised by her doctor. Indisputably, there is no "large fraction" of these women who would face a substantial obstacle to obtaining a safe abortion because of their inability to use this particular procedure. In fact, it is not clear that *any* woman would be deprived of a safe abortion by her inability to obtain a partial birth abortion. More medically sophisticated minds than ours have searched and failed to identify a single circumstance (let alone a large fraction) in which partial birth abortion is required. But no matter. The "ad hoc nullification" machine is back at full throttle. See *Thornburgh v. American College of Obstetricians and Gynecologists*, 476 U.S., at 814, 106 S.Ct. 2169 (O'CONNOR, J., dissenting); *Madsen v. Women's Health Center, Inc.*, 512 U.S. 753, 785, 114 S.Ct. 2516, 129 L.Ed.2d 593 (1994) (SCALIA, J., concurring in judgment in part and dissenting in part).* * *

Even if I were willing to assume that the partial birth method of abortion is safer for some small set of women, such a conclusion would not require invalidating the Act, because this case comes to us on a facial challenge. The only question before us is whether respondent has shown that " 'no set of circumstances exists under which the Act would be valid.' " *Ohio v. Akron Center for Reproductive Health*, 497 U.S. 502, 514, 110 S.Ct. 2972, 111 L.Ed.2d 405 (1990) (quoting *Webster v. Reproductive Health Services, supra*, at 524, 109 S.Ct. 3040 (O'CONNOR, J., concurring in part and concurring in judgment)). Courts may not invalidate on its face a state statute regulating abortion "based upon a worst-case analysis that may never occur." 497 U.S., at 514, 110 S.Ct. 2972.

Invalidation of the statute would be improper even assuming that *Casey* rejected this standard *sub silentio* (at least so far as abortion cases are concerned) in favor of a so-called " 'large fraction' " test. See *Fargo Women's Health Organization v. Schafer*, 507 U.S. 1013, 1014, 113 S.Ct. 1668, 123 L.Ed.2d 285 (1993) (O'CONNOR, J., joined by SOUTER, J., concurring) (arguing that the "no set of circumstances" standard is incompatible with *Casey*). See also *Janklow v. Planned Parenthood, Sioux Falls Clinic*, 517 U.S. 1174, 1177–1179, 116 S.Ct. 1582, 134 L.Ed.2d 679 (1996)

(SCALIA, J., dissenting from denial of certiorari). In *Casey,* the Court was presented with a facial challenge to, among other provisions, a spousal notice requirement. The question, according to the majority, was whether the spousal notice provision operated as a "substantial obstacle" to the women "whose conduct it affects," namely, "married women seeking abortions who do not wish to notify their husbands of their intentions and who do not qualify for one of the statutory exceptions to the notice requirement." 505 U.S., at 895, 112 S.Ct. 2791. The Court determined that a "large fraction" of the women in this category were victims of psychological or physical abuse. *Ibid.* For this subset of women, according to the Court, the provision would pose a substantial obstacle to the ability to obtain an abortion because their husbands could exercise an effective veto over their decision. *Id.,* at 897, 112 S.Ct. 2791.

None of the opinions supporting the majority so much as mentions the large fraction standard, undoubtedly because the Nebraska statute easily survives it. I will assume, for the sake of discussion, that the category of women whose conduct Nebraska's partial birth abortion statute might affect includes any woman who wishes to obtain a safe abortion after 16 weeks' gestation. I will also assume (although I doubt it is true) that, of these women, every one would be willing to use the partial birth abortion procedure if so advised by her doctor. Indisputably, there is no "large fraction" of these women who would face a substantial obstacle to obtaining a safe abortion because of their inability to use this particular procedure. In fact, it is not clear that *any* woman would be deprived of a safe abortion by her inability to obtain a partial birth abortion. More medically sophisticated minds than ours have searched and failed to identify a single circumstance (let alone a large fraction) in which partial birth abortion is required. But no matter. The "ad hoc nullification" machine is back at full throttle. See *Thornburgh v. American College of Obstetricians and Gynecologists,* 476 U.S., at 814, 106 S.Ct. 2169 (O'CONNOR, J., dissenting); *Madsen v. Women's Health Center, Inc.,* 512 U.S. 753, 785, 114 S.Ct. 2516, 129 L.Ed.2d 593 (1994) (SCALIA, J., concurring in judgment in part and dissenting in part).

We were reassured repeatedly in *Casey* that not all regulations of abortion are unwarranted and that the States may express profound respect for fetal life. Under *Casey,* the regulation before us today should easily pass constitutional muster. But the Court's abortion jurisprudence is a particularly virulent strain of constitutional exegesis. And so today we are told that 30 States are prohibited from banning one rarely used form of abortion that they believe to border on infanticide. It is clear that the Constitution does not compel this result.

I respectfully dissent.

After **Stenberg v. Carhart** *the following statute, known as the* **Born–Alive Infant Protection Act,** *was adopted in Pub. L. 107–207, § 2(a), Aug. 5, 2002, 116 Stat. 926:*

1 U.S.C.A., § 8.   "Person", "human being", "child", and "individual" as including born-alive infant

(a) In determining the meaning of any Act of Congress, or of any ruling, regulation, or interpretation of the various administrative bureaus and agencies of the United States, the words "person", "human being", "child", and "individual", shall include every infant member of the species homo sapiens who is born alive at any stage of development.

(b) As used in this section, the term "born alive", with respect to a member of the species homo sapiens, means the complete expulsion or extraction from his or her mother of that member, at any stage of development, who after such expulsion or extraction breathes or has a beating heart, pulsation of the umbilical cord, or definite movement of voluntary muscles, regardless of whether the umbilical cord has been cut, and regardless of whether the expulsion or extraction occurs as a result of natural or induced labor, cesarean section, or induced abortion.

(c) Nothing in this section shall be construed to affirm, deny, expand, or contract any legal status or legal right applicable to any member of the species homo sapiens at any point prior to being "born alive" as defined in this section.

Bowers v. Hardwick *has been expressly overruled by the Court. Please substitute the following for that decision and the* **NOTE** *at page 87:*

Lawrence v. Texas

Supreme Court of the United States, 2003.
539 U.S. 558, 123 S.Ct. 2472, 156 L.Ed.2d 508.

■ Justice Kennedy delivered the opinion of the Court.

Liberty protects the person from unwarranted government intrusions into a dwelling or other private places. In our tradition the State is not omnipresent in the home. And there are other spheres of our lives and existence, outside the home, where the State should not be a dominant presence. Freedom extends beyond spatial bounds. Liberty presumes an autonomy of self that includes freedom of thought, belief, expression, and certain intimate conduct. The instant case involves liberty of the person both in its spatial and more transcendent dimensions.

I

The question before the Court is the validity of a Texas statute making it a crime for two persons of the same sex to engage in certain intimate sexual conduct.

In Houston, Texas, officers of the Harris County Police Department were dispatched to a private residence in response to a reported weapons disturbance. They entered an apartment where one of the petitioners, John Geddes Lawrence, resided. The right of the police to enter does not seem to have been questioned. The officers observed Lawrence and another man, Tyron Garner, engaging in a sexual act. The two petitioners were arrested, held in custody over night, and charged and convicted before a Justice of the Peace.

The complaints described their crime as "deviate sexual intercourse, namely anal sex, with a member of the same sex (man)." App. to Pet. for Cert. 127a, 139a. The applicable state law is Tex. Penal Code Ann.

§ 21.06(a) (2003). It provides: "A person commits an offense if he engages in deviate sexual intercourse with another individual of the same sex." The statute defines "[d]eviate sexual intercourse" as follows:

"(A) any contact between any part of the genitals of one person and the mouth or anus of another person; or

"(B) the penetration of the genitals or the anus of another person with an object." § 21.01(1).

The petitioners exercised their right to a trial *de novo* in Harris County Criminal Court. They challenged the statute as a violation of the Equal Protection Clause of the Fourteenth Amendment and of a like provision of the Texas Constitution. Tex. Const., Art. 1, § 3a. Those contentions were rejected. The petitioners, having entered a plea of *nolo contendere,* were each fined $200 and assessed court costs of $141.25. App. to Pet. for Cert. 107a–110a.

The Court of Appeals for the Texas Fourteenth District considered the petitioners' federal constitutional arguments under both the Equal Protection and Due Process Clauses of the Fourteenth Amendment. After hearing the case en banc the court, in a divided opinion, rejected the constitutional arguments and affirmed the convictions. 41 S.W.3d 349 (Tex.App.2001). The majority opinion indicates that the Court of Appeals considered our decision in *Bowers v. Hardwick,* 478 U.S. 186, 106 S.Ct. 2841, 92 L.Ed.2d 140 (1986), to be controlling on the federal due process aspect of the case. *Bowers* then being authoritative, this was proper.

We granted certiorari, 537 U.S. 1044, 123 S.Ct. 661, 154 L.Ed.2d 514 (2002), to consider three questions:

"1. Whether Petitioners' criminal convictions under the Texas 'Homosexual Conduct' law—which criminalizes sexual intimacy by same-sex couples, but not identical behavior by different-sex couples—violate the Fourteenth Amendment guarantee of equal protection of laws?

"2. Whether Petitioners' criminal convictions for adult consensual sexual intimacy in the home violate their vital interests in liberty and privacy protected by the Due Process Clause of the Fourteenth Amendment?

"3. Whether *Bowers v. Hardwick,* 478 U.S. 186, 106 S.Ct. 2841, 92 L.Ed.2d 140 (1986), should be overruled?" Pet. for Cert. i.

The petitioners were adults at the time of the alleged offense. Their conduct was in private and consensual.

II

We conclude the case should be resolved by determining whether the petitioners were free as adults to engage in the private conduct in the exercise of their liberty under the Due Process Clause of the Fourteenth Amendment to the Constitution. For this inquiry we deem it necessary to reconsider the Court's holding in *Bowers.*

There are broad statements of the substantive reach of liberty under the Due Process Clause in earlier cases, including *Pierce v. Society of Sisters,* 268 U.S. 510, 45 S.Ct. 571, 69 L.Ed. 1070 (1925), and *Meyer v. Nebraska,* 262 U.S. 390, 43 S.Ct. 625, 67 L.Ed. 1042 (1923); but the most pertinent beginning point is our decision in *Griswold v. Connecticut,* 381 U.S. 479, 85 S.Ct. 1678, 14 L.Ed.2d 510 (1965).

In *Griswold* the Court invalidated a state law prohibiting the use of drugs or devices of contraception and counseling or aiding and abetting the use of contraceptives. The Court described the protected interest as a right to privacy and placed emphasis on the marriage relation and the protected space of the marital bedroom. *Id.,* at 485, 85 S.Ct. 1678.

After *Griswold* it was established that the right to make certain decisions regarding sexual conduct extends beyond the marital relationship. In *Eisenstadt v. Baird,* 405 U.S. 438, 92 S.Ct. 1029, 31 L.Ed.2d 349 (1972), the Court invalidated a law prohibiting the distribution of contraceptives to unmarried persons. The case was decided under the Equal Protection Clause, *id.,* at 454, 92 S.Ct. 1029; but with respect to unmarried persons, the Court went on to state the fundamental proposition that the law impaired the exercise of their personal rights, *ibid.* It quoted from the statement of the Court of Appeals finding the law to be in conflict with fundamental human rights, and it followed with this statement of its own:

> "It is true that in *Griswold* the right of privacy in question inhered in the marital relationship. . . . If the right of privacy means anything, it is the right of the *individual,* married or single, to be free from unwarranted governmental intrusion into matters so fundamentally affecting a person as the decision whether to bear or beget a child." *Id.,* at 453, 92 S.Ct. 1029.

The opinions in *Griswold* and *Eisenstadt* were part of the background for the decision in *Roe v. Wade,* 410 U.S. 113, 93 S.Ct. 705, 35 L.Ed.2d 147 (1973). As is well known, the case involved a challenge to the Texas law prohibiting abortions, but the laws of other States were affected as well. Although the Court held the woman's rights were not absolute, her right to elect an abortion did have real and substantial protection as an exercise of her liberty under the Due Process Clause. The Court cited cases that protect spatial freedom and cases that go well beyond it. *Roe* recognized the right of a woman to make certain fundamental decisions affecting her destiny and confirmed once more that the protection of liberty under the Due Process Clause has a substantive dimension of fundamental significance in defining the rights of the person.

In *Carey v. Population Services Int'l,* 431 U.S. 678, 97 S.Ct. 2010, 52 L.Ed.2d 675 (1977), the Court confronted a New York law forbidding sale or distribution of contraceptive devices to persons under 16 years of age. Although there was no single opinion for the Court, the law was invalidated. Both *Eisenstadt* and *Carey,* as well as the holding and rationale in *Roe,* confirmed that the reasoning of *Griswold* could not be confined to the protection of rights of married adults. This was the state of the law with respect to some of the most relevant cases when the Court considered *Bowers v. Hardwick.*

The facts in *Bowers* had some similarities to the instant case. A police officer, whose right to enter seems not to have been in question, observed Hardwick, in his own bedroom, engaging in intimate sexual conduct with another adult male. The conduct was in violation of a Georgia statute making it a criminal offense to engage in sodomy. One difference between the two cases is that the Georgia statute prohibited the conduct whether or not the participants were of the same sex, while the Texas statute, as we have seen, applies only to participants of the same sex. Hardwick was not prosecuted, but he brought an action in federal court to declare the state statute invalid. He alleged he was a practicing homosexual and that the criminal prohibition violated rights guaranteed to him by the Constitution. The Court, in an opinion by Justice White, sustained the Georgia law. Chief Justice Burger and Justice Powell joined the opinion of the Court and filed separate, concurring opinions. Four Justices dissented. 478 U.S., at 199, 106 S.Ct. 2841 (opinion of Blackmun, J., joined by Brennan, Marshall, and STEVENS, JJ.); *id.*, at 214, 106 S.Ct. 2841 (opinion of STEVENS, J., joined by Brennan and Marshall, JJ.).

The Court began its substantive discussion in *Bowers* as follows: "The issue presented is whether the Federal Constitution confers a fundamental right upon homosexuals to engage in sodomy and hence invalidates the laws of the many States that still make such conduct illegal and have done so for a very long time." *Id.*, at 190, 106 S.Ct. 2841. That statement, we now conclude, discloses the Court's own failure to appreciate the extent of the liberty at stake. To say that the issue in *Bowers* was simply the right to engage in certain sexual conduct demeans the claim the individual put forward, just as it would demean a married couple were it to be said marriage is simply about the right to have sexual intercourse. The laws involved in *Bowers* and here are, to be sure, statutes that purport to do no more than prohibit a particular sexual act. Their penalties and purposes, though, have more far-reaching consequences, touching upon the most private human conduct, sexual behavior, and in the most private of places, the home. The statutes do seek to control a personal relationship that, whether or not entitled to formal recognition in the law, is within the liberty of persons to choose without being punished as criminals.

This, as a general rule, should counsel against attempts by the State, or a court, to define the meaning of the relationship or to set its boundaries absent injury to a person or abuse of an institution the law protects. It suffices for us to acknowledge that adults may choose to enter upon this relationship in the confines of their homes and their own private lives and still retain their dignity as free persons. When sexuality finds overt expression in intimate conduct with another person, the conduct can be but one element in a personal bond that is more enduring. The liberty protected by the Constitution allows homosexual persons the right to make this choice.

Having misapprehended the claim of liberty there presented to it, and thus stating the claim to be whether there is a fundamental right to engage in consensual sodomy, the *Bowers* Court said: "Proscriptions against that conduct have ancient roots." *Id.,* at 192, 106 S.Ct. 2841. In academic writings, and in many of the scholarly *amicus* briefs filed to assist the Court in this case, there are fundamental criticisms of the historical premises relied upon by the majority and concurring opinions in *Bowers*. Brief for Cato Institute as *Amicus Curiae* 16–17; Brief for American Civil Liberties Union et al. as *Amici Curiae* 15–21; Brief for Professors of History et al. as *Amici Curiae* 3–10. We need not enter this debate in the attempt to reach a definitive historical judgment, but the following considerations counsel against adopting the definitive conclusions upon which *Bowers* placed such reliance.

At the outset it should be noted that there is no longstanding history in this country of laws directed at homosexual conduct as a distinct matter. Beginning in colonial times there were prohibitions of sodomy derived from the English criminal laws passed in the first instance by the Reformation Parliament of 1533. The English prohibition was understood to include relations between men and women as well as relations between men and men. See, *e.g., King v. Wiseman,* 92 Eng. Rep. 774, 775 (K.B.1718) (interpreting "mankind" in Act of 1533 as including women and girls). Nineteenth-century commentators similarly read American sodomy, buggery, and crime-against-nature statutes as criminalizing certain relations between men and women and between men and men. See, *e.g.,* 2 J. Bishop, Criminal Law § 1028 (1858); . . . J. May, The Law of Crimes § 203 (2d ed. 1893). The absence of legal prohibitions focusing on homosexual conduct may be explained in part by noting that according to some scholars the concept of the homosexual as a distinct category of person did not emerge until the late 19th century. See, e.g., J. Katz, The Invention of Heterosexuality 10 (1995); J. D'Emilio & E. Freedman, Intimate Matters: A History of Sexuality in America 121 (2d ed. 1997) ("The modern terms *homosexuality* and *heterosexuality* do not apply to an era that had not yet articulated these distinctions"). Thus early American sodomy laws were not directed at homosexuals as such but instead sought to prohibit nonprocreative sexual activity more generally. This does not suggest approval of homosexual conduct. It does tend to show that this particular form of conduct was not thought of as a separate category from like conduct between heterosexual persons.

Laws prohibiting sodomy do not seem to have been enforced against consenting adults acting in private. A substantial number of sodomy prosecutions and convictions for which there are surviving records were for predatory acts against those who could not or did not consent, as in the case of a minor or the victim of an assault. As to these, one purpose for the prohibitions was to ensure there would be no lack of coverage if a predator committed a sexual assault that did not constitute rape as defined by the criminal law. Thus the model sodomy indictments presented in a 19th-century treatise, see 2 Chitty, *supra,* at 49, addressed the predatory acts of an adult man against a minor girl or minor boy. Instead of targeting relations between consenting adults in private, 19th-century sodomy prosecutions typically involved relations between men and minor girls or minor boys, relations between adults involving force, relations between adults implicating disparity in status, or relations between men and animals.

To the extent that there were any prosecutions for the acts in question, 19th-century evidence rules imposed a burden that would make a conviction more difficult to obtain even taking into account the problems always inherent in prosecuting consensual acts committed in private. Under then-prevailing standards, a man could not be convicted of sodomy based upon testimony of a consenting partner, because the partner was considered an accomplice. A partner's testimony, however, was admissible if he or she had not consented to the act or was a minor, and therefore incapable of consent. See, *e.g.,* F. Wharton, Criminal Law 443 (2d ed. 1852); 1 F. Wharton, Criminal Law 512 (8th ed. 1880). The rule may explain in part the infrequency of these prosecutions. In all events that infrequency makes it difficult to say that society approved of a rigorous and systematic punishment of the consensual acts committed in private and by adults. The longstanding criminal prohibition of homosexual sodomy upon which the *Bowers* decision placed such reliance is as consistent with a general condemnation of nonprocreative sex as it is with an established tradition of prosecuting acts because of their homosexual character.

The policy of punishing consenting adults for private acts was not much discussed in the early legal literature. We can infer that one reason for this was the very private nature of the conduct. Despite the absence of prosecutions, there may have been periods in which there was public criticism of homosexuals as such and an insistence that the criminal laws be enforced to discourage their practices. But far from possessing "ancient roots," *Bowers,* 478 U.S., at 192, 106 S.Ct. 2841, American laws targeting same-sex couples did not develop until the last third of the 20th century. The reported decisions concerning the prosecution of consensual, homosexual sodomy between adults for the years 1880–1995 are not always clear in the details, but a significant number involved conduct in a public place. See Brief for American Civil Liberties Union et al. as *Amici Curiae* 14–15, and n. 18.

It was not until the 1970's that any State singled out same-sex relations for criminal prosecution, and only nine States have done so. [Cases and statutes omitted.]

In summary, the historical grounds relied upon in *Bowers* are more complex than the majority opinion and the concurring opinion by Chief Justice Burger indicate. Their historical premises are not without doubt and, at the very least, are overstated.

It must be acknowledged, of course, that the Court in *Bowers* was making the broader point that for centuries there have been powerful voices to condemn homosexual conduct as immoral. The condemnation has been shaped by religious beliefs, conceptions of right and acceptable behavior, and respect for the traditional family. For many persons these are not trivial concerns but profound and deep convictions accepted as ethical and moral principles to which they aspire and which thus determine the course of their lives. These considerations do not answer the question before us, however. The issue is whether the majority may use the power of the State to enforce these views on the whole society through operation of the criminal law. "Our obligation is to define the liberty of all, not to mandate our own moral code." *Planned Parenthood of Southeastern Pa. v. Casey,* 505 U.S. 833, 850, 112 S.Ct. 2791, 120 L.Ed.2d 674 (1992).

Chief Justice Burger joined the opinion for the Court in *Bowers* and further explained his views as follows: "Decisions of individuals relating to homosexual conduct have been subject to state intervention throughout the history of Western civilization. Condemnation of those practices is firmly rooted in Judeao–Christian moral and ethical standards." 478 U.S., at 196, 106 S.Ct. 2841. As with Justice White's assumptions about history, scholarship casts some doubt on the sweeping nature of the statement by Chief Justice Burger as it pertains to private homosexual conduct between consenting adults. See, *e.g.,* Eskridge, Hardwick and Historiography, 1999 U. Ill. L.Rev. 631, 656. In all events we think that our laws and traditions in the past half century are of most relevance here. These references show an emerging awareness that liberty gives substantial protection to adult persons in deciding how to conduct their private lives in matters pertaining to sex. "[H]istory and tradition are the starting point but not in all cases the ending point of the substantive due process inquiry." *County of Sacramento v. Lewis,* 523 U.S. 833, 857, 118 S.Ct. 1708, 140 L.Ed.2d 1043 (1998) (KENNEDY, J., concurring).

This emerging recognition should have been apparent when *Bowers* was decided. In 1955 the American Law Institute promulgated the Model Penal Code and made clear that it did not recommend or provide for "criminal penalties for consensual sexual relations conducted in private." ALI, Model Penal Code § 213.2, Comment 2, p. 372 (1980). It justified its decision on three grounds: (1) The prohibitions undermined respect for the law by penalizing conduct many people engaged in; (2) the statutes regulated private conduct not harmful to others; and (3) the laws were arbitrarily enforced and thus invited the danger of blackmail. ALI, Model Penal Code, Commentary 277–280 (Tent. Draft No. 4, 1955). In 1961 Illinois changed its laws to conform to the Model Penal Code. Other States soon followed. Brief for Cato Institute as *Amicus Curiae* 15–16.

In *Bowers* the Court referred to the fact that before 1961 all 50 States had outlawed sodomy, and that at the time of the Court's decision 24 States and the District of Columbia had sodomy laws. 478 U.S., at 192–193, 106 S.Ct. 2841. Justice Powell pointed out that these prohibitions often were being ignored, however. Georgia, for instance, had not sought to enforce its law for decades. *Id.,* at 197–198, n. 2, 106 S.Ct. 2841 ("The history of nonenforcement suggests the moribund character today of laws criminalizing this type of private, consensual conduct").

The sweeping references by Chief Justice Burger to the history of Western civilization and to Judeo–Christian moral and ethical standards did not take account of other authorities pointing in an opposite direction. A committee advising the British Parliament recommended in 1957 repeal of laws punishing homosexual conduct. The Wolfenden Report: Report of the Committee on Homosexual Offenses and Prostitution (1963). Parliament enacted the substance of those recommendations 10 years later. Sexual Offences Act 1967, § 1.

Of even more importance, almost five years before *Bowers* was decided the European Court of Human Rights considered a case with parallels to *Bowers* and to today's case. An adult male resident in Northern Ireland alleged he was a practicing homosexual who desired to engage in consensual homosexual conduct. The laws of Northern Ireland forbade him that right. He alleged that he had been questioned, his home had been searched, and he feared criminal prosecution. The court held that the laws proscribing the conduct were invalid under the European Convention on Human Rights. *Dudgeon v. United Kingdom,* 45 Eur. Ct. H.R. (1981). Authoritative in all countries that are members of the Council of Europe (21 nations then, 45 nations now), the decision is at odds with the premise in *Bowers* that the claim put forward was insubstantial in our Western civilization.

In our own constitutional system the deficiencies in *Bowers* became even more apparent in the years following its announcement. The 25 States with laws prohibiting the relevant conduct referenced in the *Bowers* decision are reduced now to 13, of which 4 enforce their laws only against homosexual conduct. In those States where sodomy is still proscribed, whether for same-sex or heterosexual conduct, there is a pattern of nonenforcement with respect to consenting adults acting in private. The State of Texas admitted in 1994 that as of that date it had not prosecuted anyone under those circumstances. *State v. Morales,* 869 S.W.2d 941, 943.

Two principal cases decided after *Bowers* cast its holding into even more doubt. In *Planned Parenthood of Southeastern Pa. v. Casey,* 505 U.S. 833, 112 S.Ct. 2791, 120 L.Ed.2d 674 (1992), the Court reaffirmed the substantive force of the liberty protected by the Due Process Clause. The *Casey* decision again confirmed that our laws and tradition afford constitutional protection to personal decisions relating to marriage, procreation, contraception, family relationships, child rearing, and education. *Id.,* at 851, 112 S.Ct. 2791. In explaining the respect the Constitution demands for the autonomy of the person in making these choices, we stated as follows:

> "These matters, involving the most intimate and personal choices a person may make in a lifetime, choices central to personal dignity and autonomy, are central to the liberty protected by the Fourteenth Amendment. At the heart of liberty is the right to define one's own concept of existence, of meaning, of the universe, and of the mystery of human life. Beliefs about these matters could not define the attributes of personhood were they formed under compulsion of the State." *Ibid.*

Persons in a homosexual relationship may seek autonomy for these purposes, just as heterosexual persons do. The decision in *Bowers* would deny them this right.

The second post-*Bowers* case of principal relevance is *Romer v. Evans,* 517 U.S. 620, 116 S.Ct. 1620, 134 L.Ed.2d 855 (1996). There the Court struck down class-based legislation directed at homosexuals as a violation of the Equal Protection Clause. *Romer* invalidated an amendment to Colorado's constitution which named as a solitary class persons who were homosexuals, lesbians, or bisexual either by "orientation, conduct, practices or relationships," *id.,* at 624, 116 S.Ct. 1620 (internal quotation marks omitted), and deprived them of protection under state antidiscrimination laws. We concluded that the provision was "born of animosity toward the class of persons affected" and further that it had no rational relation to a legitimate governmental purpose. *Id.,* at 634, 116 S.Ct. 1620.

As an alternative argument in this case, counsel for the petitioners and some *amici* contend that *Romer* provides the basis for declaring the Texas statute invalid under the Equal Protection Clause. That is a tenable argument, but we conclude the instant case requires us to address whether *Bowers* itself has continuing validity. Were we to hold the statute invalid under the Equal Protection Clause some might question whether a prohibition would be valid if drawn differently, say, to prohibit the conduct both between same-sex and different-sex participants.

Equality of treatment and the due process right to demand respect for conduct protected by the substantive guarantee of liberty are linked in important respects, and a decision on the latter point advances both interests. If protected conduct is made criminal and the law which does so remains unexamined for its substantive validity, its stigma might remain even if it were not enforceable as drawn for equal protection reasons. When homosexual conduct is made criminal by the law of the State, that declaration in and of itself is an invitation to subject homosexual persons to discrimination both in the public and in the private spheres. The central holding of *Bowers* has been brought in question by this case, and it should be addressed. Its continuance as precedent demeans the lives of homosexual persons.

The stigma this criminal statute imposes, moreover, is not trivial. The offense, to be sure, is but a class C misdemeanor, a minor offense in the Texas legal system. Still, it remains a criminal offense with all that imports for the dignity of the persons charged. The petitioners will bear on their record the history of their criminal convictions. Just this Term we rejected various challenges to state laws requiring the registration of sex offenders. *Smith v. Doe,* 538 U.S. 84, 123 S.Ct. 1140, 155 L.Ed.2d 164 (2003); *Connecticut Dept. of Public Safety v. Doe,* 538 U.S. 1, 123 S.Ct. 1160, 155 L.Ed.2d 98 (2003). We are advised that if Texas convicted an adult for private, consensual homosexual conduct under the statute here in question the convicted person would come within the registration laws of at least four States were he or she to be subject to their jurisdiction. Pet. for Cert. 13, and n. 12 (citing Idaho Code §§ 18–8301 to 18–8326 (Cum.Supp.2002); La.Code Crim. Proc. Ann., §§ 15:540–15:549 (West 2003); Miss.Code Ann. §§ 45–33–21 to 45–33–57 (Lexis 2003); S.C.Code Ann. §§ 23–3–400 to 23–3–490 (West 2002)). This underscores the consequential nature of the punishment and the state-sponsored condemnation attendant to the criminal prohibition. Furthermore, the Texas criminal conviction carries with it the other collateral consequences always following a conviction, such as notations on job application forms, to mention but one example.

The foundations of *Bowers* have sustained serious erosion from our recent decisions in *Casey* and *Romer*. When our precedent has been thus weakened, criticism from other sources is of greater significance. In the United States criticism of *Bowers* has been substantial and continuing, disapproving of its reasoning in all respects, not just as to its historical assumptions. See, *e.g.,* C. Fried, Order and Law: Arguing the Reagan Revolution—A Firsthand Account 81–84 (1991); R. Posner, Sex and Reason 341–350 (1992). The courts of five different States have declined to follow it in interpreting provisions in their own state constitutions parallel to the Due Process Clause of the Fourteenth Amendment, see *Jegley v. Picado,* 349 Ark. 600, 80 S.W.3d 332 (2002); *Powell v. State,* 270 Ga. 327, 510 S.E.2d 18, 24 (1998); *Gryczan v. State,* 283 Mont. 433, 942 P.2d 112 (1997); *Campbell v. Sundquist,* 926 S.W.2d 250 (Tenn.App.1996); *Commonwealth v. Wasson,* 842 S.W.2d 487 (Ky.1992).

To the extent *Bowers* relied on values we share with a wider civilization, it should be noted that the reasoning and holding in *Bowers* have been rejected elsewhere. The European Court of Human Rights has followed not *Bowers* but its own decision in *Dudgeon v. United Kingdom.* See *P.G. & J.H. v. United Kingdom,* App. No. 00044787/98, & ¶ 56 (Eur.Ct.H. R., Sept. 25, 2001); *Modinos v. Cyprus,* 259 Eur. Ct. H.R. (1993); *Norris v. Ireland,* 142 Eur. Ct. H.R. (1988). Other nations, too, have taken action consistent with an affirmation of the protected right of homosexual adults to engage in intimate, consensual conduct. See Brief for Mary Robinson et al. as *Amici Curiae* 11–12. The right the petitioners seek in this case has been accepted as an integral part of human freedom in many other countries. There has been no showing that in this country the governmental interest in circumscribing personal choice is somehow more legitimate or urgent.

The doctrine of *stare decisis* is essential to the respect accorded to the judgments of the Court and to the stability of the law. It is not, however, an inexorable command. *Payne v. Tennessee,* 501 U.S. 808, 828, 111 S.Ct. 2597, 115 L.Ed.2d 720 (1991) ("*Stare decisis* is not an inexorable command; rather, it 'is a principle of policy and not a mechanical formula of adherence to the latest decision' ") (quoting *Helvering v. Hallock,* 309 U.S. 106, 119, 60 S.Ct. 444, 84 L.Ed. 604 (1940)). In *Casey* we noted that when a Court is asked to overrule a precedent recognizing a constitutional liberty interest, individual or societal reliance on the existence of that liberty cautions with particular strength against reversing course. 505 U.S., at 855–856, 112 S.Ct. 2791; see also *id.,* at 844, 112 S.Ct. 2791 ("Liberty finds no refuge in a jurisprudence of doubt"). The holding in *Bowers,* however, has not induced detrimental reliance comparable to some instances where recognized individual rights are involved. Indeed, there has been no individual or societal reliance on *Bowers* of the sort that could counsel against overturning its holding once there are compelling reasons to do so. *Bowers* itself causes uncertainty, for the precedents before and after its issuance contradict its central holding.

The rationale of *Bowers* does not withstand careful analysis. In his dissenting opinion in Bowers Justice STEVENS came to these conclusions:

"Our prior cases make two propositions abundantly clear. First, the fact that the governing majority in a State has traditionally viewed a particular practice as immoral is not a sufficient reason for upholding a law prohibiting the practice; neither history nor tradition could save a law prohibiting miscegenation from constitutional attack. Second, individual decisions by married persons, concerning the intimacies of their physical relationship, even when not intended to produce offspring, are a form of 'liberty' protected by the Due Process Clause of the Fourteenth Amendment. Moreover, this protection extends to intimate choices by unmarried as well as married persons." 478 U.S., at 216, 106 S.Ct. 2841 (footnotes and citations omitted).

Justice STEVENS' analysis, in our view, should have been controlling in *Bowers* and should control here.

Bowers was not correct when it was decided, and it is not correct today. It ought not to remain binding precedent. *Bowers v. Hardwick* should be and now is overruled.

The present case does not involve minors. It does not involve persons who might be injured or coerced or who are situated in relationships where consent might not easily be refused. It does not involve public conduct or prostitution. It does not involve whether the government must give formal recognition to any relationship that homosexual persons seek to enter. The case does involve two adults who, with full and mutual consent from each other, engaged in sexual practices common to a homosexual lifestyle. The petitioners are entitled to respect for their private lives. The State cannot demean their existence or control their destiny by making their private sexual conduct a crime. Their right to liberty under the Due Process Clause gives them the full right to engage in their conduct without intervention of the government. "It is a promise of the Constitution that there is a realm of personal liberty which the government may not enter." *Casey, supra,* at 847, 112 S.Ct. 2791. The Texas statute furthers no legitimate state interest which can justify its intrusion into the personal and private life of the individual.

Had those who drew and ratified the Due Process Clauses of the Fifth Amendment or the Fourteenth Amendment known the components of liberty in its manifold possibilities, they might have been more specific. They did not presume to have this insight. They knew times can blind us to certain truths and later generations can see that laws once thought necessary and proper in fact serve only to oppress. As the Constitution endures, persons in every generation can invoke its principles in their own search for greater freedom.

The judgment of the Court of Appeals for the Texas Fourteenth District is reversed, and the case is remanded for further proceedings not inconsistent with this opinion.

■ JUSTICE O'CONNOR, concurring in the judgment.

The Court today overrules *Bowers v. Hardwick,* 478 U.S. 186, 106 S.Ct. 2841, 92 L.Ed.2d 140 (1986). I joined *Bowers,* and do not join the Court in overruling it. Nevertheless, I agree with the Court that Texas' statute banning same-sex sodomy is unconstitutional. See Tex. Penal Code Ann. § 21.06 (2003). Rather than relying on the substantive component of the Fourteenth Amendment's Due Process Clause, as the Court does, I base my conclusion on the Fourteenth Amendment's Equal Protection Clause.

The Equal Protection Clause of the Fourteenth Amendment "is essentially a direction that all persons similarly situated should be treated alike." *Cleburne v. Cleburne Living Center, Inc.,* 473 U.S. 432, 439, 105 S.Ct. 3249, 87 L.Ed.2d 313 (1985); see also *Plyler v. Doe,* 457 U.S. 202, 216, 102 S.Ct. 2382, 72 L.Ed.2d 786 (1982). Under our rational basis standard of review, "legislation is presumed to be valid and will be sustained if the classification drawn by the statute is rationally related to a legitimate state interest." *Cleburne v. Cleburne Living Center, supra,* at 440, 105 S.Ct. 3249; see also *Department of Agriculture v. Moreno,* 413 U.S. 528, 534, 93 S.Ct. 2821, 37 L.Ed.2d 782 (1973); *Romer v. Evans,* 517 U.S. 620, 632–633, 116 S.Ct. 1620, 134 L.Ed.2d 855 (1996); *Nordlinger v. Hahn,* 505 U.S. 1, 11–12, 112 S.Ct. 2326, 120 L.Ed.2d 1 (1992).

Laws such as economic or tax legislation that are scrutinized under rational basis review normally pass constitutional muster, since "the Constitution presumes that even improvident decisions will eventually be rectified by the democratic processes." *Cleburne v. Cleburne Living Center, supra,* at 440, 105 S.Ct. 3249; see also *Fitzgerald v. Racing Assn. of Central Iowa,* 539 U.S. 103, 123 S.Ct. 2156, 156 L.Ed.2d 97 (2003); *Williamson v. Lee Optical of Okla., Inc.,* 348 U.S. 483, 75 S.Ct. 461, 99 L.Ed. 563 (1955). We have consistently held, however, that some objectives, such as "a bare . . . desire to harm a politically unpopular group," are not legitimate state interests. *Department of Agriculture v. Moreno, supra,* at 534, 93 S.Ct. 2821. See also *Cleburne v. Cleburne Living Center, supra,* at 446–447, 105 S.Ct. 3249; *Romer v. Evans, supra,* at 632, 116 S.Ct. 1620. When a law exhibits such a desire to harm a politically unpopular group, we have applied a more searching form of rational basis review to strike down such laws under the Equal Protection Clause.

We have been most likely to apply rational basis review to hold a law unconstitutional under the Equal Protection Clause where, as here, the challenged legislation inhibits personal relationships. In *Department of Agriculture v. Moreno,* for example, we held that a law preventing those households containing an individual unrelated to any other member of the household from receiving food stamps violated equal protection because the purpose of the law was to " 'discriminate against hippies.' " 413 U.S., at 534, 93 S.Ct. 2821. The asserted governmental interest in preventing food stamp fraud was not deemed sufficient to satisfy rational basis review. *Id.,* at 535–538, 93 S.Ct. 2821. In *Eisenstadt v. Baird,* 405 U.S. 438, 447–455, 92 S.Ct. 1029, 31 L.Ed.2d 349 (1972), we refused to sanction a law that discriminated between married and unmarried persons by prohibiting the distribution of contraceptives to single persons. Likewise, in *Cleburne v.*

Cleburne Living Center, supra, we held that it was irrational for a State to require a home for the mentally disabled to obtain a special use permit when other residences—like fraternity houses and apartment buildings—did not have to obtain such a permit. And in *Romer v. Evans,* we disallowed a state statute that "impos[ed] a broad and undifferentiated disability on a single named group"—specifically, homosexuals. 517 U.S., at 632, 116 S.Ct. 1620.

The statute at issue here makes sodomy a crime only if a person "engages in deviate sexual intercourse with another individual of the same sex." Tex. Penal Code Ann. § 21.06(a) (2003). Sodomy between opposite-sex partners, however, is not a crime in Texas. That is, Texas treats the same conduct differently based solely on the participants. Those harmed by this law are people who have a same-sex sexual orientation and thus are more likely to engage in behavior prohibited by § 21.06.

The Texas statute makes homosexuals unequal in the eyes of the law by making particular conduct—and only that conduct—subject to criminal sanction. It appears that prosecutions under Texas' sodomy law are rare. See *State v. Morales,* 869 S.W.2d 941, 943 (Tex.1994) (noting in 1994 that § 21.06 "has not been, and in all probability will not be, enforced against private consensual conduct between adults"). This case shows, however, that prosecutions under § 21.06 *do* occur. And while the penalty imposed on petitioners in this case was relatively minor, the consequences of conviction are not. It appears that petitioner's convictions, if upheld, would disqualify them from or restrict their ability to engage in a variety of professions, including medicine, athletic training, and interior design. See, *e.g.,* Tex. Occ.Code Ann. § 164.051(a)(2)(B) (2003 Pamphlet) (physician); § 451.251(a)(1) (athletic trainer); § 1053.252(2) (interior designer). Indeed, were petitioners to move to one of four States, their convictions would require them to register as sex offenders to local law enforcement. See, *e.g.,* Idaho Code § 18–8304 (Cum.Supp.2002); La. Stat. Ann. § 15:542 (West Cum.Supp.2003); Miss.Code Ann. § 45–33–25 (West 2003); S.C.Code Ann. § 23–3–430 (West Cum.Supp.2002); cf. *ante,* at 2482.

And the effect of Texas' sodomy law is not just limited to the threat of prosecution or consequence of conviction. Texas' sodomy law brands all homosexuals as criminals, thereby making it more difficult for homosexuals to be treated in the same manner as everyone else. Indeed, Texas itself has previously acknowledged the collateral effects of the law, stipulating in a prior challenge to this action that the law "legally sanctions discrimination against [homosexuals] in a variety of ways unrelated to the criminal law," including in the areas of "employment, family issues, and housing." *State v. Morales,* 826 S.W.2d 201, 203 (Tex.App.1992).

Texas attempts to justify its law, and the effects of the law, by arguing that the statute satisfies rational basis review because it furthers the legitimate governmental interest of the promotion of morality. In *Bowers,* we held that a state law criminalizing sodomy as applied to homosexual couples did not violate substantive due process. We rejected the argument that no rational basis existed to justify the law, pointing to the government's interest in promoting morality. 478 U.S., at 196, 106 S.Ct. 2841. The only question in front of the Court in *Bowers* was whether the substantive component of the Due Process Clause protected a right to engage in homosexual sodomy. *Id.,* at 188, n. 2. *Bowers* did not hold that moral disapproval of a group is a rational basis under the Equal Protection Clause to criminalize homosexual sodomy when heterosexual sodomy is not punished.

This case raises a different issue than *Bowers:* whether, under the Equal Protection Clause, moral disapproval is a legitimate state interest to justify by itself a statute that bans homosexual sodomy, but not heterosexual sodomy. It is not. Moral disapproval of this group, like a bare desire to harm the group, is an interest that is insufficient to satisfy rational basis review under the Equal Protection Clause. See, *e.g., Department of Agriculture v. Moreno, supra,* at 534, 93 S.Ct. 2821; *Romer v. Evans,* 517 U.S., at 634–635, 116 S.Ct. 1620. Indeed, we have never held that moral disapproval, without any other asserted state interest, is a sufficient rationale under the Equal Protection Clause to justify a law that discriminates among groups of persons.

Moral disapproval of a group cannot be a legitimate governmental interest under the Equal Protection Clause because legal classifications must not be "drawn for the purpose of disadvantaging the group burdened by the law." *Id.,* at 633, 116 S.Ct. 1620. Texas' invocation of moral disapproval as a legitimate state interest proves nothing more than Texas' desire to criminalize homosexual sodomy. But the Equal Protection Clause prevents a State from creating "a classification of persons undertaken for its own sake." *Id.,* at 635, 116 S.Ct. 1620. And because Texas so rarely enforces its sodomy law as applied to private, consensual acts, the law serves more as a statement of dislike and disapproval against homosexuals than as a tool to stop criminal behavior. The Texas sodomy law "raise[s] the inevitable inference that the disadvantage imposed is born of animosity toward the class of persons affected." *Id.,* at 634, 116 S.Ct. 1620.

Texas argues, however, that the sodomy law does not discriminate against homosexual persons. Instead, the State maintains that the law discriminates only against homosexual conduct. While it is true that the law applies only to conduct, the conduct targeted by this law is conduct that is closely correlated with being homosexual. Under such circumstances, Texas' sodomy law is targeted at more than conduct. It is instead directed toward gay persons as a class. "After all, there can hardly be more palpable discrimination against a class than making the conduct that defines the class criminal." *Id.,* at 641, 116 S.Ct. 1620 (SCALIA, J., dissenting) (internal quotation marks omitted). When a State makes homosexual conduct criminal, and not "deviate sexual intercourse" committed by persons of different sexes, "that declaration in and of itself is an invitation to subject homosexual persons to discrimination both in the public and in the private spheres." *Ante,* at 2482.

Indeed, Texas law confirms that the sodomy statute is directed toward homosexuals as a class. In Texas, calling a person a homosexual is slander *per se* because the word "homosexual" "impute[s] the commission of a crime." *Plumley v. Landmark Chevrolet, Inc.,* 122 F.3d 308, 310 (C.A.5 1997) (applying Texas law); see also *Head v. Newton,* 596 S.W.2d 209, 210 (Tex.App.1980). The State has admitted that because of the sodomy law, *being* homosexual carries the presumption of being a criminal. See *State v. Morales,* 826 S.W.2d, at 202–203 ("[T]he statute brands lesbians and gay men as criminals and thereby legally sanctions discrimination against them in a variety of ways unrelated to the criminal law"). Texas' sodomy law therefore results in discrimination against homosexuals as a class in an array of areas outside the criminal law. See *ibid.* In *Romer v. Evans,* we refused to sanction a law that singled out homosexuals "for disfavored legal status." 517 U.S., at 633, 116 S.Ct. 1620. The same is true here. The Equal Protection Clause " 'neither knows nor tolerates classes among citizens.' " *Id.,* at 623, 116 S.Ct. 1620 (quoting *Plessy v. Ferguson,* 163 U.S. 537, 559, 16 S.Ct. 1138, 41 L.Ed. 256 (1896) (Harlan, J. dissenting)).

A State can of course assign certain consequences to a violation of its criminal law. But the State cannot single out one identifiable class of citizens for punishment that does not apply to everyone else, with moral disapproval as the only asserted state interest for the law. The Texas sodomy statute subjects homosexuals to "a lifelong penalty and stigma. A legislative classification that threatens the creation of an underclass ... cannot be reconciled with" the Equal Protection Clause. *Plyler v. Doe,* 457 U.S., at 239, 102 S.Ct. 2382 (Powell, J., concurring).

Whether a sodomy law that is neutral both in effect and application, see *Yick Wo v. Hopkins,* 118 U.S. 356, 6 S.Ct. 1064, 30 L.Ed. 220 (1886), would violate the substantive component of the Due Process Clause is an issue that need not be decided today. I am confident, however, that so long as the Equal Protection Clause requires a sodomy law to apply equally to the private consensual conduct of homosexuals and heterosexuals alike, such a law would not long stand in our democratic society. In the words of Justice Jackson:

> "The framers of the Constitution knew, and we should not forget today, that there is no more effective practical guaranty against arbitrary and unreasonable government than to require that the principles of law which officials would impose upon a minority be imposed generally. Conversely, nothing opens the door to arbitrary action so effectively as to allow those officials to pick and choose only a few to whom they will apply legislation and thus to escape the political retribution that might be visited upon them if larger numbers were affected." *Railway Express Agency, Inc. v. New York,* 336 U.S. 106, 112–113, 69 S.Ct. 463, 93 L.Ed. 533 (1949) (concurring opinion).

That this law as applied to private, consensual conduct is unconstitutional under the Equal Protection Clause does not mean that other laws distinguishing between heterosexuals and homosexuals would similarly fail under rational basis review. Texas cannot assert any legitimate state interest here, such as national security or preserving the traditional institution of marriage. Unlike the moral disapproval of same-sex relations—the asserted state interest in this case—other reasons exist to promote the institution of marriage beyond mere moral disapproval of an excluded group.

A law branding one class of persons as criminal based solely on the State's moral disapproval of that class and the conduct associated with that class runs contrary to the values of the Constitution and the Equal Protection Clause, under any standard of review. I therefore concur in the Court's judgment that Texas' sodomy law banning "deviate sexual intercourse" between consenting adults of the same sex, but not between consenting adults of different sexes, is unconstitutional.

■ JUSTICE SCALIA, with whom THE CHIEF JUSTICE and JUSTICE THOMAS join, dissenting.

"Liberty finds no refuge in a jurisprudence of doubt." *Planned Parenthood of Southeastern Pa. v. Casey,* 505 U.S. 833, 844, 112 S.Ct. 2791, 120 L.Ed.2d 674 (1992). That was the Court's sententious response, barely more than a decade ago, to those seeking to overrule *Roe v. Wade,* 410 U.S. 113, 93 S.Ct. 705, 35 L.Ed.2d 147 (1973). The Court's response today, to those who have engaged in a 17–year crusade to overrule *Bowers v. Hardwick,* 478 U.S. 186, 106 S.Ct. 2841, 92 L.Ed.2d 140 (1986), is very different. The need for stability and certainty presents no barrier.

Most of the rest of today's opinion has no relevance to its actual holding—that the Texas statute "furthers no legitimate state interest which can justify" its application to petitioners under rational-basis review. *Ante,* at 2484 (overruling *Bowers* to the extent it sustained Georgia's antisodomy statute under the rational-basis test). Though there is discussion of "fundamental proposition[s]," *ante,* at 2477, and "fundamental decisions," *ibid.* nowhere does the Court's opinion declare that homosexual sodomy is a "fundamental right" under the Due Process Clause; nor does it subject the Texas law to the standard of review that would be appropriate (strict scrutiny) if homosexual sodomy *were* a "fundamental right." Thus, while overruling the *outcome* of *Bowers,* the Court leaves strangely untouched its central legal conclusion: "[R]espondent would have us announce ... a fundamental right to engage in homosexual sodomy. This we are quite unwilling to do." 478 U.S., at 191, 106 S.Ct. 2841. Instead the Court simply describes petitioners' conduct as "an exercise of their liberty"—which it undoubtedly is—and proceeds to apply an unheard-of form of rational-basis review that will have far-reaching implications beyond this case. *Ante,* at 2476.

I

I begin with the Court's surprising readiness to reconsider a decision rendered a mere 17 years ago in *Bowers v. Hardwick.* I do not myself believe in rigid adherence to *stare decisis* in constitutional cases; but I do believe that we should be consistent rather than manipulative in invoking the doctrine. Today's opinions in support of reversal do not bother to distinguish—or indeed, even bother to mention—the paean to *stare decisis* coauthored by three Members of today's majority in *Planned Parenthood v.*

Casey. There, when *stare decisis* meant preservation of judicially invented abortion rights, the widespread criticism of *Roe* was strong reason to *reaffirm* it:

> "Where, in the performance of its judicial duties, the Court decides a case in such a way as to resolve the sort of intensely divisive controversy reflected in *Roe* [,] ... its decision has a dimension that the resolution of the normal case does not carry.... [T]o overrule under fire in the absence of the most compelling reason ... would subvert the Court's legitimacy beyond any serious question." 505 U.S., at 866–867, 112 S.Ct. 2791.

Today, however, the widespread opposition to *Bowers,* a decision resolving an issue as "intensely divisive" as the issue in *Roe,* is offered as a reason in favor of *overruling* it. See *ante,* at 2482–2483. Gone, too, is any "enquiry" (of the sort conducted in *Casey*) into whether the decision sought to be overruled has "proven 'unworkable,' " *Casey, supra,* at 855, 112 S.Ct. 2791.

Today's approach to *stare decisis* invites us to overrule an erroneously decided precedent (including an "intensely divisive" decision) *if:* (1) its foundations have been "eroded" by subsequent decisions, *ante,* at 2482; (2) it has been subject to "substantial and continuing" criticism, *ibid.*; and (3) it has not induced "individual or societal reliance" that counsels against overturning, *ante,* at 2483. The problem is that *Roe* itself—which today's majority surely has no disposition to overrule—satisfies these conditions to at least the same degree as *Bowers.*

A preliminary digressive observation with regard to the first factor: The Court's claim that *Planned Parenthood v. Casey, supra,* "casts some doubt" upon the holding in *Bowers* (or any other case, for that matter) does not withstand analysis. *Ante,* at 2480. As far as its holding is concerned, *Casey* provided a *less* expansive right to abortion than did *Roe, which was already on the books when* Bowers *was decided.* And if the Court is referring not to the holding of *Casey,* but to the dictum of its famed sweet-mystery-of-life passage, *ante,* at 2481 (" 'At the heart of liberty is the right to define one's own concept of existence, of meaning, of the universe, and of the mystery of human life' "): That "casts some doubt" upon either the totality of our jurisprudence or else (presumably the right answer) nothing at all. I have never heard of a law that attempted to restrict one's "right to define" certain concepts; and if the passage calls into question the government's power to regulate *actions based on* one's self-defined "concept of existence, etc.," it is the passage that ate the rule of law.

I do not quarrel with the Court's claim that *Romer v. Evans,* 517 U.S. 620, 116 S.Ct. 1620, 134 L.Ed.2d 855 (1996), "eroded" the "foundations" of *Bowers'* rational-basis holding. See *Romer, supra,* at 640–643, 116 S.Ct. 1620 (SCALIA, J., dissenting). But *Roe* and *Casey* have been equally "eroded" by *Washington v. Glucksberg,* 521 U.S. 702, 721, 117 S.Ct. 2258, 138 L.Ed.2d 772 (1997), which held that *only* fundamental rights which are " 'deeply rooted in this Nation's history and tradition' " qualify for anything other than rational basis scrutiny under the doctrine of "substantive due process." *Roe* and *Casey,* of course, subjected the restriction of abortion to heightened scrutiny without even attempting to establish that the freedom to abort *was* rooted in this Nation's tradition.

Bowers, the Court says, has been subject to "substantial and continuing [criticism], disapproving of its reasoning in all respects, not just as to its historical assumptions." *Ante,* at 2483. Exactly what those nonhistorical criticisms are, and whether the Court even agrees with them, are left unsaid, although the Court does cite two books. See *ibid.* (citing C. Fried, Order and Law: Arguing the Reagan Revolution—A Firsthand Account 81–84 (1991); R. Posner, Sex and Reason 341–350 (1992)).[1] Of course, *Roe* too (and by extension *Casey*) had been (and still is) subject to unrelenting criticism, including criticism from the two commentators cited by the Court today. See Fried, *supra,* at 75 ("Roe was a prime example of twisted judging"); Posner, *supra,* at 337 ("[The Court's] opinion in *Roe* (3)27 fails to measure up to professional expectations regarding judicial opinions"); Posner, Judicial Opinion Writing, 62 U. Chi. L.Rev. 1421, 1434 (1995) (describing the opinion in *Roe* as an "embarrassing performanc[e]").

That leaves, to distinguish the rock-solid, unamendable disposition of *Roe* from the readily overrulable *Bowers,* only the third factor. "[T]here has been," the Court says, "no individual or societal reliance on *Bowers* of the sort that could counsel against overturning its holding...." *Ante,* at 2483. It seems to me that the "societal reliance" on the principles confirmed in *Bowers* and discarded today has been overwhelming. Countless judicial decisions and legislative enactments have relied on the ancient proposition that a governing majority's belief that certain sexual behavior is "immoral and unacceptable" constitutes a rational basis for regulation. See, *e.g., Williams v. Pryor,* 240 F.3d 944, 949 (C.A.11 2001) (citing *Bowers* in upholding Alabama's prohibition on the sale of sex toys on the ground that "[t]he crafting and safeguarding of public morality ... indisputably is a legitimate government interest under rational basis scrutiny"); *Milner v. Apfel,* 148 F.3d 812, 814 (C.A.7 1998) (citing *Bowers* for the proposition that "[l]egislatures are permitted to legislate with regard to morality ... rather than confined to preventing demonstrable harms"); *Holmes v. California Army National Guard* 124 F.3d 1126, 1136 (C.A.9 1997) (relying on *Bowers* in upholding the federal statute and regulations banning from military service those who engage in homosexual conduct); *Owens v. State,* 352 Md. 663, 683, 724 A.2d 43, 53 (1999) (relying on *Bowers* in holding that "a person has no constitutional right to engage in sexual intercourse, at least outside of marriage"); *Sherman v. Henry,* 928 S.W.2d 464, 469–473 (Tex.1996) (relying on *Bowers* in rejecting a claimed constitutional right to commit adultery). We ourselves relied extensively on *Bowers* when we concluded, in *Barnes v. Glen Theatre, Inc.,* 501 U.S. 560, 569, 111 S.Ct. 2456, 115 L.Ed.2d 504 (1991), that Indiana's public indecency statute furthered "a substantial government interest in protecting order and

---

1. This last-cited critic of *Bowers* actually writes: *"[Bowers]* is correct nevertheless that the right to engage in homosexual acts is not deeply rooted in America's history and tradition." Posner, Sex and Reason, at 343.

morality," *ibid.,* (plurality opinion); see also *id.,* at 575, 111 S.Ct. 2456 (SCALIA, J., concurring in judgment). State laws against bigamy, same-sex marriage, adult incest, prostitution, masturbation, adultery, fornication, bestiality, and obscenity are likewise sustainable only in light of *Bowers'* validation of laws based on moral choices. Every single one of these laws is called into question by today's decision; the Court makes no effort to cabin the scope of its decision to exclude them from its holding. See *ante,* at 2480 (noting "an emerging awareness that liberty gives substantial protection to adult persons in deciding how to conduct their private lives *in matters pertaining to sex*" (emphasis added)). The impossibility of distinguishing homosexuality from other traditional "morals" offenses is precisely why *Bowers* rejected the rational-basis challenge. "The law," it said, "is constantly based on notions of morality, and if all laws representing essentially moral choices are to be invalidated under the Due Process Clause, the courts will be very busy indeed." 478 U.S., at 196, 106 S.Ct. 2841.[2]

What a massive disruption of the current social order, therefore, the overruling of *Bowers* entails. Not so the overruling of *Roe,* which would simply have restored the regime that existed for centuries before 1973, in which the permissibility of and restrictions upon abortion were determined legislatively State-by-State. *Casey,* however, chose to base its *stare decisis* determination on a different "sort" of reliance. "[P]eople," it said, "have organized intimate relationships and made choices that define their views of themselves and their places in society, in reliance on the availability of abortion in the event that contraception should fail." 505 U.S., at 856, 112 S.Ct. 2791. This falsely assumes that the consequence of overruling *Roe* would have been to make abortion unlawful. It would not; it would merely have *permitted* the States to do so. Many States would unquestionably have

---

2. While the Court does not overrule *Bowers* "holding that homosexual sodomy is not a 'fundamental right,'" it is worth noting that the 'societal reliance' upon that aspect of the decision has been substantial as well." See 10 U.S.C. § 654(b)(1) ("A member of the armed forces shall be separated from the armed forces ... if ... the member has engaged in ... a homosexual act or acts"); *Marcum v. McWhorter,* 308 F.3d 635, 640–642 (C.A.6 2002) (relying on *Bowers* in rejecting a claimed fundamental right to commit adultery); *Mullins v. Oregon,* 57 F.3d 789, 793–794 (C.A.9 1995) (relying on *Bowers* in rejecting a grandparent's claimed "fundamental liberty interes[t]" in the adoption of her grandchildren); *Doe v. Wigginton,* 21 F.3d 733, 739–740 (C.A.6 1994) (relying on *Bowers* in rejecting a prisoner's claimed "fundamental right" to on-demand HIV testing); *Schowengerdt v. United States,* 944 F.2d 483, 490 (C.A.9 1991) (relying on *Bowers* in upholding a bisexual's discharge from the armed services); *Charles v. Baesler,* 910 F.2d 1349, 1353 (C.A.6 1990) (relying on *Bowers* in rejecting fire department captain's claimed "fundamental" interest in a promotion); *Henne v. Wright,* 904 F.2d 1208, 1214–1215 (C.A.8 1990) (relying on *Bowers* in rejecting a claim that state law restricting surnames that could be given to children at birth implicates a "fundamental right"); *Walls v. Petersburg,* 895 F.2d 188, 193 implicates a "fundamental right"; *Walls v. Petersburg,* 895 F.2d 188, 193 (C.A.4 1990) (relying on *Bowers* in rejecting substantive-due-process challenge to a police department questionnaire that asked prospective employees about homosexual activity); *High Tech Gays v. Defense Industrial Security Clearance Office,* 895 F.2d 563, 570–571 (C.A.9 1990) (relying on *Bowers* holding that homosexual activity is not a fundamental right in rejecting—on the basis of the rational-basis standard—an equal-protection challenge to the Defense Department's policy of conducting expanded investigations into backgrounds of gay and lesbian applicants for secret and top-secret security clearance).

declined to prohibit abortion, and others would not have prohibited it within six months (after which the most significant reliance interests would have expired). Even for persons in States other than these, the choice would not have been between abortion and childbirth, but between abortion nearby and abortion in a neighboring State.

To tell the truth, it does not surprise me, and should surprise no one, that the Court has chosen today to revise the standards of *stare decisis* set forth in *Casey*. It has thereby exposed *Casey*'s extraordinary deference to precedent for the result-oriented expedient that it is.

II

Having decided that it need not adhere to *stare decisis,* the Court still must establish that *Bowers* was wrongly decided and that the Texas statute, as applied to petitioners, is unconstitutional.

Texas Penal Code Ann. § 21.06(a) (2003) undoubtedly imposes constraints on liberty. So do laws prohibiting prostitution, recreational use of heroin, and, for that matter, working more than 60 hours per week in a bakery. But there is no right to "liberty" under the Due Process Clause, though today's opinion repeatedly makes that claim. *Ante,* at 2478 ("The liberty protected by the Constitution allows homosexual persons the right to make this choice"); *ante,* at 2481 (" 'These matters . . . are central to the liberty protected by the Fourteenth Amendment' "); *ante,* at 2483 ("Their right to liberty under the Due Process Clause gives them the full right to engage in their conduct without intervention of the government"). The Fourteenth Amendment *expressly allows* States to deprive their citizens of "liberty," *so long as "due process of law" is provided:*

"No state shall . . . deprive any person of life, liberty, or property, *without due process of law."* Amdt. 14 (emphasis added).

Our opinions applying the doctrine known as "substantive due process" hold that the Due Process Clause prohibits States from infringing *fundamental* liberty interests, unless the infringement is narrowly tailored to serve a compelling state interest. *Washington v. Glucksberg,* 521 U.S., at 721, 117 S.Ct. 2258. We have held repeatedly, in cases the Court today does not overrule, that *only* fundamental rights qualify for this so-called "heightened scrutiny" protection—that is, rights which are " 'deeply rooted in this Nation's history and tradition,' " *ibid.* See *Reno v. Flores,* 507 U.S. 292, 303, 113 S.Ct. 1439, 123 L.Ed.2d 1 (1993) (fundamental liberty interests must be "so rooted in the traditions and conscience of our people as to be ranked as fundamental" (internal quotation marks and citations omitted)); *United States v. Salerno,* 481 U.S. 739, 751, 107 S.Ct. 2095, 95 L.Ed.2d 697 (1987) (same). See also *Michael H. v. Gerald D.,* 491 U.S. 110, 122, 109 S.Ct. 2333, 105 L.Ed.2d 91 (1989) ("[W]e have insisted not merely that the interest denominated as a 'liberty' be 'fundamental' . . . but also that it be an interest traditionally protected by our society"); *Moore v. East Cleveland,* 431 U.S. 494, 503, 97 S.Ct. 1932, 52 L.Ed.2d 531 (1977) (plurality opinion); *Meyer v. Nebraska,* 262 U.S. 390, 399, 43 S.Ct. 625, 67 L.Ed. 1042 (1923) (Fourteenth Amendment protects "those privileges *long recognized at common law* as essential to the orderly pursuit of happiness by free men" (emphasis added)).[3] All other liberty interests may be abridged or abrogated pursuant to a validly enacted state law if that law is rationally related to a legitimate state interest.

Bowers held, first, that criminal prohibitions of homosexual sodomy are not subject to heightened scrutiny because they do not implicate a "fundamental right" under the Due Process Clause, 478 U.S., at 191–194, 106 S.Ct. 2841. Noting that "[p]roscriptions against that conduct have ancient roots," *id.,* at 192, 106 S.Ct. 2841, that "[s]odomy was a criminal offense at common law and was forbidden by the laws of the original 13 States when they ratified the Bill of Rights," *ibid.,* and that many States had retained their bans on sodomy, *id.,* at 193, *Bowers* concluded that a right to engage in homosexual sodomy was not " 'deeply rooted in this Nation's history and tradition,' " *id.,* at 192, 106 S.Ct. 2841.

The Court today does not overrule this holding. Not once does it describe homosexual sodomy as a "fundamental right" or a "fundamental liberty interest," nor does it subject the Texas statute to strict scrutiny. Instead, having failed to establish that the right to homosexual sodomy is " 'deeply rooted in this Nation's history and tradition,' " the Court concludes that the application of Texas's statute to petitioners' conduct fails the rational-basis test, and overrules *Bowers'* holding to the contrary, see *id.,* at 196, 106 S.Ct. 2841. "The Texas statute furthers no legitimate state interest which can justify its intrusion into the personal and private life of the individual." *Ante,* at 2484.

I shall address that rational-basis holding presently. First, however, I address some aspersions that the Court casts upon *Bowers'* conclusion that homosexual sodomy is not a "fundamental right"—even though, as I have said, the Court does not have the boldness to reverse that conclusion.

III

The Court's description of "the state of the law" at the time of *Bowers* only confirms that *Bowers* was right. *Ante,* at 2477. The Court points to *Griswold v. Connecticut,* 381 U.S. 479, 481–482, 85 S.Ct. 1678, 14 L.Ed.2d 510 (1965). But that case *expressly disclaimed* any reliance on the doctrine of "substantive due process," and grounded the so-called "right to privacy" in penumbras of constitutional provisions *other than* the Due Process Clause. *Eisenstadt v. Baird,* 405 U.S. 438, 92 S.Ct. 1029, 31 L.Ed.2d 349 (1972), likewise had nothing to do with "substantive due process"; it

---

3. The Court is quite right that "history and tradition are the starting point but not in all cases the ending point of the substantive due process inquiry," *ante,* at 2480. An asserted "fundamental liberty interest" must not only be "deeply rooted in this Nation's history and tradition," *Washington v. Glucksberg,* 521 U.S. 702, 721, 117 S.Ct. 2258 (1997), but it must *also* be "implicit in the concept of ordered liberty," so that "neither liberty nor justice would exist if [it] were sacrificed," *ibid.* Moreover, liberty interests unsupported by history and tradition, though not deserving of "heightened scrutiny," are *still* protected from state laws that are not rationally related to any legitimate state interest. *Id.,* at 722, 117 S.Ct. 2258. As I proceed to discuss, it is this latter principle that the Court applies in the present case.

invalidated a Massachusetts law prohibiting the distribution of contraceptives to unmarried persons solely on the basis of the Equal Protection Clause. Of course *Eisenstadt* contains well known dictum relating to the "right to privacy," but this referred to the right recognized in *Griswold*—a right penumbral to the *specific* guarantees in the Bill of Rights, and not a "substantive due process" right.

Roe v. Wade recognized that the right to abort an unborn child was a "fundamental right" protected by the Due Process Clause. 410 U.S., at 155, 93 S.Ct. 705. The *Roe* Court, however, made no attempt to establish that this right was " 'deeply rooted in this Nation's history and tradition' ''; instead, it based its conclusion that "the Fourteenth Amendment's concept of personal liberty . . . is broad enough to encompass a woman's decision whether or not to terminate her pregnancy" on its own normative judgment that anti-abortion laws were undesirable. See *id.*, at 153, 93 S.Ct. 705. We have since rejected *Roe*'s holding that regulations of abortion must be narrowly tailored to serve a compelling state interest, see *Planned Parenthood v. Casey,* 505 U.S., at 876, 112 S.Ct. 2791 (joint opinion of O'CONNOR, KENNEDY, and SOUTER, JJ.); *id.*, at 951–953, 112 S.Ct. 2791 (REHNQUIST, C. J., concurring in judgment in part and dissenting in part)—and thus, by logical implication, *Roe*'s holding that the right to abort an unborn child is a "fundamental right." See 505 U.S., at 843–912, 112 S.Ct. 2791 (joint opinion of O'CONNOR, KENNEDY, and SOUTER, JJ.) (not once describing abortion as a "fundamental right" or a "fundamental liberty interest").

After discussing the history of antisodomy laws, *ante,* at 2478–2480, the Court proclaims that, "it should be noted that there is no longstanding history in this country of laws directed at homosexual conduct as a distinct matter," *ante,* at 2478. This observation in no way casts into doubt the "definitive [historical] conclusion," *id.*, on which *Bowers* relied: that our Nation has a longstanding history of laws prohibiting *sodomy in general*— regardless of whether it was performed by same-sex or opposite-sex couples:

> "It is obvious to us that neither of these formulations would extend a fundamental right to homosexuals to engage in acts of consensual sodomy. Proscriptions against that conduct have ancient roots. *Sodomy* was a criminal offense at common law and was forbidden by the laws of the original 13 States when they ratified the Bill of Rights. In 1868, when the Fourteenth Amendment was ratified, all but 5 of the 37 States in the Union had *criminal sodomy laws.* In fact, until 1961, all 50 States outlawed *sodomy,* and today, 24 States and the District of Columbia continue to provide criminal penalties for *sodomy* performed in private and between consenting adults. Against this background, to claim that a right to engage in such conduct is 'deeply rooted in this Nation's history and tradition' or 'implicit in the concept of ordered liberty' is, at best, facetious." 478 U.S., at 192–194, 106 S.Ct. 2841 (citations and footnotes omitted; emphasis added).

It is (as *Bowers* recognized) entirely irrelevant whether the laws in our long national tradition criminalizing homosexual sodomy were "directed at homosexual conduct as a distinct matter." *Ante,* at 2478. Whether homosexual sodomy was prohibited by a law targeted at same-sex sexual relations or by a more general law prohibiting both homosexual and heterosexual sodomy, the only relevant point is that it *was* criminalized—which suffices to establish that homosexual sodomy is not a right "deeply rooted in our Nation's history and tradition." The Court today agrees that homosexual sodomy was criminalized and thus does not dispute the facts on which *Bowers actually* relied.

Next the Court makes the claim, again unsupported by any citations, that "[l]aws prohibiting sodomy do not seem to have been enforced against consenting adults acting in private." *Ante,* at 2479. The key qualifier here is "acting in private"—since the Court admits that sodomy laws *were* enforced against consenting adults (although the Court contends that prosecutions were "infrequent," *ibid.*). I do not know what "acting in private" means; surely consensual sodomy, like heterosexual intercourse, is rarely performed on stage. If all the Court means by "acting in private" is "on private premises, with the doors closed and windows covered," it is entirely unsurprising that evidence of enforcement would be hard to come by. (Imagine the circumstances that would enable a search warrant to be obtained for a residence on the ground that there was probable cause to believe that consensual sodomy was then and there occurring.) Surely that lack of evidence would not sustain the proposition that consensual sodomy on private premises with the doors closed and windows covered was regarded as a "fundamental right," even though all other consensual sodomy was criminalized. There are 203 prosecutions for consensual, adult homosexual sodomy reported in the West Reporting system and official state reporters from the years 1880–1995. See W. Eskridge, Gaylaw: Challenging the Apartheid of the Closet 375 (1999) (hereinafter Gaylaw). There are also records of 20 sodomy prosecutions and 4 executions during the colonial period. J. Katz, Gay/Lesbian Almanac 29, 58, 663 (1983). *Bowers'* conclusion that homosexual sodomy is not a fundamental right "deeply rooted in this Nation's history and tradition" is utterly unassailable.

Realizing that fact, the Court instead says: "[W]e think that our laws and traditions in the past half century are of most relevance here. These references show *an emerging awareness* that liberty gives substantial protection to adult persons in deciding how to conduct their private lives *in matters pertaining to sex.*" *Ante,* at 2480 (emphasis added). Apart from the fact that such an "emerging awareness" does not establish a "fundamental right," the statement is factually false. States continue to prosecute all sorts of crimes by adults "in matters pertaining to sex": prostitution, adult incest, adultery, obscenity, and child pornography. Sodomy laws, too, have been enforced "in the past half century," in which there have been 134 reported cases involving prosecutions for consensual, adult, homosexual sodomy. Gaylaw 375. In relying, for evidence of an "emerging recognition," upon the American Law Institute's 1955 recommendation not to criminalize " 'consensual sexual relations conducted in private,' " *ante,* at 2480, the Court ignores the fact that this recommendation was "a point of resistance in most of the states that considered adopting the Model Penal Code." Gaylaw 159.

In any event, an "emerging awareness" is by definition not "deeply rooted in this Nation's history and tradition[s]," as we have said "fundamental right" status requires. Constitutional entitlements do not spring into existence because some States choose to lessen or eliminate criminal sanctions on certain behavior. Much less do they spring into existence, as the Court seems to believe, because *foreign nations* decriminalize conduct. The *Bowers* majority opinion *never* relied on "values we share with a wider civilization," *ante,* at 2483, but rather rejected the claimed right to sodomy on the ground that such a right was not " 'deeply rooted in *this Nation's* history and tradition,' " 478 U.S., at 193–194, 106 S.Ct. 2841 (emphasis added). *Bowers'* rational-basis holding is likewise devoid of any reliance on the views of a "wider civilization," see *id.,* at 196, 106 S.Ct. 2841. The Court's discussion of these foreign views (ignoring, of course, the many countries that have retained criminal prohibitions on sodomy) is therefore meaningless dicta. Dangerous dicta, however, since "this Court ... should not impose foreign moods, fads, or fashions on Americans." *Foster v. Florida,* 537 U.S. 990, n., 123 S.Ct. 470, 154 L.Ed.2d 359 (2002) (THOMAS, J., concurring in denial of certiorari).

IV

I turn now to the ground on which the Court squarely rests its holding: the contention that there is no rational basis for the law here under attack. This proposition is so out of accord with our jurisprudence—indeed, with the jurisprudence of *any* society we know—that it requires little discussion.

The Texas statute undeniably seeks to further the belief of its citizens that certain forms of sexual behavior are "immoral and unacceptable," *Bowers, supra,* at 196, 106 S.Ct. 2841—the same interest furthered by criminal laws against fornication, bigamy, adultery, adult incest, bestiality, and obscenity. *Bowers* held that this *was* a legitimate state interest. The Court today reaches the opposite conclusion. The Texas statute, it says, "furthers *no legitimate state interest* which can justify its intrusion into the personal and private life of the individual," *ante,* at 2484 (emphasis addded). The Court embraces instead Justice STEVENS' declaration in his *Bowers* dissent, that "the fact that the governing majority in a State has traditionally viewed a particular practice as immoral is not a sufficient reason for upholding a law prohibiting the practice," *ante,* at 2483. This effectively decrees the end of all morals legislation. If, as the Court asserts, the promotion of majoritarian sexual morality is not even a *legitimate* state interest, none of the above-mentioned laws can survive rational-basis review.

V

Finally, I turn to petitioners' equal-protection challenge, which no Member of the Court save Justice O'CONNOR, *ante,* at 2484 (opinion concurring in judgment), embraces: On its face § 21.06(a) applies equally to all persons. Men and women, heterosexuals and homosexuals, are all subject to its prohibition of deviate sexual intercourse with someone of the same sex. To be sure, § 21.06 does distinguish between the sexes insofar as concerns the partner with whom the sexual acts are performed: men can violate the law only with other men, and women only with other women. But this cannot itself be a denial of equal protection, since it is precisely the same distinction regarding partner that is drawn in state laws prohibiting marriage with someone of the same sex while permitting marriage with someone of the opposite sex.

The objection is made, however, that the antimiscegenation laws invalidated in *Loving v. Virginia,* 388 U.S. 1, 8, 87 S.Ct. 1817, 18 L.Ed.2d 1010 (1967), similarly were applicable to whites and blacks alike, and only distinguished between the races insofar as the *partner* was concerned. In *Loving,* however, we correctly applied heightened scrutiny, rather than the usual rational-basis review, because the Virginia statute was "designed to maintain White Supremacy." *Id.,* at 6, 11, 87 S.Ct. 1817. A racially discriminatory purpose is always sufficient to subject a law to strict scrutiny, even a facially neutral law that makes no mention of race. See *Washington v. Davis,* 426 U.S. 229, 241–242, 96 S.Ct. 2040, 48 L.Ed.2d 597 (1976). No purpose to discriminate against men or women as a class can be gleaned from the Texas law, so rational-basis review applies. That review is readily satisfied here by the same rational basis that satisfied it in *Bowers*—society's belief that certain forms of sexual behavior are "immoral and unacceptable," 478 U.S., at 196, 106 S.Ct. 2841. This is the same justification that supports many other laws regulating sexual behavior that make a distinction based upon the identity of the partner—for example, laws against adultery, fornication, and adult incest, and laws refusing to recognize homosexual marriage.

Justice O'CONNOR argues that the discrimination in this law which must be justified is not its discrimination with regard to the sex of the partner but its discrimination with regard to the sexual proclivity of the principal actor.

> "While it is true that the law applies only to conduct, the conduct targeted by this law is conduct that is closely correlated with being homosexual. Under such circumstances, Texas' sodomy law is targeted at more than conduct. It is instead directed toward gay persons as a class." *Ante,* at 2486–2487.

Of course the same could be said of any law. A law against public nudity targets "the conduct that is closely correlated with being a nudist," and hence "is targeted at more than conduct"; it is "directed toward nudists as a class." But be that as it may. Even if the Texas law *does* deny equal protection to "homosexuals as a class," that denial *still* does not need to be justified by anything more than a rational basis, which our cases show is satisfied by the enforcement of traditional notions of sexual morality.

JUSTICE O'CONNOR simply decrees application of "a more searching form of rational basis review" to the Texas statute. *Ante,* at 2485. The cases she cites do not recognize such a standard, and reach their conclusions only after finding, as required by conventional rational-basis analysis, that no conceivable legitimate state interest supports the classification at issue. See *Romer v. Evans,* 517 U.S., at 635, 116 S.Ct. 1620; *Cleburne v. Cleburne Living Center, Inc.,* 473 U.S. 432, 448–450, 105 S.Ct. 3249, 87 L.Ed.2d 313 (1985); *Department of Agriculture v. Moreno,* 413 U.S. 528, 534–538, 93 S.Ct. 2821, 37 L.Ed.2d 782 (1973). Nor does Justice O'CONNOR explain precisely what her "more searching form" of rational-basis review consists of. It must at least mean, however, that laws exhibiting " 'a ... desire to harm a politically unpopular group,' " *ante,* at 2485, are invalid *even though* there may be a conceivable rational basis to support them.

This reasoning leaves on pretty shaky grounds state laws limiting marriage to opposite-sex couples. Justice O'CONNOR seeks to preserve them by the conclusory statement that "preserving the traditional institution of marriage" is a legitimate state interest. *Ante,* at 2488. But "preserving the traditional institution of marriage" is just a kinder way of describing the State's *moral disapproval* of same-sex couples. Texas's interest in § 21.06 could be recast in similarly euphemistic terms: "preserving the traditional sexual mores of our society." In the jurisprudence Justice O'CONNOR has seemingly created, judges can validate laws by characterizing them as "preserving the traditions of society" (good); or invalidate them by characterizing them as "expressing moral disapproval" (bad).

* * *

Today's opinion is the product of a Court, which is the product of a law-profession culture, that has largely signed on to the so-called homosexual agenda, by which I mean the agenda promoted by some homosexual activists directed at eliminating the moral opprobrium that has traditionally attached to homosexual conduct. I noted in an earlier opinion the fact that the American Association of Law Schools (to which any reputable law school *must* seek to belong) excludes from membership any school that refuses to ban from its job-interview facilities a law firm (no matter how small) that does not wish to hire as a prospective partner a person who openly engages in homosexual conduct. See *Romer, supra,* at 653, 116 S.Ct. 1620.

One of the most revealing statements in today's opinion is the Court's grim warning that the criminalization of homosexual conduct is "an invitation to subject homosexual persons to discrimination both in the public and in the private spheres." *Ante,* at 2482. It is clear from this that the Court has taken sides in the culture war, departing from its role of assuring, as neutral observer, that the democratic rules of engagement are observed. Many Americans do not want persons who openly engage in homosexual conduct as partners in their business, as scoutmasters for their children, as teachers in their children's schools, or as boarders in their home. They view this as protecting themselves and their families from a lifestyle that they believe to be immoral and destructive. The Court views it as "discrimination" which it is the function of our judgments to deter. So imbued is the Court with the law profession's anti-anti-homosexual culture, that it is seemingly unaware that the attitudes of that culture are not obviously "mainstream"; that in most States what the Court calls "discrimination" against those who engage in homosexual acts is perfectly legal; that proposals to ban such "discrimination" under Title VII have repeatedly been rejected by Congress, see Employment Non–Discrimination Act of 1994, S. 2238, 103d Cong., 2d Sess. (1994); Civil Rights Amendments, H.R. 5452, 94th Cong., 1st Sess. (1975); that in some cases such "discrimination" is *mandated* by federal statute, see 10 U.S.C. § 654(b)(1) (mandating discharge from the armed forces of any service member who engages in or intends to engage in homosexual acts); and that in some cases such "discrimination" is a constitutional right, see *Boy Scouts of America v. Dale,* 530 U.S. 640, 120 S.Ct. 2446, 147 L.Ed.2d 554 (2000).

Let me be clear that I have nothing against homosexuals, or any other group, promoting their agenda through normal democratic means. Social perceptions of sexual and other morality change over time, and every group has the right to persuade its fellow citizens that its view of such matters is the best. That homosexuals have achieved some success in that enterprise is attested to by the fact that Texas is one of the few remaining States that criminalize private, consensual homosexual acts. But persuading one's fellow citizens is one thing, and imposing one's views in absence of democratic majority will is something else. I would no more *require* a State to criminalize homosexual acts—or, for that matter, display *any* moral disapprobation of them—than I would *forbid* it to do so. What Texas has chosen to do is well within the range of traditional democratic action, and its hand should not be stayed through the invention of a brand-new "constitutional right" by a Court that is impatient of democratic change. It is indeed true that "later generations can see that laws once thought necessary and proper in fact serve only to oppress," *ante,* at 2484; and when that happens, later generations can repeal those laws. But it is the premise of our system that those judgments are to be made by the people, and not imposed by a governing caste that knows best.

One of the benefits of leaving regulation of this matter to the people rather than to the courts is that the people, unlike judges, need not carry things to their logical conclusion. The people may feel that their disapprobation of homosexual conduct is strong enough to disallow homosexual marriage, but not strong enough to criminalize private homosexual acts—and may legislate accordingly. The Court today pretends that it possesses a similar freedom of action, so that that we need not fear judicial imposition of homosexual marriage, as has recently occurred in Canada (in a decision that the Canadian Government has chosen not to appeal). See *Halpern v. Toronto,* 2003 WL 34950 (Ontario Ct.App.); Cohen, Dozens in Canada Follow Gay Couple's Lead, Washington Post, June 12, 2003, p. A25. At the end of its opinion—after having laid waste the foundations of our rational-basis jurisprudence—the Court says that the present case "does not involve whether the government must give formal recognition to any relationship that homosexual persons seek to enter." *Ante,* at 2484. Do not believe it. More illuminating than this bald, unreasoned disclaimer is the progression of thought displayed by an earlier passage in the Court's opinion, which notes the constitutional protections afforded to "personal decisions relating to *marriage,* procreation, contraception, family relationships, child rearing, and education," and then declares that "[p]ersons in a homosexual relationship may seek autonomy for these purposes, just as heterosexual persons do." *Ante,* at 2482 (emphasis added). Today's opinion dismantles the structure of constitutional law that has permitted a distinction to be made between heterosexual and homosexual unions, insofar as formal recognition in marriage is concerned. If moral disapprobation of homosexual conduct is "no legitimate state interest" for purposes of proscribing that conduct, *ante,* at 2484; and if, as the Court coos (casting aside all pretense of neutrality), "[w]hen sexuality finds overt expression in intimate conduct with another person, the conduct can be but one element in a personal bond that is more enduring," *ante,* at 2478; what justification could there possibly be for denying the benefits of marriage to homosexual couples exercising "[t]he liberty protected by the Constitution," *ibid.*? Surely not the encouragement of procreation, since the sterile and the elderly are allowed to marry. This case "does not involve" the issue of homosexual marriage only if one entertains the belief that principle and logic have nothing to do with the decisions of this Court. Many will hope that, as the Court comfortingly assures us, this is so.

The matters appropriate for this Court's resolution are only three: Texas's prohibition of sodomy neither infringes a "fundamental right" (which the Court does not dispute), nor is unsupported by a rational relation to what the Constitution considers a legitimate state interest, nor denies the equal protection of the laws. I dissent.

■ JUSTICE THOMAS, dissenting.

I join Justice SCALIA's dissenting opinion. I write separately to note that the law before the Court today "is . . . uncommonly silly." *Griswold v. Connecticut,* 381 U.S. 479, 527, 85 S.Ct. 1678, 14 L.Ed.2d 510 (1965) (Stewart, J., dissenting). If I were a member of the Texas Legislature, I would vote to repeal it. Punishing someone for expressing his sexual preference through noncommercial consensual conduct with another adult does not appear to be a worthy way to expend valuable law enforcement resources.

Notwithstanding this, I recognize that as a member of this Court I am not empowered to help petitioners and others similarly situated. My duty, rather, is to "decide cases 'agreeably to the Constitution and laws of the United States.' " *Id.,* at 530, 85 S.Ct. 1678. And, just like Justice Stewart, I "can find [neither in the Bill of Rights nor any other part of the Constitution a] general right of privacy," *ibid.,* or as the Court terms it today, the "liberty of the person both in its spatial and more transcendent dimensions," *ante,* at 2475.

NOTE

The aftermath of the Supreme Court's majority decision, especially the dissent by Justice Antonin Scalia, has been less than anticipated. For example, the U.S. District Court for the District of Utah has affirmed federal and state prohibition of polygamy. The challenge to the polygamy ban was based on *Lawrence,* and as a violation of free exercise of religion, freedom of association, and the right to privacy. Bronson v. Swensen, 2005 WL 1310538 (D. Utah 2005). Also, in New York, legislation that allows only opposite sex couples to marry is rationally related to procreation and child-rearing and thus constitutional in spite of the *Lawrence* decision. Seymour v. Holcomb, 7 Misc.3d 530, 790 N.Y.S.2d 858 (Sup. Ct. 2005). But see Hernandez v. Robles, 7 Misc.3d 459, 794 N.Y.S.2d 579 (N.Y. Sup. Ct. 2005), holding that denial of marriage licenses to same-sex couples violates equal protection and due process guarantees in the state constitution. Likewise, *Lawrence* does not provide that same-sex couples have a fundamental right to marry. Lofton v. Secretary of the Department of Children & Family Servs., 358 F.3d 804 (11th Cir. 2004); Wilson v. Ake, 354 F.Supp.2d 1298 (M.D. Fla. 2005). As to sexual mores, Virginia's anti-fornication statute is void as it cannot be distinguished from the sodomy statute in *Lawrence* and therefore infringes on a person's liberty interest. Martin v. Ziherl, 269 Va. 35, 607 S.E.2d 367 (2005). But after *Lawrence,* Alabama can continue to criminalize the sale of sexual devices marketed primarily for sexual stimulation. Williams v. Attorney Gen. of Ala., 378 F.3d 1232 (11th Cir. 2004).

Following the case of **Singer v. Hara,** *add the following decision and* **NOTES** *at page 116:*

Goodridge v. Department of Public Health

Supreme Judicial Court of Massachusetts, 2003.
440 Mass. 309, 798 N.E.2d 941.

■ MARSHALL, C.J.

Marriage is a vital social institution. The exclusive commitment of two individuals to each other nurtures love and mutual support; it brings stability to our society. For those who choose to marry, and for their children, marriage provides an abundance of legal, financial, and social benefits. In return it imposes weighty legal, financial, and social obligations. The question before us is whether, consistent with the Massachusetts Constitution, the Commonwealth may deny the protections, benefits, and obligations conferred by civil marriage to two individuals of the same sex who wish to marry. We conclude that it may not. The Massachusetts Constitution affirms the dignity and equality of all individuals. It forbids the creation of second-class citizens. In reaching our conclusion we have given full deference to the arguments made by the Commonwealth. But it has failed to identify any constitutionally adequate reason for denying civil marriage to same-sex couples.

We are mindful that our decision marks a change in the history of our marriage law. Many people hold deep-seated religious, moral, and ethical convictions that marriage should be limited to the union of one man and one woman, and that homosexual conduct is immoral. Many hold equally strong religious, moral, and ethical convictions that same-sex couples are entitled to be married, and that homosexual persons should be treated no differently than their heterosexual neighbors. Neither view answers the question before us. Our concern is with the Massachusetts Constitution as a charter of governance for every person properly within its reach. "Our obligation is to define the liberty of all, not to mandate our own moral code." *Lawrence v. Texas,* 539 U.S. 558, ___, 123 S.Ct. 2472, 2480, 156 L.Ed.2d 508 (2003) (*Lawrence*), quoting *Planned Parenthood of Southeastern Pa. v. Casey,* 505 U.S. 833, 850, 112 S.Ct. 2791, 120 L.Ed.2d 674 (1992).

Whether the Commonwealth may use its formidable regulatory authority to bar same-sex couples from civil marriage is a question not previously addressed by a Massachusetts appellate court. It is a question the United States Supreme Court left open as a matter of Federal law in *Lawrence, supra* at 2484, where it was not an issue. There, the Court affirmed that the core concept of common human dignity protected by the Fourteenth Amendment to the United States Constitution precludes government intrusion into the deeply personal realms of consensual adult expressions of intimacy and one's choice of an intimate partner. The Court also reaffirmed the central role that decisions whether to marry or have children bear in shaping one's identity. *Id.* at 2481. The Massachusetts Constitution is, if anything, more protective of individual liberty and equality than the Federal Constitution; it may demand broader protection for fundamental rights; and it is less tolerant of government intrusion into the protected spheres of private life.

Barred access to the protections, benefits, and obligations of civil marriage, a person who enters into an intimate, exclusive union with another of the same sex is arbitrarily deprived of membership in one of our community's most rewarding and cherished institutions. That exclusion is incompatible with the constitutional principles of respect for individual autonomy and equality under law.

I

The plaintiffs are fourteen individuals from five Massachusetts counties. As of April 11, 2001, the date they filed their complaint, the plaintiffs Gloria Bailey, sixty years old, and Linda Davies, fifty-five years old, had been in a committed relationship for thirty years; the plaintiffs Maureen Brodoff, forty-nine years old, and Ellen Wade, fifty-two years old, had been in a committed relationship for twenty years and lived with their twelve year old daughter; the plaintiffs Hillary Goodridge, forty-four years old, and Julie Goodridge, forty-three years old, had been in a committed relationship for thirteen years and lived with their five year old daughter; the plaintiffs Gary Chalmers, thirty-five years old, and Richard Linnell, thirty-seven years old, had been in a committed relationship for thirteen years and lived with their eight year old daughter and Richard's mother; the plaintiffs Heidi Norton, thirty-six years old, and Gina Smith, thirty-six years old, had been in a committed relationship for eleven years and lived with their two sons, ages five years and one year; the plaintiffs Michael Horgan, forty-one years old, and Edward Balmelli, forty-one years old, had been in a committed relationship for seven years; and the plaintiffs David Wilson, fifty-seven years old, and Robert Compton, fifty-one years old, had been in a committed relationship for four years and had cared for David's mother in their home after a serious illness until she died.

The plaintiffs include business executives, lawyers, an investment banker, educators, therapists, and a computer engineer. Many are active in church, community, and school groups. They have employed such legal means as are available to them—for example, joint adoption, powers of attorney, and joint ownership of real property—to secure aspects of their relationships. Each plaintiff attests a desire to marry his or her partner in order to affirm publicly their commitment to each other and to secure the legal protections and benefits afforded to married couples and their children.

. . .

In March and April, 2001, each of the plaintiff couples attempted to obtain a marriage license from a city or town clerk's office. As required under G.L. c. 207, they completed notices of intention to marry on forms provided by the registry, see G.L. c. 207, § 20, and presented these forms to a Massachusetts town or city clerk, together with the required health forms and marriage license fees. See G.L. c. 207, § 19. In each case, the clerk either refused to accept the notice of intention to marry or denied a marriage license to the couple on the ground that Massachusetts does not recognize same-sex marriage. Because obtaining a marriage license is a necessary prerequisite to civil marriage in Massachusetts, denying marriage licenses to the plaintiffs was tantamount to denying them access to civil marriage itself, with its appurtenant social and legal protections, benefits, and obligations.

On April 11, 2001, the plaintiffs filed suit in the Superior Court against the department and the commissioner seeking a judgment that "the exclusion of the [p]laintiff couples and other qualified same-sex couples from access to marriage licenses, and the legal and social status of civil marriage, as well as the protections, benefits and obligations of marriage, violates Massachusetts law." See G.L. c. 231A. The plaintiffs alleged violation of the laws of the Commonwealth, including but not limited to their rights under arts. 1, 6, 7, 10, 12, and 16, and Part II, c. 1, § 1, art. 4, of the Massachusetts Constitution.[7] The department, represented by the

---

7. Article 1, as amended by art. 106 of the Amendments to the Massachusetts Constitution, provides: "All people are born free and equal and have certain natural, essential and unalienable rights; among which may be reckoned the right of enjoying and defending their lives and liberties; that of acquiring, possessing and protecting property; in fine, that of seeking and obtaining their safety and happiness. Equality under the law shall not be denied or abridged because of sex, race, color, creed or national origin."

Article 6 provides: "No man, nor corporation, or association of men, have any other title to obtain advantages, or particular and exclusive privileges, distinct from those of the community, than what arises from the consideration of services rendered to the public...."

Article 7 provides: "Government is instituted for the common good; for the protection, safety, prosperity, and happiness of the people; and not for the profit, honor, or private interest of any one man, family or class of men: Therefore the people alone have an incontestable, unalienable, and indefeasible right to institute government; and to reform,

Attorney General, admitted to a policy and practice of denying marriage licenses to same-sex couples. It denied that its actions violated any law or that the plaintiffs were entitled to relief. The parties filed cross motions for summary judgment.

A Superior Court judge ruled for the department. In a memorandum of decision and order dated May 7, 2002, he dismissed the plaintiffs' claim that the marriage statutes should be construed to permit marriage between persons of the same sex, holding that the plain wording of G.L. c. 207, as well as the wording of other marriage statutes, precluded that interpretation. Turning to the constitutional claims, he held that the marriage exclusion does not offend the liberty, freedom, equality, or due process provisions of the Massachusetts Constitution, and that the Massachusetts Declaration of Rights does not guarantee "the fundamental right to marry a person of the same sex." He concluded that prohibiting same-sex marriage rationally furthers the Legislature's legitimate interest in safeguarding the "primary purpose" of marriage, "procreation." The Legislature may rationally limit marriage to opposite-sex couples, he concluded, because those couples are "theoretically . . . capable of procreation," they do not rely on "inherently more cumbersome" noncoital means of reproduction, and they are more likely than same-sex couples to have children, or more children.

After the complaint was dismissed and summary judgment entered for the defendants, the plaintiffs appealed. Both parties requested direct appellate review, which we granted.

II

. . .

We interpret statutes to carry out the Legislature's intent, determined by the words of a statute interpreted according to "the ordinary and approved usage of the language." *Hanlon v. Rollins*, 286 Mass. 444, 447, 190 N.E. 606 (1934). The everyday meaning of "marriage" is "[t]he legal union of a man and woman as husband and wife," Black's Law Dictionary 986 (7th ed.1999), and the plaintiffs do not argue that the term "marriage"

alter, or totally change the same, when their protection, safety, prosperity and happiness require it."

Article 10 provides, in relevant part: "Each individual of the society has a right to be protected by it in the enjoyment of his life, liberty and property, according to standing laws. . . ."

Article 12 provides, in relevant part: "[N]o subject shall be . . . deprived of his property, immunities, or privileges, put out of the protection of the law . . . or deprived of his life, liberty, or estate, but by the judgment of his peers, or the law of the land." Article 16, as amended by art. 77 of the

Amendments, provides, in relevant part: "The right of free speech shall not be abridged." Part II, c. 1, § 1, art. 4, as amended by art. 112, provides, in pertinent part, that "full power and authority are hereby given and granted to the said general court, from time to time, to make, ordain, and establish all manner of wholesome and reasonable orders, laws, statutes, and ordinances, directions and instructions, either with penalties or without; so as the same be not repugnant or contrary to this constitution, as they shall judge to be for the good and welfare of this Commonwealth."

has ever had a different meaning under Massachusetts law. See, e.g., *Milford v. Worcester,* 7 Mass. 48, 52 (1810) (marriage "is an engagement, by which a single man and a single woman, of sufficient discretion, take each other for husband and wife"). This definition of marriage, as both the department and the Superior Court judge point out, derives from the common law. See *Commonwealth v. Knowlton,* 2 Mass. 530, 535 (1807) (Massachusetts common law derives from English common law except as otherwise altered by Massachusetts statutes and Constitution). See also *Commonwealth v. Lane,* 113 Mass. 458, 462–463 (1873) ("when the statutes are silent, questions of the validity of marriages are to be determined by the jus gentium, the common law of nations"); C.P. Kindregan, Jr., & M.L. Inker, Family Law and Practice § 1.2 (3d ed.2002). Far from being ambiguous, the undefined word "marriage," as used in G.L. c. 207, confirms the General Court's intent to hew to the term's common-law and quotidian meaning concerning the genders of the marriage partners.

.   .   .

The intended scope of G.L. c. 207 is also evident in its consanguinity provisions. See *Chandler v. County Comm'rs of Nantucket County,* 437 Mass. 430, 435, 772 N.E.2d 578 (2002) (statute's various provisions may offer insight into legislative intent). Sections 1 and 2 of G.L. c. 207 prohibit marriages between a man and certain female relatives and a woman and certain male relatives, but are silent as to the consanguinity of male-male or female-female marriage applicants. See G.L. c. 207, §§ 1–2. The only reasonable explanation is that the Legislature did not intend that same-sex couples be licensed to marry. We conclude, as did the judge, that G.L. c. 207 may not be construed to permit same-sex couples to marry.[11]

The plaintiffs' claim that the marriage restriction violates the Massachusetts Constitution can be analyzed in two ways. Does it offend the Constitution's guarantees of equality before the law? Or do the liberty and due process provisions of the Massachusetts Constitution secure the plaintiffs' right to marry their chosen partner? In matters implicating marriage, family life, and the upbringing of children, the two constitutional concepts frequently overlap, as they do here. See, e.g., *M.L.B. v. S.L.J.,* 519 U.S. 102, 120, 117 S.Ct. 555, 136 L.Ed.2d 473 (1996) (noting convergence of due process and equal protection principles in cases concerning parent-child relationships); *Perez v. Sharp,* 32 Cal.2d 711, 728, 198 P.2d 17 (1948) (analyzing statutory ban on interracial marriage as equal protection violation concerning regulation of fundamental right). See also *Lawrence, supra* at 2482 ("Equality of treatment and the due process right to demand respect for conduct protected by the substantive guarantee of liberty are

---

11. We use the terms "same sex" and "opposite sex" when characterizing the couples in question, because these terms are more accurate in this context than the terms "homosexual" or "heterosexual," although at times we use those terms when we consider them appropriate. Nothing in our marriage law precludes people who identify themselves (or who are identified by others) as gay, lesbian, or bisexual from marrying persons of the opposite sex. See *Baehr v. Lewin,* 74 Haw. 530, 543 n. 11, 547 n. 14, 852 P.2d 44 (1993).

linked in important respects, and a decision on the latter point advances both interests"); *Bolling v. Sharpe,* 347 U.S. 497, 74 S.Ct. 693, 98 L.Ed. 884 (1954) (racial segregation in District of Columbia public schools violates the due process clause of Fifth Amendment to United States Constitution), decided the same day as *Brown v. Board of Educ. of Topeka,* 347 U.S. 483, 74 S.Ct. 686, 98 L.Ed. 873 (1954) (holding that segregation of public schools in States violates equal protection clause of Fourteenth Amendment). Much of what we say concerning one standard applies to the other.

We begin by considering the nature of civil marriage itself. Simply put, the government creates civil marriage. In Massachusetts, civil marriage is, and since pre-Colonial days has been, precisely what its name implies: a wholly secular institution. See *Commonwealth v. Munson,* 127 Mass. 459, 460–466 (1879) (noting that "[i]n Massachusetts, from very early times, the requisites of a valid marriage have been regulated by statutes of the Colony, Province, and Commonwealth," and surveying marriage statutes from 1639 through 1834). No religious ceremony has ever been required to validate a Massachusetts marriage. *Id.*

In a real sense, there are three partners to every civil marriage: two willing spouses and an approving State. See *DeMatteo v. DeMatteo,* 436 Mass. 18, 31, 762 N.E.2d 797 (2002) ("Marriage is not a mere contract between two parties but a legal status from which certain rights and obligations arise"); *Smith v. Smith,* 171 Mass. 404, 409, 50 N.E. 933 (1898) (on marriage, the parties "assume[ ] new relations to each other and to the State"). See also *French v. McAnarney,* 290 Mass. 544, 546, 195 N.E. 714 (1935). While only the parties can mutually assent to marriage, the terms of the marriage—who may marry and what obligations, benefits, and liabilities attach to civil marriage—are set by the Commonwealth. Conversely, while only the parties can agree to end the marriage (absent the death of one of them or a marriage void ab initio), the Commonwealth defines the exit terms. See G.L. c. 208.

Civil marriage is created and regulated through exercise of the police power. See *Commonwealth v. Stowell,* 389 Mass. 171, 175, 449 N.E.2d 357 (1983) (regulation of marriage is properly within the scope of the police power). "Police power" (now more commonly termed the State's regulatory authority) is an old-fashioned term for the Commonwealth's lawmaking authority, as bounded by the liberty and equality guarantees of the Massachusetts Constitution and its express delegation of power from the people to their government. In broad terms, it is the Legislature's power to enact rules to regulate conduct, to the extent that such laws are "necessary to secure the health, safety, good order, comfort, or general welfare of the community" (citations omitted). *Opinion of the Justices,* 341 Mass. 760, 785, 168 N.E.2d 858 (1960). See *Commonwealth v. Alger,* 61 Mass. 53, 7 Cush. 53, 85 (1851).

Without question, civil marriage enhances the "welfare of the community." It is a "social institution of the highest importance." *French v. McAnarney, supra.* Civil marriage anchors an ordered society by encouraging stable relationships over transient ones. It is central to the way the

Commonwealth identifies individuals, provides for the orderly distribution of property, ensures that children and adults are cared for and supported whenever possible from private rather than public funds, and tracks important epidemiological and demographic data.

Marriage also bestows enormous private and social advantages on those who choose to marry. Civil marriage is at once a deeply personal commitment to another human being and a highly public celebration of the ideals of mutuality, companionship, intimacy, fidelity, and family. "It is an association that promotes a way of life, not causes; a harmony in living, not political faiths; a bilateral loyalty, not commercial or social projects." *Griswold v. Connecticut,* 381 U.S. 479, 486, 85 S.Ct. 1678, 14 L.Ed.2d 510 (1965). Because it fulfils yearnings for security, safe haven, and connection that express our common humanity, civil marriage is an esteemed institution, and the decision whether and whom to marry is among life's momentous acts of self-definition.

Tangible as well as intangible benefits flow from marriage. The marriage license grants valuable property rights to those who meet the entry requirements, and who agree to what might otherwise be a burdensome degree of government regulation of their activities.[13] See *Leduc v. Commonwealth,* 421 Mass. 433, 435, 657 N.E.2d 755 (1995), cert. denied, 519 U.S. 827, 117 S.Ct. 91, 136 L.Ed.2d 47 (1996) ("The historical aim of licensure generally is preservation of public health, safety, and welfare by extending the public trust only to those with proven qualifications"). The Legislature has conferred on "each party [in a civil marriage] substantial rights concerning the assets of the other which unmarried cohabitants do not have." *Wilcox v. Trautz,* 427 Mass. 326, 334, 693 N.E.2d 141 (1998). See *Collins v. Guggenheim,* 417 Mass. 615, 618, 631 N.E.2d 1016 (1994) (rejecting claim for equitable distribution of property where plaintiff cohabited with but did not marry defendant); *Feliciano v. Rosemar Silver Co.,* 401 Mass. 141, 142, 514 N.E.2d 1095 (1987) (government interest in promoting marriage would be "subverted" by recognition of "a right to recover for loss of consortium by a person who has not accepted the correlative responsibilities of marriage"); *Davis v. Misiano,* 373 Mass. 261, 263, 366 N.E.2d 752 (1977) (unmarried partners not entitled to rights of separate support or alimony). See generally *Attorney Gen. v. Desilets,* 418 Mass. 316, 327–328 & nn. 10, 11, 636 N.E.2d 233 (1994).

The benefits accessible only by way of a marriage license are enormous, touching nearly every aspect of life and death. The department states that "hundreds of statutes" are related to marriage and to marital benefits. With no attempt to be comprehensive, we note that some of the statutory benefits conferred by the Legislature on those who enter into civil marriage include, as to property: joint Massachusetts income tax filing (G.L. c. 62C, § 6); tenancy by the entirety (a form of ownership that provides certain

---

13. For example, married persons face substantial restrictions, simply because they are married, on their ability freely to dispose of their assets. See, e.g., G.L. c. 208, § 34 (providing for payment of alimony and the equitable division of property on divorce); G.L. c. 191, § 15, and G.L. c. 189 (rights of elective share and dower).

protections against creditors and allows for the automatic descent of property to the surviving spouse without probate) (G.L. c. 184, § 7); extension of the benefit of the homestead protection (securing up to $300,000 in equity from creditors) to one's spouse and children (G.L. c. 188, § 1); automatic rights to inherit the property of a deceased spouse who does not leave a will (G.L. c. 190, § 1); the rights of elective share and of dower (which allow surviving spouses certain property rights where the decedent spouse has not made adequate provision for the survivor in a will) (G.L. c. 191, § 15, and G.L. c. 189); entitlement to wages owed to a deceased employee (G.L. c. 149, § 178A [general] and G.L. c. 149, § 178C [public employees]); eligibility to continue certain businesses of a deceased spouse (e.g., G.L. c. 112, § 53 [dentist]); the right to share the medical policy of one's spouse (e.g., G.L. c. 175, § 108, Second [*a*] [3] [defining insured's "dependent" to include one's spouse]), (see *Connors v. Boston*, 430 Mass. 31, 43, 714 N.E.2d 335 (1999) [domestic partners of city employees not included within term "dependent" as used in G.L. c. 32B, § 2]); thirty-nine week continuation of health coverage for the spouse of a person who is laid off or dies (e.g., G.L. c. 175, § 110G); preferential options under the Commonwealth's pension system (see G.L. c. 32, § 12[2] ["Joint and Last Survivor Allowance"]); preferential benefits in the Commonwealth's medical program, MassHealth (e.g., 130 Code Mass. Regs. § 515.012[A], prohibiting placing lien on long-term care patient's former home if spouse still lives there); access to veterans' spousal benefits and preferences (e.g., G.L. c. 115, § 1 [defining "dependents"] and G.L. c. 31, § 26 [State employment] and § 28 [municipal employees]); financial protections for spouses of certain Commonwealth employees (fire fighters, police officers, and prosecutors, among others) killed in the performance of duty (e.g., G.L. c. 32, §§ 100–103); the equitable division of marital property on divorce (G.L. c. 208, § 34); temporary and permanent alimony rights (G.L. c. 208, §§ 17 and 34); the right to separate support on separation of the parties that does not result in divorce (G.L. c. 209, § 32); and the right to bring claims for wrongful death and loss of consortium, and for funeral and burial expenses and punitive damages resulting from tort actions (G.L. c. 229, §§ 1 and 2; G.L. c. 228, § 1. See *Feliciano v. Rosemar Silver Co.*, *supra*).

Exclusive marital benefits that are not directly tied to property rights include the presumptions of legitimacy and parentage of children born to a married couple (G.L. c. 209C, § 6, and G.L. c. 46, § 4B); and evidentiary rights, such as the prohibition against spouses testifying against one another about their private conversations, applicable in both civil and criminal cases (G.L. c. 233, § 20). Other statutory benefits of a personal nature available only to married individuals include qualification for bereavement or medical leave to care for individuals related by blood or marriage (G.L. c. 149, § 52D); an automatic "family member" preference to make medical decisions for an incompetent or disabled spouse who does not have a contrary health care proxy, see *Shine v. Vega*, 429 Mass. 456, 466, 709 N.E.2d 58 (1999); the application of predictable rules of child custody, visitation, support, and removal out-of-State when married parents divorce (e.g., G.L. c. 208, § 19 [temporary custody], § 20 [temporary support], § 28 [custody and support on judgment of divorce], § 30 [removal from Commonwealth], and § 31 [shared custody plan]); priority rights to administer the estate of a deceased spouse who dies without a will, and the requirement that a surviving spouse must consent to the appointment of any other person as administrator (G.L. c. 38, § 13 [disposition of body], and G.L. c. 113, § 8 [anatomical gifts]); and the right to interment in the lot or tomb owned by one's deceased spouse (G.L. c. 114, §§ 29–33).

Where a married couple has children, their children are also directly or indirectly, but no less auspiciously, the recipients of the special legal and economic protections obtained by civil marriage. Notwithstanding the Commonwealth's strong public policy to abolish legal distinctions between marital and nonmarital children in providing for the support and care of minors, see *Department of Revenue v. Mason M.,* 439 Mass. 665, 790 N.E.2d 671 (2003); *Woodward v. Commissioner of Social Sec.,* 435 Mass. 536, 546, 760 N.E.2d 257 (2002), the fact remains that marital children reap a measure of family stability and economic security based on their parents' legally privileged status that is largely inaccessible, or not as readily accessible, to nonmarital children. Some of these benefits are social, such as the enhanced approval that still attends the status of being a marital child. Others are material, such as the greater ease of access to family-based State and Federal benefits that attend the presumptions of one's parentage.

It is undoubtedly for these concrete reasons, as well as for its intimately personal significance, that civil marriage has long been termed a "civil right." See, e.g., *Loving v. Virginia,* 388 U.S. 1, 12, 87 S.Ct. 1817, 18 L.Ed.2d 1010 (1967) ("Marriage is one of the 'basic civil rights of man,' fundamental to our very existence and survival"), quoting *Skinner v. Oklahoma,* 316 U.S. 535, 541, 62 S.Ct. 1110, 86 L.Ed. 1655 (1942); *Milford v. Worcester,* 7 Mass. 48, 56 (1810) (referring to "civil rights incident to marriages"). See also *Baehr v. Lewin,* 74 Haw. 530, 561, 852 P.2d 44 (1993) (identifying marriage as "civil right[ ]"); *Baker v. State,* 170 Vt. 194, 242, 744 A.2d 864 (1999) (Johnson, J., concurring in part and dissenting in part) (same). The United States Supreme Court has described the right to marry as "of fundamental importance for all individuals" and as "part of the fundamental 'right of privacy' implicit in the Fourteenth Amendment's Due Process Clause." *Zablocki v. Redhail,* 434 U.S. 374, 384, 98 S.Ct. 673, 54 L.Ed.2d 618 (1978). See *Loving v. Virginia, supra* ("The freedom to marry has long been recognized as one of the vital personal rights essential to the orderly pursuit of happiness by free men").

.   .   .

For decades, indeed centuries, in much of this country (including Massachusetts) no lawful marriage was possible between white and black Americans. That long history availed not when the Supreme Court of California held in 1948 that a legislative prohibition against interracial marriage violated the due process and equality guarantees of the Fourteenth Amendment, *Perez v. Sharp,* 32 Cal.2d 711, 728, 198 P.2d 17 (1948), or when, nineteen years later, the United States Supreme Court also held that a statutory bar to interracial marriage violated the Fourteenth Amendment, *Loving v. Virginia,* 388 U.S. 1, 87 S.Ct. 1817, 18 L.Ed.2d 1010 (1967). As both *Perez* and *Loving* make clear, the right to marry means little if it does not include the right to marry the person of one's choice, subject to appropriate government restrictions in the interests of public health, safety, and welfare. See *Perez v. Sharp, supra* at 717, 198 P.2d 17 ("the essence of the right to marry is freedom to join in marriage with the person of one's choice"). See also *Loving v. Virginia, supra* at 12, 87 S.Ct. 1817. In this case, as in *Perez* and *Loving,* a statute deprives individuals of access to an institution of fundamental legal, personal, and social significance—the institution of marriage—because of a single trait: skin color in *Perez* and *Loving,* sexual orientation here. As it did in *Perez* and *Loving,* history must yield to a more fully developed understanding of the invidious quality of the discrimination.

The Massachusetts Constitution protects matters of personal liberty against government incursion as zealously, and often more so, than does the Federal Constitution, even where both Constitutions employ essentially the same language. See *Planned Parenthood League of Mass., Inc. v. Attorney Gen.,* 424 Mass. 586, 590, 677 N.E.2d 101 (1997); *Corning Glass Works v. Ann & Hope, Inc. of Danvers,* 363 Mass. 409, 416, 294 N.E.2d 354 (1973). That the Massachusetts Constitution is in some instances more protective of individual liberty interests than is the Federal Constitution is not surprising. Fundamental to the vigor of our Federal system of government is that "state courts are absolutely free to interpret state constitutional provisions to accord greater protection to individual rights than do similar provisions of the United States Constitution." [*Arizona v. Evans,* 514 U.S. 1, 8, 115 S.Ct. 1185, 131 L.Ed.2d 34 (1995).]

. . .

The plaintiffs challenge the marriage statute on both equal protection and due process grounds. With respect to each such claim, we must first determine the appropriate standard of review. Where a statute implicates a fundamental right or uses a suspect classification, we employ "strict judicial scrutiny." *Lowell v. Kowalski,* 380 Mass. 663, 666, 405 N.E.2d 135 (1980). For all other statutes, we employ the " 'rational basis' test." *English v. New England Med. Ctr.,* 405 Mass. 423, 428, 541 N.E.2d 329 (1989). For due process claims, rational basis analysis requires that statutes "bear[ ] a real and substantial relation to the public health, safety, morals, or some other phase of the general welfare." *Coffee-Rich, Inc. v. Commissioner of Pub. Health, supra,* quoting *Sperry & Hutchinson Co. v. Director of the Div. on the Necessaries of Life,* 307 Mass. 408, 418, 30 N.E.2d 269 (1940). For equal protection challenges, the rational basis test requires that "an impartial lawmaker could logically believe that the classification would serve a legitimate public purpose that transcends the harm to the members of the disadvantaged class." *English v. New England Med. Ctr., supra* at 429, 541 N.E.2d 329, quoting *Cleburne v. Cleburne Living Ctr., Inc.,* 473 U.S. 432, 452, 105 S.Ct. 3249, 87 L.Ed.2d 313 (1985) (Stevens, J., concurring).

The department argues that no fundamental right or "suspect" class is at issue here,[21] and rational basis is the appropriate standard of review. For the reasons we explain below, we conclude that the marriage ban does not meet the rational basis test for either due process or equal protection. Because the statute does not survive rational basis review, we do not consider the plaintiffs' arguments that this case merits strict judicial scrutiny.

The department posits three legislative rationales for prohibiting same-sex couples from marrying: (1) providing a "favorable setting for procreation"; (2) ensuring the optimal setting for child rearing, which the department defines as "a two-parent family with one parent of each sex"; and (3) preserving scarce State and private financial resources. We consider each in turn.

The judge in the Superior Court endorsed the first rationale, holding that "the state's interest in regulating marriage is based on the traditional concept that marriage's primary purpose is procreation." This is incorrect. Our laws of civil marriage do not privilege procreative heterosexual intercourse between married people above every other form of adult intimacy and every other means of creating a family. General Laws c. 207 contains no requirement that the applicants for a marriage license attest to their ability or intention to conceive children by coitus. Fertility is not a condition of marriage, nor is it grounds for divorce. People who have never consummated their marriage, and never plan to, may be and stay married. See *Franklin v. Franklin,* 154 Mass. 515, 516, 28 N.E. 681 (1891) ("The consummation of a marriage by coition is not necessary to its validity").[22] People who cannot stir from their deathbed may marry. See G.L. c. 207, § 28A. While it is certainly true that many, perhaps most, married couples have children together (assisted or unassisted), it is the exclusive and

---

21. Article 1 of the Massachusetts Constitution specifically prohibits sex-based discrimination. See *post* at 344–345, 798 N.E.2d at 970–971 (Greaney, J., concurring). We have not previously considered whether "sexual orientation" is a "suspect" classification. Our resolution of this case does not require that inquiry here.

22. Our marriage law does recognize that the inability to participate in intimate relations may have a bearing on one of the central expectations of marriage. Since the earliest days of the Commonwealth, the divorce statutes have permitted (but not required) a spouse to choose to divorce his or her impotent mate. See St. 1785, c. 69, § 3. While infertility is not a ground to void or terminate a marriage, impotency (the inability to engage in sexual intercourse) is, at the election of the disaffected spouse. See G.L. c. 207, § 14 (annulment); G.L. c. 208, § 1 (di-

vorce). Cf. *Martin v. Otis,* 233 Mass. 491, 495, 124 N.E. 294 (1919) ("impotency does not render a marriage void, but only voidable at the suit of the party conceiving himself or herself to be wronged"); *Smith v. Smith,* 171 Mass. 404, 408, 50 N.E. 933 (1898) (marriage nullified because husband's incurable syphilis "leaves him no foundation on which the marriage relation could properly rest"). See also G.L. c. 207, § 28A. However, in *Hanson v. Hanson,* 287 Mass. 154, 191 N.E. 673 (1934), a decree of annulment for nonconsummation was reversed where the wife knew before the marriage that her husband had syphilis and voluntarily chose to marry him. We held that, given the circumstances of the wife's prior knowledge of the full extent of the disease and her consent to be married, the husband's condition did not go "to the essence" of the marriage. *Id.* at 159, 191 N.E. 673.

permanent commitment of the marriage partners to one another, not the begetting of children, that is the sine qua non of civil marriage.[23]

Moreover, the Commonwealth affirmatively facilitates bringing children into a family regardless of whether the intended parent is married or unmarried, whether the child is adopted or born into a family, whether assistive technology was used to conceive the child, and whether the parent or her partner is heterosexual, homosexual, or bisexual.[24] If procreation were a necessary component of civil marriage, our statutes would draw a tighter circle around the permissible bounds of nonmarital child bearing and the creation of families by noncoital means. The attempt to isolate procreation as "the source of a fundamental right to arry," 440 Mass. at 370 (Cordy, J., dissenting), overlooks the integrated way in which courts have examined the complex and overlapping realms of personal autonomy, marriage, family life, and child rearing. Our jurisprudence recognizes that, in these nuanced and fundamentally private areas of life, such a narrow focus is inappropriate.

The "marriage is procreation" argument singles out the one unbridgeable difference between same-sex and opposite-sex couples, and transforms that difference into the essence of legal marriage. Like "Amendment 2" to the Constitution of Colorado, which effectively denied homosexual persons equality under the law and full access to the political process, the marriage restriction impermissibly "identifies persons by a single trait and then denies them protection across the board." *Romer v. Evans,* 517 U.S. 620, 633, 116 S.Ct. 1620, 134 L.Ed.2d 855 (1996). In so doing, the State's action confers an official stamp of approval on the destructive stereotype that same-sex relationships are inherently unstable and inferior to opposite-sex relationships and are not worthy of respect.[25]

---

23. It is hardly surprising that civil marriage developed historically as a means to regulate heterosexual conduct and to promote child rearing, because until very recently unassisted heterosexual relations were the only means short of adoption by which children could come into the world, and the absence of widely available and effective contraceptives made the link between heterosexual sex and procreation very strong indeed. Punitive notions of illegitimacy, see *Powers v. Wilkinson,* 399 Mass. 650, 661, 506 N.E.2d 842 (1987), and of homosexual identity, see *Lawrence, supra* at 2478–2479, further cemented the common and legal understanding of marriage as an unquestionably heterosexual institution. But it is circular reasoning, not analysis, to maintain that marriage must remain a heterosexual institution because that is what it historically has been. As one dissent acknowledges, in "the modern age," "heterosexual intercourse, procreation, and child care are not necessarily conjoined." *Post*

at 382, 798 N.E.2d at 995–996 (Cordy, J., dissenting).

24. Adoption and certain insurance coverage for assisted reproductive technology are available to married couples, same-sex couples, and single individuals alike. See G.L. c. 210, § 1; *Adoption of Tammy,* 416 Mass. 205, 619 N.E.2d 315 (1993) (adoption); G.L. c. 175, § 47H; G.L. c. 176A, § 8K; G.L. c. 176B, § 4J; and G.L. c. 176G, § 4 (insurance coverage). See also *Woodward v. Commissioner of Social Sec.,* 435 Mass. 536, 546, 760 N.E.2d 257 (2002) (posthumous reproduction); *Culliton v. Beth Israel Deaconess Med. Ctr.,* 435 Mass. 285, 293, 756 N.E.2d 1133 (2001) (gestational surrogacy).

25. Because our laws expressly or implicitly sanction so many kinds of opposite-sex marriages that do not or will never result in unassisted reproduction, it is erroneous to claim, as the dissent does, that the "theoretical[ ]" procreative capacity of opposite-sex couples, *post* at 391, 798 N.E.2d at 1002

The department's first stated rationale, equating marriage with unassisted heterosexual procreation, shades imperceptibly into its second: that confining marriage to opposite-sex couples ensures that children are raised in the "optimal" setting. Protecting the welfare of children is a paramount State policy. Restricting marriage to opposite-sex couples, however, cannot plausibly further this policy. "The demographic changes of the past century make it difficult to speak of an average American family. The composition of families varies greatly from household to household." *Troxel v. Granville,* 530 U.S. 57, 63, 120 S.Ct. 2054, 147 L.Ed.2d 49 (2000). Massachusetts has responded supportively to "the changing realities of the American family," *id.* at 64, 120 S.Ct. 2054, and has moved vigorously to strengthen the modern family in its many variations. See, e.g., G.L. c. 209C (paternity statute); G.L. c. 119, § 39D (grandparent visitation statute); *Blixt v. Blixt,* 437 Mass. 649, 774 N.E.2d 1052 (2002), cert. denied, 537 U.S. 1189, 123 S.Ct. 1259, 154 L.Ed.2d 1022 (2003) (same); *E.N.O. v. L.M.M.,* 429 Mass. 824, 711 N.E.2d 886, cert. denied, 528 U.S. 1005, 120 S.Ct. 500, 145 L.Ed.2d 386 (1999) (de facto parent); *Youmans v. Ramos,* 429 Mass. 774, 782, 711 N.E.2d 165 (1999) (same); and *Adoption of Tammy,* 416 Mass. 205, 619 N.E.2d 315 (1993) (coparent adoption). Moreover, we have repudiated the common-law power of the State to provide varying levels of protection to children based on the circumstances of birth. See G.L. c. 209C (paternity statute); *Powers v. Wilkinson,* 399 Mass. 650, 661, 506 N.E.2d 842 (1987) ("Ours is an era in which logic and compassion have impelled the law toward unburdening children from the stigma and the disadvantages heretofore attendant upon the status of illegitimacy"). The "best interests of the child" standard does not turn on a parent's sexual orientation or marital status. See e.g., *Doe v. Doe,* 16 Mass.App.Ct. 499, 503, 452 N.E.2d 293 (1983) (parent's sexual orientation insufficient ground to deny custody of child in divorce action). See also *E.N.O. v. L.M.M., supra* at 829–830, 711 N.E.2d 886 (best interests of child determined by considering child's relationship with biological and de facto same-sex parents); *Silvia v. Silvia,* 9 Mass.App.Ct. 339, 341 & n. 3, 400 N.E.2d 1330 (1980) (collecting support and custody statutes containing no gender distinction).

The department has offered no evidence that forbidding marriage to people of the same sex will increase the number of couples choosing to enter into opposite-sex marriages in order to have and raise children. There is thus no rational relationship between the marriage statute and the Commonwealth's proffered goal of protecting the "optimal" child rearing unit. Moreover, the department readily concedes that people in same-sex couples may be "excellent" parents. These couples (including four of the plaintiff couples) have children for the reasons others do—to love them, to care for them, to nurture them. But the task of child rearing for same-sex couples is made infinitely harder by their status as outliers to the marriage laws. While establishing the parentage of children as soon as possible is

(Cordy, J., dissenting), sufficiently justifies excluding from civil marriage same-sex cou- ples who actually have children.

crucial to the safety and welfare of children, see *Culliton v. Beth Israel Deaconess Med. Ctr.,* 435 Mass. 285, 292, 756 N.E.2d 1133 (2001), same-sex couples must undergo the sometimes lengthy and intrusive process of second-parent adoption to establish their joint parentage. While the enhanced income provided by marital benefits is an important source of security and stability for married couples and their children, those benefits are denied to families headed by same-sex couples. See, e.g., note 6, *supra.* While the laws of divorce provide clear and reasonably predictable guidelines for child support, child custody, and property division on dissolution of a marriage, same-sex couples who dissolve their relationships find themselves and their children in the highly unpredictable terrain of equity jurisdiction. See *E.N.O. v. L.M.M., supra.* Given the wide range of public benefits reserved only for married couples, we do not credit the department's contention that the absence of access to civil marriage amounts to little more than an inconvenience to same-sex couples and their children. Excluding same-sex couples from civil marriage will not make children of opposite-sex marriages more secure, but it does prevent children of same-sex couples from enjoying the immeasurable advantages that flow from the assurance of "a stable family structure in which children will be reared, educated, and socialized." 440 Mass. at 381 (Cordy, J., dissenting).[26]

No one disputes that the plaintiff couples are families, that many are parents, and that the children they are raising, like all children, need and should have the fullest opportunity to grow up in a secure, protected family unit. Similarly, no one disputes that, under the rubric of marriage, the State provides a cornucopia of substantial benefits to married parents and their children. The preferential treatment of civil marriage reflects the Legislature's conclusion that marriage "is the foremost setting for the education and socialization of children" precisely because it "encourages parents to remain committed to each other and to their children as they grow." 440 Mass. at 383, 798 N.E.2d at 996 (Cordy, J., dissenting).

In this case, we are confronted with an entire, sizeable class of parents raising children who have absolutely no access to civil marriage and its protections because they are forbidden from procuring a marriage license. It cannot be rational under our laws, and indeed it is not permitted, to penalize children by depriving them of State benefits because the State disapproves of their parents' sexual orientation.

The third rationale advanced by the department is that limiting marriage to opposite-sex couples furthers the Legislature's interest in conserving scarce State and private financial resources. The marriage restriction is rational, it argues, because the General Court logically could assume that same-sex couples are more financially independent than mar-

---

26. The claim that the constitutional rights to bear and raise a child are "not implicated or infringed" by the marriage ban, *post* at 371, 798 N.E.2d at 988 (Cordy, J., dissenting), does not stand up to scrutiny. The absolute foreclosure of the marriage option for the class of parents and would-be parents at issue here imposes a heavy burden on their decision to have and raise children that is not suffered by any other class of parent.

ried couples and thus less needy of public marital benefits, such as tax advantages, or private marital benefits, such as employer-financed health plans that include spouses in their coverage.

An absolute statutory ban on same-sex marriage bears no rational relationship to the goal of economy. First, the department's conclusory generalization—that same-sex couples are less financially dependent on each other than opposite-sex couples—ignores that many same-sex couples, such as many of the plaintiffs in this case, have children and other dependents (here, aged parents) in their care. The department does not contend, nor could it, that these dependents are less needy or deserving than the dependents of married couples. Second, Massachusetts marriage laws do not condition receipt of public and private financial benefits to married individuals on a demonstration of financial dependence on each other; the benefits are available to married couples regardless of whether they mingle their finances or actually depend on each other for support.

The department suggests additional rationales for prohibiting same-sex couples from marrying, which are developed by some amici. It argues that broadening civil marriage to include same-sex couples will trivialize or destroy the institution of marriage as it has historically been fashioned. Certainly our decision today marks a significant change in the definition of marriage as it has been inherited from the common law, and understood by many societies for centuries. But it does not disturb the fundamental value of marriage in our society.

Here, the plaintiffs seek only to be married, not to undermine the institution of civil marriage. They do not want marriage abolished. They do not attack the binary nature of marriage, the consanguinity provisions, or any of the other gate-keeping provisions of the marriage licensing law. Recognizing the right of an individual to marry a person of the same sex will not diminish the validity or dignity of opposite-sex marriage, any more than recognizing the right of an individual to marry a person of a different race devalues the marriage of a person who marries someone of her own race. If anything, extending civil marriage to same-sex couples reinforces the importance of marriage to individuals and communities. That same-sex couples are willing to embrace marriage's solemn obligations of exclusivity, mutual support, and commitment to one another is a testament to the enduring place of marriage in our laws and in the human spirit.

It has been argued that, due to the State's strong interest in the institution of marriage as a stabilizing social structure, only the Legislature can control and define its boundaries. Accordingly, our elected representatives legitimately may choose to exclude same-sex couples from civil marriage in order to assure all citizens of the Commonwealth that (1) the benefits of our marriage laws are available explicitly to create and support a family setting that is, in the Legislature's view, optimal for child rearing, and (2) the State does not endorse gay and lesbian parenthood as the equivalent of being raised by one's married biological parents. These arguments miss the point. The Massachusetts Constitution requires that legislation meet certain criteria and not extend beyond certain limits. It is the function of courts to determine whether these criteria are met and whether these limits are exceeded. In most instances, these limits are defined by whether a rational basis exists to conclude that legislation will bring about a rational result. The Legislature in the first instance, and the courts in the last instance, must ascertain whether such a rational basis exists. To label the court's role as usurping that of the Legislature, see, e.g., *post* at 394–395 (Cordy, J., dissenting), is to misunderstand the nature and purpose of judicial review. We owe great deference to the Legislature to decide social and policy issues, but it is the traditional and settled role of courts to decide constitutional issues.[31]

The history of constitutional law "is the story of the extension of constitutional rights and protections to people once ignored or excluded." *United States v. Virginia,* 518 U.S. 515, 557, 116 S.Ct. 2264, 135 L.Ed.2d 735 (1996) (construing equal protection clause of Fourteenth Amendment to prohibit categorical exclusion of women from public military institute). This statement is as true in the area of civil marriage as in any other area of civil rights. See, e.g., *Turner v. Safley,* 482 U.S. 78, 107 S.Ct. 2254, 96 L.Ed.2d 64 (1987); *Loving v. Virginia,* 388 U.S. 1, 87 S.Ct. 1817, 18 L.Ed.2d 1010 (1967); *Perez v. Sharp,* 32 Cal.2d 711, 198 P.2d 17 (1948). As a public institution and a right of fundamental importance, civil marriage is an evolving paradigm. The common law was exceptionally harsh toward women who became wives: a woman's legal identity all but evaporated into that of her husband. See generally C.P. Kindregan, Jr., & M.L. Inker, Family Law and Practice §§ 1.9 and 1.10 (3d ed.2002). Thus, one early Nineteenth Century jurist could observe matter of factly that, prior to the abolition of slavery in Massachusetts, "the condition of a slave resembled the connection of a wife with her husband, and of infant children with their father. He is obliged to maintain them, and they cannot be separated from him."

---

31. If total deference to the Legislature were the case, the judiciary would be stripped of its constitutional authority to decide challenges to statutes pertaining to marriage, child rearing, and family relationships, and, conceivably, unconstitutional laws that provided for the forced sterilization of habitual criminals; prohibited miscegenation; required court approval for the marriage of persons with child support obligations; compelled a pregnant unmarried minor to obtain the consent of both parents before undergoing an abortion; and made sodomy a criminal offense, to name just a few, would stand.

Indeed, every State court that has recently considered the issue we decide today has exercised its duty in the same way, by carefully scrutinizing the statutory ban on same-sex marriages in light of relevant State constitutional provisions. See *Brause v. Bureau of Vital Statistics,* No. 3AN–95–6562CI, 1998 WL 88743 (Alaska Super.Ct., Feb. 27, 1998) (concluding marriage statute violated right to privacy provision in Alaska Constitution) (superseded by constitutional amendment, art. I, § 25 of Constitution of Alaska); *Baehr v. Lewin,* 74 Haw. 530, 571–580, 852 P.2d 44 (1993) (concluding marriage statute implicated Hawaii Constitution's equal protection clause; remanding case to lower court for further proceedings); *Baker v. State,* 170 Vt. 194, 197–198, 744 A.2d 864 (1999) (concluding marriage statute violated Vermont Constitution's common benefits clause). But see *Standhardt v. Superior Court,* 77 P.3d 451 (Ariz.Ct.App.2003) (marriage statute does not violate liberty interests under either Federal or Arizona Constitution). See also *Halpern v. Toronto (City),* 172 O.A.C. 276 (2003) (concluding marriage statute violated equal protection provisions of Canada's Charter of Rights and Freedoms); *Eagle Canada, Inc.* v. *Canada (Attorney Gen.),* 13 B.C.L.R. (4th) 1 (2003) (same).

Winchendon v. Hatfield, 4 Mass. 123, 129 (1808). But since at least the middle of the Nineteenth Century, both the courts and the Legislature have acted to ameliorate the harshness of the common-law regime. In *Bradford v. Worcester,* 184 Mass. 557, 562, 69 N.E. 310 (1904), we refused to apply the common-law rule that the wife's legal residence was that of her husband to defeat her claim to a municipal "settlement of paupers." In *Lewis v. Lewis,* 370 Mass. 619, 629, 351 N.E.2d 526 (1976), we abrogated the common-law doctrine immunizing a husband against certain suits because the common-law rule was predicated on "antediluvian assumptions concerning the role and status of women in marriage and in society." *Id.* at 621, 351 N.E.2d 526. Alarms about the imminent erosion of the "natural" order of marriage were sounded over the demise of antimiscegenation laws, the expansion of the rights of married women, and the introduction of "no-fault" divorce. Marriage has survived all of these transformations, and we have no doubt that marriage will continue to be a vibrant and revered institution.

. . .

The marriage ban works a deep and scarring hardship on a very real segment of the community for no rational reason. The absence of any reasonable relationship between, on the one hand, an absolute disqualification of same-sex couples who wish to enter into civil marriage and, on the other, protection of public health, safety, or general welfare, suggests that the marriage restriction is rooted in persistent prejudices against persons who are (or who are believed to be) homosexual.[33] "The Constitution

---

33. It is not dispositive, for purposes of our constitutional analysis, whether the Legislature, at the time it incorporated the common-law definition of marriage into the first marriage laws nearly three centuries ago, did so with the intent of discriminating against or harming persons who wish to marry another of the same sex. We are not required to impute an invidious intent to the Legislature in determining that a statute of long standing has no applicability to present circumstances or violates the rights of individuals under the Massachusetts Constitution. That the Legislature may have intended what at the time of enactment was a perfectly reasonable form of discrimination—or a result not recognized as a form of discrimination—was not enough to salvage from later constitutional challenge laws burdening nonmarital children or denying women's equal partnership in marriage. See, e.g., *Trimble v. Gordon,* 430 U.S. 762, 97 S.Ct. 1459, 52 L.Ed.2d 31 (1977) (nonmarital children); *Angelini v. OMD Corp.,* 410 Mass. 653, 662, 663, 575 N.E.2d 41 (1991) ("The traditional common law rules which discriminated against children born out of wedlock have been discard-

ed" and "[w]e have recognized that placing additional burdens on [nonmarital] children is unfair because they are not responsible for their [status]"); *Silvia v. Silvia,* 9 Mass.App. Ct. 339, 340–341, 400 N.E.2d 1330 (1980) (there now exists "a comprehensive statutory and common law pattern which places marital and parental obligations on both the husband and wife"). We are concerned with the operation of challenged laws on the parties before us, and we do not inhibit our inquiry on the ground that a statute's original enactors had a benign or at the time constitutionally unassailable purpose. See *Colo v. Treasurer & Receiver Gen.,* 378 Mass. 550, 557, 392 N.E.2d 1195 (1979), quoting *Walz v. Tax Comm'n of the City of N.Y.,* 397 U.S. 664, 678, 90 S.Ct. 1409, 25 L.Ed.2d 697 (1970) ("the mere fact that a certain practice has gone unchallenged for a long period of time cannot alone immunize it from constitutional invalidity, 'even when that span of time covers our entire national existence and indeed predates it' "); *Merit Oil Co. v. Director of Div. of Necessaries of Life,* 319 Mass. 301, 305, 65 N.E.2d 529 (1946) (constitutional

cannot control such prejudices but neither can it tolerate them. Private biases may be outside the reach of the law, but the law cannot, directly or indirectly, give them effect." *Palmore v. Sidoti,* 466 U.S. 429, 433, 104 S.Ct. 1879, 80 L.Ed.2d 421 (1984) (construing Fourteenth Amendment). Limiting the protections, benefits, and obligations of civil marriage to opposite-sex couples violates the basic premises of individual liberty and equality under law protected by the Massachusetts Constitution.

IV

. . .

We construe civil marriage to mean the voluntary union of two persons as spouses, to the exclusion of all others. This reformulation redresses the plaintiffs' constitutional injury and furthers the aim of marriage to promote stable, exclusive relationships. It advances the two legitimate State interests the department has identified: providing a stable setting for child rearing and conserving State resources. It leaves intact the Legislature's broad discretion to regulate marriage. See *Commonwealth v. Stowell,* 389 Mass. 171, 175, 449 N.E.2d 357 (1983).

In their complaint the plaintiffs request only a declaration that their exclusion and the exclusion of other qualified same-sex couples from access to civil marriage violates Massachusetts law. We declare that barring an individual from the protections, benefits, and obligations of civil marriage solely because that person would marry a person of the same sex violates the Massachusetts Constitution. We vacate the summary judgment for the department. We remand this case to the Superior Court for entry of judgment consistent with this opinion. Entry of judgment shall be stayed for 180 days to permit the Legislature to take such action as it may deem appropriate in light of this opinion. See, e.g., *Michaud v. Sheriff of Essex County,* 390 Mass. 523, 535–536, 458 N.E.2d 702 (1983).

So ordered.

[The concurring opinion of GREANEY, J. and the dissenting opinion of SPINA, J. have been omitted.]

■ SOSMAN, J. (dissenting, with whom SPINA and CORDY, JJ., join).

In applying the rational basis test to any challenged statutory scheme, the issue is not whether the Legislature's rationale behind that scheme is persuasive to us, but only whether it satisfies a minimal threshold of rationality. Today, rather than apply that test, the court announces that, because it is persuaded that there are no differences between same-sex and opposite-sex couples, the Legislature has no rational basis for treating them differently with respect to the granting of marriage licenses.[1] Reduced to its

---

contours of State's regulatory authority coextensive "with the changing needs of society").

1. The one difference that the court acknowledges—that sexual relations between persons of the same sex does not result in pregnancy and childbirth—it immediately brushes aside on the theory that civil marriage somehow has nothing to do with begetting children. *Ante* at 331–333, 798 N.E.2d at

essence, the court's opinion concludes that, because same-sex couples are now raising children, and withholding the benefits of civil marriage from their union makes it harder for them to raise those children, the State must therefore provide the benefits of civil marriage to same-sex couples just as it does to opposite-sex couples. Of course, many people are raising children outside the confines of traditional marriage, and, by definition, those children are being deprived of the various benefits that would flow if they were being raised in a household with married parents. That does not mean that the Legislature must accord the full benefits of marital status on every household raising children. Rather, the Legislature need only have some rational basis for concluding that, at present, those alternate family structures have not yet been conclusively shown to be the equivalent of the marital family structure that has established itself as a successful one over a period of centuries. People are of course at liberty to raise their children in various family structures, so long as they are not literally harming their children by doing so. See *Blixt v. Blixt,* 437 Mass. 649, 668–670, 774 N.E.2d 1052 (2002) (Sosman, J., dissenting), cert. denied, 537 U.S. 1189, 123 S.Ct. 1259, 154 L.Ed.2d 1022 (2003). That does not mean that the State is required to provide identical forms of encouragement, endorsement, and support to all of the infinite variety of household structures that a free society permits.

Based on our own philosophy of child rearing, and on our observations of the children being raised by same-sex couples to whom we are personally close, we may be of the view that what matters to children is not the gender, or sexual orientation, or even the number of the adults who raise them, but rather whether those adults provide the children with a nurturing, stable, safe, consistent, and supportive environment in which to mature. Same-sex couples can provide their children with the requisite nurturing, stable, safe, consistent, and supportive environment in which to mature, just as opposite-sex couples do. It is therefore understandable that the court might view the traditional definition of marriage as an unnecessary anachronism, rooted in historical prejudices that modern society has in large measure rejected and biological limitations that modern science has overcome.

It is not, however, our assessment that matters. Conspicuously absent from the court's opinion today is any acknowledgment that the attempts at scientific study of the ramifications of raising children in same-sex couple households are themselves in their infancy and have so far produced inconclusive and conflicting results. Notwithstanding our belief that gender and sexual orientation of parents should not matter to the success of the child rearing venture, studies to date reveal that there are still some observable differences between children raised by opposite-sex couples and

961–962. For the reasons explained in detail in Justice Cordy's dissent, in which I join, the reasons justifying the civil marriage laws are inextricably linked to the fact that human sexual intercourse between a man and a woman frequently results in pregnancy and childbirth. Indeed, as Justice Cordy outlines, that fact lies at the core of why society fashioned the institution of marriage in the first place. *Post* at 381–382, 798 N.E.2d at 995–996 (Cordy, J., dissenting).

children raised by same-sex couples. See *post* at 386–387, 798 N.E.2d at 998–999 (Cordy, J., dissenting). Interpretation of the data gathered by those studies then becomes clouded by the personal and political beliefs of the investigators, both as to whether the differences identified are positive or negative, and as to the untested explanations of what might account for those differences. (This is hardly the first time in history that the ostensible steel of the scientific method has melted and buckled under the intense heat of political and religious passions.) Even in the absence of bias or political agenda behind the various studies of children raised by same-sex couples, the most neutral and strict application of scientific principles to this field would be constrained by the limited period of observation that has been available. Gay and lesbian couples living together openly, and official recognition of them as their children's sole parents, comprise a very recent phenomenon, and the recency of that phenomenon has not yet permitted any study of how those children fare as adults and at best minimal study of how they fare during their adolescent years. The Legislature can rationally view the state of the scientific evidence as unsettled on the critical question it now faces: are families headed by same-sex parents equally successful in rearing children from infancy to adulthood as families headed by parents of opposite sexes? Our belief that children raised by same-sex couples *should* fare the same as children raised in traditional families is just that: a passionately held but utterly untested belief. The Legislature is not required to share that belief but may, as the creator of the institution of civil marriage, wish to see the proof before making a fundamental alteration to that institution.

.   .   .

As a matter of social history, today's opinion may represent a great turning point that many will hail as a tremendous step toward a more just society. As a matter of constitutional jurisprudence, however, the case stands as an aberration. To reach the result it does, the court has tortured the rational basis test beyond recognition. I fully appreciate the strength of the temptation to find this particular law unconstitutional—there is much to be said for the argument that excluding gay and lesbian couples from the benefits of civil marriage is cruelly unfair and hopelessly outdated; the inability to marry has a profound impact on the personal lives of committed gay and lesbian couples (and their children) to whom we are personally close (our friends, neighbors, family members, classmates, and co-workers); and our resolution of this issue takes place under the intense glare of national and international publicity. Speaking metaphorically, these factors have combined to turn the case before us into a ''perfect storm'' of a constitutional question. In my view, however, such factors make it all the more imperative that we adhere precisely and scrupulously to the established guideposts of our constitutional jurisprudence, a jurisprudence that makes the rational basis test an extremely deferential one that focuses on the rationality, not the persuasiveness, of the potential justifications for the classifications in the legislative scheme. I trust that, once this particular ''storm'' clears, we will return to the rational basis test as it has always been understood and applied. Applying that deferential test in the manner it is customarily applied, the exclusion of gay and lesbian couples from the institution of civil marriage passes constitutional muster. I respectfully dissent.

■ CORDY, J. (dissenting, with whom SPINA and SOSMAN, JJ., join).

The court's opinion concludes that the Department of Public Health has failed to identify any "constitutionally adequate reason" for limiting civil marriage to opposite-sex unions, and that there is no "reasonable relationship" between a disqualification of same-sex couples who wish to enter into a civil marriage and the protection of public health, safety, or general welfare. Consequently, it holds that the marriage statute cannot withstand scrutiny under the Massachusetts Constitution. Because I find these conclusions to be unsupportable in light of the nature of the rights and regulations at issue, the presumption of constitutional validity and significant deference afforded to legislative enactments, and the "undesirability of the judiciary substituting its notions of correct policy for that of a popularly elected Legislature" responsible for making such policy, *Zayre Corp. v. Attorney Gen.*, 372 Mass. 423, 433, 362 N.E.2d 878 (1977), I respectfully dissent. Although it may be desirable for many reasons to extend to same-sex couples the benefits and burdens of civil marriage (and the plaintiffs have made a powerfully reasoned case for that extension), that decision must be made by the Legislature, not the court.

.   .   .

The Massachusetts marriage statute does not impair the exercise of a recognized fundamental right, or discriminate on the basis of sex in violation of the equal rights amendment to the Massachusetts Constitution. Consequently, it is subject to review only to determine whether it satisfies the rational basis test. Because a conceivable rational basis exists upon which the Legislature could conclude that the marriage statute furthers the legitimate State purpose of ensuring, promoting, and supporting an optimal social structure for the bearing and raising of children, it is a valid exercise of the State's police power.

A.   *Limiting marriage to the union of one man and one woman does not impair the exercise of a fundamental right.* Civil marriage is an institution created by the State. In Massachusetts, the marriage statutes are derived from English common law, see *Commonwealth v. Knowlton,* 2 Mass. 530, 534 (1807), and were first enacted in colonial times. *Commonwealth v. Munson,* 127 Mass. 459, 460 (1879). They were enacted to secure public interests and not for religious purposes or to promote personal interests or aspirations. (See discussion *infra* at 381–385). As the court notes in its opinion, the institution of marriage is "the legal union of a man and woman as husband and wife," *ante* at 319, 798 N.E.2d at 952, and it has always been so under Massachusetts law, colonial or otherwise.

The plaintiffs contend that because the right to choose to marry is a "fundamental" right, the right to marry the person of one's choice, including a member of the same sex, must also be a "fundamental" right.

While the court stops short of deciding that the right to marry someone of the same sex is "fundamental" such that strict scrutiny must be applied to any statute that impairs it, it nevertheless agrees with the plaintiffs that the right to choose to marry is of fundamental importance ("among the most basic" of every person's "liberty and due process rights") and would be "hollow" if an individual was foreclosed from "freely choosing the person with whom to share ... the ... institution of civil marriage." *Ante* at 329, 798 N.E.2d at 959. Hence, it concludes that a marriage license cannot be denied to an individual who wishes to marry someone of the same sex. In reaching this result the court has transmuted the "right" to marry into a right to change the institution of marriage itself. This feat of reasoning succeeds only if one accepts the proposition that the definition of the institution of marriage as a union between a man and a woman is merely "conclusory" (as suggested, *ante* at 348, 798 N.E.2d at 972 [Greaney, J., concurring]), rather than the basis on which the "right" to partake in it has been deemed to be of fundamental importance. In other words, only by assuming that "marriage" includes the union of two persons of the same sex does the court conclude that restricting marriage to opposite-sex couples infringes on the "right" of same-sex couples to "marry."

. . .

In Massachusetts jurisprudence, protected decisions generally have been limited to those concerning "whether or not to beget or bear a child," *Matter of Moe,* 385 Mass. 555, 564, 432 N.E.2d 712 (1982) (see *Opinion of the Justices,* 423 Mass. 1201, 1234–1235 [1996] ["focus of (the *Griswold* and *Roe* cases) and the cases following them has been the intrusion ... into the especially intimate aspects of a person's life implicated in procreation and childbearing"]); how to raise a child, see *Care & Protection of Robert,* 408 Mass. 52, 58, 60, 556 N.E.2d 993 (1990); or whether or not to accept medical treatment, see *Brophy v. New England Sinai Hosp., Inc.,* 398 Mass. 417, 430, 497 N.E.2d 626 (1986); *Superintendent of Belchertown State Sch. v. Saikewicz,* 373 Mass. 728, 742, 370 N.E.2d 417 (1977), none of which is at issue here. See also *Commonwealth v. Balthazar,* 366 Mass. 298, 301, 318 N.E.2d 478 (1974) (statute punishing unnatural and lascivious acts does not apply to sexual conduct engaged in by adults in private, in light of "articulation of the constitutional right of an individual to be free from government regulation of certain sex related activities").

The marriage statute, which regulates only the act of obtaining a marriage license, does not implicate privacy in the sense that it has found constitutional protection under Massachusetts and Federal law. Cf. *Commonwealth v. King,* 374 Mass. 5, 14, 372 N.E.2d 196 (1977) (solicitation of prostitution "while in a place to which the public had access" implicated no "constitutionally protected rights of privacy"); *Marcoux v. Attorney Gen., supra* at 68, 375 N.E.2d 688 (right to privacy, at most, protects conduct "limited more or less to the hearth"). It does not intrude on any right that the plaintiffs have to privacy in their choices regarding procreation, an intimate partner or sexual relations.[6] The plaintiffs' right to privacy in such matters does not require that the State officially endorse their choices in order for the right to be constitutionally vindicated.

. . .

Because the rights and interests discussed above do not afford the plaintiffs any fundamental right that would be impaired by a statute limiting marriage to members of the opposite sex, they have no fundamental right to be declared "married" by the State.

Insofar as the right to marry someone of the same sex is neither found in the unique historical context of our Constitution nor compelled by the meaning ascribed by this court to the liberty and due process protections contained within it, should the court nevertheless recognize it as a fundamental right? The consequences of deeming a right to be "fundamental" are profound, and this court, as well as the Supreme Court, has been very cautious in recognizing them. Such caution is required by separation of powers principles. If a right is found to be "fundamental," it is, to a great extent, removed from "the arena of public debate and legislative action"; utmost care must be taken when breaking new ground in this field "lest the liberty protected by the Due Process Clause be subtly transformed into the policy preferences of [judges]." *Washington v. Glucksberg,* 521 U.S. 702, 720, 117 S.Ct. 2258 (1997).

. . .

Although public attitudes toward marriage in general and same-sex marriage in particular have changed and are still evolving, "the asserted contemporary concept of marriage and societal interests for which [plaintiffs] contend" are "manifestly [less] deeply founded" than the "historic institution" of marriage. *Matter of Cooper,* 187 A.D.2d 128, 133–134, 592 N.Y.S.2d 797 (1993). Indeed, it is not readily apparent to what extent contemporary values have embraced the concept of same-sex marriage. Perhaps the "clearest and most reliable objective evidence of contemporary values is the legislation enacted by the country's legislatures," *Atkins v. Virginia,* 536 U.S. 304, 312, 122 S.Ct. 2242, 153 L.Ed.2d 335 (2002), quoting *Penry v. Lynaugh,* 492 U.S. 302, 331, 109 S.Ct. 2934, 106 L.Ed.2d 256 (1989). No State Legislature has enacted laws permitting same-sex marriages; and a large majority of States, as well as the United States Congress, have affirmatively prohibited the recognition of such marriages for any purpose. See P. Greenberg, State Laws Affecting Lesbians and Gays, National Conference of State Legislatures Legisbriefs at 1 (April/May 2001) (reporting that, as of May, 2001, thirty-six States had enacted "defense of marriage" statutes); 1 U.S.C. § 7 (2000); 28 U.S.C. § 1738C (2000) (Federal Defense of Marriage Act).

---

6. Contrast *Lawrence v. Texas,* 539 U.S. 558, 123 S.Ct. 2472, 156 L.Ed.2d 508 (2003), in which the United States Supreme Court struck down the Texas criminal sodomy statute because it constituted State intrusion on some of these very choices.

Given this history and the current state of public opinion, as reflected in the actions of the people's elected representatives, it cannot be said that "a right to same-sex marriage is so rooted in the traditions and collective conscience of our people that failure to recognize it would violate the fundamental principles of liberty and justice that lie at the base of all our civil and political institutions. Neither ... [is] a right to same-sex marriage ... implicit in the concept of ordered liberty, such that neither liberty nor justice would exist if it were sacrificed." *Baehr v. Lewin,* 74 Haw. 530, 556–557, 852 P.2d 44 (1993). See *Dean v. District of Columbia,* 653 A.2d 307, 333 (D.C.1995) (per curiam) (Ferren, J., concurring in part and dissenting in part); *Baker v. Nelson,* 291 Minn. 310, 312, 191 N.W.2d 185 (1971), appeal dismissed, 409 U.S. 810, 93 S.Ct. 37, 34 L.Ed.2d 65 (1972); *Storrs v. Holcomb,* 168 Misc.2d 898, 899–900, 645 N.Y.S.2d 286 (N.Y.Sup.Ct.1996), dismissed, 245 A.D.2d 943, 666 N.Y.S.2d 835 (1997).[11] The one exception was the Alaska Superior Court, which relied on that State's Constitution's express and broadly construed right to privacy. *Brause,* 1998 WL 88743 at *3–*4 (Alaska Super 1998). In such circumstances, the law with respect to same-sex marriages must be left to develop through legislative processes, subject to the constraints of rationality, lest the court be viewed as using the liberty and due process clauses as vehicles merely to enforce its own views regarding better social policies, a role that the strongly worded separation of powers principles in art. 30 of the Declaration of Rights of our Constitution forbids, and for which the court is particularly ill suited.

. . .

In analyzing whether a statute satisfies the rational basis standard, we look to the nature of the classification embodied in the enactment, then to whether the statute serves a legitimate State purpose, and finally to whether the classification is reasonably related to the furtherance of that purpose. With this framework, we turn to the challenged statute, G.L. c. 207, which authorizes local town officials to issue licenses to couples of the opposite sex authorizing them to enter the institution of civil marriage.

1. *Classification.* The nature of the classification at issue is readily apparent. Opposite-sex couples can obtain a license and same-sex couples cannot. The granting of this license, and the completion of the required solemnization of the marriage, opens the door to many statutory benefits and imposes numerous responsibilities. The fact that the statute does not permit such licenses to be issued to couples of the same sex thus bars them

---

11. Because of the absence of deep historical roots, every court but one that has considered recognizing a fundamental right to same-sex marriage has declined to do so. See, e.g., *Standhardt v. Superior Court,* 77 P.3d 451 (Ariz.Ct.App.2003); *Dean v. District of Columbia,* 653 A.2d 307, 333 (D.C.1995) (per curiam) (Ferren, J., concurring in part and dissenting in part); *Baehr v. Lewin,* 74 Haw. 530, 556–557, 852 P.2d 44 (1993); *Baker v. Nelson,* 291 Minn. 310, 312–314, 191 N.W.2d 185 (1971); *Storrs v. Holcomb,* 168 Misc.2d 898, 899–900, 645 N.Y.S.2d 286 (N.Y.Sup.Ct.1996), dismissed, 245 A.D.2d 943, 666 N.Y.S.2d 835 (1997). The one exception was the Alaska Superior Court, which relied on that State's Constitution's express and broadly construed right to privacy. *Brause v. Bureau of Vital Statistics,* No. 3AN–95–6562CI, 1998 WL 88743 (Alaska Super.Ct. Feb. 27, 1998).

from civil marriage. The classification is not drawn between men and women or between heterosexuals and homosexuals, any of whom can obtain a license to marry a member of the opposite sex; rather, it is drawn between same-sex couples and opposite-sex couples.

2. *State purpose.* The court's opinion concedes that the civil marriage statute serves legitimate State purposes, but further investigation and elaboration of those purposes is both helpful and necessary.

Civil marriage is the institutional mechanism by which societies have sanctioned and recognized particular family structures, and the institution of marriage has existed as one of the fundamental organizing principles of human society. See C.N. Degler, The Emergence of the Modern American Family, in The American Family in Social–Historical Perspective 61 (3d ed.1983); A.J. Hawkins, Introduction, in Revitalizing the Institution of Marriage for the Twenty–First Century: An Agenda for Strengthening Marriage xiv (2002); C. Lasch, Social Pathologists and the Socialization of Reproduction, in The American Family in Social–Historical Perspective, *supra* at 80; W.J. O'Donnell & D.A. Jones, Marriage and Marital Alternatives 1 (1982); L. Saxton, The Individual, Marriage, and the Family 229–230, 260 (1968); M.A. Schwartz & B.M. Scott, Marriages and Families: Diversity and Change 4 (1994); Wardle, "Multiply and Replenish": Considering Same–Sex Marriage in Light of State Interests in Marital Procreation, 24 Harv. J.L. & Pub. Pol'y 771, 777–780 (2001); J.Q. Wilson, The Marriage Problem: How Our Culture Has Weakened Families 28, 40, 66–67 (2002). Marriage has not been merely a contractual arrangement for legally defining the private relationship between two individuals (although that is certainly part of any marriage). Rather, on an institutional level, marriage is the "very basis of the whole fabric of civilized society," J.P. Bishop, Commentaries on the Law of Marriage and Divorce, and Evidence in Matrimonial Suits § 32 (1852), and it serves many important political, economic, social, educational, procreational, and personal functions.

Paramount among its many important functions, the institution of marriage has systematically provided for the regulation of heterosexual behavior, brought order to the resulting procreation, and ensured a stable family structure in which children will be reared, educated, and socialized. See *Milford v. Worcester,* 7 Mass. 48, 52 (1810) (civil marriage "intended to regulate, chasten, and refine, the intercourse between the sexes; and to multiply, preserve, and improve the species"). See also P. Blumstein & P. Schwartz, American Couples: Money, Work, Sex 29 (1983); C.N. Degler, *supra* at 61; G. Douglas, Marriage, Cohabitation, and Parenthood—From Contract to Status?, in Cross Currents: Family Law and Policy in the United States and England 223 (2000); S.L. Nock, The Social Costs of De-Institutionalizing Marriage, in Revitalizing the Institution of Marriage for the Twenty–First Century: An Agenda for Strengthening Marriage, *supra* at 7; L. Saxton, *supra* at 239–240, 242; M.A. Schwartz & B.M. Scott, *supra* at 4–6; Wardle, *supra* at 781–796; J.Q. Wilson, *supra* at 23–32. Admittedly, heterosexual intercourse, procreation, and child care are not necessarily conjoined (particularly in the modern age of widespread effective contraception and supportive social welfare programs), but an orderly society requires some mechanism for coping with the fact that sexual intercourse commonly results in pregnancy and childbirth. The institution of marriage is that mechanism.

The institution of marriage provides the important legal and normative link between heterosexual intercourse and procreation on the one hand and family responsibilities on the other. The partners in a marriage are expected to engage in exclusive sexual relations, with children the probable result and paternity presumed. See G.L. c. 209C, § 6 ("a man is presumed to be the father of a child . . . if he is or has been married to the mother and the child was born during the marriage, or within three hundred days after the marriage was terminated by death, annulment or divorce"). Whereas the relationship between mother and child is demonstratively and predictably created and recognizable through the biological process of pregnancy and childbirth, there is no corresponding process for creating a relationship between father and child.[16] Similarly, aside from an act of heterosexual intercourse nine months prior to childbirth, there is no process for creating a relationship between a man and a woman as the parents of a particular child. The institution of marriage fills this void by formally binding the husband-father to his wife and child, and imposing on him the responsibilities of fatherhood. See J.Q. Wilson, *supra* at 23–32. See also P. Blumstein & P. Schwartz, *supra* at 29; C.N. Degler, *supra* at 61; G. Douglas, *supra* at 223; S.L. Nock, *supra* at 7; L. Saxton, *supra* at 239–240, 242; M.A. Schwartz & B.M. Scott, *supra* at 4–6; Wardle, *supra* at 781–796. The alternative, a society without the institution of marriage, in which heterosexual intercourse, procreation, and child care are largely disconnected processes, would be chaotic.

The marital family is also the foremost setting for the education and socialization of children. Children learn about the world and their place in it primarily from those who raise them, and those children eventually grow up to exert some influence, great or small, positive or negative, on society. The institution of marriage encourages parents to remain committed to each other and to their children as they grow, thereby encouraging a stable venue for the education and socialization of children. See P. Blumstein & P. Schwartz, *supra* at 26; C.N. Degler, *supra* at 61; S.L. Nock, *supra* at 2–3; C. Lasch, *supra* at 81; M.A. Schwartz & B.M. Scott, *supra* at 6–7. More macroscopically, construction of a family through marriage also formalizes the bonds between people in an ordered and institutional manner, thereby facilitating a foundation of interconnectedness and interdependency on which more intricate stabilizing social structures might be built. See M. Grossberg, Governing the Hearth: Law and Family in Nineteenth–Century America 10 (1985); C. Lasch, *supra;* L. Saxton, *supra* at 260; J.Q. Wilson, *supra* at 221.

---

16. Modern DNA testing may reveal actual paternity, but it establishes only a genetic relationship between father and child.

This court, among others, has consistently acknowledged both the institutional importance of marriage as an organizing principle of society, and the State's interest in regulating it. See *French v. McAnarney,* 290 Mass. 544, 546, 195 N.E. 714 (1935) ("Marriage is not merely a contract between the parties. It is the foundation of the family. It is a social institution of the highest importance. The Commonwealth has a deep interest that its integrity is not jeopardized"); *Milford v. Worcester,* 7 Mass. 48, 52 (1810) ("Marriage, being essential to the peace and harmony, and to the virtues and improvements of civil society, it has been, in all well-regulated governments, among the first attentions of the civil magistrate to regulate [it]"). See also *Skinner v. Oklahoma,* 316 U.S. 535, 541, 62 S.Ct. 1110, 86 L.Ed. 1655 (1942) ("Marriage and procreation are fundamental to the very existence and survival of the [human] race"); *Maynard v. Hill,* 125 U.S. 190, 211, 8 S.Ct.

The marital family is also the foremost setting for the education and socialization of children. Children learn about the world and their place in it primarily from those who raise them, and those children eventually grow up to exert some influence, great or small, positive or negative, on society. The institution of marriage encourages parents to remain committed to each other and to their children as they grow, thereby encouraging a stable venue for the education and socialization of children. See P. Blumstein & P. Schwartz, *supra* at 26; C.N. Degler, *supra* at 61; S.L. Nock, *supra* at 2–3; C. Lasch, *supra* at 81; M.A. Schwartz & B.M. Scott, *supra* at 6–7. More macroscopically, construction of a family through marriage also formalizes the bonds between people in an ordered and institutional manner, thereby facilitating a foundation of interconnectedness and interdependency on which more intricate stabilizing social structures might be built. See M. Grossberg, Governing the Hearth: Law and Family in Nineteenth–Century America 10 (1985); C. Lasch, *supra;* L. Saxton, *supra* at 260; J.Q. Wilson, *supra* at 221.

This court, among others, has consistently acknowledged both the institutional importance of marriage as an organizing principle of society, and the State's interest in regulating it. See *French v. McAnarney,* 290 Mass. 544, 546, 195 N.E. 714 (1935) ("Marriage is not merely a contract between the parties. It is the foundation of the family. It is a social institution of the highest importance. The Commonwealth has a deep interest that its integrity is not jeopardized"); *Milford v. Worcester,* 7 Mass. 48, 52 (1810) ("Marriage, being essential to the peace and harmony, and to the virtues and improvements of civil society, it has been, in all well-regulated governments, among the first attentions of the civil magistrate to regulate [it]"). See also *Skinner v. Oklahoma,* 316 U.S. 535, 541, 62 S.Ct. 1110, 86 L.Ed. 1655 (1942) ("Marriage and procreation are fundamental to the very existence and survival of the [human] race"); *Maynard v. Hill,* 125 U.S. 190, 211, 8 S.Ct. 723, 31 L.Ed. 654 (1888) (marriage "is an institution, in the maintenance of which in its purity the public is deeply interested, for it is the foundation of the family and of society, without which there would be neither civilization nor progress"); *Murphy v. Ramsey,* 114 U.S. 15, 45, 5 S.Ct. 747, 29 L.Ed. 47 (1885) ("no legislation can be supposed more wholesome and necessary in the founding of a free, self-governing common-wealth ... than that which seeks to establish it on the basis of the idea of the family, as consisting in and springing from the union for life of one man and one woman ... the sure foundation of all that is stable and noble in our civilization; the best guaranty of that reverent morality which is the source of all beneficent progress in social and political improvement''); *Reynolds v. United States,* 98 U.S. 145, 165, 25 L.Ed. 244 (1878) (''Upon [marriage] society may be said to be built, and out of its fruits spring social relations and social obligations and duties, with which government is necessarily required to deal'').

It is undeniably true that dramatic historical shifts in our cultural, political, and economic landscape have altered some of our traditional notions about marriage, including the interpersonal dynamics within it, the range of responsibilities required of it as an institution, and the legal environment in which it exists. Nevertheless, the institution of marriage remains the principal weave of our social fabric. See C.N. Degler, *supra* at 61; A.J. Hawkins, Introduction, in Revitalizing the Institution of Marriage for the Twenty–First Century: An Agenda for Strengthening Marriage xiv (2002); C. Lasch, *supra* at 80; W.J. O'Donnell & D.A. Jones, Marriage and Marital Alternatives 1 (1982); L. Saxton, *supra* at 229–230, 260; M.A. Schwartz & B.M. Scott, *supra* at 4; Wardle, *supra* at 777–780; J.Q. Wilson, *supra* at 28, 40, 66–67. A family defined by heterosexual marriage contin-ues to be the most prevalent social structure into which the vast majority of children are born, nurtured, and prepared for productive participation in civil society, see Children's Living Arrangements and Characteristics: March, 2002, United States Census Bureau Current Population Reports at 3 (June, 2003) (in 2002, 69% of children lived with two married parents, 23% lived with their mother, 5% lived with their father, and 4% lived in households with neither parent present).

. . .

There is no question that many same-sex couples are capable of being good parents, and should be (and are) permitted to be so. The policy question that a legislator must resolve is a different one, and turns on an assessment of whether the marriage structure proposed by the plaintiffs will, over time, if endorsed and supported by the State, prove to be as stable and successful a model as the one that has formed a cornerstone of our society since colonial times, or prove to be less than optimal, and result in consequences, perhaps now unforeseen, adverse to the State's legitimate interest in promoting and supporting the best possible social structure in which children should be born and raised. Given the critical importance of civil marriage as an organizing and stabilizing institution of society, it is eminently rational for the Legislature to postpone making fundamental changes to it until such time as there is unanimous scientific evidence, or popular consensus, or both, that such changes can safely be made.

There is no reason to believe that legislative processes are inadequate to effectuate legal changes in response to evolving evidence, social values, and views of fairness on the subject of same-sex relationships.[38] Deliberate consideration of, and incremental responses to rapidly evolving scientific and social understanding is the norm of the political process—that it may seem painfully slow to those who are already persuaded by the arguments in favor of change is not a sufficient basis to conclude that the processes are constitutionally infirm. See, e.g., *Massachusetts Fed'n of Teachers v. Board of Educ.,* 436 Mass. 763, 778, 767 N.E.2d 549 (2002); *Mobil Oil v. Attorney Gen.,* 361 Mass. 401, 417, 280 N.E.2d 406 (1972) (Legislature may proceed piecemeal in addressing perceived injustices or problems). The advancement of the rights, privileges, and protections afforded to homosexual members of our community in the last three decades has been significant, and there is no reason to believe that that evolution will not continue. Changes of attitude in the civic, social, and professional communities have been even more profound. Thirty years ago, The Diagnostic and Statistical Manual, the seminal handbook of the American Psychiatric Association, still listed homosexuality as a mental disorder. Today, the Massachusetts Psychiatric Society, the American Psychoanalytic Association, and many other psychiatric, psychological, and social science organizations have joined in an amicus brief on behalf of the plaintiffs' cause. A body of experience and evidence has provided the basis for change, and that body continues to mount. The Legislature is the appropriate branch, both constitutionally and practically, to consider and respond to it. It is not enough that we as Justices might be personally of the view that we have learned enough to decide what is best. So long as the question is at all debatable, it must be the Legislature that decides. The marriage statute thus meets the requirements of the rational basis test. Accord *Standhardt v. Superior Court,* 77 P.3d 451 (Ariz.Ct.App.2003) (marriage statutes rationally related to State's legitimate interest in encouraging procreation and child rearing within marriage); *Baker v. Nelson,* 291 Minn. 310, 313, 191 N.W.2d 185 (1971) ("equal protection clause of the Fourteenth Amendment, like the due process clause, is not offended by the state's classification of persons authorized to marry"); *Singer v. Hara,* 11 Wash.App. 247, 262–263, 522 P.2d 1187 (1974) ("There can be no doubt that there exists a rational basis for the state to limit the definition of marriage to exclude same-sex relationships").

D.   *Conclusion.* While "[t]he Massachusetts Constitution protects matters of personal liberty against government incursion as zealously, and often more so, than does the Federal Constitution," *ante* at 328, 798 N.E.2d at 958–959, this case is not about government intrusions into matters of

---

38. Legislatures in many parts of the country continue to consider various means of affording same-sex couples the types of benefits and legal structures that married couples enjoy. For example, in 1999 the California Legislature established the first State-wide domestic partner registry in the nation, and in each of the years 2001, 2002, and 2003 substantially expanded the rights and bene-fits accruing to registered partners. Cal. Fam. Code §§ 297 et seq. (West Supp.2003). See also comments of Massachusetts Senate President Robert Travaglini to the effect that he intends to bring civil union legislation to the floor of the Senate for a vote. Mass. Senate Eyes Civil Unions: Move Comes as SJC Mulls Gay Marriages, Boston Globe, Sept. 7, 2003, at A1.

personal liberty. It is not about the rights of same-sex couples to choose to live together, or to be intimate with each other, or to adopt and raise children together. It is about whether the State must endorse and support their choices by changing the institution of civil marriage to make its benefits, obligations, and responsibilities applicable to them. While the courageous efforts of many have resulted in increased dignity, rights, and respect for gay and lesbian members of our community, the issue presented here is a profound one, deeply rooted in social policy, that must, for now, be the subject of legislative not judicial action.

NOTES

Voting in the November 2, 2004 presidential election, voters in Arkansas, Georgia, Kentucky, Michigan, Mississippi, Montana, North Dakota, Ohio, Oklahoma, Oregon, and Utah added state constitutional amendments barring same-sex marriage. *Eleven States Ban Same–Sex Marriage Through Constitutional Amendments*, 31 Fam. L. Rep. (BNA) 1022 (Nov. 9, 2004). Additional states already had similar bans: Alaska, Hawaii, Louisiana, Missouri, Nebraska, and Nevada. *Id.* Litigation continues over the constitutionality of state statutes barring same-sex marriage. For example, the Indiana Court of Appeals upheld the constitutionality of the state's statute banning same-sex marriage because it furthers the state's interest in responsible procreation. Morrison v. Sadler, 821 N.E.2d 15 (Ind. Ct. App. 2005). And the state's supreme court ruled that Louisiana's constitutional amendment banning same-sex marriage was validly enacted in spite of irregularities. Forum for Equality PAC v. McKeithen, 893 So.2d 738 (La. 2005). Nonetheless, in California, the San Francisco County Superior Court held that same-sex marriage cannot be prohibited simply because California has always prohibited same-sex marriages. Coordination Proceeding (Marriage Cases), 2005 WL 583129 (Cal. Super. Ct. 2005). Likewise, one New York Supreme Court decision ruled that prohibiting same-sex couples from marrying is a denial of equal protection and due process. Hernandez v. Robles, 7 Misc.3d 459, 794 N.Y.S.2d 579 (2005). But another decision from the same court held that legislation prohibiting same-sex marriage is rationally related to procreation and child-rearing. Seymour v. Holcomb, 7 Misc.3d 530, 790 N.Y.S.2d 858 (Sup. Ct. 2005).

Foreign recognition of the right to same-sex marriage continues. For example, the Supreme Court of Canada approved a constitutional amendment that would expand the country's definition of marriage to include same-sex couples, but also allow "religious groups to refuse to perform marriages that are not in accordance with their religious beliefs." *In re* Section 53 of the Supreme Court Act, R.S.C. 1985, c. S–26, [2004] 3 S.C.R. 698, 716 (Can.). And in South Africa the Supreme Court of Appeals ruled that same-sex persons may enter into common law marriage. *South African Court Revises Common–Law Definition of Marriage*, 31 Fam. L. Rep. (BNA) 1068 (Dec. 7, 2004).

Suggested Reading: **Mark Strasser, Lawrence** *and Same–Sex Marriage Bans: On Constitutional Interpretation and Sophisticated Rhetoric,* 69 BROOK. L. REV. 1003–1036 (2004); **Melissa A. Glidden,** *Recent Development. Federal Marriage Amendment,* 41 HARV. J. ON LEGIS. 483–499 (2004); **M. Isabel Medina,** *Of Constitutional Amendments, Human Rights, and Same–Sex Marriage,* 64 LA. L. REV. 459–475 (2004); **Andrew Koppelman,** *Interstate Recognition of Same–Sex Civil Unions After Lawrence v. Texas,* 65 OHIO L. J. 1265–1282 (2004).

CHAPTER II

GETTING MARRIED

C. MARRIAGE PROCEDURES, FORMAL, AND INFORMAL

1. INFORMAL OR "COMMON LAW" MARRIAGE

At Utah Code Annotated at page 147, the statute has been amended to read:

(1) A marriage which is not solemnized according to this chapter shall be legal and valid if a court or administrative order establishes that it arises out of a contract between *a man and a woman* who: (change in italics)

3. STATUTORILY REQUIRED FORMALITIES

At page 153, under NOTES, *Licensure, please add:*

The Idaho Supreme Court interpreted its newly enacted state statute specifying that "consent alone will not constitute marriage; it must be followed by the issuance of a license," as establishing a requirement that a license must be issued before there can be a valid marriage. Dire v. Dire–Blodgett, 140 Idaho 777, 102 P.3d 1096, 1098 (2004).

D. ANNULMENT AND ITS EFFECTS

2. PUTATIVE MARRIAGE

At Putative Marriage, page 162, please add the following case:

Williams v. Williams
Nevada Supreme Court, 2004.
97 P.3d 1124.

■ PER CURIAM.

This is a case of first impression involving the application of the putative spouse doctrine in an annulment proceeding. Under the doctrine, an individual whose marriage is void due to a prior legal impediment is treated as a spouse so long as the party seeking equitable relief participated in the marriage ceremony with the good-faith belief that the ceremony was legally valid. A majority of states recognize the doctrine when dividing property acquired during the marriage, applying equitable principles, based on community property law, to the division. However, absent fraud, the doctrine does not apply to awards of spousal support. While some states have extended the doctrine to permit spousal support awards, they have done so under the authority of state statutes.

We agree with the majority view. Consequently, we adopt the putative spouse doctrine in annulment proceedings for purposes of property division and affirm the district court's division of the property. However, we reject the doctrine as a basis of awarding equitable spousal support. Because Nevada's annulment statutes do not provide for an award of support upon annulment, we reverse the district court's award of spousal support.

On August 26, 1973, appellant Richard E. Williams underwent a marriage ceremony with respondent Marcie C. Williams. At that time, Marcie believed that she was divorced from John Allmaras. However, neither Marcie nor Allmaras had obtained a divorce. Richard and Marcie believed they were legally married and lived together, as husband and wife, for 27 years. In March 2000, Richard discovered that Marcie was not divorced from Allmaras at the time of their marriage ceremony.

In August 2000, Richard and Marcie permanently separated. In February 2001, Richard filed a complaint for an annulment. Marcie answered and counterclaimed for one-half of the property and spousal support as a putative spouse. In April 2002, the parties engaged in a one-day bench trial to resolve the matter.

At trial, Richard testified that had he known Marcie was still married, he would not have married her. He claimed that Marcie knew she was not divorced when she married him or had knowledge that would put a reasonable person on notice to check if the prior marriage had been dissolved. Specifically, Richard stated that Marcie should not have relied on statements from Allmaras that he had obtained a divorce because Marcie never received any legal notice of divorce proceedings. In addition, Richard claimed that in March 2000, when Marcie received a social security check in the name of Marcie Allmaras, Marcie told him that she had never been divorced from Allmaras. Marcie denied making the statement.

Marcie testified that she believed she was not married to her former husband, John Allmaras, and was able to marry again because Allmaras told her they were divorced. Marcie further testified that in 1971, she ran into Allmaras at a Reno bus station, where he specifically told her that they were divorced and he was living with another woman. According to Marcie, she discovered she was still married to Allmaras during the course of the annulment proceedings with Richard. Marcie testified that if she had known at any time that she was still married to Allmaras, she would have obtained a divorce from him.

During the 27 years that the parties believed themselves to be married, Marcie was a homemaker and a mother. From 1981 to 1999, Marcie was a licensed child-care provider for six children. During that time, she earned $460 a week. At trial, Marcie had a certificate of General Educational Development (G.E.D.) and earned $8.50 an hour at a retirement home. She was 63 years old and lived with her daughter because she could not afford to live on her own.

Both parties stipulated to the value of most of their jointly-owned property. At the time of the annulment proceeding, the parties held various items in their joint names, including bank accounts, vehicles, life insurance policies, a Sparks home, a radiator business, and a motorcycle.

The district court found that Marcie had limited ability to support herself. The district court also concluded that both parties believed they were legally married, acted as husband and wife, and conceived and raised two children. Marcie stayed home to care for and raise their children. Based upon these facts, the district court granted the annulment and awarded Marcie one-half of all the jointly-held property and spousal support. The district court did not indicate whether its award was based on the putative spouse doctrine or an implied contract and quantum meruit theory. The final judgment divided the parties' property so that each received assets of approximately the same value. It also ordered Richard to pay Marcie the sum of $500 per month for a period of four years as "reimbursement and compensation for the benefit received by [Richard] by way of [Marcie's] forgoing a career outside the home in order to care for [Richard] and their children." Richard timely appealed the district court's judgment.

A marriage is void if either of the parties to the marriage has a former husband or wife then living.[2] Richard and Marcie's marriage was void because Marcie was still married to another man when she married Richard. Although their marriage was void, an annulment proceeding was necessary to legally sever their relationship. An annulment proceeding is the proper manner to dissolve a void marriage and resolve other issues arising from the dissolution of the relationship.

First, Richard contends that Marcie is not entitled to one-half of their joint property because their marriage was void. Richard asserts that application of the putative spouse doctrine and quasi-community property principles was improper. Alternatively, Richard argues that if the district court relied on implied contract and quantum meruit theories, the district court should have divided the parties' residence according to this court's decision in *Sack v. Tomlin,*[4] which would provide Richard with 67 percent of the assets instead of 50 percent.

Second, Richard argues that the district court erred in awarding spousal support. Richard contends support is not permitted, absent statutory authority, under the putative spouse doctrine and that there is no basis in Nevada law for awarding compensation for services rendered during the marriage under a theory of quantum meruit.

Because the record does not reflect the basis for the district court's decision, resolution of Richard's contentions requires us to address the putative spouse doctrine.

Under the putative spouse doctrine, when a marriage is legally void, the civil effects of a legal marriage flow to the parties who contracted to

---

2. NRS 125.290(2).   **4.** 110 Nev. 204, 871 P.2d 298 (1994).

marry in good faith.[5] That is, a putative spouse is entitled to many of the rights of an actual spouse. A majority of states have recognized some form of the doctrine through case law or statute.[7] States differ, however, on what exactly constitutes a "civil effect." The doctrine was developed to avoid depriving innocent parties who believe in good faith that they are married from being denied the economic and status-related benefits of marriage, such as property division, pension, and health benefits.[8]

The doctrine has two elements: (1) a proper marriage ceremony was performed, and (2) one or both of the parties had a good-faith belief that there was no impediment to the marriage and the marriage was valid and proper.[9] "Good faith" has been defined as an "honest and reasonable belief that the marriage was valid at the time of the ceremony."[10] Good faith is presumed. The party asserting lack of good faith has the burden of proving bad faith.] Whether the party acted in good faith is a question of fact.[12] Unconfirmed rumors or mere suspicions of a legal impediment do not vitiate good faith " 'so long as no certain or authoritative knowledge of some legal impediment comes to him or her.' "[13] However, when a person receives reliable information that an impediment exists, the individual cannot ignore the information, but instead has a duty to investigate further. Persons cannot act " 'blindly or without reasonable precaution.' "[15] Finally, once a spouse learns of the impediment, the putative marriage ends.

We have not previously considered the putative spouse doctrine, but we are persuaded by the rationale of our sister states that public policy supports adopting the doctrine in Nevada. Fairness and equity favor recognizing putative spouses when parties enter into a marriage ceremony in good faith and without knowledge that there is a factual or legal impediment to their marriage. Nor does the doctrine conflict with Nevada's policy in refusing to recognize common-law marriages or palimony suits. In the putative spouse doctrine, the parties have actually attempted to enter into a formal relationship with the solemnization of a marriage ceremony, a missing element in common-law marriages and palimony suits. As a majority of our sister states have recognized, the sanctity of marriage is not

---

5. *Hicklin,* 509 N.W.2d at 631.

7. Christopher L. Blakesley, *The Putative Marriage Doctrine,* 60 Tul. L.Rev. 1 (1985); *see* Cal. Fam.Code § 2251 (West 1994); Colo.Rev.Stat. Ann. § 14–2–111 (West 2003); 750 Ill. Comp. Stat. Ann. 5/305 (West 1999); La. Civ.Code Ann. art. 96 (West 1999); Minn.Stat. Ann. § 518.055 (West 1990); Mont.Code Ann. § 40–1–404 (2003).

8. *See Cortes v. Fleming,* 307 So.2d 611, 613 (La.1973) (noting that the doctrine has been applied to issues involving legitimacy of children, workers' compensation benefits, community property, and inheritance).

9. Blakesley, *supra* note 7, at 6.

10. *Hicklin,* 509 N.W.2d at 631

12. *Galbraith v. Galbraith,* 396 So.2d 1364, 1369 (La.Ct.App.1981).

13. *Garduno v. Garduno,* 760 S.W.2d 735, 740 (Tex.App.1988) (quoting *Succession of Chavis,* 211 La. 313, 29 So.2d 860, 862 (1947)).

15. *Id.* (quoting *Chavis,* 29 So.2d at 863).

undermined, but rather enhanced, by the recognition of the putative spouse doctrine. We therefore adopt the doctrine in Nevada.

We now apply the doctrine to the instant case. The district court found that the parties obtained a license and participated in a marriage ceremony on August 26, 1973, in Verdi, Nevada. The district court also found that Marcie erroneously believed that her prior husband, Allmaras, had terminated their marriage by divorce and that she was legally able to marry Richard. In so finding, the district court also necessarily rejected Richard's argument that Marcie acted unreasonably in relying on Allmaras' statements because she had never been served with divorce papers and that she had a duty to inquire about the validity of her former marriage before marrying Richard.

Although Richard's and Marcie's testimony conflicted on this issue, judging the credibility of the witnesses and the weight to be given to their testimony are matters within the discretion of the district court.[17] "This court reviews district court decisions concerning divorce proceedings for an abuse of discretion. Rulings supported by substantial evidence will not be disturbed on appeal."[18] Substantial evidence is that which a sensible person may accept as adequate to sustain a judgment.[19] We apply the same standard in annulment proceedings. The district court was free to disregard Richard's testimony, and substantial evidence supports the district court's finding that Marcie did not act unreasonably in relying upon Allmaras' representations. The record reflects no reason for Marcie to have disbelieved him and, thus, no reason to have investigated the truth of his representations. Although older case law suggests that a party cannot rely on a former spouse's representation of divorce, more recent cases indicate this is just a factor for the judge to consider in determining good faith. We conclude that the district court did not err in finding that Marcie entered into the marriage in good faith. She therefore qualifies as a putative spouse. We now turn to the effect of the doctrine on the issues of property division and alimony.

Community property states that recognize the putative spouse doctrine apply community property principles to the division of property, including determinations of what constitutes community and separate property. Since putative spouses believe themselves to be married, they are already under the assumption that community property laws would apply to a termination of their relationship. There is no point, therefore, in devising a completely separate set of rules for dividing property differently in a putative spouse scenario. We agree with this reasoning.

In some states, courts apply community property principles to divide property acquired during the purported marriage.[22] In other states, the

17. *Castle v. Simmons,* 120 Nev. 98, —, 86 P.3d 1042, 1046 (2004).

18. *Shydler v. Shydler,* 114 Nev. 192, 196, 954 P.2d 37, 39 (1998).

19. *See Schmanski v. Schmanski,* 115 Nev. 247, 251, 984 P.2d 752, 755 (1999).

22. *Sanguinetti v. Sanguinetti,* 69 P.2d 845, 847 (1937).

property is considered to be held under joint tenancy principles and is divided equally between the parties. Regardless of the approach, all states that recognize the putative spouse doctrine divide assets acquired during the marriage in an equitable fashion. We conclude that the application of community property principles to a putative marriage, as indicated in *Sanguinetti v. Sanguinetti*,[24] is the better approach to the division of property in such cases.[25] In this case, the district court treated the parties' property as quasi-community property and equally divided the joint property between the parties. Substantial evidence supports the district court's division, and we affirm the district court's distribution of the property.

States are divided on whether spousal support is a benefit or civil effect that may be awarded under the putative spouse doctrine. Although some states permit the award of alimony, they do so because their annulment statutes permit an award of rehabilitative or permanent alimony. At least one state, however, has found alimony to be a civil effect under the putative spouse doctrine even in the absence of a specific statute permitting an award of alimony.[28]

Nevada statutes do not provide for an award of alimony after an annulment. Thus, the cases in which alimony was awarded pursuant to statute are of little help in resolving this issue. In those cases, state legislatures had codified the putative spouse doctrine and specifically indicated that issues such as property division and alimony were to be resolved in the same manner as if the void marriage had been valid. Absent such a determination by the Nevada Legislature, we must look to the cases in which courts have either refused to award alimony in the absence of statutory authority, despite recognizing the doctrine for other purposes, or awarded spousal support based on the putative spouse doctrine.

In *McKinney v. McKinney,* the Georgia Supreme Court summarily stated that alimony is not available in an equitable action for annulment because the right to alimony depends upon a valid marriage.[31] This reflects the general rule expressed in *Poupart*. However, unlike *Poupart*, the Georgia Supreme Court does appear to have relied on the putative spouse doctrine in dividing the parties' property since it discussed concepts of good faith. Thus, it appears that the Georgia court declined to award alimony under the doctrine.

---

24. 69 P.2d at 847

25. Different rules may apply when one of the parties qualifies as a putative spouse and the other does not. When a person enters into the relationship with knowledge of an impediment and knowledge the marriage is not valid, some states have found the person who acted in bad faith is not entitled to benefit from the marriage. We do not reach this issue because the facts of this case involve two innocent putative spouses.

28. *Cortes v. Fleming,* 307 So.2d 611 (La.1973). While the Louisiana Supreme Court did not rely on a statute specifically granting a putative spouse the right to alimony in its decision, the court did use an annulment statute as a basis of the award. The court indicated the term "civil effect" in the annulment statute was broad enough to include alimony. Nevada does not have similar language in its annulment statutes.

31. 242 Ga. 607, 250 S.E.2d 470, 472 (1978).

The California Supreme Court followed the same rationale in *Sanguinetti,* noting that a putative spouse has no right to an allowance of alimony. However, the California Supreme Court found that a putative spouse could maintain a claim under quantum meruit for the reasonable value of the services that the putative spouse rendered to the marriage if there was fraud or fault (such as cruelty) committed by the party opposing alimony.

In a similar case, Kindle v. Kindle,[35] the Florida Court of Appeals upheld an award of alimony when the husband failed to disclose his previous marriage and was not divorced when he entered into a second marriage ceremony. Preston and Kikeu Kindle were married for 20 years when the court granted an annulment. At the time the couple married, Preston was already married, but he never disclosed this to Kikeu. The trial court found that Kikeu was an innocent victim of Preston's wrongdoing and awarded Kikeu permanent alimony. The Florida Court of Appeals upheld the permanent alimony award based on equitable principles. The court further stated that "[i]t would be grossly inequitable to deny alimony to a putative wife of a twenty-year marriage because the husband fraudulently entered into a marriage ceremony."[37]

Sanguinetti and *Kindle,* however, are distinguishable from the instant case. In those cases, the courts found fraud, bad faith or bad conduct, such as cruelty, to support the award of equitable alimony. In the instant case, Richard and Marcie each acted in good faith. Neither Richard nor Marcie knowingly defrauded the other, and there is no evidence of misconduct or bad faith.

We can find no case, and Marcie has cited to none, in which spousal support was awarded to a putative spouse absent statutory authority, fraud, bad faith or bad conduct. Although one commentator favors such awards on the theory that the purpose of the putative spouse doctrine is to fulfill the reasonable expectations of the parties,[38] we are unaware of any court adopting such a standard.

The putative spouse doctrine did not traditionally provide for an award of spousal support. Extensions of the doctrine have come through statute or findings of fraud and bad faith. As neither is present in this case, we decline to extend the doctrine to permit an award of spousal support when both parties act in good faith. Richard and Marcie's marriage was void, and there was no showing of bad faith or fraud by either party. Absent an equitable basis of bad faith or fraud or a statutory basis, the district court had no authority to grant the spousal support award, and we reverse that part of the judgment awarding spousal support.

We conclude that an annulment proceeding is the proper method for documenting the existence of a void marriage and resolving the rights of the parties arising out of the void relationship. We adopt the putative spouse doctrine and conclude that common-law community property princi-

---

35. 629 So.2d 176 (Fla.Dist.Ct.App. 1993).

37. *Id.* at 177.

38. Blakesley, *supra* note 7, at 43.

ples apply by analogy to the division of property acquired during a putative marriage. However, the putative spouse doctrine does not permit an award of spousal support in the absence of bad faith, fraud or statutory authority. Therefore, we affirm that portion of the district court's order equally dividing the parties' property and reverse that portion of the order awarding spousal support.

E.   DETERMINING LEGAL ELIGIBILITY
3.   PHYSICAL OR MENTAL INCAPACITY

Following **M.T. v. J.T.** *and transsexual marriage, please add the following case at page 201:*

Kantaras v. Kantaras

District Court of Appeal of Florida, Second District, 2004.
884 So.2d 155.

■ FULMER, JUDGE.

Linda Kantaras appeals from a final judgment dissolving her marriage to Michael Kantaras. This appeal presents an issue of first impression in Florida: whether a postoperative female-to-male transsexual person can validly marry a female under the current law of this state. We hold that the law of this state does not provide for or allow such a marriage; therefore, we reverse the final judgment and remand for the trial court to declare the marriage of the parties void ab initio.

In 1959 Margo Kantaras was born a female in Ohio. In 1986 Margo changed her name to Michael John Kantaras, and in 1987 Michael underwent sex reassignment, which included hormonal treatments, a total hysterectomy, and a double mastectomy. In 1988 Michael met Linda, and Linda learned of Michael's surgeries. Linda, who was pregnant by a former boyfriend, gave birth to a son in June 1989. Linda and Michael applied for a marriage license with Michael representing that he[1] was male. The two married in July 1989 in Florida. In September 1989, Michael applied to adopt Linda's son, with Michael representing to the court that he was Linda's husband. Linda gave birth to a daughter in 1992 after Linda underwent artificial insemination with the sperm of Michael's brother.

In 1998 Michael filed a petition for dissolution of marriage seeking to dissolve his marriage to Linda and to obtain custody of both children. Linda answered and counterpetitioned for dissolution and/or annulment claiming that the marriage was void ab initio because it violated Florida law that bans same-sex marriage. Linda claimed that the adoption of her son was void because it violated Florida's ban on homosexual adoption, and she claimed that Michael was not the biological or legal father of her daughter.

---

1. Our references to Michael Kantaras as "he" throughout this opinion are not intended to carry a legal significance.

After a lengthy trial, the trial court entered an order finding that Michael was legally a male at the time of the marriage, and thus, the trial court concluded that the marriage was valid. The trial court also concluded that Michael was entitled to primary residential custody of the two children.

In outlining its reasons for determining that Michael was male at the time of the marriage, the trial court stated, in part:

24. Michael at the date of marriage was a male based on the persuasive weight of all the medical evidence and the testimony of lay witnesses in this case, including the following:

(a) As a child, while born female, Michael's parents and siblings observed his male characteristics and agreed he should have been born a "boy."

(b) Michael always has perceived himself as a male and assumed the male role doing house chores growing up, played male sports, refused to wear female clothing at home or in school and had his high school picture taken in male clothing.

(c) Prior to marriage he successfully completed the full process of transsexual reassignment, involving hormone treatment, irreversible medical surgery that removed all of his female organs inside of his body, including having a male reconstructed chest, a male voice, a male configured body and hair with beard and moustache, and a naturally developed penis.

(d) At the time of the marriage his bride, Linda was fully informed about his sex reassignment status, she accepted along with his friends, family and wor[k] colleagues that Michael in his appearance, characteristics and behavior was perceived as a man. At the time of the marriage he could not assume the role of a woman.

(e) Before and after the marriage he has been accepted as a man in a variety of social and legal ways, such as having a male driving license; male passport; male name change; male modification of his birth certificate by legal ruling; male participation in legal adoption proceedings in court; and as a male in an artificial insemination program, and participating for years in school activities with the children of this marriage as their father. All of this, was no different than what Michael presented himself as at the date of marriage.

25. Michael was born a heterosexual transsexual female. That condition [which] is now called "Gender Identity Dysphoria," was diagnosed for Michael in adulthood some twenty (20) years after birth. Today and at the date of marriage, Michael had no secondary female identifying characteristics and all reproductive female organs were absent, such as ovaries, fallopian tubes, cervix, womb, and breasts. The only feature left is a vagina which Dr. Cole testified was not typically female because it now had a penis or enlarged, elongate[d] clitoris.

26. Michael after sex reassignment or triatic treatments would still have a chromosomal patter [sic] (XX) of a woman but that is a presumption. No chromosomal tests were performed on Michael during the course of his treatment at the Rosenberg Clinic.

27. Chromosomes are only one factor in the determination of sex and they do not overrule gender or self identity, which is the true test or identifying mark of sex. Michael has always, for a lifetime, had a self-identity of a male. Dr. Walter Bockting, Dr. Ted Huang and Dr. Collier Cole, all testified that Michael Kantaras is now and at the date of marriage was medically and legally "male."

28. Under the marriage statute of Florida, Michael is deemed to be male, and the marriage ceremony performed in the Sandford [sic] County Court house on July 18, 1989, was legal.

The issue in this case involves the interplay between the Florida statutes governing marriage and the question of whether Michael Kantaras was legally male or female when he married Linda. We first address the relevant statutes and then discuss our reasons for concluding that the trial court erred in finding that Michael was male at the time of the marriage.

The Florida Legislature has expressly banned same-sex marriage. As amended in 1977 by chapter 77–139, Laws of Florida, the statute governing the issuance of a marriage license, at the time one was issued in this case, provided that no license shall be issued unless one party is a male and the other a female:No county court judge or clerk of the circuit court in this state shall issue a license for the marriage of any person unless there shall be first presented and filed with him an affidavit in writing, signed by both parties to the marriage, made and subscribed before some person authorized by law to administer an oath, . . . and unless one party is a male and the other party is a female. § 741.04(1), Fla. Stat. (1987). In 1997, the legislature enacted the Florida Defense of Marriage Act, prohibiting marriage between persons of the same sex:

(1) Marriages between persons of the same sex entered into in any jurisdiction, whether within or outside the State of Florida, the United States, or any other jurisdiction, either domestic or foreign, or any other place or location, or relationships between persons of the same sex which are treated as marriages in any jurisdiction, whether within or outside the State of Florida, the United States, or any other jurisdiction, either domestic or foreign, or any other place or location, are not recognized for any purpose in this state.

(2) The state, its agencies, and its political subdivisions may not give effect to any public act, record, or judicial proceeding of any state, territory, possession, or tribe of the United States or of any other jurisdiction, either domestic or foreign, or any other place or location respecting either a marriage or relationship not recognized under subsection (1) or a claim arising from such a marriage or relationship.

(3) For purposes of interpreting any state statute or rule, the term "marriage" means only a legal union between one man and one

woman as husband and wife, and the term "spouse" applies only to a member of such a union.

§ 741.212, Fla. Stat. (Supp.1998).

Courts in Ohio, Kansas, Texas, and New York have addressed issues involving the marriage of a postoperative transsexual person, and in all cases the courts have invalidated or refused to allow the marriage on the grounds that it violated state statutes or public policy. In the case of *In re Ladrach,* 32 Ohio Misc.2d 6, 513 N.E.2d 828 (Probate 1987), the court found that a postoperative male-to-female transsexual was not permitted to marry a male.

> "[T]here is no authority in Ohio for the issuance of a marriage license to consummate a marriage between a post-operative male to female transsexual person and a male person." *Id.* at 832.

> This court is charged with the responsibility of interpreting the statutes of this state.... Since the case at bar is apparently one of first impression in Ohio, it is this court's opinion that the legislature should change the statutes, if it is to be the public policy of the state of Ohio to issue marriage licenses to post-operative transsexuals.

> *Id.*

More recently an Ohio appellate court agreed with the decision in *Ladrach* and affirmed a trial court's denial of a marriage license to a postoperative female-to-male transsexual and a female. *See In re A Marriage License for Nash,* Nos.2002–T–0149, 2002–T–0179, 2003 WL 23097095 (Ohio Ct.App. Dec. 31, 2003). Noting that "Ohio, like most states, has a clear public policy that authorizes and recognizes marriages only between members of the opposite sex," the court concluded that the term "male" as used in the marriage statute does not include a female-to-male postoperative transsexual. *Id.* at 5–6. Agreeing with the court in *Ladrach* that it was the responsibility of the legislature to change the public policy, the court stated that it was "loath to expand the statutory designation of individuals who may marry through judicial legislation." *Id.* at 7.

The Kansas Supreme Court declared a marriage void after it found that a postoperative male-to-female transsexual was not a woman. *See In re Estate of Gardiner,* 273 Kan. 191, 42 P.3d 120 (2002), *cert. denied,* 537 U.S. 825, 123 S.Ct. 113, 154 L.Ed.2d 36 (2002). *Gardiner,* a probate case, involved the question of who was the rightful heir to the intestate estate of Marshall Gardiner: Gardiner's son, Joe, or J'Noel Gardiner, a male-to-female transsexual who married Marshall Gardiner the year before his death. *Id.* at 122. Joe sought summary judgment on the ground that J'Noel's marriage to Marshall was void. *Id.* at 123. The district court granted summary judgment concluding that the marriage was void under Kansas law on the ground that J'Noel was a male. *Id.* The court of appeals reversed and directed the district court to determine whether J'Noel was male or female at the time the marriage license was issued, taking into account a number of factors in addition to chromosomes. *Id.* at 132–34. The Supreme Court of Kansas granted Joe's petition for review and reversed the decision of the court of appeals, concluding that the district court had properly entered summary judgment on the ground that J'Noel's marriage to Marshall was void. *Id.* at 136–37.

The supreme court concluded that the issue on appeal was one of law, not fact, and it involved the interpretation of the Kansas statutes. *Id.* at 135. The court recognized that "[t]he fundamental rule of statutory construction is that the intent of the legislature governs." *Id.* After discussing the common meaning of the terms sex, male, and female, the court stated:

> The words "sex," "male," and "female" in everyday understanding do not encompass transsexuals. The plain, ordinary meaning of "persons of the opposite sex" contemplates a biological man and a biological woman and not persons who are experiencing gender dysphoria. A male-to-female post-operative transsexual does not fit the definition of a female. The male organs have been removed, but the ability to "produce ova and bear offspring" does not and never did exist. There is no womb, cervix, or ovaries, nor is there any change in his chromosomes. As the *Littleton* court noted, the transsexual still "inhabits . . . a male body in all aspects other than what the physicians have supplied." 9 S.W.3d at 231. J'Noel does not fit the common meaning of female.

Id. at 135.

In response to the court of appeals' conclusion that a question remained as to whether J'Noel was a female at the time the license was issued for the purpose of the statute, the supreme court stated:

> We do not agree that the question remains. We view the legislative silence to indicate that transsexuals are not included. If the legislature intended to include transsexuals, it could have been a simple matter to have done so. We apply the rules of statutory construction to ascertain the legislative intent as expressed in the statute. We do not read into a statute something that does not come within the wording of the statute.

Id. at 136 (citation omitted). The supreme court stated further:

> [T]he legislature clearly viewed "opposite sex" in the narrow traditional sense. . . . We cannot ignore what the legislature has declared to be the public policy of this state. Our responsibility is to interpret [the statute] and not to rewrite it. . . . If the legislature wishes to change public policy, it is free to do so; we are not. To conclude that J'Noel is of the opposite sex of Marshall would require that we rewrite [the statute].

Id. at 136–37. The supreme court concluded that "the validity of J'Noel's marriage to Marshall is a question of public policy to be addressed by the legislature and not by this court." *Id.* at 137.

In *Littleton v. Prange,* 9 S.W.3d 223 (Tex.App.1999), the Texas court found a marriage between a man and a postoperative male-to-female transsexual void. Christie Littleton, the transsexual, married Jonathon

Mark Littleton in Kentucky in 1989. *Id.* at 225. After Jonathon's death in 1996, Christie sued Dr. Prange for medical malpractice in her capacity as Jonathon's surviving spouse. *Id.* The doctor moved for summary judgment asserting that Christie was a man and could not be the surviving spouse of another man. *Id.* The trial court agreed and granted summary judgment. *Id.*

> The appeals court concluded that the case presented a pure question of law.

Id. at 230.

> In our system of government it is for the legislature, should it choose to do so, to determine what guidelines should govern the recognition of marriages involving transsexuals. . . .
>
> It would be intellectually possible for this court to write a protocol for when transsexuals would be recognized as having successfully changed their sex. . . . But this court has no authority to fashion a new law on transsexuals, or anything else. We cannot make law when no law exists: we can only interpret the written word of our sister branch of government, the legislature.

Id. at 230. The court concluded "as a matter of law, that Christie Littleton is a male. As a male, Christie cannot be married to another male. Her marriage to Jonathon was invalid, and she cannot bring a cause of action as his surviving spouse." *Id.* at 231.

New York courts have also refused to recognize transsexual marriage. *See Anonymous v. Anonymous,* 67 Misc.2d 982, 325 N.Y.S.2d 499 (1971); *Frances B. v. Mark B.,* 78 Misc.2d 112, 355 N.Y.S.2d 712 (1974). In *Frances B.,* the plaintiff, a woman, filed an annulment action claiming that, prior to the marriage, the defendant (a postoperative female-to-male transsexual) fraudulently represented himself as a male, although the defendant did not have male sex organs and was still a woman. 355 N.Y.S.2d at 713. The defendant moved to amend his answer to include a counterclaim for divorce on the ground of abandonment. *Id.* at 714. The court, noting the public policy that the marriage relationship exists for the purpose of begetting offspring, concluded that the defendant's sex reassignment surgery did not enable the defendant to perform male sexual functions in a marriage:

> Assuming, as urged, that defendant was a male entrapped in the body of a female, the record does not show that the entrapped male successfully escaped to enable defendant to perform male functions in a marriage. Attempted sex reassignment by mastectomy, hysterectomy, and androgenous hormonal therapy, has not achieved that result.

Id. at 717.

Thus, the court concluded that, as a matter of law, the defendant had no basis to counterclaim for divorce. *Id.* at 716–17.

There is one case in the United States that has permitted transsexual marriage. In *M.T. v. J.T.,* 140 N.J.Super. 77, 355 A.2d 204 (1976), the husband sought an annulment on the ground that his wife was a male-to-female transsexual. The New Jersey court rejected the husband's argument, upheld the validity of the marriage, and affirmed a judgment of the lower court obligating the husband to support the transsexual as his wife. 355 A.2d at 211. After considering the medical evidence, the court held that when a transsexual person has successfully undergone sex-reassignment and can fully function sexually in the reassigned sex, then the person could marry legally as a member of the sex finally indicated. *Id.* at 210–11.

> In sum, it has been established that an individual suffering from the condition of transsexualism is one with a disparity between his or her genitalia or anatomical sex and his or her gender, that is, the individual's strong and consistent emotional and psychological sense of sexual being. A transsexual in a proper case can be treated medically by certain supportive measures and through surgery to remove and replace existing genitalia with sex organs which will coincide with the person's gender. If such sex reassignment surgery is successful and the postoperative transsexual is, by virtue of medical treatment, thereby possessed of the full capacity to function sexually as a male or female, as the case may be, we perceive no legal barrier, cognizable social taboo, or reason grounded in public policy to prevent that person's identification at least for purposes of marriage to the sex finally indicated.

Id. at 210–11.

In the case before us, the trial court relied heavily on the approach taken by an Australian family court in *In re Kevin*, (2001) 28 Fam. L.R. 158, *aff'd*, 30 Fam. L.R. 1 (Austl.Fam.Ct.2003) (pagination of Lexis printout), which the trial court believed "correctly states the law in modern society's approach to transsexualism." In that case, the Australian court took the view that courts must recognize advances in medical knowledge and practice and found that a female-to-male transsexual should be considered a man for purposes of marriage. Australia prohibits same-sex marriage; nevertheless, the court ruled that a marriage between a woman and a postoperative female-to-male transsexual was valid. In affirming the trial court, the Family Court of Australia stated in its conclusion:

> Should the words "man" and "marriage" as used in the Marriage Act 1961 bear their contemporary ordinary everyday meaning?
>
> . . . .
>
> Unless the context requires a different interpretation, the words "man" and "woman" when used in legislation have their ordinary contemporary meaning according to Australian usage. That meaning includes post-operative transsexuals as men or women in accordance with their sexual reassignment. . . .

30 Fam. L.R. 1 at 48.

On appeal, Michael argues that the trial court properly adopted the approach taken by the Australian court.

He further argues that the approach taken by the majority of courts in the United States that have addressed the issue of transsexual marriage ignore modern medical science. We disagree.

The controlling issue in this case is whether, as a matter of law, the Florida statutes governing marriage authorize a postoperative transsexual to marry in the reassigned sex. We conclude they do not. We agree with the Kansas, Ohio, and Texas courts in their understanding of the common meaning of male and female, as those terms are used statutorily, to refer to immutable traits determined at birth. Therefore, we also conclude that the trial court erred by declaring that Michael is male for the purpose of the marriage statutes. Whether advances in medical science support a change in the meaning commonly attributed to the terms male and female as they are used in the Florida marriage statutes is a question that raises issues of public policy that should be addressed by the legislature. Thus, the question of whether a postoperative transsexual is authorized to marry a member of their birth sex is a matter for the Florida legislature and not the Florida courts to decide. Until the Florida legislature recognizes sex-reassignment procedures and amends the marriage statutes to clarify the marital rights of a postoperative transsexual person, we must adhere to the common meaning of the statutory terms and invalidate any marriage that is not between persons of the opposite sex determined by their biological sex at birth. Therefore, we hold that the marriage in this case is void ab initio.

Our holding that the marriage is void ab initio does not take into consideration the best interests of the children involved in this case. While we recognize that the trial judge went to great lengths to determine the best interests of the children, the issue of deciding primary residential custody was dependent on the trial court's conclusion that the marriage was valid. We do not attempt to undertake a determination of the legal status of the children resulting from our conclusion that the marriage is void. The legal status of the children and the parties' property rights will be issues for the trial court to examine in the first instance on remand.

Reversed and remanded with directions to grant the counterpetition for annulment declaring the marriage between the parties void ab initio.

■ COVINGTON and WALLACE, JJ., Concur.

CHAPTER III

HUSBAND AND WIFE: CHANGING ROLES, RIGHTS AND DUTIES

B. NAMES IN THE FAMILY

2. NAMES FOR CHILDREN

Please add at end of NOTES *section "Disputes between parents," the following at page 238:*

The New Jersey Supreme Court takes the position that the child's primary caretaker has a presumptive right to change the name of the child and that the primary caretaker does not need to show how the change would promote the child's best interest before doing so. In moving away from a "best interest" test the court holds that the other parent, the non-caretaker, has the burden to rebut the presumption. Ronan v. Adely, 182 N.J. 103, 861 A.2d 822 (2004). Other courts still rely on the best interest of the child in deciding cases involving disputes over names. *See, e.g.,* Poindexter v. Poindexter, 2005 WL 318689 (S.Ct. Ark. 2005); *In re* Name Change of Perez, 822 N.E.2d 811 (Ohio 2005).

E. TESTIMONIAL PRIVILEGE, TORTS AND CRIMES BETWEEN SPOUSES

1. TESTIMONIAL PRIVILEGE

Following Trammel v. United States *and testimonial privilege, please add at page 258:*

Commonwealth v. Kirkner

Pennsylvania Supreme Court, 2002.
569 Pa. 499, 805 A.2d 514.

■ JUSTICE EAKIN.

On July 4, 1999, police responded to a domestic disturbance at the home of Joseph and Kellie Kirkner. Mrs. Kirkner told police her husband choked her, struck her in the face, and shoved her to the ground. She accompanied police to their barracks where she permitted them to photograph her bruises and abrasions. She wrote a two-page statement about the incident.

Appellee was charged with simple assault and harassment. At the preliminary hearing, the Commonwealth presented sufficient evidence to hold him for trial, despite his wife's failure to appear. The Commonwealth issued a trial subpoena to Mrs. Kirkner which her attorney moved to quash.

After conducting a colloquy with wife, the trial court granted the motion, relying on *Commonwealth v. Hatfield,* 406 Pa.Super. 139, 593 A.2d 1275 (1991), *aff'd per curiam,* 530 Pa. 590, 610 A.2d 466 (1992), *reargument granted,* 534 Pa. 255, 628 A.2d 840 (1993). The trial court concluded: "the decision to force an unwilling spouse to testify is a matter for the trial [c]ourt's discretion." Trial Court Opinion, 12/15/99, at 2. In deciding to quash the subpoena, the court found: (1) wife's decision not to testify was her choice and not the product of coercion by husband; (2) wife did not fear for her personal safety; (3) wife was not financially dependent on husband; (4) wife was an educated woman with training in law; and (5) wife's decision not to testify was motivated by her desire to preserve her marriage and family. The Commonwealth filed an interlocutory appeal. The Superior Court affirmed the trial court's order, determining it was bound by its *Hatfield* decision. *Commonwealth v. Kirkner,* No. 3317 EDA 1999, 768 A.2d 884 (Pa.Super.2000)

This Court granted allowance of appeal to address whether *Hatfield* contradicts the mandatory language of 42 Pa.C.S. § 5913 (relating to spouses as witnesses against each other). The facts in *Hatfield* parallel those in the instant case. Elaine Hatfield was beaten by her husband; she sustained a bloody nose, black eye and multiple contusions. Mr. Hatfield was charged, and despite Mrs. Hatfield's refusal to testify at the preliminary hearing, was held for court based on testimony by other witnesses. A subpoena was issued for Mrs. Hatfield to testify at trial; she filed a motion to quash because of spousal privilege. The trial court quashed the subpoena, relying on the assurances of counsel that the circumstances surrounding the assault were unique and that the Hatfields were in counseling. The Commonwealth appealed; the Superior Court stated: "[w]hether to force the unwilling spouse to give evidence thus becomes a matter for the trial court's discretion." *Id.,* at 1276. For this proposition, the court cited *Commonwealth v. Hess,* 270 Pa.Super. 501, 411 A.2d 830 (1979), a case of first impression dealing with competency, not statutory privilege. The Superior Court felt itself constrained to defer to the trial court's decision that "nullifying the prosecution" best served the interests of justice. *Hatfield,* at 1276–77.

The Commonwealth argues if the trial court has discretion to determine whether a victim should testify against an accused spouse, then the trial court will effectively be establishing spousal privilege on a case-by-case basis; the Commonwealth contends the use of "shall" in 42 Pa.C.S. § 5913 signals the General Assembly's intent to eliminate the privilege, and hence the discretion, in this circumstance.

Spousal privilege in the common law can be traced to canons of medieval jurisprudence: "the rule that an accused was not permitted to testify in his own behalf because of his interest in the proceeding; [and] the concept that husband and wife were one" and married women had no recognized separate legal existence. *Trammel v. United States,* 445 U.S. 40, 44, 100 S.Ct. 906, 63 L.Ed.2d 186 (1980). However, "[e]ven at common law the [spousal] privilege was withheld from the husband in criminal prosecutions against him for wrongs directly against the person of the wife." McCormick, *Evidence* § 66 at 162 (3d ed.1984) (citing 1 Blackstone, Commentaries 443 (1765); 8 Wigmore, Evidence § 2239 (McNaughton rev. 1961)). In 1887, when the General Assembly codified the common law prohibition of one spouse testifying against the other, it delineated specific circumstances when spouses would be competent to testify against each other.

> Nor shall husband and wife be competent or permitted to testify against each other, or in support of a criminal charge of adultery alleged to have been committed by or with the other, except that in proceedings for desertion and maintenance, and in any criminal proceeding against either for bodily injury or violence attempted, done or threatened upon the other, or upon the minor children of said husband and wife, or the minor children of either of them, or any minor child in their care or custody, or in the care or custody of either of them, each shall be a competent witness against the other, and except also that either of them shall be competent merely to prove the fact of marriage, in support of a criminal charge of adultery or bigamy alleged to have been committed by or with the other.

See Commonwealth v. Moore, 453 Pa. 302, 309 A.2d 569, 570 n. 4 (1973) (citing Act of May 23, 1887, P.L. 158, § 2(b), *as amended,* 19 P.S. § 683).

While the rule of testimonial competency became one of testimonial privilege in 1989, the exceptions found in the original Act survive today. Section 5913 provides:

> Except as otherwise provided in this subchapter, in a criminal proceeding a person shall have the privilege, which he or she may waive, not to testify against his or her then lawful spouse except that *there shall be no such privilege:*

> (1) in proceedings for desertion and maintenance;

> (2) in any criminal proceeding against either for bodily injury or violence attempted, done or threatened upon the other, or upon the minor children of said husband and wife, or the minor children of either of them, or any minor child in their care or custody, or in the care or custody of either of them;

> (3) applicable to proof of the fact of marriage, in support of a criminal charge of bigamy alleged to have been committed by or with the other; or

> (4) in any criminal proceeding in which one of the charges pending against the defendant includes murder, involuntary deviate sexual intercourse or rape.

42 Pa.C.S. § 5913 (emphasis added).

Adhering to the Statutory Construction Act, "[w]hen the words of a statute are clear and free from all ambiguity, the letter of it is not to be disregarded under the pretext of pursuing its spirit." 1 Pa.C.S. § 1921(b). In this clear and unambiguous statute, " 'shall' is mandatory." *Oberneder v. Link Computer Corp.,* 548 Pa. 201, 696 A.2d 148, 150 (1997).

Section 5913 uses the phrase "shall be no such privilege" in criminal proceedings for bodily injury between husband and wife. The statute cannot be modified by judicial discretion, no matter how well-intentioned the trial court might be. *See Commonwealth v. Newman,* 534 Pa. 424, 633 A.2d 1069, 1072 (1993); *Commonwealth v. Scott,* 516 Pa. 346, 532 A.2d 426, 429 (1987). While reliance on *Hatfield* by the trial and appellate courts was understandable, *Hatfield* is in error. Such discretion as exists reposes in the District Attorney, who has the obligation of determining the merits of any prosecution, and the responsibility of requiring appropriate witnesses to testify. As there is no privilege excusing this witness in this case, it was error to quash the subpoena.

If the victim's goal of preserving her relationship with her spouse through forgiveness and understanding is to be achieved, appellee may offer her equal forgiveness and understanding of her truthful testimony. If there is a conviction, or an understanding and forgiving plea, an appropriate sentence may, of course, be fashioned.

The decision in *Hatfield* contradicts the express intention of the legislature in 42 Pa.C.S. § 5913. Therefore, the decision in *Hatfield* is overruled. There being no privilege, the decision of the Superior Court is reversed; this case is remanded to the trial court for reinstatement of the subpoena.

Order reversed; case remanded. Jurisdiction relinquished.

■ CHIEF JUSTICE ZAPPALA concurs in the result.

[The concurring opinion of Justice Cappy has been omitted.]

2.   SEXUAL ASSAULT OR RAPE

Replace the Virginia Code provision at page 264 with the following:

CODE OF VIRGINIA (West 2002, and Cum. Supp. 2004)

§ 18.2–61.   Rape

A.   If any person has sexual intercourse with a complaining witness who is not his or her spouse or causes a complaining witness, whether or not his or her spouse, to engage in sexual intercourse with any other person and such act is accomplished (i) against the complaining witness's will, by force, threat or intimidation of or against the complaining witness or another person, or (ii) through the use of the complaining witness's mental incapacity or physical helplessness, or (iii) with a child under age thirteen as the victim, he or she shall be guilty of rape.

B. If any person has sexual intercourse with his or her spouse and such act is accomplished against the spouse's will by force, threat or intimidation of or against the spouse or another, he or she shall be guilty of rape.

C. A violation of this section shall be punishable, in the discretion of the court or jury, by confinement in a state correctional facility for life or for any term not less than five years. There shall be a rebuttable presumption that a juvenile over the age of 10 but less than 12, does not possess the physical capacity to commit a violation of this section. In any case deemed appropriate by the court, all or part of any sentence imposed for a violation of subsection B may be suspended upon the defendant's completion of counseling or therapy, if not already provided, in the manner prescribed under § 19.2–218.1 if, after consideration of the views of the complaining witness and such other evidence as may be relevant, the court finds such action will promote maintenance of the family unit and will be in the best interest of the complaining witness.

D. Upon a finding of guilt under subsection B in any case tried by the court without a jury, the court, without entering a judgment of guilt, upon motion of the defendant and with the consent of the complaining witness and the attorney for the Commonwealth, may defer further proceedings and place the defendant on probation pending completion of counseling or therapy, if not already provided, in the manner prescribed under § 19.2–218.1. If the defendant fails to so complete such counseling or therapy, the court may make final disposition of the case and proceed as otherwise provided. If such counseling is completed as prescribed under § 19.2–218.1, the court may discharge the defendant and dismiss the proceedings against him if, after consideration of the views of the complaining witness and such other evidence as may be relevant, the court finds such action will promote maintenance of the family unit and be in the best interest of the complaining witness.

4. INSTITUTIONAL RESPONSES TO VIOLENCE BETWEEN SPOUSES

Following Cladd v. State *and the* NOTE *after it, please add at page 270:*

H.E.S. v. J.C.S.

New Jersey Supreme Court, 2003.
175 N.J. 309, 815 A.2d 405.

■ COLEMAN, J.

This case requires us to address procedural and substantive issues concerning New Jersey's Domestic Violence Act, *N.J.S.A.* 2C:25–17 to –35. Procedurally, the issues presented are whether defendant's right to due process was violated when he received notice of a domestic violence complaint less than twenty-four hours before trial and when a finding of domestic violence was based on an allegation that was not contained in the complaint. We also must address the novel issue of whether video surveillance by one spouse of the other spouse's bedroom can constitute one of the predicate offenses of domestic violence. The trial court held that defendant had received due process, and that he had committed both harassment in violation of *N.J.S.A.* 2C:33–4 and stalking in violation of *N.J.S.A.* 2C:12–10. The Appellate Division agreed that defendant's due process rights had not been violated, but concluded that the surveillance constituted stalking but not harassment. We reverse and hold that the trial procedures violated defendant's right to due process. We agree with the trial court that the conduct complained of can constitute both stalking and harassment.

When this litigation began in August 2000, plaintiff H.E.S. and her husband, defendant J.C.S., had been married for eighteen years. Although they lived in the same house with their two daughters, defendant had occupied a separate bedroom since November 1999. Plaintiff had filed for divorce in June 2000 but defendant may not have been served until August 2000.

Between August 17 and 19, 2000, plaintiff and defendant engaged in numerous altercations resulting in both parties filing domestic violence complaints. On August 21, 2000, defendant filed a domestic violence complaint against plaintiff. The typed complaint specified the following acts allegedly were committed by plaintiff:

> ON 8/17/00 DEF[ENDANT, H.E.S.] HAS HAD HER BROTHERS HARASSING AND STALKING PLA[INTIFF, J.C.S.] DUE TO SOME CHURCH PROBLEMS. DEF[ENDANT'S] BROTHERS BROKE WINDOWS IN BOTH OF PLA[INTIFF'S] CARS.

An additional handwritten notation reads:

> Pla[intiff] states that def[endant] is constantly harassing him by calling police and making false accusations against him[,] by telling police he is assaulting her [and] locking her in the house.

That complaint was filed on a pre-printed form designed for domestic violence complaints. In answer to the question, "Any prior history of domestic violence?" an "X" was typed next to the printed answer "yes," but the spaces following the instruction "explain & dates" contain only the typed words "NOT REPORTED." A temporary restraining order (TRO) was entered against plaintiff, with a final hearing scheduled for August 31, 2000.

Before a hearing was conducted on defendant's complaint, plaintiff filed a separate domestic violence complaint against defendant on August 22, 2000. That complaint listed the following acts allegedly committed by defendant:

> ON 8–18–00 PLA[INTIFF] CAME HOME FROM CHURCH WITH THE CHILDREN. PLA [INTIFF] COULDN'T GET INTO HER GARAGE BECAUSE DEF[ENDANT] LOCKED SAME. DEF [ENDANT] BEGAN TO YELL AND SCREAM ABOUT HOW HE WAS GOING TO DESTROY PLA [INTIFF] & HER FAMILY. AND THE ONLY WAY PLA[INTIFF] WOULD GET OUT OF THIS MARRIAGE IS BY DEATH.

Plaintiff's complaint was filed on the same previously described pre-printed domestic violence complaint form. The form contained a section for selecting the predicate criminal offenses constituting domestic violence. On plaintiff's complaint, an "X" was typed next to "Terroristic Threats." Neither "Harassment," "Stalking," nor any other predicate offense was checked. In answer to the question, "Any prior history of domestic violence?" an "X" was typed next to the printed answer "yes." However, the only information following the instruction "explain & dates" is the cross-reference "SEE FV 01 321 01C" (referring to defendant's August 21, 2000, complaint against plaintiff).

As a result of plaintiff's complaint, a TRO was entered against defendant with a final hearing scheduled for August 24, 2000. Defendant asserts that on August 23, 2000, a court clerk called him and requested to reschedule the hearing on his complaint to August 24. Defendant agreed. Defendant maintains that he was served with plaintiff's complaint and TRO on August 23, 2000. At the beginning of court proceedings on the complaints on August 24, 2000, defendant's counsel requested a continuance. The court denied the motion and proceeded with trial on both complaints, dismissing defendant's complaint after finding the evidence was insufficient. That matter is not before us.

As for plaintiff's complaint, H.E.S. testified that on August 18, 2000, before she left for church, defendant told plaintiff that if she refused to drop the divorce complaint he would "destroy" her. When plaintiff returned from church and was unable to open the garage door, she and the children went to the front door where defendant met them. Plaintiff testified that defendant let the girls into the house and then told her, "[H.E.S.], it's over. You're doomed. I will destroy you. The only way you're going to get out of this marriage is by death." She then entered the house, where he allegedly proceeded to "rant and rave," threatening to press charges against her brothers and to have her parents incarcerated.

Plaintiff's counsel then asked plaintiff whether defendant had ever acted that way before. Defense counsel objected, arguing that the complaint failed to give notice of past acts of domestic violence. The court ruled that "what may be in that form may be an issue for cross-examination and credibility, but it doesn't preclude in any way testimony regarding past incidences which are admissible in the court proceeding."

Plaintiff then testified about prior incidents of domestic violence that were not mentioned in her complaint. Specifically, she stated that defendant 1) twice left her stranded without transportation to or from work; 2) locked her in a bedroom, pinned her down and bruised her during an altercation in 1999; 3) verbally abused her in 1991; and 4) on another occasion, hit her and knocked her unconscious.

Next, plaintiff described the video surveillance involved in this appeal. Her attorney produced a "microchip" and plaintiff explained that the "microchip" was a camera and microphone she had found hidden in a picture in her bedroom. Plaintiff called the police, who came to her home and took photographs of the device and the wiring leading from plaintiff's bedroom, over defendant's office, to the attic, and finally into a VCR in defendant's bedroom. Upon finding the surveillance equipment, plaintiff realized how defendant seemed to know details about her daily activity that he otherwise could not have known. Plaintiff was "devastated" by the discovery and felt that this incident was one more reason to "get out." Plaintiff explained that defendant had made several statements to her to the effect that "he understands why husbands kill their wives because it's women like me that make men kill their wives." She testified that defendant had attempted to force himself on her sexually several times since moving out of their bedroom in November 1999, and that in general she was "terrified" of defendant because "[h]e is over the edge."

During cross-examination, plaintiff was questioned with respect to her failure to specify any prior incidents of domestic violence in her complaint. She stated that she had described other incidents on the Victim Information Sheet that she filled out prior to the preparation of her complaint. That sheet apparently was neither served on defendant nor introduced into evidence.

Defendant objected to having to defend against charges of domestic violence that were not included in the complaint and of which he had no notice. However, the trial court concluded that "[t]hese are summary matters. The complaint does not in and of itself exclude what evidence will be admissible. It does not in any way preclude testimony of past acts of domestic violence." In an attempt to ameliorate due process concerns, the trial court allowed a brief continuance until the next day to permit counsel to consult with defendant. The next day defense counsel asked for another continuance. He argued that he had insufficient time to prepare his defense to allegations of prior acts of domestic violence that he had not known about until the previous day, and that time had not permitted him to subpoena police officers who had been called to the parties' home. The court denied a continuance. The only witness defendant presented was a private investigator, and most of his testimony (regarding police reports of domestic violence at the parties' home) was excluded for hearsay reasons.

The trial court declined to consider many of plaintiff's allegations of prior domestic violence because they were too remote or did not indicate a pattern of violence. The court stated that "[t]his matter contends two things, one, that a terroristic threat was made and/or stalking or even harassment committed on or about [the] 18th of August. So I'm not considering the past acts of domestic violence in making my decision regarding the restraining order filed by [plaintiff] against [defendant]."

The trial court found that the verbal "threat" allegedly made by defendant was not domestic violence but rather was "simply the type of vindictiveness that ... precedes a divorce." However, the court held that defendant's placement of the camera and microphone in plaintiff's bedroom did constitute domestic violence. The court found that defendant's act constituted harassment because it was "designed to alarm or annoy," and also stalking "because it's repetitive activity ... [and was] designed to put an individual in fear ... of harm." Based on the incidents of harassment and stalking, advanced for the first time during the hearing, the trial court issued a final restraining order (FRO) against defendant.

The Appellate Division held that the trial court did not violate defendant's due process rights when it based its finding of domestic violence on incidents not alleged in the complaint. *H.E.S. v. J.C.S.,* 349 *N.J.Super.* 332, 336, 793 *A.*2d 780 (2002). The court stated that " '[t]he previous history of domestic violence between the plaintiff and defendant, including threats, harassment and physical abuse' " must be considered in evaluating a domestic violence claim. *Id.* at 341, 793 *A.*2d 780 (quoting *N.J.S.A.* 2C:25–29a(1); citing *Cesare v. Cesare,* 154 *N.J.* 394, 402, 713 *A.*2d 390 (1998); *Corrente v. Corrente,* 281 *N.J.Super.* 243, 248, 657 *A.*2d 440 (App.Div. 1995)). The Appellate Division noted that although each act of prior (or subsequent) domestic violence need not be listed in the complaint, the predicate act of domestic violence may not be based on allegations of which a defendant was not given notice. *Id.* at 341–43, 793 *A.*2d 780. The panel, nevertheless, concluded that the notice given here ("overnight") was sufficient. *Id.* at 343, 793 *A.*2d 780. The Appellate Division distinguished *J.F. v. B.K.,* 308 *N.J.Super.* 387, 391–92, 706 *A.*2d 203 (App.Div.1998) (holding that same-day notice of domestic violence charges violated due process) because that defendant was denied any chance to respond to the complaint and an FRO was issued the same day. In contrast, in this case defendant had overnight to prepare, presented one witness, did not describe what exculpatory evidence he could possibly offer, and most significantly did not take the stand. *Id.* at 343–44, 793 *A.*2d 780. The Appellate Division also noted that court personnel, rather than plaintiff, were to blame for exclusion from the complaint of the hidden microphone and camera, and that administrative failure "should not inure to plaintiff's detriment any more than to defendant's." *Id.* at 344, 793 *A.*2d 780. The panel concluded that:

> What is critical, consistent with *J.F. v. B.K.,* is that a defendant receive notice of the conduct alleged to constitute a predicate offense. The complaint served upon defendant in this case did not provide such notice; nevertheless, we are satisfied that defendant did have actual notice and the opportunity to defend against plaintiff's allegations arising from her August 19 discovery. By allowing trial on those allegations to proceed, the judge effectively allowed plaintiff to amend her complaint. In the alternative, the judge could have required plaintiff to file a new complaint, which then could have been served upon defendant while all the parties were in court.... We see no error in the procedure the judge adopted.

[*Id.* at 345–46, 793 *A.*2d 780.]

The Appellate Division also suggested remedial procedures that should be adopted by domestic violence intake workers to ensure proper notice to future defendants, specifically, the inclusion of sufficient space on the complaint form for listing prior acts of domestic violence, and instruction of intake personnel on the importance of including each prior act in the complaint. *Id.* at 345, 793 *A.*2d 780.

The Appellate Division held that defendant's behavior constituted stalking under *N.J.S.A.* 2C:12–10, but not harassment under *N.J.S.A.* 2C:33–4. *H.E.S., supra,* 349 *N.J.Super.* at 336, 793 *A.*2d 780. The applicable provision of the harassment statute requires that a defendant's purpose is "to alarm or seriously annoy." *N.J.S.A.* 2C:33–4c. The Appellate Division held that "the evidence does not support a finding that the perpetrator had either the purpose to harass or to alarm or seriously annoy plaintiff" because he intended the camera to remain hidden. *H.E.S., supra,* 349 *N.J.Super.* at 349, 793 *A.*2d 780. On the other hand, in its discussion of stalking, the Appellate Division noted plaintiff's testimony that "defendant had seemed to know plaintiff's every move for some time before August 19." The court held that placement of the camera met the definition of stalking, which requires behavior that "would cause fear in a reasonable person, irrespective of whether the perpetrator intended to instill such fear." *Id.* at 350–51, 793 *A.*2d 780.

We granted defendant's petition for certification. 174 *N.J.* 40, 803 *A.*2d 636 (2002).

Defendant asserts two due process violations. First, he argues that the trial court erred in requiring him to defend against imposition of a final restraining order less than twenty-four hours after receiving the complaint. Second, he contends that refusing to grant an adjournment after plaintiff asserted allegations not contained in the complaint constituted error. Plaintiff responds that defendant had a sufficient amount of time, more than twenty-four hours, to prepare a defense, and that the claimed lack of time did not prejudice his case. We agree with defendant on both of his due process claims.

The Fourteenth Amendment of the United States Constitution provides that no State shall "deprive any person of life, liberty, or property, without due process of law." *U.S. Const.* amend. XIV, § 1. This Court has held that although "Article I, paragraph 1 of the New Jersey Constitution does not [specifically] enumerate the right to due process, [it] protects against injustice and, to that extent, protects 'values like those encompassed by the principle[s] of due process.' " *Doe v. Poritz,* 142 *N.J.* 1, 99, 662 *A.*2d 367 (1995) (internal citation omitted).

Due process is "a flexible [concept] that depends on the particular circumstances." *Id.* at 106, 662 *A.*2d 367 (citing *Zinermon v. Burch,* 494 *U.S.* 113, 127, 110 *S.Ct.* 975, 984, 108 *L.Ed.*2d 100, 114–15 (1990); *Mathews v. Eldridge,* 424 *U.S.* 319, 334, 96 *S.Ct.* 893, 902, 47 *L. Ed.*2d 18, 33 (1976); *Nicoletta v. North Jersey Dist. Water Supply Comm'n,* 77 *N.J.* 145, 165, 390 *A.*2d 90 (1978)). At a minimum, due process requires that a party in a judicial hearing receive "notice defining the issues and an adequate opportunity to prepare and respond." *McKeown-Brand v. Trump Castle Hotel & Casino,* 132 *N.J.* 546, 559, 626 *A.*2d 425 (1993) (citing *Nicoletta, supra,* 77 *N.J.* at 162, 390 *A.*2d 90). As we stated in *Nicoletta,* " '[t]here can be no adequate preparation where the notice does not reasonably apprise the party of the charges, or where the issues litigated at the hearing differ substantially from those outlined in the notice.' " *Supra,* 77 *N.J.* at 162,

390 A.2d 90 (quoting *Department of Law and Pub. Safety v. Miller,* 115 *N.J.Super.* 122, 126, 278 A.2d 495 (App.Div.1971)).

Although this Court has never addressed the scope of procedural due process protection required in domestic violence proceedings, several Appellate Division opinions have. In *J.F. v. B.K., supra,* 308 *N.J.Super.* at 389, 706 A.2d 203, the plaintiff's first domestic violence complaint against the defendant was filed on June 28, 1996, and dismissed after a hearing on July 2, 1996. The plaintiff filed a second complaint against the defendant on February 24, 1997, alleging that he had left notes on her car following a history of domestic violence. *Ibid.* At the final hearing on March 4, 1997, the plaintiff described prior events of domestic violence as well as the note that was the basis for her second complaint. *Id.* at 389–90, 706 A.2d 203. The court found that the defendant had harassed the plaintiff and ordered a final restraining order. *Id.* at 390–91, 706 A.2d 203. The court's opinion did not mention the note that was the subject of the plaintiff's complaint, but instead based its decision on the alleged prior acts of domestic violence described by the plaintiff during her oral testimony. *Ibid.*

The Appellate Division reversed, concluding that it was "clearly improper" for the trial court to find that the defendant had committed domestic violence by relying on a prior course of conduct not mentioned in the complaint. *Id.* at 391, 706 A.2d 203. Noting that the "[d]efendant could not prepare a defense to charges that he was not even told about until the day of the hearing [,]" the court held that "[i]t constitutes a fundamental violation of due process to convert a hearing on a complaint alleging one act of domestic violence into a hearing on other acts of domestic violence which are not even alleged in the complaint." *Id.* at 391–92, 706 A.2d 203 (citing *Nicoletta, supra,* 77 *N.J.* at 162–63, 390 A.2d 90; *Miller, supra,* 115 *N.J.Super.* at 126, 278 A.2d 495).

In *Depos v. Depos,* 307 *N.J.Super.* 396, 704 A.2d 1049 (Ch.Div.1997), the trial court addressed a defendant's due process rights in a domestic violence action. The court ruled that, pursuant to *R.* 5:5–1, the defendant had no right to take the plaintiff's deposition. *Id.* at 399, 704 A.2d 1049. The defendant made the due process argument that failure to allow a deposition "would put him in the position of defending against 'things he doesn't know about' at the time of the trial." *Id.* at 402, 704 A.2d 1049. The court responded that the defendant had a remedy to that situation "if and when matters are testified to which go beyond what plaintiff has alleged in the complaint[,]" the defendant could "request a continuance of the trial in order to prepare a defense[,]" either at the end of the plaintiff's direct testimony or after the plaintiff's case. *Id.* at 402–03, 704 A.2d 1049 (citing *Nicoletta, supra,* 77 *N.J.* at 162, 390 A.2d 90).

The Domestic Violence Act requires that a final hearing be held "within 10 days of the filing of a complaint . . . in the county where the ex parte restraints were ordered. . . ." *N.J.S.A.* 2C:25–29a. But, as the Appellate Division acknowledged, "the ten-day provision does not preclude a continuance where fundamental fairness dictates allowing a defendant additional time." *H.E.S., supra,* 349 *N.J.Super.* at 342–43, 793 A.2d 780.

Indeed, to the extent that compliance with the ten-day provision precludes meaningful notice and an opportunity to defend, the provision must yield to due process requirements. *See McKeown–Brand, supra,* 132 *N.J.* at 559, 626 A.2d 425; *Nicoletta, supra,* 77 *N.J.* at 162, 390 A.2d 90; *cf. In re Commitment of M.G.,* 331 *N.J.Super.* 365, 385, 751 A.2d 1101 (App.Div. 2000) (holding that due process notice requirement takes precedence over statute requiring execution of sexually violent predator certifications no less than three days before commitment).

Further, we reject plaintiff's argument that in this case defendant had ample time to prepare a defense because the hearing did not begin as scheduled at 8:30 a.m. on August 24, 2000. It is not disputed that defendant was served with the complaint on August 23, 2000, and that the matter was scheduled for 8:30 a.m. the following day. That was not adequate time for preparation. Plaintiff's claim that she was acting under similar time constraints is likewise unavailing because she was aware of the allegations in her complaint at least as early as August 22, 2000, when she filed the complaint.

We agree with plaintiff that one reason for holding an expedited hearing to evaluate domestic violence complaints is to protect the interest of both the victim and the accused as quickly as possible. That purpose could have been achieved within the ten-day rule had the trial court granted an adjournment until as late as September 1, 2000. Plaintiff would not have been affected adversely by an adjournment because the TRO would have remained in place until the hearing. Even the Appellate Division agreed that granting a continuance would have been "preferable." *H.E.S., supra,* 349 *N.J.Super.* at 344, 793 A.2d 780.

Defendant's due process rights were further violated by the trial court's refusal to grant an adjournment after plaintiff alleged an incident of domestic violence not contained in the complaint, namely, use of the hidden camera and microphone in plaintiff's bedroom, and by the court's decision to grant a FRO on the basis of that allegation. *See J.F., supra,* 308 *N.J.Super.* at 392, 706 A.2d 203.

It is undisputed that plaintiff's domestic violence complaint did not allege that defendant had harassed or stalked her. Plaintiff argues that she informed domestic violence intake personnel of the incident, and that she should not be prejudiced for their failure to detail the incident in the complaint. However, the record does not contain any asserted prejudice had the trial court granted either of defendant's requests for a continuance because plaintiff would still have been protected by the TRO. As was observed in *J.F.,* "[i]t constitutes a fundamental violation of due process to convert a hearing on a complaint alleging one act of domestic violence into a hearing on other acts of domestic violence which are not even alleged in the complaint." *J.F., supra,* 308 *N.J.Super.* at 391–92, 706 A.2d 203 (citing *Nicoletta, supra,* 77 *N.J.* at 162–63, 390 A.2d 90; *Miller, supra,* 115 *N.J.Super.* at 126, 278 A.2d 495). The court's attempt in *H.E.S.* to distinguish *J.F.* on its facts is not persuasive. The fact that defendant's counsel had "overnight to consider his response," *H.E.S., supra,* 349

N.J.Super. at 343, 793 A.2d 780, does not diminish defendant's due process rights in this case.

We also reject plaintiff's argument that any due process violations were harmless. To support that argument, plaintiff asserts that defendant would be unable to provide any defense if given any amount of time because he has not denied responsibility for placing the microphone and camera in plaintiff's bedroom. We find that argument unpersuasive given the novelty of the factual circumstances and the legal issue involved. Although it is questionable whether defendant would have been able to obtain evidence exonerating him from responsibility for installing the microphone and camera in his wife's bedroom and connecting them to a VCR in his bedroom, enforcement of due process does not depend on guilt or innocence. The procedure employed here "involves such a probability that prejudice will result that it is deemed inherently lacking in due process." *Estes v. Texas*, 381 *U.S.* 532, 542–43, 85 *S.Ct.* 1628, 1632–33, 14 *L.Ed.*2d 543, 549–50 (1965). Accordingly, the FRO is vacated because of due process violations. Next we consider whether the video surveillance of plaintiff's bedroom presents a prima facie case of stalking or harassment under the Domestic Violence Act. Defendant contends that it does not. The answer determines whether a new hearing on the FRO should be conducted. The trial court found that defendant's behavior constituted harassment and stalking in violation of the Domestic Violence Act. The Appellate Division, however, held that installation of the video surveillance equipment did "not satisfy the elements of harassment as a matter of law." *H.E.S., supra,* 349 *N.J.Super.* at 336, 793 A.2d 780. It affirmed the finding of stalking.

Although there are several ways to prove harassment, for the purposes of this case the relevant criteria are those stated in *N.J.S.A.* 2C:33–4c. A defendant is guilty of the petty disorderly persons offense of harassment if, "with purpose to harass another, he ... [e]ngages in any other course of alarming conduct or of repeatedly committed acts with purpose to alarm or seriously annoy such other person." *Ibid.* The Appellate Division found that defendant did not engage in harassment because he placed the camera and microphone in plaintiff's bedroom, not to alarm or annoy her, but simply to watch her covertly. *H.E.S., supra,* 349 *N.J.Super.* at 349, 793 A.2d 780. Because defendant obviously did not want plaintiff to find the camera, the Appellate Division held that he could not have intended to annoy or alarm her, and thus one of the elements of *N.J.S.A.* 2C:33–4c is missing. *H.E.S., supra,* 349 *N.J.Super.* at 349, 793 A.2d 780. The Appellate Division relied on *State v. Fuchs*, 230 *N.J.Super.* 420, 426–27, 553 A.2d 853 (App.Div.1989), and *State v. Zarin*, 220 *N.J.Super.* 99, 101–02, 531 A.2d 411 (Law Div.1987), both of which concluded that the harassment statute did not apply to "peeping Toms" because those defendants intended to observe their victims without being discovered. *H.E.S., supra,* 349 *N.J.Super.* at 349, 793 A.2d 780.

The Appellate Division, however, failed to consider defendant's behavior that went beyond merely observing his wife in her bedroom. As we noted previously, "courts must consider the totality of the circumstances to determine whether the harassment statute has been violated." *Cesare, supra,* 154 *N.J.* at 404, 713 *A.*2d 390 (citing *State v. Hoffman,* 149 *N.J.* 564, 585, 695 *A.*2d 236 (1997)). The circumstances of this case, according to plaintiff, reveal that defendant often knew to whom she spoke on the phone, even though her phone only had one line. Plaintiff often saw defendant while she was traveling for her job, even though she knew he had no way of knowing where she would be at a certain time. Plaintiff also alleged that defendant had stolen checks and important papers that she had hidden in her bedroom. She testified that defendant's conduct made her feel as though he "knew [her] every move, [her] every step." In addition, the parties' past history, when properly presented, helps to inform the court regarding defendant's purpose, motive, and intended use of information obtained through the video and audio surveillance of plaintiff's private acts and conversations in her bedroom. If plaintiff is found to be credible, a sufficient evidentiary basis can be found to support a conclusion that defendant had the purpose to harass plaintiff by "repeatedly committ[ing] acts with purpose to alarm or seriously annoy" plaintiff. *N.J.S.A.* 2C:33–4c.

"A finding of a purpose to harass may be inferred from the evidence presented" and from common sense and experience. *Hoffman, supra,* 149 *N.J.* at 577, 695 *A.*2d 236 (internal citations omitted). The alternative requirement that defendant's purpose was to alarm plaintiff requires proof of anxiety or distress. *Id.* at 579, 695 *A.*2d 236. The serious annoyance requirement "under subsection (c) means to weary, worry, trouble, or offend." *Id.* at 581, 695 *A.*2d 236. "Thus, the difference between 'annoyance' and 'serious annoyance' is a matter of degree" and that determination must be made on a case-by-case basis. *Ibid.* We therefore hold that the Appellate Division erred when it concluded that, apparently as a matter of law, defendant's conduct could not constitute harassment under *N.J.S.A.* 2C:33–4c. Under the totality of the circumstances and viewing the evidence presented in a light most favorable to plaintiff, a prima facie case of harassment was established.

Defendant argues that the Appellate Division erroneously concluded that his conduct amounted to stalking under *N.J.S.A.* 2C:12–10. Specifically, defendant contends that, although the behavior complained of constitutes "boorish and offensive" "snooping," "surveillance by a spouse in the marital home does not constitute domestic violence" as a matter of law. We disagree, and affirm the Appellate Division's interpretation of the stalking statute to include the type of behavior involved here when viewed in the context of the parties' history.

The New Jersey Legislature created the crime of stalking in 1992. *L.* 1992, *c.* 209, effective January 5, 1993. The stalking statute was "intended to protect victims who are repeatedly followed and threatened." *Committee Statement, Senate,* No. 256, *L.* 1992, *c.* 209. The statute has been amended several times since 1992 and currently provides, in pertinent part:

a. As used in this act:

(1) "Course of conduct" means repeatedly maintaining a visual or physical proximity to a person or repeatedly conveying, or causing to

be conveyed, verbal or written threats or threats conveyed by any other means of communication or threats implied by conduct or a combination thereof directed at or toward a person.

(2) "Repeatedly" means on two or more occasions.

. . . .

b. A person is guilty of stalking . . . if he purposefully or knowingly engages in a course of conduct directed at a specific person that would cause a reasonable person to fear bodily injury to himself or a member of his immediate family or to fear the death of himself or a member of his immediate family.

[*N.J.S.A.* 2C:12–10.]

Defendant argues that his behavior was not stalking under New Jersey law because he did not behave in a "threatening" manner, but merely hid the camera and microphone in plaintiff's bedroom. He alleges that plaintiff did not feel threatened because she continued to live in the same house as he and did not apply for a TRO until after he had obtained one against her. Defendant argues that he "had constant opportunities to be violent if he wanted to" because he lived in the same house with plaintiff, and that conducting surveillance of plaintiff's bedroom "did not create opportunities for violence that were not already there." In other words, defendant argues that such behavior within a marital home cannot constitute stalking because it would not cause a reasonable person to fear bodily injury. Defendant asserts that the Appellate Division "trivialize[s]" the Domestic Violence Act (quoting *Kamen v. Egan,* 322 *N.J.Super.* 222, 229, 730 A.2d 873 (App.Div.1999)) by applying it to his nonviolent "snooping." We reject defendant's arguments.

The law is clear that acts of actual violence are not required to support a finding of domestic violence. The stalking statute was intended "to intervene in repetitive harassing or threatening behavior before the victim has actually been physically attacked." *State v. Saunders,* 302 *N.J.Super.* 509, 520, 695 A.2d 722 (App.Div.) (citations omitted), *certif. denied,* 151 *N.J.* 470, 700 A.2d 881 (1997). In the domestic violence context, granting a FRO when the defendant has been stalking the plaintiff furthers the Domestic Violence Act's goal of " 'assur[ing] the victims of domestic violence the *maximum protection* from abuse the law can provide.' " *Cesare, supra,* 154 *N.J.* at 399, 713 A.2d 390 (quoting *N.J.S.A.* 2C:25–18).

The elements of stalking are that: 1) defendant engaged in speech or conduct that was directed at or toward a person, 2) that speech or conduct occurred on at least two occasions, 3) defendant purposely engaged in speech or a course of conduct that is capable of causing a reasonable person to fear for herself or her immediate family bodily injury or death, and 4) defendant knowingly, recklessly or negligently caused a reasonable fear of bodily injury or death. *State v. Cardell,* 318 *N.J.Super.* 175, 183, 723 A.2d 111 (App.Div.) (quoting *N.J.S.A.* 2C:12–10), *certif. denied,* 158 *N.J.* 687, 731 A.2d 46 (1999). The mental culpability element, however, was changed to "purposefully or knowingly" by *L.* 1999, *c.* 47, § 1, effective March 12, 1999 and codified at *N.J.S.A.* 2C:12–10b.

In this case, it is reasonable to infer that defendant is responsible for installing the surveillance equipment and that he acted "purposefully or knowingly" against "a specific person," his wife. *N.J.S.A.* 2C:12–10. If believed, defendant's behavior would constitute a "course of conduct" because he had "repeatedly ['over a sufficient period or on a sufficient number of occasions to establish a "course of conduct" under the statute,' *H.E.S., supra,* 349 *N.J.Super.* at 350, 793 *A.*2d 780)] maintain[ed] a visual ... proximity to" plaintiff. *N.J.S.A.* 2C:12–10a(1), (2). Also, based on the totality of the circumstances, defendant's surveillance of plaintiff's bedroom, listening to her conversations and then following her after threatening to kill her if she did not drop the divorce action could "cause a reasonable person to fear bodily injury to [her]self." *N.J.S.A.* 2C:12–10.

The reasonable standard refers to persons in the victim's position and with the victim's knowledge of the defendant. *Cesare, supra,* 154 *N.J.* at 403, 713 *A.*2d 390. "Courts must ... consider plaintiff's individual circumstances and background in determining whether a reasonable person in that situation would have believed the defendant's threat." *Ibid.* (citations omitted). The relevant inquiry in this case is whether a reasonable person in plaintiff's situation, knowing what plaintiff knew about her husband under the totality of the circumstances, would have feared bodily injury as a result of his alleged speech and conduct.

Much of our harassment analysis applies here as well. Defendant observed plaintiff's behavior and listened to private conversations that took place in the privacy of her own bedroom. Defendant allegedly followed plaintiff while she was working, appearing in places where he otherwise could not have known she would be, and allegedly stole items from her bedroom that she had hidden from him. She claims he threatened to kill her unless she dropped the divorce proceedings. We hold that a finder of fact could reasonably have found, based on the totality of the circumstances, that defendant's behavior would have placed a reasonable person in fear of bodily injury. If plaintiff's testimony is believed, she feared her husband not only because of several sporadic prior incidents of physical violence, but also because of his more recent threats that the only way he would let her leave the marriage was "by death." Such threats may be understood to indicate defendant's desire to maintain control over his wife by any means necessary. Appearing while she was traveling for work, seemingly able to know where she would be without being told, could have enhanced plaintiff's feeling of helplessness and inability to escape defendant. This is the sort of behavior that New Jersey's anti-stalking statute was designed to prevent.

We, therefore, remand the matter to the trial court to conduct new proceedings on the FRO. On remand, the court must consider the totality of the circumstances surrounding the complaint, including past incidents of domestic violence and defendant's behavior after he placed the camera and microphone in plaintiff's bedroom.

Finally, defendant asserted during oral argument before this Court that he declined to testify with respect to the camera and microphone at the FRO hearing because he feared that doing so would expose him to criminal charges under the Wiretapping and Electronic Surveillance Control Act, *N.J.S.A.* 2A:156A–1 to –34. That Act provides that "any person who: a. Purposely intercepts [or] endeavors to intercept ... any wire, electronic or oral communication ... shall be guilty of a crime of the third degree." *N.J.S.A.* 2A:156A–3. Appellate Division cases have held that, following the federal wiretap statute, videotape surveillance is not violative of the New Jersey wiretap statute even if there is simultaneous audio surveillance. *Hornberger v. American Broadcasting Cos.*, 351 *N.J.Super.* 577, 619, 799 A.2d 566 (App.Div.2002); *State v. Diaz*, 308 *N.J.Super.* 504, 512, 706 A.2d 264 (App.Div.1998). However, defendant's audio surveillance of plaintiff with the microphone component of the camera may fit within that definition. The microphone component of the device planted in plaintiff's bedroom may be an intercepting "device" under *N.J.S.A.* 2A:156A–2d. With that device, he allegedly endeavored to intercept the oral communications of plaintiff while in her bedroom, either with another person or on her private telephone line. *See N.J.S.A.* 2A:156A–2b, –2c. In any event, we comment on that issue only to suggest to the trial court that an unfavorable inference should not be drawn against defendant if he elects not to testify on the remand.

V.

The judgment of the Appellate Division with respect to due process violations and harassment is reversed. Its judgment finding that the conduct may constitute stalking is affirmed. The matter is remanded to the trial court for new proceedings on the FRO consistent with this opinion.

At page 280, please add to the **NOTE** *on Remedies for Failure of Officials to Act the following:*

The en banc Court of Appeals for the Tenth Circuit, during spring of 2004, held that a state statute that promised a process by which a restraining order issued against an abusive spouse would be given vitality through careful and prompt consideration by law enforcement officials, provided a basis for a procedural due process claim against the local municipality. Gonzales v. City of Castle Rock, 366 F.3d 1093 (10th Cir. 2004). Oral arguments at the Supreme Court emphasized the distinction between the procedural and the substantive claim, but on June 27, 2005, the Supreme Court, in a 7-2 decision ruled that the city police could not be sued under a 14th Amendment procedural claim. Castle Rock, Colo. v. Gonzales, 2005 WL 1499788.

5. TORT ACTIONS BETWEEN SPOUSES

Following Tort Actions Between Spouses, please add at page 285:

Bozman v. Bozman

Maryland Court of Appeals, 2003.
376 Md. 461, 830 A.2d 450.

■ BELL, CHIEF JUDGE.

Whether the common-law doctrine of interspousal tort immunity shall remain viable in Maryland is the issue we decide in this appeal. The Circuit

Court for Baltimore County dismissed the complaint alleging malicious prosecution filed by William E. Bozman, the petitioner, against Nancie L. Bozman, the respondent, a judgment which the Court of Special Appeals affirmed. We shall reverse the judgment of the intermediate appellate court and, as urged by the petitioner, abrogate the doctrine of interspousal immunity.

The petitioner and the respondent were married in this State on August 16, 1968. On February 24, 2000, the petitioner initiated divorce proceedings against the respondent. As grounds, he pled adultery. The parties were divorced on March 12, 2001.

Shortly before the divorce was finalized, on January 20, 2001, the petitioner filed in the Circuit Court for Baltimore County a complaint sounding in malicious prosecution against the respondent. In that complaint, which consisted of one count, the petitioner alleged that, as a result of criminal charges, which the respondent brought against him on February 17, 2000, May 3, 2000 and July 19, 2000, he was arrested and charged with stalking, harassment and multiple counts of violation of a Protective Order. The petitioner further alleged that the charges were brought without probable cause, were deliberately fabricated to ensure that the petitioner would be arrested, and were in retaliation for the petitioner's initiation of the divorce proceedings and his unwillingness to make concessions in those proceedings. The respondent moved to dismiss the complaint. She argued, in support of that motion, *inter alia,* that the action was barred based upon the common law doctrine of interspousal tort immunity.

The Circuit Court granted the respondent's Motion to Dismiss, but with leave to amend. Thereafter, the petitioner filed an Amended Complaint. As she had done earlier, the respondent filed a motion to dismiss, relying, also as she had done before, on the doctrine of interspousal immunity. Responding to the motion to dismiss and relying on this Court's decision in *Lusby v. Lusby,* 283 Md. 334, 390 A.2d 77 (1978), in which the Court held that interspousal immunity was not a defense to a tort action between spouses where the conduct constituting the tort was "outrageous [and] intentional," *id.* at 335, 390 A.2d at 77, the petitioner argued that the defense was inapplicable under the facts he alleged; his multiple incarcerations and his being subjected to house arrest were sufficiently outrageous and intentional as to fall within the *Lusby* rule. Altogether, the petitioner claims, as a result of the respondent's false accusations, that he was incarcerated on five separate occasions, for periods ranging between one (1) and ten (10) days, and placed on home detention, which required that he wear an ankle monitoring bracelet for approximately eight (8) months.

On the same day that a hearing on the motion to dismiss was held, the petitioner filed a Second Amended Complaint. That complaint reiterated the allegations of the earlier complaint as Count I and added a second malicious prosecution count. That second malicious prosecution count alleged that, on February 2, 2001, the respondent filed, against the petitioner, additional charges of violating an *ex parte* order, which although ultimately dismissed, again resulted in the petitioner's incarceration and incurring an expense to be released. As he did in the initial complaint, the petitioner claimed that the respondent fabricated the charges, although, on this occasion, the momentum was different; it was in response to the initial malicious prosecution action and the respondent's inability to "prevail in her position" in the divorce proceedings. The petitioner specifically alleged that the dismissal of the charges referred to in Count II, one of the elements of a successful malicious prosecution action, occurred after the parties were divorced. Thus, he argued that that count was not subject to the interspousal immunity defense.

The trial court granted the respondent's Motion to Dismiss, ruling that the action was barred by the doctrine of interspousal immunity. The petitioner noted a timely appeal to the Court of Special Appeals.

In the intermediate appellate court, the petitioner challenged the trial court's dismissal of Count I of the Second Amended Complaint, arguing that it was error in light of this Court's decision in *Lusby,* because malicious prosecution is an outrageous, intentional tort to which interspousal immunity is not a defense. As to the dismissal of Count II of the Second Amended Complaint, the petitioner submitted that, not only was the conduct outrageous and intentional, but the cause of action for the malicious prosecution alleged in that count arose after the parties were legally divorced. Consequently, he argues, the doctrine of interspousal immunity is rendered inapplicable to that count, as well.

To be sure, the Court of Special Appeals "questioned the continued viability of" the doctrine of interspousal immunity. *Bozman v. Bozman,* 146 Md.App. 183, 195, 806 A.2d 740, 747 (2002), citing *Boblitz v. Boblitz,* 296 Md. 242, 462 A.2d 506, (1983). Characterizing it as an "antiquated doctrine" and stating that it "runs counter to present-day norms," *id.,* the intermediate appellate court commented:

> "We recognize that the doctrine may serve some practical purpose of preventing spouses from instituting suits in tort as a means of gaining an advantage in pending divorce proceedings or for some other improper reason. We remain unconvinced, however, that retention of this doctrine best reflects the will of the people of this State as evidence by, among other reforms, enactment of the Equal Rights Amendment in 1972."

Id. Nevertheless, it recognized that:

> "Regardless, we are bound to follow the dictates of the law as it presently exists in Maryland. The law is that interspousal immunity may be raised as a defense to a viable cause of action alleging an intentional tort so long as the tort is not 'outrageous,' as that term is used in *Lusby* and *Doe [v. Doe,* 358 Md. 113, 747 A.2d 617]."

Id. at 196, 806 A.2d at 747.

Therefore, the Court of Special Appeals addressed the issue that lay at the heart of the case, as submitted to it, the quality of the respondent's conduct and, more generally, the nature of the tort of malicious prosecution. More specifically, the court considered whether the tort, or at least the conduct that constituted the tort, came within the term, "outrageous," as defined in, and contemplated by, *Lusby*. It concluded:

> "Without minimizing in any way the harsh consequences to appellant wrought by appellee's behavior in this case, we cannot say that it is of comparable character to that addressed by the Court in *Lusby*. Appellee's actions in the instant case no doubt caused appellant to suffer significant humiliation and hardship. But they did not involve extreme violence of the most personal and invasive sort, the threat of death and a display of the means by which to carry out that threat, or the physical and psychic trauma that the victim in *Lusby* endured. We conclude, therefore, that the conduct that underlies appellant's claim of malicious prosecution is not, in and of itself, indicative of the sort of outrageous conduct contemplated by the *Lusby* exception to interspousal immunity."

Id. at 197–98, 806 A.2d at 748.[3] Accordingly, the intermediate appellate court held that "malicious prosecution is not so outrageous as to bring it within the narrow exception to the doctrine of interspousal immunity." The court affirmed the trial court's dismissal of Count I of the Second Amended Complaint. *Id.* at 186, 806 A.2d at 741.

Turning to Count II, the intermediate appellate court vacated the trial court's dismissal of that count and remanded the case for further proceedings. It explained that the respondent "failed to demonstrate that the parties were married when the cause of action in Count II arose." *Id.*

Both the petitioner and the respondent filed a petition for Writ of Certiorari in this Court. The petitioner's petition sought review of the correctness of the Court of Special Appeals' judgment dismissing Count I of

---

3. Because one of the elements of the tort of intentional infliction of emotional distress, recognized by this Court in *Harris v. Jones*, 281 Md. 560, 566, 380 A.2d 611 (1977), is that the conduct must be "extreme and outrageous," the Court of Special Appeals relied heavily on this Court's cases addressing that tort. *Bozman v. Bozman,* 146 Md. App. 183, 198–200, 806 A.2d 740, 748–750 (2002). Noting that liability has been found in those cases only " 'where the conduct has been so outrageous in character, and so extreme in degree, as to go beyond all possible bounds of decency, and to be regarded as atrocious, and utterly intolerable in a civilized community,' " *id.* (quoting *Harris,* 281 Md. at 567, 380 A.2d at 615, in turn quoting Restatement (Second) of Torts, ch. 2, Emotional Distress, § 46 (1965)), the court cited *B.N. v. K.K.,* 312 Md. 135, 146, 538 A.2d 1175 (1988) ("one who knowingly engages in conduct that is highly likely to infect another with an incurable disease … has committed extreme and outrageous conduct.") and *Figueiredo–Torres v. Nickel,* 321 Md. 642, 654, 584 A.2d 69 (1991) (a psychologist retained to improve a marital relationship acts outrageously when he facilitates a romantic, sexual relationship with the spouse of a patient). The court also relied on those parent-child immunity doctrine cases, in which a minor child has been the victim of "cruel, inhuman or outrageous conduct at the hands of a parent." *Bozman,* 146 Md.App. at 199, 806 A.2d at 749, quoting *Eagan v. Calhoun,* 347 Md. 72, 75, 698 A.2d 1097 (1997) (father committed voluntary manslaughter of his children's mother); *see Mahnke v. Moore,* 197 Md. 61, 68, 77 A.2d 923 (1951) (father shot child's mother in child's presence, kept the child with the body for six days, then shooting self in front of the child).

the Second Amended Complaint, both as to the grounds, interspousal immunity, and the standard for defining "outrageous" conduct, to measure whether the conduct met the standard established in *Harris v. Jones,* 281 Md. 560, 380 A.2d 611 (1977). In her cross-petition, the respondent sought review of the propriety of the dismissal of Count II of the Second Amended Complaint.

We granted both petitions. *Bozman v. Bozman,* 372 Md. 429, 813 A.2d 257 (2002). We agree with the Court of Special Appeals, that the interspousal immunity doctrine is an antiquated rule of law which, in our view, runs counter to prevailing societal norms and, therefore, has lived out its usefulness. Accordingly, we shall answer the petitioner's first question in the affirmative and, so, complete the abrogation of the doctrine from the common law of this State. As a result, we need not, and shall not, address the other questions raised by the petitioner's petition or the respondent's cross-petition.

In the case *sub judice,* the petitioner states that the "fundamental issue before this Honorable Court is whether the doctrine of interspousal immunity should be abolished." (Petitioner's Brief at 6). Thus, the petitioner directly and un-apologetically asks us to reexamine our holdings in the line of cases from *Furstenburg v. Furstenburg,* 152 Md. 247, 136 A. 534 (1927) to *Doe v. Doe,* 358 Md. 113, 747 A.2d 617 (2000) and to conclude that the rule of interspousal tort immunity has outlived its usefulness in this State. The petitioner relies on many of the cases cited in *Boblitz,* to be sure, but he bolsters his argument with decisions speaking on the issue filed by our sister jurisdictions since *Boblitz* was decided.

The respondent, not unexpectedly, urges "that this Court [should] defer such drastic and far reaching action [as abrogating the interspousal immunity doctrine] to the legislature of this State." (Respondent's Brief at 3). Some of the arguments the respondent offers in support of our staying our hand, in deference to legislative action, if any, are reminiscent of those that this Court identified in *Boblitz* as the rationales on which those courts retaining interspousal immunity relied to justify its retention and those courts abrogating the doctrine, fully or partially, addressed, and rejected. She offers six such arguments: Husbands and Wives are Treated Differently by the Law; Status of the Doctrine in other States; Other remedies; Stare Decisis; Boblitz Should Not Be a Springboard.

The doctrine of interspousal immunity in tort cases is a rule of law existing in the common law of Maryland. *Doe, supra,* 358 Md. at 119, 747 A.2d at 619 ("Prior to *Lusby,* the doctrine of interspousal immunity in tort cases was clearly recognized as part of the common law of this state."). In *Boblitz,* we noted that it is a rule of "ancient origin" and created "exclusively from judicial decisions." 296 Md. at 244, 462 A.2d at 507. "The rule at common law [was] that a married woman cannot maintain an action against her husband for injuries caused by his negligent or tortious act." *David v. David,* 161 Md. 532, 534, 157 A. 755, 756 (1932).

The rationale underlying the interspousal immunity rule has been discussed in our cases. In *David,* the Court stated: "The reason usually

given for that rule is the presumed legal identity of the husband and wife."
Id. at 534, 157 A. at 756, quoting *Philips v. Barnet* 1 QB 436 (1876). A
more complete statement of the rationale was provided in *Lusby*, 283 Md.
at 338, 390 A.2d at 78–79, with attribution to Blackstone, (1 W. Blackstone,
Commentaries, Book 1, Ch. 15, p. 442, 443):

> " 'By marriage, the husband and wife are one person in the law:
> that is, the very being of legal existence of the woman is suspended
> during the marriage, or at least is incorporated and consolidated into
> that of the husband: under whose wing, protection, and cover, she
> performs everything; and is therefore called in our law french a *feme-
> covert, foemina viro co-operta;* is said to be a *covert-baron,* or under the
> protection and influence of her husband, her *baron,* or *lord;* and her
> condition during her marriage is called *coverture.* Upon this principle,
> of a union of person in husband and wife, depend almost all the legal
> rights, duties and disabilities, that either of them acquire by the
> marriage.'

> "He adds, in discussing the consequences of this union of husband and
> wife, 'If the wife be injured in her person or her property, she can bring no
> action for redress without her husband's concurrence, and in his name, as
> well as her own: neither can she be sued without making the husband a
> defendant.' "

See also, Boblitz, 296 Md. at 244, 462 A.2d at 507. The *Lusby* Court, again
quoting Blackstone, Book 1, Ch. 15, pp. 444–45, also addressed another
aspect of the relationship between husband and wife at common law, which
it characterized as "hard to comprehend":

> " 'The husband also, by the old law, might give his wife moderate
> correction. For, as he is to answer for her misbehavior, the law thought
> it reasonable to intrust him with this power of restraining her, by
> domestic chastisement, in the same moderation that a man is allowed
> to correct his apprentices or children; for whom the master or parent is
> also liable in some cases to answer. But this power of correction was
> confined within reasonable bounds, and the husband was prohibited
> from using any violence to his wife, *aliter quam ad virum, ex causa
> regiminis et castigationis uxoris suae, licite et rationabiliter pertinet.*
> The civil law gave the husband the same, or a larger, authority over his
> wife: allowing him, for some misdemeanors, *flagellis et fustibus acriter
> verberare uxorem* [to beat his wife severely with scourges and cudgels];
> for others, only *modicam castigationem adhibere* [to use moderate
> chastisement]. But with us, in the politer reign of Charles the Second,
> this power of correction began to be doubted; and a wife may now have
> security of the peace against her husband; or, in return, a husband
> against his wife. Yet the lower rank of people, who were always fond of
> the old common law, still claim and exert their ancient privilege: and
> the courts of law will still permit a husband to restrain a wife of her
> liberty, in case of any gross misbehavior.'

> " 'These are the chief legal effects of marriage during the cover-
> ture; upon which we may observe, that even the disabilities which the

wife lies under are for the most part intended for her protection and benefit: so great a favorite is the female sex of the laws of England.' "

283 Md. at 338–39, 390 A.2d at 79. The *Boblitz* Court, too, commented on the effect of the doctrine on women:

"Application of the words interspousal immunity to this ancient rule of law borders on mockery. It would more aptly be called a 'rule in derogation of married women.' Under it the person or property of a woman upon marriage came under the 'protection and influence' of her husband—for good or ill. She became subservient to his will and fitted with a distasteful yoke of servitude and compelled obeisance that was galling at best and crushing at worst."

296 Md. at 245, 462 A.2d at 507.

Our laws pertaining to the rights of married women were completely revised in 1898, with the enactment of the Married Women's Act,[6] see Ch. 457 of the Acts of 1898, now codified at Md.Code 1984, 1999 Repl.Vol. §§ 4–203–4–205 of the Family Law Article. It was the effect of the Married Women's Act on this common law impediment to, or prohibition against, married women and, thus, the construction of that Act, that has resulted in the bulk of our jurisprudence in this area. From *Furstenburg* until *Lusby,* without exception, "Maryland would not entertain a suit by one spouse against the other for his or her tort, committed during the marital status." *Tobin v. Hoffman,* 202 Md. 382, 391, 96 A.2d 597, 601 (1953) (applying District of Columbia law, interspousal immunity does not apply where wife sues her husband's co-partner in his individual capacity for a tort he committed by his own hand, albeit, within the ambit of partnership activities). See *Stokes v. Assoc. of Independent Taxi Operators,* 248 Md. 690, 237 A.2d 762 (1968) (suit against husband's employer for injuries wife suffered while a paying passenger in taxicab driven by her husband); *Hudson v. Hudson,* 226 Md. 521, 174 A.2d 339 (1961) (action by wife against husband for injuries sustained in a pre-marriage automobile accident caused by husband's negligence); *Ennis v. Donovan,* 222 Md. 536, 161 A.2d 698 (1960) (third party claim against husband by defendant in negligence action, brought by the husband, as administrator of wife's estate); *Fernandez v. Fernandez,* 214 Md. 519, 135 A.2d 886 (1957) (action by the wife, during period of separation, against husband for replevin); *Gregg v. Gregg,* 199 Md. 662, 87 A.2d 581 (1952) (suit for necessaries by

---

6. As enacted, the Act provided:

"Married women shall have power to engage in any business, and to contract, whether engaged in business or not, and to sue upon their contracts, and also to sue for the recovery, security or protection of their property, and for torts committed against them, as fully as if they were unmarried; contracts may also be made with them, and they may also be sued separately upon their contracts, whether made before or during marriage, and for wrongs independent of contract committed by them before or during their marriage, as fully as if they were unmarried; and upon judgments recovered against them, execution may be issued as if they were unmarried; nor shall any husband be liable upon any contract made by his wife in her own name and upon her own responsibility, nor for any tort committed separately by her out of his presence, without his participation or sanction."

the wife against the husband for period not covered by the award of alimony); *Riegger v. Bruton Brewing Company,* 178 Md. 518, 16 A.2d 99 (1940) (suit by wife against husband's employer for husband's negligence); *David v. David,* 161 Md. 532, 157 A. 755 (1932) (suit by wife against partnership of which husband was a member for injuries sustained on the business premises); *Furstenburg v. Furstenburg,* 152 Md. 247, 136 A. 534 (1927) (suit by wife against husband for injuries sustained in automobile accident caused by husband's negligence). That is because the Court in *Furstenburg,* 152 Md. at 252–53, 136 A. at 536, relying on *Thompson v. Thompson,* 218 U.S. 611, 31 S.Ct. 111,54 L.Ed. 1180 (1910), in which the Supreme Court construed a similar District of Columbia statute, concluded that the Maryland Act "g[a]ve the wife a remedy, by her suit alone, for actionable wrongs which could not theretofore be thus independently redressed," and did not "create, as between husband and wife, personal causes of action which did not exist before the act."

Two years later, see Ch. 633, Sec. 19(a) of Acts of 1900, the General Assembly added:

> "A married woman may contract with her husband and may form a copartnership with her husband or with any other person or persons in the same manner as if she were a feme sole, and upon all such contracts, partnership or otherwise, a married woman may sue and be sued as fully as if she were a feme sole."

That the Court uniformly applied the doctrine, without exception, did not mean that it did not recognize its flaws. As was pointed out in *Boblitz, supra,* 296 Md. at 251, 462 A.2d at 510, "The opinions in decisions of this Court upon the issue demonstrate that we had misgiving concerning our holdings [relating to the doctrine's applicability] in the line of cases from *Furstenburg* to *Stokes.*" In fact, the Court did not hesitate to criticize the application of the doctrine and the rationale supporting it. In *David,* 161 Md. at 535, 157 A. at 756, while accepting "the broader sociological and political ground that it [permitting suit for tort between spouses] would introduce into the home, the basic unit of organized society, discord, suspicion and distrust, and would be inconsistent with the common welfare," the Court characterized as "technical and artificial" the ground based on the identity of husband and wife. The Court in *Gregg,* 199 Md. at 666, 87 A.2d at 583 labeled the domestic tranquility rationale for the interspousal immunity doctrine "as artificial as" the unity of husband and wife rationale. Expounding on that theme, it pointed out:

> "It applies to a post-bellum situation a theory which is clearly only applicable to conditions prior to the difficulty which caused the bringing of the legal action. After discord, suspicion and distrust have entered the home, it is idle to say that one of the parties shall not be allowed to sue the other because of fear of bringing in what is already there."

Id. at 667, 87 A.2d at 583. In *Fernandez,* although not permitting a replevin action to be prosecuted by a wife against her husband, from whom she then was separated, the Court acknowledged "the appeal to reason and convenience" of the contrary rule, 214 Md. at 521, 135 A.2d at 887, and that "the literal language of the [Married Women's] Act authorizes both [a right for the wife to sue her husband for the tort against her person] and [a right to sue him for a tort against her property interest], as well as a right to sue him in contract." *Id.* at 524, 135 A.2d at 889.

Our reluctance to change the common law and, thus, our continued adherence to the interspousal immunity doctrine, was in deference to the Legislature. *Stokes, supra,* 248 Md. at 692, 237 A.2d at 763 (declining to change the interspousal immunity rule and noting that change, if any, would be left to Legislature); *Ennis, supra,* 222 Md. at 542, 161 A.2d at 702 ("We can only repeat that if it be desirable to permit a married woman, under certain circumstances, to sue her husband in tort, this authorization should emanate from the Legislature, not from the courts"); *Fernandez,* 214 Md. at 524, 135 A.2d at 889 ("Those in the situation of the appellant must proceed in equity until the Legislature sees fit to change the law."); *Gregg, supra,* 199 Md. at 667, 87 A.2d at 583 ("these ancient theories which form a part of the common law have to be followed by us unless they have been changed by legislative action, and the clear import of the decision in the *David* case is that the emancipatory statutes must be strictly construed.").

The first breach of the interspousal immunity doctrine in Maryland occurred with our decision in *Lusby.* There, the wife brought a tort action against her husband for damages. As reported by the Court (283 Md. at 335, 390 A.2d at 77),

> "She alleged that while she was operating her motor vehicle on a public highway the husband 'pulled alongside of [her] in his pick-up truck and pointed a highpowered rifle at her.' She attempted to flee by increasing the speed of her car. She claimed that then 'another truck occupied by two (2) men, whose identities are unknown to [her] and who, [t]hereinafter are referred to [in the declaration] as John Doe and Richard Roe, cut and forced her off the road, nearly causing a collision.' ... After she stopped her car, the husband 'approached her automobile with a rifle pointed at her, opened her left door, ordered her to move over, forced his way into the automobile and began to drive the automobile.' They were followed by Doe in the husband's truck and Roe in the second truck. Thereafter, the wife 'was forced to enter [the husband's] truck with [the husband] and Richard Roe.' John Doe drove the wife's vehicle and the second truck was left parked. She alleged that her husband then struck her, 'tore [her] clothes off and did forcefully and violently, despite [her] desperate attempts to protect herself, carnally know [her] against her will and without her consent.' She further claimed that, with the aid and assistance of her husband, both Doe and Roe attempted to rape her. She said that following those events her husband 'and his two companions released [her] and [her husband] told [her] that he would kill her if she informed anyone of the aforesaid events; and that he has continued to harass and threaten [her]."

Id. at 335–36, 390 A.2d at 77–78. On these facts, the Court held, "under the facts and circumstances of this case, amounting to an outrageous, intentional tort, a wife may sue her husband for damages." *Id.* at 335, 390 A.2d at 77.

In rendering our decision, we stated, having noted the Legislature's inaction with regard to amending the Married Women's Act to ameliorate the effect of the interspousal immunity defense and the purpose of statutory construction in the interpretation of statutes:

> "For purposes of our decision here today ... we need not be involved with statutory construction nor need we be involved with our prior cases other than for dicta appearing in them to the effect that one spouse may not sue another for tort. None of our prior cases has involved an intentional tort."

Id. at 357–58, 390 A.2d at 89. Nevertheless, before doing so, and, presumably, to inform the decision, we reviewed all of our cases addressing the interspousal immunity doctrine, *id.* at 340–46, 390 A.2d at 80–82, surveyed the cases on the subject from our sister jurisdictions, *id.* at 346–49, 390 A.2d at 82–84, considered the opinions of the commentators as to the doctrine's viability and justification, *id.* at 350, 390 A.2d at 84–85, and "examined the foundation upon which our [prior] holdings rest." *Id.* at 354–57, 390 A.2d at 86–88.

The review of our cases revealed consistent and uniform application of the doctrine, some questioning of the doctrine's underpinnings and that in none of those cases "has there been an allegation of an intentional tort, much less the outrageous conduct" involved in that case. *Id.* at 352, 390 A.2d at 86. Cases from other jurisdictions, the survey found, reflected a division on the issue of the continued viability of the interspousal immunity doctrine. *Id.* at 350, 390 A.2d at 84. On the other hand, the Court noted, the commentators were near unanimous in their criticism of the common law rule of immunity. *Id.* With regard to the examination of the prior holdings on the subject, the Court said:

> . . .
>
> Merely five years after *Lusby,* we were asked "to reexamine the interspousal immunity rule ... and to declare that rule to be no longer viable in tort cases involving personal injury to a spouse resulting from the negligence of the other spouse." *Boblitz, supra,* 296 Md. at 244, 462 A.2d at 506. In that case, a wife sued her husband for injuries she sustained almost a year before the marriage, as a result, she alleged, of his negligence in the operation of an automobile. Pleading the parties' marital status and relying on *Hudson,* the husband moved for summary judgment, arguing that the wife's alleged cause of action had been extinguished by the marriage. *Id.* at 243, 462 A.2d at 506. The motion was granted and we issued the writ of certiorari to review the question previously stated. *Id.* at 244, 462 A.2d at 506. We reversed the summary judgment, in the process abrogating the interspousal immunity rule in this State as to cases sounding in negligence. *Id.* at 275, 462 A.2d at 522. We explained:
>
> > "We share the view now held by the vast majority of American States that the interspousal immunity rule is unsound in the circum-

stances of modern life in such cases as the subject. It is a vestige of the past. We are persuaded that the reasons asserted for its retention do not survive careful scrutiny. They furnish no reasonable basis for denial of recovery for tortious personal injury. We find no subsisting public policy that justifies retention of a judicially created immunity that would bar recovery for injured victims in such cases as the present."

Id. at 273, 462 A.2d at 521. (citation omitted).

We arrived at that holding only after conducting a thorough and exhaustive review of the doctrine of interspousal immunity, including its history and rationale, the impact and effect of the doctrine on women and women's rights, the Maryland cases applying the doctrine and the foundation on which they rested, the application and acceptance of the doctrine in our sister states, and, in particular, the change that has occurred over time in the acceptance of the doctrine by the courts of those States, the views of the legal scholars and the academic community as to the continued viability of the doctrine, and the impact of abrogating the doctrine in negligence cases.

Much of the analysis undertaken by the Court as to the historical description and the historical underpinnings of the interspousal immunity doctrine had already been conducted by the Court in *Lusby,* as was the review of both the effect of the doctrine on women and of the Maryland cases applying it, albeit some with misgivings. These matters have also been addressed already in this opinion and, for that reason, need not be repeated further. It is sufficient to note, again, the observation that the doctrine was more aptly called a "rule in derogation of married women," because it subjected her and her property to her husband's will, "fitted with a distasteful yoke of servitude and compelled obeisance that was galling at best and crushing at worst," *Boblitz,* 296 Md. at 245, 462 A.2d at 507, and the criticism of the rationale for the continued adherence to the doctrine voiced in *David, Gregg* and *Fernandez.*

To be sure, the Court in *Lusby* considered the extent to which the interspousal immunity doctrine was accepted in our sister states; however, that review was not intended to be an exhaustive survey of all of the decided cases, just those cases that had abolished, in whole or in part, the doctrine before and after this Court's decision in *Stokes.* 283 Md. at 346, 390 A.2d at 82–83. As indicated, that survey revealed five cases, two of which were from California, before *Stokes, id.,* and twelve after *Stokes* was decided. *Id.* at 346–49, 390 A.2d at 83–84. By contrast, the Court identified eight states that continued to adhere to the interspousal immunity doctrine. *Id.* at 349, 390 A.2d at 84. The *Boblitz* Court conducted an exhaustive review of the decisions with respect to the doctrine, finding all 49 states, excluding Maryland, had addressed the issue. 296 Md. at 252, 462 A.2d at 511. Characterizing "[t]he changes occurring since 1965[as] astounding," it reported that twelve (12) States continued to recognize the doctrine, thirty-five (35) States had abrogated the doctrine fully or partially, and in two States, a rule of immunity was imposed by statute. *Id.* Twenty seven (27) of the abrogating States did so fully. *Id.* at 258, 462 A.2d at 514.

Because it was concerned with deciding whether to retain the rule in Maryland, the Court undertook an analysis to determine why the interspousal immunity doctrine, once the long-standing majority rule, was no longer widely favored and why those states applying it were, in fact, now in the minority. For the answer, we reviewed decisions of the minority of states retaining the interspousal immunity doctrine and those from the states that had abrogated the doctrine fully and partially, focusing on the arguments and justifications offered for the retention or abrogation. Although quoting liberally from only three, *Alfree v. Alfree,* 410 A.2d 161, 162–63 (Del.1979); *Raisen v. Raisen,* 379 So.2d 352, 355 (Fla.1979); and *Robeson v. Int'l. Indemnity Co.,* 248 Ga. 306, 282 S.E.2d 896, 898 (1981), of the twelve decisions retaining intact the interspousal immunity doctrine, the Court identified, "[f]rom the totality of decisions in the twelve states," six reasons, given by one or more of the twelve courts, for the retention of the doctrine:

"1. The unity of husband and wife;

"2. Interspousal tort actions will destroy the harmony of the marital relationship;

"3. Retention of the doctrine will prevent collusive and fraudulent claims;

"4. Retention of the doctrine will guard against an increase in trivial claims;

"5. Divorce and criminal courts to furnish adequate redress;

"6. Change is solely within the purview of the Legislature.

Id. at 253–57, 462 A.2d at 511–13 (citations omitted).

. . .

On two occasions in the last twenty-five years, this court has done an analysis of the interspousal immunity doctrine and its rational underpinnings, the reasons or justification offered for its existence and continued viability, and, on each occasion, found the doctrine and the foundation on which it was built to be lacking. We found the trend and, indeed, the great weight of authority, to be to move away from the doctrine and in favor of changing the common law to abolish it, either fully or partially. The majority of the States, we discovered, were of the view that the doctrine was outdated and served no useful purpose, that "there presently exists no cogent or logical reason why the doctrine of interspousal tort immunity should be continued." *Merenoff,* 388 A.2d at 962. As we have seen, this Court, in *Boblitz* expressed its adherence to this majority view, characterizing the doctrine as "unsound in the circumstances of modern life" and "a vestige of the past," for which "the reasons asserted for its retention do not survive careful scrutiny." 296 Md. at 273, 462 A.2d at 521. We continue of that view and, the trend toward abrogation having continued and the weight of authority having grown larger, we are fortified in that view.

. . .

We are not convinced. It has been held that "insofar as interspousal liability for tort is concerned there is no logical or legal reason for drawing a distinction between the two." *Klein v. Klein,* 58 Cal.2d 692, 26 Cal.Rptr. 102, 376 P.2d 70, 71 (1962). *See Beattie v. Beattie,* 630 A.2d 1096, 1101

("[I]t appears that the rationale underlying the abrogation of the Doctrine in the context of negligence actions would apply to intentional torts."). *See also Price v. Price,* 732 S.W.2d 316, 319–320 (Tex.1987), expressing concern that partial abrogation of the doctrine, which would leave in place a bar to other actionable torts that would not exist in the case of unmarried persons, would amount to a repudiation of the state constitutional guarantee of equal protection of the laws.

In any event, California abrogated the doctrine in intentional tort cases in 1962. The respondent has not provided any demonstrative evidence that any of the questions or problems she posits as possible and, indeed, "undoubtedly will arise" have arisen in California or any where else for that matter. Moreover, the other States that have fully abrogated the doctrine or in cases of intentional torts, some quite a long time ago, e.g. *Brown v. Brown, supra,* 88 Conn. 42, 89 A. 889 (1914); *Gilman v. Gilman,* 78 N.H. 4, 95 A. 657 (N.H.1915); *Crowell v. Crowell,* 180 N.C. 516, 105 S.E. 206 (1920); *Penton v. Penton,* 223 Ala. 282, 135 So. 481 (1931); *Pardue v. Pardue,* 167 S.C. 129, 166 S.E. 101 (1932), provide an accurate barometer of what can be expected after abrogation and what they reveal is far different from the picture the respondent paints.

The overwhelming weight of authority supports the petitioner's argument that the interspousal immunity doctrine should be abrogated. Joining the many of our sister States that have already done so, we abrogate the interspousal immunity rule, a vestige of the past, whose time has come and gone, as to all cases alleging an intentional tort. As we did in *Boblitz,* 296 Md. at 275, 462 A.2d at 522, we shall apply the abrogation to this case and to all causes of action accruing after the date of the filing of this opinion.

JUDGMENT OF THE COURT OF SPECIAL APPEALS REVERSED. CASE REMANDED TO THAT COURT, WITH INSTRUCTIONS TO REVERSE THE JUDGMENT OF THE CIRCUIT COURT FOR BALTIMORE COUNTY AND REMAND THE CASE TO THAT COURT FOR PROCEEDINGS CONSISTENT WITH THIS OPINION. COSTS IN THIS COURT AND IN THE COURT OF SPECIAL APPEALS TO BE PAID BY THE RESPONDENT.

Editor's Note:

[An Appendix on the Present status of the Interspousal Immunity Rule in 49 States other than Maryland, in the District of Columbia, and in Admiralty, has been omitted.]

G. MEDICAL CARE

Bush v. Schiavo

Supreme Court of Florida, 2004.
885 So.2d 321.

■ PARIENTE, C.J.

The narrow issue in this case requires this Court to decide the constitutionality of a law passed by the Legislature that directly affected

Theresa Schiavo, who has been in a persistent vegetative state since 1990.[7] This Court, after careful consideration of the arguments of the parties and amici, the constitutional issues raised, the precise wording of the challenged law, and the underlying procedural history of this case, concludes that the law violates the fundamental constitutional tenet of separation of powers and is therefore unconstitutional both on its face and as applied to Theresa Schiavo. Accordingly, we affirm the trial court's order declaring the law unconstitutional.

The resolution of the discrete separation of powers issue presented in this case does not turn on the facts of the underlying guardianship proceedings that resulted in the removal of Theresa's nutrition and hydration tube. The underlying litigation, which has pitted Theresa's husband, Michael Schiavo, against Theresa's parents, turned on whether the procedures sustaining Theresa's life should be discontinued. However, the procedural history is important because it provides the backdrop to the Legislature's enactment of the challenged law. We also detail the facts and procedural history in light of the Governor's assertion that chapter 2003–418, Laws of Florida (hereinafter sometimes referred to as "the Act"), was passed in order to protect the due process rights of Theresa and other individuals in her position.

As set forth in the Second District's first opinion in this case, which upheld the guardianship court's final order,

Theresa Marie Schindler was born on December 3, 1963, and lived with or near her parents in Pennsylvania until she married Michael Schiavo on November 10, 1984. Michael and Theresa moved to Florida in 1986. They were happily married and both were employed. They had no children.

On February 25, 1990, their lives changed. Theresa, age 27, suffered a cardiac arrest as a result of a potassium imbalance. Michael called 911, and Theresa was rushed to the hospital. She never regained consciousness.

Since 1990, Theresa has lived in nursing homes with constant care. She is fed and hydrated by tubes. The staff changes her diapers regularly. She has had numerous health problems, but none have been life threatening. *In re Guardianship of Schiavo*, 780 So.2d 176, 177 (Fla. 2d DCA 2001) (*Schiavo I*).

For the first three years after this tragedy, Michael and Theresa's parents, Robert and Mary Schindler, enjoyed an amicable relationship. However, that relationship ended in 1993 and the parties literally stopped speaking to each other. In May of 1998, eight years after Theresa lost consciousness, Michael petitioned the guardianship court to authorize the

---

7. The trial court, in an extensive written order, declared that the law was unconstitutional as a violation of separation of powers, as a violation of the right of privacy and as unconstitutional retroactive legislation. The Second District Court of Appeal certified this case as one of great public importance and requiring immediate resolution by this Court. We have jurisdiction. *See* art. V, § 3(b)(5), Fla. Const.

termination of life-prolonging procedures. *See id.* By filing this petition, which the Schindlers opposed, Michael placed the difficult decision in the hands of the court.

The trial court, in an extensive written order, declared that the law was unconstitutional as a violation of separation of powers, as a violation of the right of privacy and as unconstitutional retroactive legislation. The Second District Court of Appeal certified this case as one of great public importance and requiring immediate resolution by this Court. We have jurisdiction. *See* art. V, § 3(b)(5), Fla. Const.

After a trial, at which both Michael and the Schindlers presented evidence, the guardianship court issued an extensive written order authorizing the discontinuance of artificial life support. The trial court found by clear and convincing evidence that Theresa Schiavo was in a persistent vegetative state and that Theresa would elect to cease life-prolonging procedures if she were competent to make her own decision. This order was affirmed on direct appeal, *see Schiavo I,* 780 So.2d at 177, and we denied review. *See In re Guardianship of Schiavo,* 789 So.2d 348 (Fla.2001).

The severity of Theresa's medical condition was explained by the Second District as follows

> The evidence is overwhelming that Theresa is in a permanent or persistent vegetative state. It is important to understand that a persistent vegetative state is not simply a coma. She is not asleep. She has cycles of apparent wakefulness and apparent sleep without any cognition or awareness. As she breathes, she often makes moaning sounds. Theresa has severe contractures of her hands, elbows, knees, and feet.

> Over the span of this last decade, Theresa's brain has deteriorated because of the lack of oxygen it suffered at the time of the heart attack. By mid 1996, the CAT scans of her brain showed a severely abnormal structure. At this point, much of her cerebral cortex is simply gone and has been replaced by cerebral spinal fluid. Medicine cannot cure this condition. Unless an act of God, a true miracle, were to recreate her brain, Theresa will always remain in an unconscious, reflexive state, totally dependent upon others to feed her and care for her most private needs. She could remain in this state for many years.

Schiavo I, 780 So.2d at 177. In affirming the trial court's order, the Second District concluded by stating:

> In the final analysis, the difficult question that faced the trial court was whether Theresa Marie Schindler Schiavo, not after a few weeks in a coma, but after ten years in a persistent vegetative state that has robbed her of most of her cerebrum and all but the most instinctive of neurological functions, with no hope of a medical cure but with sufficient money and strength of body to live indefinitely, would choose to continue the constant nursing care and the supporting tubes in hopes that a miracle would somehow recreate her missing brain tissue, or whether she would wish to permit a natural death process to take its course and for her family members and loved ones

to be free to continue their lives. After due consideration, we conclude that the trial judge had clear and convincing evidence to answer this question as he did.

Schiavo I, 780 So.2d at 180.

Although the guardianship court's final order authorizing the termination of life-prolonging procedures was affirmed on direct appeal, the litigation continued because the Schindlers began an attack on the final order. The Schindlers filed a motion for relief from judgment under Florida Rule of Civil Procedure 1.540(b)(2) and (3) in the guardianship court, alleging newly discovered evidence and intrinsic fraud. The Schindlers also filed a separate complaint in the civil division of the circuit court, challenging the final judgment of the guardianship court. *See In re Guardianship of Schiavo,* 792 So.2d 551, 555–56 (Fla. 2d DCA 2001) (*Schiavo II*).

The trial court determined that the post-judgment motion was untimely and the Schindlers appealed. The Second District agreed that the guardianship court had appropriately denied the rule 1.540(b)(2) and (3) motion as untimely. *See Schiavo II,* 792 So.2d at 558. The Second District also reversed an injunction entered in the case pending before the civil division of the circuit court. *See id.* at 562. However, the Second District determined that the Schindlers, as "interested parties," had standing to file either a motion for relief from judgment under Florida Rule of Civil Procedure 1.540(b)(5) or an independent action in the guardianship court to challenge the judgment on the ground that it is "no longer equitable for the trial court to enforce its earlier order." *Schiavo II,* 792 So.2d at 560 (quotation marks omitted). Nonetheless, the Second District pointedly cautioned

> that any proceeding to challenge a final order on this basis is extraordinary and should not be filed merely to delay an order with which an interested party disagrees or to retry an adversary proceeding. The interested party must establish that new circumstances make it no longer equitable to enforce the earlier order. In this case, if the Schindlers believe a valid basis for relief from the order exists, they must plead and prove newly discovered evidence of such a substantial nature that it proves either (1) that Mrs. Schiavo would not have made the decision to withdraw life-prolonging procedures fourteen months earlier when the final order was entered, or (2) that Mrs. Schiavo would make a different decision at this time based on developments subsequent to the earlier court order.

Id. at 554.

On remand, the Schindlers filed a timely motion for relief from judgment pursuant to rule 1.540(b)(5). *See In re Guardianship of Schiavo,* 800 So.2d 640, 642 (Fla. 2d DCA 2001) (*Schiavo III*). The trial court summarily denied the motion but the Second District reversed and remanded to the guardianship court for the purpose of conducting a limited evidentiary hearing:

Of the four issues resolved in the original trial ..., we conclude that the motion establishes a colorable entitlement only as to the fourth issue. As to that issue-whether there was clear and convincing evidence to support the determination that Mrs. Schiavo would choose to withdraw the life-prolonging procedures-the motion for relief from judgment alleges evidence of a new treatment that could dramatically improve Mrs. Schiavo's condition and allow her to have cognitive function to the level of speech. In our last opinion we stated that the Schindlers had "presented no medical evidence suggesting that any new treatment could restore to Mrs. Schiavo a level of function within the cerebral cortex that would allow her to understand her perceptions of sight and sound or to communicate or respond cognitively to those perceptions." *Schiavo II,* 792 So.2d at 560. Although we have expressed some lay skepticism about the new affidavits, the Schindlers now have presented some evidence, in the form of the affidavit of Dr. [Fred] Webber, of such a potential new treatment.

Id. at 645.

The Second District permitted the Schindlers to present evidence to establish by a preponderance of the evidence that the judgment was no longer equitable and specifically held:

To meet this burden, they must establish that new treatment offers sufficient promise of increased cognitive function in Mrs. Schiavo's cerebral cortex-significantly improving the quality of Mrs. Schiavo's life-so that she herself would elect to undergo this treatment and would reverse the prior decision to withdraw life-prolonging procedures.

Id. The Second District required an additional set of medical examinations of Theresa and instructed that one of the physicians must be a new, independent physician selected either by the agreement of the parties or, if they could not agree, by the appointment of the guardianship court. *See id.* at 646.

After conducting a hearing for the purpose set forth in the Second District's decision, the guardianship court denied the Schindlers' motion for relief from judgment. *See In re Guardianship of Schiavo,* 851 So.2d 182, 183 (Fla. 2d DCA 2003) (*Schiavo IV*). In reviewing the trial court's order, the Second District explained that it was "not reviewing a final judgment in this appellate proceeding. The final judgment was entered several years ago and has already been affirmed by this court." *Id.* at 185–86. However, the Second District carefully examined the record:

Despite our decision that the appropriate standard of review is abuse of discretion, this court has closely examined all of the evidence in this record. We have repeatedly examined the videotapes, not merely watching short segments but carefully observing the tapes in their entirety. We have examined the brain scans with the eyes of educated laypersons and considered the explanations provided by the doctors in the transcripts. We have concluded that, if we were called upon to review the guardianship court's decision de novo, we would still affirm it.

Id. at 186. Finally, the Second District concluded its fourth opinion in the Schiavo case with the following observation:

> The judges on this panel are called upon to make a collective, objective decision concerning a question of law. Each of us, however, has our own family, our own loved ones, our own children. From our review of the videotapes of Mrs. Schiavo, despite the irrefutable evidence that her cerebral cortex has sustained the most severe of irreparable injuries, we understand why a parent who had raised and nurtured a child from conception would hold out hope that some level of cognitive function remained. If Mrs. Schiavo were our own daughter, we could not but hold to such a faith.

> But in the end, this case is not about the aspirations that loving parents have for their children. It is about Theresa Schiavo's right to make her own decision, independent of her parents and independent of her husband.... It may be unfortunate that when families cannot agree, the best forum we can offer for this private, personal decision is a public courtroom and the best decision-maker we can provide is a judge with no prior knowledge of the ward, but the law currently provides no better solution that adequately protects the interests of promoting the value of life. We have previously affirmed the guardianship court's decision in this regard, and we now affirm the denial of a motion for relief from that judgment.

Id. at 186–87. We denied review, *see In re Guardianship of Schiavo,* 855 So.2d 621 (Fla.2003), and Theresa's nutrition and hydration tube was removed on October 15, 2003.

On October 21, 2003, the Legislature enacted chapter 2003–418, the Governor signed the Act into law, and the Governor issued executive order No. 03–201 to stay the continued withholding of nutrition and hydration from Theresa. The nutrition and hydration tube was reinserted pursuant to the Governor's executive order.

On the same day, Michael Schiavo brought the action for declaratory judgment in the circuit court. Relying on undisputed facts and legal argument, the circuit court entered a final summary judgment on May 6, 2004, in favor of Michael Schiavo, finding the Act unconstitutional both on its face and as applied to Theresa. Specifically, the circuit court found that chapter 2003–418 was unconstitutional on its face as an unlawful delegation of legislative authority and as a violation of the right to privacy, and unconstitutional as applied because it allowed the Governor to encroach upon the judicial power and to retroactively abolish Theresa's vested right to privacy.[2]

---

2. Because we find the separation of powers issue to be dispositive in this case, we do not reach the other constitutional issues addressed by the circuit court.

We begin our discussion by emphasizing that our task in this case is to review the constitutionality of chapter 2003–418, not to reexamine the guardianship court's orders directing the removal of Theresa's nutrition and hydration tube, or to review the Second District's numerous decisions in the guardianship case. Although we recognize that the parties continue to dispute the findings made in the prior proceedings, these proceedings are relevant to our decision only to the extent that they occurred and resulted in a final judgment directing the withdrawal of life-prolonging procedures.

The language of chapter 2003–418 is clear. It states in full:

Section 1. (1) The Governor shall have the authority to issue a one-time stay to prevent the withholding of nutrition and hydration from a patient if, as of October 15, 2003:

(a) That patient has no written advance directive;

(b) The court has found that patient to be in a persistent vegetative state;

(c) That patient has had nutrition and hydration withheld; and

(d) A member of that patient's family has challenged the withholding of nutrition and hydration.

(2) The Governor's authority to issue the stay expires 15 days after the effective date of this act, and the expiration of the authority does not impact the validity or the effect of any stay issued pursuant to this act. The Governor may lift the stay authorized under this act at any time. A person may not be held civilly liable and is not subject to regulatory or disciplinary sanctions for taking any action to comply with a stay issued by the Governor pursuant to this act.

(3) Upon issuance of a stay, the chief judge of the circuit court shall appoint a guardian ad litem for the patient to make recommendations to the Governor and the court.

Section 2. This act shall take effect upon becoming a law.

Ch.2003–418, Laws of Fla.

Thus, chapter 2003–418 allowed the Governor to issue a stay to prevent the withholding of nutrition and hydration from a patient under the circumstances provided for in subsections (1)(a)–(d). Under the fifteen-day sunset provision, the Governor's authority to issue the stay expired on November 5, 2003. *See id.* The Governor's authority to lift the stay continues indefinitely.

The cornerstone of American democracy known as separation of powers recognizes three separate branches of government-the executive, the legislative, and the judicial-each with its own powers and responsibilities. In Florida, the constitutional doctrine has been expressly codified in article II, section 3 of the Florida Constitution, which not only divides state government into three branches but also expressly prohibits one branch from exercising the powers of the other two branches:

Branches of Government.—The powers of the state government shall be divided into legislative, executive and judicial branches. No person belonging to one branch shall exercise any powers appertaining to either of the other branches unless expressly provided herein.

"This Court ... has traditionally applied a strict separation of powers doctrine," *State v. Cotton,* 769 So.2d 345, 353 (Fla.2000), and has explained that this doctrine "encompasses two fundamental prohibitions. The first is that no branch may encroach upon the powers of another. The second is that no branch may delegate to another branch its constitutionally assigned power." *Chiles v. Children A, B, C, D, E, & F,* 589 So.2d 260, 264 (Fla.1991) (citation omitted).

The circuit court found that chapter 2003–418 violates both of these prohibitions, and we address each separately below. Our standard of review is de novo. *See Major League Baseball v. Morsani,* 790 So.2d 1071, 1074 (Fla.2001) (stating that a trial court's ruling on a motion for summary judgment posing a pure question of law is subject to de novo review).

. . .

Under the express separation of powers provision in our state constitution, "the judiciary is a coequal branch of the Florida government vested with the sole authority to exercise the judicial power," and "the legislature cannot, short of constitutional amendment, reallocate the balance of power expressly delineated in the constitution among the three coequal branches." *Children A, B, C, D, E, & F,* 589 So.2d at 268–69; *see also Office of State Attorney v. Parrotino,* 628 So.2d 1097, 1099 (Fla.1993) ("[T]he legislature cannot take actions that would undermine the independence of Florida's judicial ... offices.").

As the United States Supreme Court has explained, the power of the judiciary is "not merely to rule on cases, but to *decide* them, subject to review only by superior courts" and "[h]aving achieved finality ... a judicial decision becomes the last word of the judicial department with regard to a particular case or controversy." *Plaut,* 514 U.S. at 218–19, 227, 115 S.Ct. 1447. Moreover, "purely judicial acts ... are not subject to review as to their accuracy by the Governor." *In re Advisory Opinion to the Governor,* 213 So.2d 716, 720 (Fla.1968); *see also Children A, B, C, D, E, & F,* 589 So.2d at 269 ("The judicial branch cannot be subject in *331 any manner to oversight by the executive branch.").

In *Advisory Opinion,* the Governor asked the Court whether he had the "constitutional authority to review the judicial accuracy and propriety of [a judge] and to suspend him from office if it does not appear ... that the Judge has exercised proper judicial discretion and wisdom." 213 So.2d at 718. The Court agreed that the Governor had the authority to suspend a judge on the grounds of incompetency "if the physical or mental incompetency is established and determined within the Judicial Branch by a court of competent jurisdiction." *Id.* at 720. However, the Court held that the Governor did not have the power to "review the judicial discretion and wisdom of a ... Judge while he is engaged in the judicial process." *Id.* The

Court explained that article V of the Florida Constitution provides for appellate review for the benefit of litigants aggrieved by the decisions of the lower court, and that "[a]ppeal is the exclusive remedy." *Id.*

In this case, the undisputed facts show that the guardianship court authorized Michael to proceed with the discontinuance of Theresa's life support after the issue was fully litigated in a proceeding in which the Schindlers were afforded the opportunity to present evidence on all issues. This order as well as the order denying the Schindlers' motion for relief from judgment were affirmed on direct appeal. *See Schiavo I*, 780 So.2d at 177; *Schiavo IV*, 851 So.2d at 183. The Schindlers sought review in this Court, which was denied. Thereafter, the tube was removed. Subsequently, pursuant to the Governor's executive order, the nutrition and hydration tube was reinserted. Thus, the Act, as applied in this case, resulted in an executive order that effectively reversed a properly rendered final judgment and thereby constituted an unconstitutional encroachment on the power that has been reserved for the independent judiciary. *Cf. Bailey*, 10 Fla. at 249–50 (noting that had the statute under review "directed a rehearing, the hearing of the case would necessarily carry with it the right to set aside the judgment of the Court, and there would be unquestionably an exercise of judicial power").

The Governor and amici assert that the Act does not reverse a final court order because an order to discontinue life-prolonging procedures may be challenged at any time prior to the death of the ward. In advancing this argument, the Governor and amici rely on the Second District's conclusion that as long as the ward is alive, an order discontinuing life-prolonging procedures "is subject to recall and is executory in nature." *Schiavo II*, 792 So.2d at 559. However, the Second District did not hold that the guardian-ship court's order was not a final judgment but, rather, that the Schindlers, as interested parties, could file a motion for relief from judgment under Florida Rule of Civil Procedure 1.540(b)(5) if they sufficiently alleged that it is no longer equitable that the judgment have prospective application. *See id.* at 561. Rule 1.540(b) expressly states that a motion filed pursuant to its terms "does not affect the finality of a judgment." Further, the fact that a final judgment may be subject to recall under a rule of procedure, if certain circumstances can be proved, does not negate its finality. Unless and until the judgment is vacated by judicial order, it is "the last word of the judicial department with regard to a particular case or controversy." *Plaut*, 514 U.S. at 227, 115 S.Ct. 1447.

Under procedures enacted by the Legislature, effective both before the passage of the Act and after its fifteen-day effective period expired, circuit courts are charged with adjudicating issues regarding incompetent individ-uals. The trial courts of this State are called upon to make many of the most difficult decisions facing society. In proceedings under chapter 765, Florida Statutes (2003), these decisions literally affect the lives or deaths of patients. The trial courts also handle other weighty decisions affecting the welfare of children such as termination of parental rights and child custo-dy. *See* § 61.13(2)(b)(1), Fla. Stat. (2003) ("The court shall determine all matters relating to custody of each minor child of the parties in accordance with the best interests of the child and in accordance with the Uniform Child Custody Jurisdiction and Enforcement Act."); § 39.801(2), Fla. Stat. (2003) ("The circuit court shall have exclusive original jurisdiction of a proceeding involving termination of parental rights."). When the prescribed procedures are followed according to our rules of court and the governing statutes, a final judgment is issued, and all post-judgment procedures are followed, it is without question an invasion of the authority of the judicial branch for the Legislature to pass a law that allows the executive branch to interfere with the final judicial determination in a case. That is precisely what occurred here and for that reason the Act is unconstitutional as applied to Theresa Schiavo.

In addition to concluding that the Act is unconstitutional as applied in this case because it encroaches on the power of the judicial branch, we further conclude that the Act is unconstitutional on its face because it delegates legislative power to the Governor. The Legislature is permitted to transfer subordinate functions "to permit administration of legislative policy by an agency with the expertise and flexibility to deal with complex and fluid conditions." *Microtel, Inc. v. Fla. Public Serv. Comm'n,* 464 So.2d 1189, 1191 (Fla.1985). However, under article II, section 3 of the constitution the Legislature "may not delegate the power to enact a law or the right to exercise unrestricted discretion in applying the law." *Sims v. State,* 754 So.2d 657, 668 (Fla.2000). This prohibition, known as the nondelegation doctrine, requires that "fundamental and primary policy decisions ... be made by members of the legislature who are elected to perform those tasks, and [that the] administration of legislative programs must be pursuant to some minimal standards and guidelines ascertainable by reference to the enactment establishing the program." *Askew v. Cross Key Waterways,* 372 So.2d 913, 925 (Fla.1978); *see also Avatar Dev. Corp. v. State,* 723 So.2d 199, 202 (Fla.1998) (citing *Askew* with approval). In other words, statutes granting power to the executive branch "must clearly announce adequate standards to guide ... in the execution of the powers delegated. The statute must so clearly define the power delegated that the [executive] is precluded from acting through whim, showing favoritism, or exercising unbridled discretion." *Lewis v. Bank of Pasco County,* 346 So.2d 53, 55–56 (Fla.1976). The requirement that the Legislature provide sufficient guidelines also ensures the availability of meaningful judicial review:

> In the final analysis it is the courts, upon a challenge to the exercise or nonexercise of administrative action, which must determine whether the administrative agency has performed consistently with the mandate of the legislature. When legislation is so lacking in guidelines that neither the agency nor the courts can determine whether the agency is carrying out the intent of the legislature in its conduct, then, in fact, the agency becomes the lawgiver rather than the administrator of the law.

Askew, 372 So.2d at 918–19.

We have recognized that the "specificity of the guidelines [set forth in the legislation] will depend on the complexity of the subject and the 'degree of difficulty involved in articulating finite standards.' " *Brown v. Apalachee Regional Planning Council,* 560 So.2d 782, 784 (Fla.1990) (quoting *Askew,* 372 So.2d at 918). However, we have also made clear that "[e]ven where a general approach would be more practical than a detailed scheme of legislation, enactments may not be drafted in terms so general and unrestrictive that administrators are left without standards for the guidance of their official acts." *State Dep't of Citrus v. Griffin,* 239 So.2d 577, 581 (Fla.1970).

In both *Askew* and *Lewis,* this Court held that the respective statutes under review violated the nondelegation doctrine because they failed to provide the executive branch with adequate guidelines and criteria. In *Askew,* the Court invalidated a statute that directed the executive branch to designate certain areas of the state as areas of critical state concern but did not contain sufficient standards to allow "a reviewing court to ascertain whether the priorities recognized by the Administration Commission comport with the intent of the legislature." 372 So.2d at 919. The statute in question enunciated the following criteria for the Division of State Planning to use in identifying a particular area as one of critical state concern:

(a) An area containing, or having a significant impact upon, environmental, historical, natural, or archaeological resources of regional or statewide importance.

(b) An area significantly affected by, or having a significant effect upon, an existing or proposed major public facility or other area of major public investment.

(c) A proposed area of major development potential, which may include a proposed site of a new community, designated in a state land development plan.

Id. at 914–15 (quoting section 380.05(2), Florida Statutes (1975)). The Court concluded that the criteria for designation of an area of critical concern set forth in subsections (a) and (b) were defective because they gave the executive agency "the fundamental legislative task of determining which geographic areas and resources [were] in greatest need of protection." *Id.* at 919. With regard to subsection (a), this Court agreed with the district court that the deficiency resulted from the Legislature's failure to "establish or provide for establishing priorities or other means for identifying and choosing among the resources the Act is intended to preserve." *Id.* (quoting *Cross Key Waterways v. Askew,* 351 So.2d 1062, 1069 (Fla. 1st DCA 1977)). Subsection (b) suffered a similar defect by expanding "the choice to include areas which in unstated ways affect or are affected by any 'major public facility' which is defined in Section 380.031(10), or any 'major public investment,' which is not." *Id.*

Lewis involved a statute that gave the state comptroller the unrestricted power to release banking records to the public that were otherwise considered confidential under the Public Records Act. *See* 346 So.2d at 55. The statute at issue provided in pertinent part:

Division records.

All bank or trust company applications, investigation reports, examination reports, and related information, including any duly authorized copies in possession of any banking organization, foreign banking corporation, or any other person or agency, shall be confidential communications, other than such documents as are required by law to be published, and shall not be made public, unless *with the consent of the department,* pursuant to a court order, or in response to legislative subpoena as provided by law.

Lewis, 346 So.2d at 54 (quoting section 658.10, Florida Statutes (1975)) (alteration in original).

This Court held that the law was "couched in vague and uncertain terms or is so broad in scope that ... it must be held unconstitutional as attempting to grant to the ... [comptroller] the power to say *what the law shall be.*" 346 So.2d at 56 (quoting *Sarasota County v. Barg,* 302 So.2d 737, 742 (Fla.1974)) (alterations in original).

In this case, the circuit court found that chapter 2003–418 contains no guidelines or standards that "would serve to limit the Governor from exercising completely unrestricted discretion in applying the law to" those who fall within its terms. The circuit court explained:

The terms of the Act affirmatively confirm the discretionary power conferred upon the Governor. He is given the "authority to issue a one-time stay to prevent the withholding of nutrition and hydration from a patient" under certain circumstances but, he is not required to do so. Likewise, the act provides that the Governor "*may* lift the stay authorized under this act at any time. The Governor *may* revoke the stay upon a finding that a change in the condition of the patient warrants revocation." (Emphasis added). In both instances there is nothing to provide the Governor with any direction or guidelines for the exercise of this delegated authority. The Act does not suggest what constitutes "a change in condition of the patient" that could "warrant revocation." Even when such an undefined "change" occurs, the Governor is not compelled to act. The Act confers upon the Governor the unfettered discretion to determine what the terms of the Act mean and when, or if, he may act under it.

We agree with this analysis. In enacting chapter 2003–418, the Legislature failed to provide any standards by which the Governor should determine whether, in any given case, a stay should be issued and how long a stay should remain in effect. Further, the Legislature has failed to provide any criteria for lifting the stay. This absolute, unfettered discretion to decide whether to issue and then when to lift a stay makes the Governor's decision virtually unreviewable.

The Governor asserts that by enacting chapter 2003–418 the Legislature determined that he should be permitted to act as proxy for an incompetent patient in very narrow circumstances and, therefore, that his discretion is limited by the provisions of chapter 765. However, the Act does not refer to the provisions of chapter 765. Specifically, the Act does not amend section 765.401(1), Florida Statutes (2003), which sets forth an order of priority for determining who should act as proxy for an incapacitated patient who has no advance directive. Nor does the Act require that the Governor's decision be made in conformity with the requirement of section 765.401 that the proxy's decision be based on "the decision the proxy reasonably believes that patient would have made under the circumstances" or, if there is no indication of what the patient would have chosen, in the patient's best interests. § 765.401(2)–(3), Fla. Stat. (2003). Finally, the Act does not provide for review of the Governor's decision as proxy as required by section 765.105, Florida Statutes (2003). In short, there is no indication in the language of chapter 2003–418 that the Legislature intended the Governor's discretion to be limited in any way. Even if we were to read chapter 2003–418 in pari materia with chapter 765, as the Governor suggests, there is nothing in chapter 765 to guide the Governor's discretion in issuing a stay because chapter 765 does not contemplate that a proxy will have the type of open-ended power delegated to the Governor under the Act.

We also reject the Governor's argument that this legislation provides an additional layer of due process protection to those who are unable to communicate their wishes regarding end-of-life decisions. Parts I, II, III, and IV of chapter 765, enacted by the Legislature in 1992 and amended several times,[4] provide detailed protections for those who are adjudicated

---

4. Prior to this Court's decision in *In re Guardianship of Browning,* 568 So.2d 4 (Fla. 1990), statutory law provided a procedure by which a competent adult could provide a declaration instructing his or her physician to withhold or withdraw life-prolonging procedures, or designating another to make the treatment decision. *See* §§ 765.01–765.17, Fla. Stat. (1991). This law had been in effect since 1984.

... [I]n 1999, the Legislature rewrote the definitions section and defined life-prolonging procedures as:

> any medical procedure, treatment, or intervention, including artificially provided sustenance and hydration, which sustains, restores, or supplants a spontaneous vital function. The term does not include the administration of medication or performance of medical procedure, when such medication or procedure is deemed necessary to provide comfort care or to alleviate pain.

Ch. 99–331, § 16 at 3464, Laws of Fla.; § 765.101(10), Fla. Stat. (2003).

In order to determine who is to act as a patient's proxy, the Legislature set forth a detailed order of priority. *See* ch. 92–199, § 5 at 1851. This order of priority has been amended only once since 1992 to allow a clinical social worker to act as the patient's proxy if none of the other potential proxies are available. *See* ch.2003–57, § 5, Laws of Fla. The Legislature also provided that a "proxy's decision to withhold or withdraw life-prolonging procedures must by supported by clear and convincing evidence that the decision would have been the one the patient would have chosen had [the patient] been competent." Ch. 92–199, § 5 at 1851, Laws of Fla.; *see also* § 765.401(3), Fla. Stat. (2003).

Finally, the Legislature provided for judicial review of a proxy's decision if "[t]he patient's family, the health care facility, or the attending physician, or any other interested person who may reasonably be expected to be directly affected by the surrogate or proxy's decision ... believes (1) The surrogate or proxy's decision is incompetent, including that the proxy's decision be based on what the patient would have chosen under the circumstances or is in the patient's best interest, and be supported by competent, substantial evidence. *See* § 765.401(2)–(3). Chapter 765 also provides for judicial review if "[t]he patient's family, the health care facility, or the attending physician, or any other interested person who may reasonably be expected to be directly affected by the surrogate or proxy's decision ... believes [that] [t]he surrogate or proxy's decision is not in accord with the patient's known desires or the provisions of this chapter." § 765.105(1), Fla. Stat. (2003).

In contrast to the protections set forth in chapter 765, chapter 2003–418's standardless, open-ended delegation of authority by the Legislature to the Governor provides no guarantee that the incompetent patient's right to withdraw life-prolonging procedures will in fact be honored. *See In re Guardianship of Browning,* 568 So.2d 4, 12 (Fla.1990) (reaffirming that an incompetent person has the same right to refuse medical treatment as a competent person). As noted above, the Act does not even require that the Governor consider the patient's wishes in deciding whether to issue a stay, and instead allows a unilateral decision by the Governor to stay the withholding of life-prolonging procedures without affording any procedural process to the patient.

Finally, we reject the Governor's argument that the Legislature's grant of authority to issue the stay under chapter 2003–418 is a valid exercise of the state's parens patriae power. Although unquestionably the Legislature may enact laws to protect those citizens who are incapable of protecting their own interests, *see, e.g., In re Byrne,* 402 So.2d 383 (Fla.1981), such laws must comply with the constitution. Chapter 2003–418 fails to do so.

Moreover, the argument that the Act broadly protects those who cannot protect themselves is belied by the case-specific criteria under which the Governor can exercise his discretion. The Act applies only if a court has found the individual to be in a persistent vegetative state and food and hydration have been ordered withdrawn. It does not authorize the Governor to intervene if a person in a persistent vegetative state is dependent upon another form of life support. Nor does the Act apply to a person who is not in a persistent vegetative state but a court finds, contrary to the wishes of another family member, that life support should be withdrawn. In theory, the Act could have applied during its fifteen-day window to more than one person, but it is undeniable that in fact the criteria fit only Theresa Schiavo.

In sum, although chapter 2003–418 applies to a limited class of people, it provides no criteria to guide the Governor's decision about whether to act. In addition, once the Governor has issued a stay as provided for in the Act, there are no criteria for the Governor to evaluate in deciding whether to lift the stay. Thus, chapter 2003–418 allows the Governor to act "through whim, show [ ] favoritism, or exercis[e] unbridled discretion,"

not in accord with the patient's known desires or the provisions of this chapter." Ch. 92–199, § 2 at 1842, Laws of Fla.; § 765.105, Fla. Stat. (2003).

Lewis, 346 So.2d at 56, and is therefore an unconstitutional delegation of legislative authority.

We recognize that the tragic circumstances underlying this case make it difficult to put emotions aside and focus solely on the legal issue presented. We are not insensitive to the struggle that all members of Theresa's family have endured since she fell unconscious in 1990. However, we are a nation of laws and we must govern our decisions by the rule of law and not by our own emotions. Our hearts can fully comprehend the grief so fully demonstrated by Theresa's family members on this record. But our hearts are not the law. What is in the Constitution always must prevail over emotion. Our oaths as judges require that this principle is our polestar, and it alone.

As the Second District noted in one of the multiple appeals in this case, we "are called upon to make a collective, objective decision concerning a question of law. Each of us, however, has our own family, our own loved ones, our own children.... But in the end, this case is not about the aspirations that loving parents have for their children." *Schiavo IV,* 851 So.2d at 186. Rather, as our decision today makes clear, this case is about maintaining the integrity of a constitutional system of government with three independent and coequal branches, none of which can either encroach upon the powers of another branch or improperly delegate its own responsibilities.

The continuing vitality of our system of separation of powers precludes the other two branches from nullifying the judicial branch's final orders. If the Legislature with the assent of the Governor can do what was attempted here, the judicial branch would be subordinated to the final directive of the other branches. Also subordinated would be the rights of individuals, including the well established privacy right to self determination. *See Browning,* 568 So.2d at 11–13. No court judgment could ever be considered truly final and no constitutional right truly secure, because the precedent of this case would hold to the contrary. Vested rights could be stripped away based on popular clamor. The essential core of what the Founding Fathers sought to change from their experience with English rule would be lost, especially their belief that our courts exist precisely to preserve the rights of individuals, even when doing so is contrary to popular will.

The trial court's decision regarding Theresa Schiavo was made in accordance with the procedures and protections set forth by the judicial branch and in accordance with the statutes passed by the Legislature in effect at that time. That decision is final and the Legislature's attempt to alter that final adjudication is unconstitutional as applied to Theresa Schiavo. Further, even if there had been no final judgment in this case, the Legislature provided the Governor constitutionally inadequate standards for the application of the legislative authority delegated in chapter 2003–418. Because chapter 2003–418 runs afoul of article II, section 3 of the Florida Constitution in both respects, we affirm the circuit court's final summary judgment.

■ WELLS, ANSTEAD, LEWIS, QUINCE, CANTERO and Bell, JJ., CONCUR.

NOTE

The contest between Michael Schiavo, Terri Schiavo's husband, and her parents over who should have the authority to remove Terri's nutrition and hydration tube, precipitated intense national debate. The contest concerned who should make the medical decisions when the incapacitated person has not made his or her wishes known. Following the Florida Supreme Court decision *supra*, the United States Supreme Court refused to hear an appeal brought by the governor in January 2005. Then, one day prior to when Terri Schiavo's feeding tube was to be removed at the request of the husband, the Florida Circuit Judge ordered a temporary stay upon a motion made by the parents that Terri's husband was not acting in his wife's best interests because of his personal involvement with another woman. The court eventually rejected the parents' assertion, the stay was then lifted, and the tube was removed on March 18, 2005. Consistently, the husband's position was that his wife had told him she would not want to continue living as she was then.

Sensing the federal courts would not intervene to overrule the husband's decision, the United States Senate and House of Representatives deliberated overnight to pass emergency legislation "for the relief of the parents of" Terri Schiavo. The president signed the legislation—The Schiavo Bill—during the pre-dawn hours on March 21, 2005. In essence, the federal legislation sought to provide to the parents of Terri Schiavo a federal cause of action regardless of whether there still remained state causes of action, and to issue any injunctive relief to safeguard Terri Schiavo's rights to continued medical treatment. In spite of the federal statute, the federal district court refused to issue injunctive relief, most importantly to reinsert the feeding tube, and the parents appealed again to the Florida Supreme Court and the United States Supreme Court. Both courts declined to intervene and Terri Schiavo died on March 31, 2005, thirteen days after the feeding tube was removed. Her husband ordered an autopsy on his wife to discover the extent of her brain damage, and then her body was cremated over the objections of her parents. *See* Laura Stanton, *The Battle over Terri Schiavo*, WASH. POST, Apr. 1, 2005, at A13.

The legal struggle between the spouse and the parents sparked intense legal, medical and religious controversy. *See, e.g.*, Timothy E. Quill, *Terri Schiavo—A Tragedy Compounded*, 352 NEW ENG. J. MED. 1630 (2005); Editorial, *Extraordinary Means*, COMMONWEAL, Apr. 8, 2005, at 5. The cost in Medicaid dollars of caring for persons such as Terri Schiavo is also being debated. *See, e.g.*, Jonathan Weisman & Ceci Connolly, *Schiavo Case Puts Face on Rising Medical Costs*, WASH. POST, Mar. 28, 2005, at A13. But the most significant impact may be the intense interest in advance medical planning as citizens wish to avoid placing themselves or their families in similar circumstances. A number of web sites offer information and forms concerning health care directives. *See, e.g.*, AGING WITH DIGNITY, at http://www.agingwithdignity.org (last visited Apr. 12, 2005); NAT'L HOSPICE & PALLIATIVE CARE ORG., at http://www.nhpco.org (last visited Apr. 12, 2005); MAYO CLINIC'S ADVANCE DIRECTIVE RES., at http://www.mayoclinic.com (last visited Apr. 12, 2005).

CHAPTER IV

MATRIMONIAL BREAKDOWN: GROUNDS AND JURISDICTION FOR DISSOLUTION OF MARRIAGE

B. GROUNDS AND DEFENSES FOR DIVORCE

1. THE FAULT SCHEME

After the section on proving adultery, please add at page 305:

In re Blanchflower

New Hampshire Supreme Court, 2003.
150 N.H. 226, 834 A.2d 1010.

■ NADEAU, J.

Robin Mayer, co-respondent in the divorce proceedings of the petitioner, David G. Blanchflower, and the respondent, Sian E. Blanchflower, challenges an order of the Lebanon Family Division (*Cyr*, J.) denying her motion to dismiss the petitioner's amended ground for divorce of adultery. *See* RSA 458:7, II (Supp.2002). We accepted this matter as an interlocutory appeal under Supreme Court Rule 8, and now reverse and remand.

The record supports the following facts. The petitioner filed for divorce from the respondent on grounds of irreconcilable differences. He subsequently moved to amend the petition to assert the fault ground of adultery under RSA 458:7, II. Specifically, the petitioner alleged that the respondent has been involved in a "continuing adulterous affair" with the co-respondent, a woman, resulting in the irremediable breakdown of the parties' marriage. The co-respondent sought to dismiss the amended petition, contending that a homosexual relationship between two people, one of whom is married, does not constitute adultery under RSA 458:7, II. The trial court disagreed, and the co-respondent brought this appeal.

Before addressing the merits, we note this appeal is not about the status of homosexual relationships in our society or the formal recognition of homosexual unions. The narrow question before us is whether a homosexual sexual relationship between a married person and another constitutes adultery within the meaning of RSA 458:7, II.

RSA 458:7 provides, in part: "A divorce from the bonds of matrimony shall be decreed in favor of the innocent party for any of the following causes: ... II. Adultery of either party." The statute does not define adultery. *Id.* Accordingly, we must discern its meaning according to our rules of statutory construction.

"In matters of statutory interpretation, this court is the final arbiter of the intent of the legislature as expressed in the words of a statute considered as a whole." *Wegner v. Prudential Prop. & Cas. Ins. Co.,* 148 N.H. 107, 108, 803 A.2d 598 (2002) (quotation omitted). We first look to the language of the statute itself and, where terms are not defined therein, "we ascribe to them their plain and ordinary meanings." *Id.*

The plain and ordinary meaning of adultery is "voluntary sexual intercourse between a married man and someone other than his wife or between a married woman and someone other than her husband." *Webster's Third New International Dictionary 30* (unabridged ed.1961). Although the definition does not specifically state that the "someone" with whom one commits adultery must be of the opposite gender, it does require sexual intercourse.

The plain and ordinary meaning of sexual intercourse is "sexual connection esp. between humans: COITUS, COPULATION." *Webster's Third New International Dictionary* 2082. Coitus is defined to require "insertion of the penis in the vagina[ ]," *Webster's Third New International Dictionary* 441, which clearly can only take place between persons of the opposite gender.

We also note that "[a] law means what it meant to its framers and its mere repassage does not alter that meaning." *Appeal of Naswa Motor Inn,* 144 N.H. 89, 91, 738 A.2d 349 (1999) (quotation omitted). The statutory compilation in which the provision now codified as RSA 458:7 first appeared is the Revised Statutes of 1842. *See RS 148:3* (1842). No definition of adultery was contained in that statute. *See id.* Our cases from that approximate time period, however, support the inference that adultery meant intercourse. *See Adams v. Adams,* 20 N.H. 299, 301 (1850); *Burns v. Burns,* 68 N.H. 33, 34, 44 A. 76 (1894).

Cases from this period also indicate that adultery as a ground for divorce was equated with the crime of adultery and was alleged as such in libels for divorce. *See, e.g., Sheafe v. Sheafe,* 24 N.H. 564, 564 (1852); *White v. White,* 45 N.H. 121, 121 (1863). Although the criminal adultery statute in the 1842 compilation also did not define adultery, *see RS 219:1* (1842), roughly contemporaneous case law is instructive: "Adultery is committed whenever there is an intercourse from which spurious issue may arise...." *State v. Wallace,* 9 N.H. 515, 517 (1838); *see also State v. Taylor,* 58 N.H. 331, 331 (1878) (same). As "spurious issue" can only arise from intercourse between a man and a woman, criminal adultery could only be committed with a person of the opposite gender.

We note that the current criminal adultery statute still requires sexual intercourse: "A person is guilty of a class B misdemeanor if, being a married person, he engages in sexual intercourse with another not his spouse or, being unmarried, engages in sexual intercourse with another known by him to be married." RSA 645:3 (1996). Based upon the foregoing, we conclude that adultery under RSA 458:7, II does not include homosexual relationships.

We reject the petitioner's argument that an interpretation of adultery that excludes homosexual conduct subjects homosexuals and heterosexuals to unequal treatment, "contrary to New Hampshire's public policy of equality and prohibition of discrimination based on sex and sexual orientation." Homosexuals and heterosexuals engaging in the same acts are treated the same because our interpretation of the term "adultery" excludes all non-coital sex acts, whether between persons of the same or opposite gender. The only distinction is that persons of the same gender cannot, by definition, engage in the one act that constitutes adultery under the statute.

The petitioner also argues that "[p]ublic policy would be well served by applying the same law to a cheating spouse, whether the promiscuous spouse chooses a paramour of the same sex or the opposite sex." This argument is tied to the premise, as argued by the petitioner, that "[t]he purpose underlying [the adultery] fault ground is based upon the fundamental concept of marital loyalty and public policy's disfavor of one spouse's violation of the marriage contract with another."

We have not, however, seen any such purpose expressed by the legislature. As noted above, the concept of adultery was premised upon a specific act. To include in that concept other acts of a sexual nature, whether between heterosexuals or homosexuals, would change beyond recognition this well-established ground for divorce and likely lead to countless new marital cases alleging adultery, for strategic purposes. In any event, "it is not the function of the judiciary to provide for present needs by an extension of past legislation." *Naswa Motor Inn*, 144 N.H. at 92, 738 A.2d 349 (quotation and brackets omitted). Similarly, "we will not undertake the extraordinary step of creating legislation where none exists. Rather, matters of public policy are reserved for the legislature." In the *Matter of Plaisted & Plaisted*, 149 N.H. 522, 526, 824 A.2d 148 (2003).

The dissent defines adultery not as a specific act of intercourse, but as "extramarital intimate sexual activity with another." This standard would permit a hundred different judges and masters to decide just what individual acts are so sexually intimate as to meet the definition. The dilemma faced by Justice Stewart and his fellow justices applying their personal standards to the issue of pornography in movies demonstrates the value of a clear objective definition of adultery in marital cases. *See Jacobellis v. Ohio*, 378 U.S. 184, 84 S.Ct. 1676, 12 L.Ed.2d 793 (1964).

We are also unpersuaded by the dissent's contention that "[i]t is improbable that the legislature intended to require an innocent spouse in a divorce action to prove the specific intimate sexual acts in which the guilty spouse engaged." Citing *Jeanson v. Jeanson*, 96 N.H. 308, 309, 75 A.2d 718 (1950), the dissent notes that adultery usually has no eyewitnesses and therefore "ordinarily must be proved by circumstantial evidence." While this is true, it does not support the dissent's point. For over a hundred and fifty years judges, lawyers and clients have understood that adultery meant intercourse as we have defined it. It is an act determined not by the subjective test of an individual justice but by an objective determination based upon the facts. What must be proved to establish adultery and what evidence may be used to prove it are separate issues. Adultery cases have always required proof of the specific sexual act engaged in, namely, sexual intercourse. That circumstantial evidence may be used to establish the act does not negate or undermine the requirement of proof that the act actually occurred. "*Jeanson* is no authority for the proposition that evidence justifying nothing more than suspicion will suffice to prove the adultery suspected." *Yergeau v. Yergeau,* 132 N.H. 659, 663, 569 A.2d 237 (1990).

Finally the petitioner contends that this appeal is procedurally improper because it was based upon the trial court's denial of an interlocutory appeal and lacked the trial court's signature. On January 24, 2003, we invited the parties to file memoranda addressing whether the trial court's denial of the co-respondent's motion for interlocutory appeal should be reversed and the case accepted for appellate review. The petitioner submitted a memorandum, as did the other parties. After considering the parties' submissions, we issued an order waiving the formal requirements of New Hampshire Supreme Court Rule 8 and treating the co-respondent's motion to dismiss amended petition as an interlocutory appeal pursuant to Rule 8. We have thus already ruled on the issue the petitioner now asserts and we decline to reconsider it.

Reversed and remanded.

■ DALIANIS and DUGGAN, JJ., concurred; BROCK, C.J., and BRODERICK, J., dissented.

■ BROCK, C.J., and BRODERICK, J., dissenting.

. . .

The purpose of permitting fault-based divorces is to provide some measure of relief to an innocent spouse for the offending conduct of a guilty spouse. *See Robinson v. Robinson,* 66 N.H. 600, 610, 23 A. 362 (1891). The law allows the court to consider fault in assessing the equitable division of the marital assets, *see* RSA 458:16–a, II(*l*) (1992), and in so doing, as in the case of adultery, seeks to justly resolve the unseemly dissolution of a confidential and trusting relationship. We should therefore view the purpose and fabric of our divorce law in a meaningful context, as the legislature presumably intended, and not so narrow our focus as to undermine its public goals. *See S.B. v. S.J.B.,* 258 N.J.Super. 151, 609 A.2d 124, 126 (1992).

From the perspective of the injured spouse, the very party fault-based divorce law is designed to protect, "[a]n extramarital relationship . . . is just as devastating . . . irrespective of the specific sexual act performed by the promiscuous spouse or the sex of the new paramour." *Id.* Indeed, to some, a homosexual betrayal may be more devastating. Accordingly, consistent with the overall purpose of New Hampshire's fault-based divorce law, we would interpret the word "adultery" in RSA 458:7, II to mean a spouse's extramarital intimate sexual activity with another, regardless of the specific intimate sexual acts performed, the marital status, or the gender of the third party. *See id.* at 127.

. . .

At end of the **NOTE** *on "Corroboration" at page 305, please add the following:*

An attorney who represented a client in a divorce action may not testify in a criminal trial where the client is accused of plotting to have her husband killed. The attorney heard the client plan the crime and was willing to testify. The court applied the attorney-client testimonial privilege to bar the attorney from testifying, holding that since the attorney and the client were involved in a separate legal matter, the crime-fraud exception to the privilege did not apply. Newman v. State, 863 A.2d 321 (Md. 2004).

D. Special Problems of Service of Process

Following the **NOTES** *on long arm statutes, please add at page 364:*

Cooke v. Cooke

Supreme Court of Georgia, 2004.
277 Ga. 731, 594 S.E.2d 370.

■ Sears, Presiding Justice.

Appellant Hugh Cooke appeals the trial court's dismissal of his complaint for divorce due to jurisdictional infirmities. Having reviewed the record, we conclude the trial court erred in determining that the appellee, Miranda Cooke, is not subject to long-arm jurisdiction in Georgia and that Fulton County is not the proper venue for this case. To the extent the trial court found that Hugh Cooke failed to establish he is a domiciliary of Georgia, that conclusion, too, is erroneous. Therefore, we reverse.

Hugh Cooke is an Irish citizen and Miranda Cooke is a citizen of Great Britain. In 1991, the parties were married in Britain and then moved to Ohio to oversee the management of their company, which is registered to conduct business in the United States. In 1992, the Cookes relocated their business to Georgia and bought a home in Fulton County. In 1997, Hugh, Miranda, and their five oldest children obtained permanent resident status in the United States (the youngest child being an American citizen by birthright). Since moving to this country in 1991, the Cookes have maintained a second home in Great Britain, where Miranda and the children currently reside.

All of the Cookes' six children were born in Great Britain except the youngest, who was born in Georgia. The children were educated in Fulton County public schools until 1999, when the older children enrolled in British schools. At that time, Miranda and the children returned to Britain, where they have since remained while Hugh has continued to reside at the couple's Georgia residence. Miranda and the children have returned to

Georgia for brief periods during school vacations and in the summer, and Hugh has traveled to Britain to see his family.

In 2000, 2001 and 2002, the Cookes filed joint tax returns with the Georgia Department of Revenue, in which they declared themselves to be year-round residents of Georgia. In 2003, the Cookes received tax statements from British authorities showing they had declared themselves to be non-residents of that nation for tax purposes.

In March 2003, Hugh filed in Fulton County Superior Court for divorce, equitable division of property and child custody. In April 2003, Miranda filed a motion to dismiss the complaint due to lack of personal jurisdiction, improper venue, and *forum non conveniens*. Miranda also initiated a separate divorce action in Great Britain. On Miranda's motion, the Georgia trial court dismissed Hugh's suit, holding that she was not subject to personal jurisdiction in Georgia and that Fulton County was not the proper venue for the proceedings. Although not entirely clear, the trial court also appears to have held that Hugh failed to establish he is presently domiciled in Georgia. The trial court did not address Miranda's argument concerning *forum non conveniens*.

1. Pretermitting whether Miranda is a Georgia resident and hence subject to personal jurisdiction in the state, it is clear that she is subject to jurisdiction under Georgia's domestic relations long-arm statute.

A court of this state may exercise personal jurisdiction over any nonresident ... [w]ith respect to proceedings for alimony, child support, or division of property in connection with an action for divorce [if the person] maintains a matrimonial domicile in this state at the time of the commencement of this action or if the defendant resided in this state preceding commencement of the action, whether cohabitating during that time or not.[1]

Georgia's domestic relations long-arm statute authorizes our courts to exercise personal jurisdiction over a party to a divorce action who has become a non-resident of this state if he or she resided in this state prior to commencement of the action. Residency, of course, refers to living in a particular locality and requires only that one be bodily present and inhabiting that locale. It being irrefuted that Miranda Cooke maintained her residence in Georgia from 1992 until at least 1997, she falls within the ambit of our domestic relations long-arm statute.

Of course, before permitting the exercise of long-arm jurisdiction, due process requires that a defendant, if she is not present in the forum state, "have certain minimum contacts with it such that the maintenance of the suit does not offend 'traditional notions of fair play and substantial justice.' "[4] In this case, Miranda Cooke purposefully availed herself of the privilege of maintaining a matrimonial domicile in Georgia—notably, her final such domicile in this country before returning to Britain. In connec-

1. OCGA § 9–10–91(5).

4. *International Shoe v. Washington*, 326 U.S. 310, 316, 66 S.Ct. 154, 90 L.Ed. 95 (1945).

tion with her domicile, she obtained certain rights and incurred several significant obligations. As we have recently held in a similar case, that is a sufficient basis upon which to conclude that the exercise of long-arm jurisdiction over Miranda Cooke comports with due process precepts of "fair play" and "substantial justice."[6]

2. The trial court erred in dismissing this matter due to improper venue.

Divorce cases shall be tried in the county where the defendant resides, if a resident of this state; if the defendant is not a resident of this state, then in the county in which plaintiff resides.

Simply put, where (as here) a defendant in a divorce action lives outside of Georgia, the action may be brought in the plaintiff's county of residence. Accordingly, Fulton County, where Hugh Cooke maintains his residence, is the proper venue for this action.

3. The trial court also held that because:

[T]here has not been a showing of the requisite intention of remaining at the Georgia residence, a new domicile has not been established in this State for the purpose of allowing this legal proceeding.

We take this to mean that the trial court concluded Hugh Cooke had failed to establish that he is a domiciliary of Georgia by showing he had been a bona fide resident of the state for six months preceding his filing of the divorce claim and intends to maintain his Georgia residence indefinitely. However, the record establishes that the Cookes lived together as a couple in Fulton County for seven years, until 1999. Thereafter, Hugh Cooke elected to remain in Georgia even though his wife and children had returned to Great Britain. Hugh Cooke's unrebutted affidavit shows that his intention has been to maintain his domicile in Georgia, where his employment, primary source of income, and residence are located. The fact that Hugh Cooke obtained permanent resident alien status in 1997 is a strong indicator that he intended to establish and maintain his domicile in this country. Moreover, he has designated himself a year-round resident of Georgia on state tax returns, and declared himself to be a non-resident of Britain for tax purposes. Accordingly, to the extent the trial court concluded that Hugh Cooke failed to establish that he is a domiciliary of Georgia, that conclusion was erroneous.

Judgment reversed.

All the Justices concur.

6. *Walters v. Walters,* 277 Ga. 221, 223–24, 586 S.E.2d 663 (2003). We note, however, that Georgia's domestic long-arm statute permits the exercise of jurisdiction over Miranda only with regard to claims for divorce, alimony, child support, and property division. Whether Georgia's courts may exercise jurisdiction over Hugh's claim for child custody must be determined in accordance with the Uniform Child Custody Jurisdiction and Enforcement Act, OCGA § 19–9–40 et seq., as well as any relevant international agreements and/or treaties.

CHAPTER V

MARITAL BREAKDOWN: RESOLVING THE FINANCIAL CONCERNS

C. PERMANENT ALIMONY AND MAINTENANCE

Following California code provisions relating to orders of support, please add at page 398:

Murphy v. Murphy

Supreme Court of Maine, 2003.
816 A.2d 814.

■ CLIFFORD, J.

Michael J. Murphy appeals and Stephanie Murphy cross-appeals from a divorce judgment entered in the District Court (Bangor, *Russell, J.*). Michael contends that the trial court erred in awarding transitional spousal support to cover Stephanie's dental and medical expenses. Michael also challenges the amount of the spousal support. Stephanie contends that the trial court erred in its determination and valuation of marital property, its division of marital property, and its failure to order Michael to pay her legal fees. We affirm the judgment.

The parties met and began living together over twenty-six years ago in New York. In 1980, they moved to Massachusetts and purchased a home as joint tenants. Michael worked for New England Electric for about ten years. During this time, the parties held themselves out as married. On July 5, 1985, their son Brendon was born, and the parties agreed that Stephanie would stay at home and take care of him. Stephanie also home schooled Brendon. After approximately ten years in Massachusetts, Michael accepted a job with an engineering firm in Maine. Two years later, the parties bought the current marital home in Hampden using about $25,000 realized from the sale of their Massachusetts home. In 1993, Stephanie decided that they needed to be married because she was concerned that if anything happened to Michael she and Brendon would not be taken care of, so the couple married in October of 1993. In 1995, Michael started his own engineering consultant business. Stephanie helped Michael with the management of this business for about one year. In the fall of 1998, Stephanie began work as a psychiatric technician at Acadia Hospital. She was trained at the hospital and currently works full time.

The divorce proceeding was commenced in September of 2000. Prior to the trial, the couple sold real estate they owned in Brewer, and the net proceeds of approximately $4600 went to Stephanie.

After the parties separated, Michael and Brendon continued to live in the marital home in Hampden. The parties agreed that after the divorce, Brendon would continue to live with Michael, but would visit Stephanie whenever Brendon wanted and the parties would share parental rights and responsibilities. Stephanie lives in an apartment and shares expenses with a domestic partner, who earns approximately $28,000 a year. Stephanie previously took a sign language course and would like to go to college to earn a degree so that she could become an American sign language interpreter. She would be able to take some electives near where she lives, but would have to attend the University of Southern Maine for two years to take the core courses in sign language.

Stephanie testified that she is in need of a substantial amount of dental work. She estimated that the cost of the extractions and bridge work needed would be about $11,250. Stephanie also testified that she would like to continue in therapy to treat her depression, for which she takes prescription medication.

In Michael's financial statement, the marital home is valued at $119,300. Philip Cormier, a licensed real estate broker who conducted an appraisal on the property, testified that, if the property were placed on the market, he would suggest a listing price of $119,000 to $125,000 in order to sell the property within three or four months, and said that the property would probably yield a price of approximately $117,000. He acknowledged that the real estate market was doing well and that some houses were actually selling at list price or higher.

Michael has a retirement account from his ten years of employment in Massachusetts, prior to his marriage, which he rolled over into an account with A.G. Edwards when he left his job in Massachusetts. Michael testified that he has not added any money to this account since that time. The account has a value of approximately $115,000 and stands in Michael's name alone.

Michael's mother died in the late 1990s, and left an estate worth nearly half a million dollars. Prior to her death, Michael and his mother had a joint account with a value of about $43,000. After her death, Michael separated this account into two accounts in local banks. One account worth about $30,000 was placed in the parties' joint names, but was used only to pay costs of his mother's estate. Stephanie had a debit card for this joint account, but she never used it. After the parties had separated and the estate costs had been paid, Michael placed this money in his separate account. Michael was expected to receive $240,000 from his mother's estate and Brendon was expected to receive $120,000.

The court found the Hampden marital home to be worth $119,300 and awarded the property to Michael, with Michael assuming the balance on the mortgage of approximately $91,000. The court awarded the $4000 car to Michael and the $9000 car to Stephanie. The court set apart various other items of tangible personal property to each party, with items valued at $15,000 to Michael, and items worth $5000 to Stephanie.

The court determined that the $115,000 retirement account was Michael's nonmarital property. The court also determined that the money Michael is to receive from his mother's estate is nonmarital property. Thus, the court concluded that Michael had nonmarital assets of approximately $355,000, and Stephanie had none. Michael received approximately $78,300 and Stephanie $18,600 from the court's initial division of the marital estate,[1] but to ensure a more equitable division, the court ordered Michael to pay Stephanie $50,000.

The court found Stephanie's earning potential is approximately $18,000, and Michael's earning capacity to be about $90,000 a year. Although Stephanie has less income potential than Michael, given Stephanie and her partner's combined income, the court concluded that she could "maintain a reasonable standard of living without general support." Taking into account Stephanie's medical, dental, and educational needs, as well as her attorney fees obligation, the court awarded her transitional spousal support in the amount of $60,000.

II. MICHAEL MURPHY'S APPEAL

A. Spousal Support—Purposes

In contending that the trial court erred in awarding Stephanie transitional spousal support to cover her dental and medical expenses, Michael argues that those two categories do not fall within the definition of transitional support. We disagree.

Issues regarding spousal support are within the sound discretion of the trial court. *Noyes v. Noyes,* 662 A.2d 921, 922 (Me.1995). Title 19–A M.R.S.A. § 951–A(2) (Supp.2002), lists the five possible types of spousal support that a trial court may award, including general support and transitional support.[2] There is a rebuttable presumption that general

---

1. Stephanie received a car worth $9000, tangible personal property worth $5000, and $4600 from the proceeds of the sale of the parties' Brewer property, which reaches a total of $18,600. Michael received the marital home worth $119,300, but also assumed the $91,000 mortgage. Michael also received a car worth $4000, tangible personal property worth $15,000, a business account totaling $13,000, and personal accounts totaling $1800. The actual total of these items is $62,100, but the court's order states it is $78,300. Neither party pointed out this mathematical inconsistency. It is possible that the $1800 figure was a typographical error that should have been $18,000, which would put Michael's total award of marital property at $78,300.

2. Title 19–A M.R.S.A. § 951–A(2) in pertinent part provides as follows:

2. Types of spousal support. The court may, after consideration of all factors set forth in subsection 5, award or modify spousal support for one or more of the following reasons.

A. General support may be awarded to provide financial assistance to a spouse with substantially less income potential than the other spouse so that both spouses can maintain a reasonable standard of living after the divorce.

(1) There is a rebuttable presumption that general support may not be awarded if the parties were married for less than 10 years as of the date of the filing of the action for divorce. There is also a rebuttable presumption that general support may not be awarded for a term exceeding 1/2 the length of the marriage if the parties were married for

support will not be awarded when the marriage is less than ten years in duration.[3] 19–A M.R.S.A. § 951–A(2)(A).

Id.

Transitional support, "may be awarded to provide for a spouse's transitional needs, including, *but not limited to:* (1) Short-term needs resulting from financial dislocations associated with the dissolution of the marriage; or (2) Reentry or advancement in the work force, including, but not limited to, physical or emotional rehabilitation services, vocational training and education." 19–A M.R.S.A. § 951–A(2)(B) (emphasis added). In determining an award of spousal support, the court must consider a number of factors, which include "health and disabilities of each party," and "any other factors the court considers appropriate."[4]

at least 10 years but not more than 20 years as of the date of the filing of the action for divorce.

(2) If the court finds that a spousal support award based upon a presumption established by this paragraph would be inequitable or unjust, that finding is sufficient to rebut the applicable presumption.

B. Transitional support may be awarded to provide for a spouse's transitional needs, including, but not limited to:

(1) Short-term needs resulting from financial dislocations associated with the dissolution of the marriage; or

(2) Reentry or advancement in the work force, including, but not limited to, physical or emotional rehabilitation services, vocational training and education.

. . .

Id.

3. Although Stephanie contends that she is entitled to an award of general support, the length of the marriage was eight years, and the trial court was not compelled to find that she overcame the presumption. *See* 19–A M.R.S.A. § 951–A(2).

4. Title 19–A M.R.S.A. § 951–A (5) provides as follows:

5. Factors. The court shall consider the following factors when determining an award of spousal support;

A. The length of the marriage;

B. The ability of each party to pay;

C. The age of each party;

D. The employment history and employment potential of each party;

E. The income history and income potential of each party;

F. The education and training of each party;

G. The provisions for retirement and health insurance benefits of each party;

H. The tax consequences of the division of marital property, including the tax consequences of the sale of the marital home, if applicable;

I. The health and disabilities of each party;

J. The tax consequences of a spousal support award;

K. The contributions of either party as homemaker;

L. The contributions of either party to the education or earning potential of the other party;

M. Economic misconduct by either party resulting in the diminution of marital property or income; N. The standard of living of the parties during the marriage;

O. The ability of the party seeking support to become self-supporting within a reasonable period of time;

P. The effect of the following on a party's need for spousal support or a party's ability to pay spousal support:

(1) Actual or potential income from marital or nonmarital property awarded or set apart to each party as part of the court's distributive order pursuant to section 953; and

The court's transitional support award in this case is based partly on Stephanie's health issues, her desire to receive counseling, her need for dental work, her obligation to pay attorney fees, and her need for more education and training. Michael challenges the court's consideration of Stephanie's counseling and dental work and contends that these items are not "transitional needs." The spousal support statute, however, does not specifically define the limits of "transitional needs," but rather provides that transitional needs "includ[e] but [are] not limited to" two broad categories. 19–A M.R.S.A. § 951–A (2)(B). Moreover, in determining an award of alimony, the court is required to consider the factors listed in § 951–A (5), including the health of the parties. 19–A M.R.S.A. § 951–A (5)(I). Accordingly, the transitional alimony award based in part on Stephanie's need for counseling and dental work is well within the trial court's discretion. *See Noyes,* 662 A.2d at 922.

B.   Spousal Support—Amount

Michael also argues that the trial court's award of $60,000 for transitional spousal support was excessive and beyond its discretion, contending that the evidence supports a transitional award of no more than $27,700. We disagree.

Stephanie has demonstrated a need for dental work, the need for legal representation in connection with this appeal, and that she will have to limit her work hours to accommodate her class schedule, and will be required to move to or commute to USM for two years. Furthermore, the statute provides that in determining an award of spousal support, the court must consider, among other factors, the income potential of the parties, their age, their standard of living, training and education, and their ability to pay spousal support. 19–A M.R.S.A. § 951–A(5). Contrary to Michael's contention, the transitional award of $60,000 was reasonable, was in keeping with the purpose of transitional support and well within the trial court's discretion. *See Noyes,* 662 A.2d at 922.

II.   STEPHANIE MURPHY'S CROSS–APPEAL

A.   Determination, Valuation, and Distribution of Marital Property

Stephanie contends that the trial court erred in its determination, valuation, and division of the marital property. She argues that the court erred in its valuation of the marital home, that the IRA account in Michael's name was marital property, that the $30,000 previously in a joint account was marital property as well, and that the division of the marital property was not equitable.

1.   The marital home in Hampden

The trial court's valuation of marital property is reviewed for clear error. *Robinson v. Robinson,* 2000 ME 101, ¶ 12, 751 A.2d 457, 460. The

---

(2) Child support for the support of a minor child or children of the marriage pursuant to chapter 63; and

Q.   Any other factors the court considers appropriate.

Id.

Hampden property was valued at $119,300 in Michael's financial statement, there was expert testimony that the property would be listed at $119,000 to $125,000, and that the market was doing well, and some homes were selling at list price or higher. The court's valuation of the marital home at $119,300 was not clear error. *See Robinson*, 2000 ME 101, ¶ 12, 751 A.2d at 460 (holding trial court's valuation of a business was not clearly erroneous because the court based its determination on an independent review of the evidence and the value was within the range provided by expert opinion).

2. Retirement account

A trial court's determination of whether property owned by the parties is part of the marital estate or is nonmarital, is reviewed for clear error. *Doucette v. Washburn*, 2001 ME 38, ¶ 7, 766 A.2d 578, 581. Such a determination made by the trial court will not be disturbed if it is supported by competent evidence in the record. *Id.*

Title 19–A M.R.S.A. § 953(2) (1998 & Supp.2002) defines "marital property" as "all property acquired by either spouse subsequent to the marriage" with five listed exceptions.[5] All property that is acquired during the marriage is presumed to be marital property, pursuant to 19–A M.R.S.A. § 953(3), but the presumption can be overcome by the applicability of one or more of the exceptions.[6] One such exception, the increase in

---

5. Title 19–A M.R.S.A. § 953(2) provides as follows:

2. Definition. For purposes of this section, "marital property" means all property acquired by either spouse subsequent to the marriage, except:

A. Property acquired by gift, bequest, devise or descent; B. Property acquired in exchange for property acquired prior to the marriage or in exchange for property acquired by gift, bequest, devise or descent;

C. Property acquired by a spouse after a decree of legal separation;

D. Property excluded by valid agreement of the parties; and

E. The increase in value of property acquired prior to the marriage and the increase in value of a spouse's nonmarital property as defined in paragraphs A to D.

(1) "Increase in value" includes:

(a) Appreciation resulting from market forces; and

(b) Appreciation resulting from reinvested income and capital gain unless either or both spouses had a substantial active role during the marriage in managing, preserving or improving the property.

(2) "Increase in value" does not include:

(a) Appreciation resulting from the investment of marital funds or property in the nonmarital property;

(b) Appreciation resulting from marital labor; and

(c) Appreciation resulting from reinvested income and capital gain if either or both spouses had a substantial active role during the marriage in managing, preserving or improving the property.

6. Title 19–A M.R.S.A. § 953(3) provides as follows:

3. Acquired subsequent to marriage. All property acquired by either spouse subsequent to the marriage and prior to a decree of legal separation is presumed to be marital property regardless of whether title is held individually or by the spouses in some form of coownership such as joint tenancy, tenancy in common, tenancy by the entirety or community property. The presumption of marital property is overcome by a showing that the property was acquired by a method listed in subsection 2.

value of property that one spouse acquired prior to the marriage, contained in section 953(2)(E), was recently addressed in *Warner v. Warner,* 2002 ME 156, ¶¶ 27–35, 807 A.2d 607. In *Warner,* we explained the newly revised section 953(2)(E) as it related to one spouse's nonmarital stock as follows:

Revised section 953(2)(E)(1)(a) establishes that to the extent a party demonstrates that the increase in value of a spouse's nonmarital stock resulted from "market forces," the increased value is nonmarital property regardless of whether the spouse or spouses played a substantial active role in managing the stock. In addition, sections 953(2)(E)(1)(b) and (2)(c) establish that to the extent a party demonstrates that the increase in value of a spouse's nonmarital stock resulted from reinvested income and capital gain, the increased value is nonmarital property unless it is also established that "either or both spouses had a substantial active role during the marriage in managing, preserving or improving the property." 19-A M.R.S.A. 953(2)(E)(1)(b) & (2)(c) (Supp.2002). *Warner,* 2002 ME 156, ¶ 31, 807 A.2d 607. Thus, the revised section 953(2)(E) makes clear that the increase of one spouse's nonmarital property that is attributable solely to market forces is also considered nonmarital property. *Id.* ¶ 27.

Michael's retirement account is a rollover account from his ten years of employment in Massachusetts prior to the parties' marriage, and Michael testified that the account has not been added to since that time. The account remains in Michael's name alone. Stephanie did not contest that the account was a rollover account from Michael's previous employer in Massachusetts. She provided no documents showing that her name had ever been on the account, nor did she show that any marital funds or effort had been applied to the account. The court's finding that the IRA account was Michael's nonmarital property and was valued at $115,000 was not clear error. *See Doucette,* 2001 ME 38, ¶ 7, 766 A.2d at 581.

3.   The $30,000 briefly held in a joint account

Stephanie challenges the trial court's determination that a $30,000 account standing in Michael's name was nonmarital property. She contends that because it had been in a joint account, it is marital property. Although property acquired by one spouse during the marriage is presumed to be marital property, that presumption may be rebutted by showing that the property falls under one of the exclusions listed in section 953(2), which includes property acquired by gift, bequest, or descent. 19-A M.R.S.A. § 953(2), (2)(A) & (3).

In *Chamberlin v. Chamberlin,* 2001 ME 167, 785 A.2d 1247, we upheld the trial court's determination that the plaintiff's property remained non-marital even though it passed through the parties' joint checking account. The plaintiff's father had died and left the plaintiff an inheritance, which included $50,000 that was briefly placed in the parties' joint checking account before the plaintiff placed the funds in various investments in her own name. *Id.* ¶ 7, 785 A.2d at 1250. The plaintiff testified that she and the defendant had previously agreed that $50,000 of the inheritance was strictly her property. *Id.* In upholding the trial court's determination that the funds were nonmarital, we stated that "[i]n contrast to our holding in *Long* [*v. Long,* 1997 ME 171, ¶¶ 16–18, 697 A.2d 1317, 1323–24], we have never held that deposit accounts are subject to such automatic treatment as marital assets when funds are placed briefly in accounts, and we decline to do so now."[7] *Id.* ¶ 6, 785 A.2d at 1249.

After his mother's death, Michael placed $30,000 of a $43,000 joint account he held with his mother, into a joint account with Stephanie, for a brief period of time, but with the understanding that this money would be used for paying taxes of his mother's estate. Stephanie never accessed any of the funds from this account, which is now in Michael's name. Section 953(2)(A) excludes property acquired after a marriage by descent from being classified as marital property. 19–A M.R.S.A. § 953(2)(A). Contrary to Stephanie's contention, *Long* does not require that the $30,000 be considered marital property. The trial court's determination that inherited money briefly placed in a joint account remains nonmarital property is not clear error. *Chamberlin,* 2001 ME 167, ¶¶ 5–7, 785 A.2d at 1249–50.

4. The division of the marital property

Stephanie challenges the trial court's division of the marital property. Following the court's initial division of the marital property, it ordered Michael to pay $50,000 to Stephanie to make the distribution more equitable.

Trial courts have broad discretion when dividing marital property, and we review the court's action for an abuse of discretion. *Robinson,* 2000 ME 101, ¶ 9, 751 A.2d at 459. Title 19–A M.R.S.A. § 953(1) provides that in a divorce action, "the court shall set apart to each spouse the spouse's property and shall divide the marital property in proportions the court considers just after considering all relevant factors."[8] The statute provides for a just distribution, which "is not synonymous with an equal distribution.... [w]e have made it clear that a court is not required to divide the marital property equally, but is required to make the division fair and just considering all of the circumstances of the parties." *Doucette,* 2001 ME 38, ¶ 24, 766 A.2d 578, 586.

---

7. In *Long,* the defendant placed $35,000 that he realized from the sale of his nonmarital property in a joint savings account, and then invested that money in property in Maine that he owned in joint tenancy with his wife. 1997 ME 171, ¶ 2, 697 A.2d at 1319. We refused to apply the source of funds rule and held that real estate owned jointly by spouses was marital property regardless of who supplied the purchasing funds. *Id.* ¶¶ 16–18, 697 A.2d at 1323–24.

8. Title 19–A M.R.S.A. § 953(1) (1998) provides that the court must consider all relevant factors, which include the following:

A. The contribution of each spouse to the acquisition of the marital property, including the contribution of a spouse as homemaker;

B. The value of the property set apart to each spouse; and

C. The economic circumstances of each spouse at the time the division of property is to become effective, including the desirability of awarding the family home or the right to live in the home for reasonable periods to the spouse having custody of the children. *Id.*

Stephanie argues that she should be awarded more marital property because of her contributions to the home over the course of their relationship and because Michael has nonmarital property. The trial court, however, considered the factors set out in section 953 in dividing the property and required Michael to pay Stephanie $50,000. The division of marital property was within the trial court's discretion. *Robinson*, 2000 ME 101, ¶ 9, 751 A.2d at 459.

C.   Attorney fees

Attorney fees awards in divorce actions are reviewed by this Court only for an abuse of discretion. *Warner*, 2002 ME 156, ¶ 54, 807 A.2d 607. Title 19–A M.R.S.A. § 952(3) (1998) provides that "[w]hen making a final decree, the court may order a party to pay reasonable attorney[ ] fees. Attorney[ ] fees awarded in the nature of support may be payable immediately or in installments." *Id.* This Court has previously recognized that the legislature has given trial courts broad discretion in determining whether or not to award attorney fees to a party in a divorce action. *Rosen v. Rosen*, 651 A.2d 335, 336 (Me.1994).

The trial court based its $60,000 transitional support award to Stephanie in part on her need to pay her divorce attorney. The court declined to directly award either party counsel fees, and determined that the parties should be responsible for their own attorney fees. Stephanie argues that Michael is in a better financial position and is more able to pay attorney fees. In *Rosen*, we said the parties' financial position is not the only factor to consider in determining an award of attorney fees. *Rosen*, 651 A.2d at 336–37. Rather, all relevant factors must be considered to reach a fair and just award. *Id.* at 336. As the trial court considered Stephanie's need to pay her attorney in awarding her transitional spousal support, the court did not abuse its discretion by failing to award her attorney fees directly.

The entry is:

Judgment affirmed.

Following the California Family Code provision on attorney-mediator at page 412, please add to the NOTE *the following:*

Mediation cases continue to be decided. For example, in interpreting the state's Domestic Relations Arbitration Act, the Michigan Court of Appeals held that the statute required a hearing before an arbitrator may settle any matter by mediation. When the arbitrator met with the parties ex parte without holding a hearing, the couple is not bound by the arbitrator's award. Miller v. Miller, 264 Mich.App. 497, 691 N.W.2d 788 (2004). Likewise, the West Virginia Supreme Court of Appeals held that when one of the parties to a custody dispute withdrew consent to the mediated plan prior to the court's order adopting it, the court lacked the right to adopt a mediated agreement. Mason v. Mason, 216 W.Va. 328, 607 S.E.2d 434 (2004).

D.   Dividing Property Upon Divorce

After NOTES *on professional degrees, please add at page 447:*

Christianson v. Christianson

Supreme Court of North Dakota, 2003.
671 N.W.2d 801.

■ Sandstrom, Justice.

Gerald Christianson is appealing a Northwest Judicial District Court judgment awarding Cecelia Christianson $900.00 per month in spousal support. Gerald Christianson argues that the district court erred in imputing income to him when determining his ability to pay, that Cecelia Christianson's needs as a disadvantaged spouse were not supported by the evidence, that temporary support should have been awarded, and that equalizing their income was inappropriate. Because we are unable to fully review the district court's finding that Cecelia Christianson is a disadvantaged spouse entitled to permanent support, we affirm that portion of its decision. Concluding the district court improperly calculated the amount of spousal support, we reverse and remand for proper calculation.

Gerald and Cecelia Christianson married in June 1968. Gerald Christianson sued Cecelia Christianson for divorce in January 2001. At the time of trial, Gerald Christianson was 56 and Cecelia Christianson was 58. Gerald Christianson has a Bachelor of Science Degree in Biology, a Master's Degree in School Administration, and a Specialist's Degree in Educational Leadership.

Gerald Christianson had been working as a Superintendent at Parshall High School in Parshall, North Dakota. Following the 1999–2000 school year, he retired and began drawing benefits from the North Dakota Teachers' Fund for Retirement. He gave up his position in anticipation of obtaining a "state job" as a grant administrator, but the job never materialized. Before retiring, Gerald Christianson had an annual salary of $56,000, and with benefits, his compensation was close to $65,000.

Gerald Christianson enrolled at North Dakota State University in Fargo, North Dakota, in August of 2000 to pursue a Specialist's Degree in Educational Leadership. The salary range for a person with this degree is between $50,000 and $90,000. While attending school at North Dakota State University, Gerald Christianson earned $692.00 per month as a graduate teaching assistant and $800.00 per month as a sales associate at Marshall Field's. Gerald Christianson's retirement income at the time gave him $2,273.86 per month. He forwarded $1,050.00 of that amount to Cecelia Christianson. Gerald Christianson is in good health, aside from occasional back pain.

Cecelia Christianson has a Bachelor of Science Degree in Elementary Education. She is employed as an elementary school teacher at Plaza

School in Plaza, North Dakota, earning $24,500. She also works part-time at the Cenex Convenience Store in Parshall, earning from $300 to $350 per month.

On October 15, 2001, the district court awarded 60 percent of the marital property to Cecelia Christianson and 40 percent to Gerald Christianson. The district court found Cecelia Christianson to be a disadvantaged spouse and determined she could not be rehabilitated. The court awarded her permanent support in the amount of zero ($0.00) dollars. Given the fact that Gerald Christianson did not have full-time employment and was pursuing a degree, the court deferred setting the amount of spousal support until October 15, 2002.

The district court found Cecelia Christianson had low job security; the school where she teaches has declining enrollment, and at some point it may no longer be feasible to keep the school open. It found that she may find it difficult to obtain other employment as a teacher because there are many elementary school teachers and she is 58 years old and does not have a portfolio, which is required by many schools.

The district court also found the parties moved to different communities nine times during their marriage. It found these moves were made solely to advance Gerald Christianson's career, and little consideration was given to whether Cecelia Christianson could obtain a teaching job. It also found Cecelia Christianson's teaching career was interrupted by these moves; extended time away from the classroom does not look good on a resume. The district court found that being away from teaching also made it difficult for Cecelia Christianson to build retirement. Because the parties dipped into her retirement fund on four occasions, her retirement is a fraction of what it could have been. It also found that Cecelia Christianson has heel spurs in both feet and will eventually require surgery. Judgment was entered November 6, 2001.

On January 16, 2003, the district court again reviewed the issue of support. The court found Cecelia Christianson's needs as a disadvantaged spouse had become more pronounced since the divorce judgment had been entered; the A.G. Edwards stock portfolio awarded to her as part of the property division had sharply declined in value. The court also found that despite a concerted and good-faith attempt to obtain employment, Gerald Christianson has been unable to secure a position in the field of school administration. The court recognized that Gerald Christianson voluntarily gave up a $56,000 job, that the salary range for an individual possessing his type of degree is $50,000 to $90,000, and that his present earnings are significantly less than the prevailing amounts earned in the community by persons with a similar work history and occupational qualifications. The court found Gerald Christianson to be underemployed. The court used an equalization-of-income approach and imputed income to Gerald Christianson to set the support award at $900.00 per month. The amended judgment was entered on April 3, 2003.

Gerald Christianson argues that no authority exists for imputing income to him for the purpose of calculating spousal support, that equalization of income was inappropriate for this case, and that the district court improperly assessed his ability to pay.

He argues spousal support is not the same as child support, in which the imputation of income is authorized, and claims no such authority exists in the case of spousal support.

"Spousal support awards must be made in consideration of the disadvantaged spouse's needs and of the supporting spouse's needs and ability to pay." *Shields v. Shields,* 2003 ND 16, ¶ 10, 656 N.W.2d 712.

Cecelia Christianson can point to no North Dakota statutory or case law providing for the imputation of income in spousal support cases. Other states have permitted imputing income in some cases. *See, e.g., Moore v. Moore,* 242 Mich.App. 652, 619 N.W.2d 723, 724–25 (2000); *In re Marriage of Carrick,* 560 N.W.2d 407, 410 (Minn.Ct.App.1997); *Grady v. Grady,* 295 Ark. 94, 747 S.W.2d 77, 78–79 (1988). Even if it were allowed, it would not be appropriate for this case. *See id.* The district court found that despite a concerted and good-faith attempt on Gerald Christianson's part to obtain employment, he has come up empty-handed in his job search.[2]

Gerald Christianson claims that the use of an income-equalization approach to spousal support was not appropriate.

Equalization is not a goal of spousal support, and equalization of income between divorcing spouses is not a measure of spousal support although it is a factor that can be considered. *Sommers,* 2003 ND 77, ¶ 17, 660 N.W.2d 586. The amount of support ordered greatly exceeds Gerald Christianson's ability to pay and is not justified by "equalization of income."

We reverse, concluding the district court improperly imputed income to Gerald Christianson when it sought to equalize the parties' incomes. We remand to the district court for proper calculation of spousal support based upon the parties' needs and ability to pay.

Cecelia Christianson argues she should be awarded attorney fees on appeal because Gerald Christianson's actions have unreasonably increased the time and effort spent on the dispute.

"The principal factors to be considered for deciding the amount of attorney fees are need and ability to pay." *Mahoney v. Mahoney,* 1997 ND 149, ¶ 40, 567 N.W.2d 206. "An award of attorney's fees in litigation about marital obligations between former spouses does not depend entirely on the merits of each position, although whether one party's actions unreasonably increased the time and effort spent on the dispute can be a factor." *Id.*

Section 14–05–23, N.D.C.C., states that "during any time in which an action for separation or divorce is pending, the court, upon application of a party, may issue an order requiring ... payment of attorney fees." Under this section we have concurrent original jurisdiction with the district court

2. Contrary to the concurring and dissenting opinion's statement, at ¶ 36, the district court did *not* implicitly or explicitly find Gerald Christianson was "voluntarily underemployed."

to award attorney fees on appeal. *Severson v. Severson,* 482 N.W.2d 594, 596 (N.D.1992).

> [A]s we are an appellate court and exercise original jurisdiction rarely, as attorney's fees and costs involve the necessity of determining facts, and as we ordinarily do not determine facts, we prefer that the district court initially make the determination of attorney's fees even in conjunction with an appeal to our Court. *McIntee v. McIntee,* 413 N.W.2d 366, 367 (N.D.1987). When a party to a divorce action makes a motion in this Court for an award of attorney's fees on appeal, we generally remand the issue to the district court for a determination. *Roen v. Roen,* 438 N.W.2d at 174.

Severson, at 596.

We remand this case to the district court for a determination of whether attorney fees should be awarded to Cecelia Christianson and, if so, for what amount.

We reverse the district court's judgment as to the amount of spousal support and remand for further proceedings.

■ CAROL RONNING KAPSMER, J., concurs. GERALD W. VANDE WALLE, C.J., I concur in the result remanding this case for further proceedings.

[The separate opinion of NEUMANN, JUSTICE, concurring in the result, has been omitted.]

■ MARING, JUSTICE, concurring in part and dissenting in part.

I respectfully dissent from that part of the majority opinion holding that no authority exists allowing imputation of income for the purpose of calculating spousal support and that part holding equalization of income is inappropriate in this case. I concur in the remaining parts of the opinion, but would affirm the judgment of the trial court.

Gerald and Cecelia were married 33 years before divorcing and in dispute is the ultimate amount of the trial court's award of permanent spousal support to Cecelia. Gerald worked as superintendent at Parshall High School for the 1999–2000 school year and earned a total compensation package of $65,000. He voluntarily quit his position at the end of the school year in anticipation of a "state job" as a grant administrator. However, the "state job" never materialized and he enrolled at North Dakota State University ("NDSU") in August of 2000 to pursue a Specialist's Degree in Educational Leadership, which he obtained in May of 2002.

During his advanced degree education, Gerald, who was then 56 years of age, began drawing from his teacher's retirement fund. Gerald testified the salary range for an Education Leader in this area of the country is $50,000 to $90,000. He testified at trial that he had already applied for forty positions region-wide and had not been able to secure one.

The trial court found that while attending NDSU, Gerald was receiving $692 a month as a Graduate Teaching Assistant, $800 a month as a part-time salesperson at Marshall Fields, and $2,273.86 a month of retirement funds. Gerald testified he was sending Cecelia $1,050 a month. The trial court also found Gerald had voluntarily relinquished his superintendent position and that the decision was not a "truly joint decision" by Gerald and Cecelia. The trial court concluded Gerald's actions constituted economic fault. Additionally, the trial court determined Gerald spent $22,704.18 of the proceeds from annuities, in part, on costs associated with obtaining his advanced degree from NDSU. Accordingly, marital funds were used by Gerald to obtain his advanced education.

Cecelia is 58 years old and earns a salary of $24,500 a year as an elementary teacher plus $300 to $350 a month as a part-time worker at the Parshall Cenex Convenience Store. The trial court found that Cecelia supported Gerald's career advancement to the detriment of her own. They moved nine times to advance Gerald's career with little or no consideration for Cecelia's teaching career. Due to the frequent moves, Cecelia could not build her retirement, and what retirement she did have, was invaded on four separate occasions to help pay moving expenses or to pay for Gerald's advanced education. The trial court concluded that Cecelia is a disadvantaged spouse and is entitled to spousal support, but declined to set the amount until Gerald finished at NDSU and obtained full-time employment and, "in any event (i.e., whether Gerald obtains full-time employment or not) . . . no later than *October 15, 2002*."

On October 15, 2002, Cecelia requested that the trial court review the spousal support award and alleged Gerald had a greater ability to pay than he did at the time of trial. On review, the trial court found that Cecelia's needs have become even more pronounced since the divorce judgment. It also found that "[d]espite a concerted and good faith attempt . . . ," Gerald has come up empty in his job search, ". . . *at least in the field of school administration*." (Emphasis added.) The trial court further found:

> Realistically, Cecelia cannot wait any longer to begin receiving support from Gerald. Recognizing that: 1. Gerald *voluntarily* gave up a $56,000.00 per year (plus benefits) superintendent's position at Parshall High School in order to obtain his advanced degree; 2. the salary range for an individual possessing this degree is $50,000.00 to $90,000.00; and, 3. Gerald's present earnings are significantly less than prevailing amounts earned in the community (of Bismarck, ND) by persons with similar work history and occupational qualifications, Gerald is "underemployed"—and equity dictates that the Court impute annual income of $50,000.00 to Gerald in calculating his spousal support obligation. When this is done, it can readily be seen that there is a substantial disparity between the incomes of Cecelia and Gerald—a disparity which the property division ordered by the Court did not ameliorate and which the Court believes *cannot* be readily adjusted by rehabilitative support given Cecelia's circumstances.

Our Court has held that the trial courts must consider the *Ruff-Fischer* guidelines in determining both the amount and duration of spousal support. *Sommer v. Sommer*, 2001 ND 191, ¶ 9, 636 N.W.2d 423. The factors include:

the respective ages of the parties, their earning ability, the duration of the marriage and conduct of the parties during the marriage, their station in life, the circumstances and necessities of each, their health and physical condition, their financial circumstances as shown by the property owned at the time, its value at the time, its income-producing capacity, if any, whether accumulated before or after the marriage, and such other matters as may be material.

Id. (citation omitted).

The trial court in this case very carefully considered all the *Ruff-Fischer* factors including the needs of each party and the ability of the supporting spouse to pay. The trial court imputed income of $50,000 to Gerald based on Gerald's testimony that the salary range for an individual with his degree was $50,000 to $90,000 and that Gerald last earned a total compensation package of $65,000.

The majority opinion states that spousal support awards are to be made in consideration of need and ability to pay, without ever mentioning the *Ruff-Fischer* guidelines; that there is no authority to impute income; and that even if it were allowed the trial court found Gerald made a good faith attempt to obtain employment. The majority opinion overlooks that the trial court found Gerald had "voluntarily" quit his job and that this act constituted economic fault. The majority opinion also overlooks that the trial court noted Gerald may need to find full-time employment in another field and that he made no attempt to do this. With regard to Gerald's good faith attempt to find a job, the trial court clearly referenced only Gerald's attempt to find a school administration job as being made in "good faith." Implicitly the trial court found Gerald was "voluntarily" underemployed, and after having given him one year to resolve his employment status, the court imputed income.

A number of jurisdictions have found that where a party has voluntarily reduced his income, the court may impute income to arrive at an amount for spousal support. *See, e.g., Moore v. Moore,* 242 Mich.App. 652, 619 N.W.2d 723, 724–25 (2000) (citing *Healy v. Healy,* 175 Mich.App. 187, 437 N.W.2d 355 (1989)) (holding that a court can consider a voluntary reduction of income to determine the proper amount of alimony, and that if a court finds a party voluntarily reduced the party's income, the court may impute additional income to arrive at an appropriate alimony award); *Weller v. Weller,* 2002 Ohio 7125, ¶ 47, 2002 WL 31862681, 8 (Ohio Ct.App.2002) (quoting *Motycka v. Motycka,* 2001 Ohio 2162, 2001 WL 688886 *14) (holding that a trial court has the discretion to impute income to parties for purposes of spousal support, "even if it is determined that a party has no income"); *Cox v. Cox,* 877 P.2d 1262, 1267 (Utah Ct.App.1994) (holding that after first determining a spouse is voluntarily unemployed or underemployed, it is appropriate to impute income) (citations omitted); *Grady v. Grady,* 295 Ark. 94, 747 S.W.2d 77, 78–79 (1988) (holding, in the proper circumstances, a trial court may impute income to a supporting spouse who voluntarily changes employment); *Grable v. Grable,* 307 Ark. 410, 821 S.W.2d 16, 20 (1991) (holding that a trial court may impute income); *In re Marriage of Stephenson,* 39 Cal.App.4th 71, 46 Cal.Rptr.2d 8, 14 (1995) (holding that if a "supporting spouse elects to retire early and to not seek reasonably remunerative available employment under the circumstances, then the court can properly impute income to that supporting spouse ..."); *Kovar v. Kovar,* 648 So.2d 177, 178 (Fla.Dist.Ct.App.1994) (holding that when a supporting spouse voluntarily reduces his income, it is in the trial court's discretion to impute income); *Bronson v. Bronson,* 793 So.2d 1109, 1111 (Fla.Dist.Ct.App.2001) (same); *In re Marriage of Carrick,* 560 N.W.2d 407, 410 (Minn.Ct.App.1997) (holding that a trial court may impute a party's income to set maintenance, if it first finds that the party was underemployed in bad faith); *In re Marriage of Warwick,* 438 N.W.2d 673, 677 (Minn.Ct.App.1989) (extending earning capacity determination as an appropriate measure of income from child support to spousal support and concluding the rationale for child support is persuasive for maintenance).

In the present case, the trial court did not err in imputing income where it found Gerald was voluntarily underemployed; had only attempted a good faith search for employment as a school superintendent and not for other full-time employment; and the imputed amount of income was within the range of Gerald's testimony as to what he could earn as well as the history of his earnings.

To the extent that the majority opinion stands for the proposition that equalization of income is never appropriate when setting spousal support, I dissent. We have stated that "[a] valid consideration in awarding spousal support is balancing the burden created by divorce." *Marschner v. Marschner,* 2001 ND 4, 621 N.W.2d 339. We also have stated that "[r]elevant to a spousal support determination is the distribution of marital property, the liquid nature of the property, and the income-producing nature of property." *Id.* In this case, the parties net marital estate was minimal being only $38,885. Here, the evidence is that the award of $14,000 in the AG Edwards Account had been reduced to $7,000 and would provide little income to Cecilia.

Cecelia significantly contributed to Gerald's increased earning ability over a period of 33 years. Cecelia's earning ability will never approach Gerald's. Our Court has stated that a valid consideration in an award of spousal support is:

> whether there is a need to *equitably* balance the burdens created by the divorce where the parties cannot maintain the same standard of living apart as they enjoyed together. *See Wald v. Wald,* 556 N.W.2d 291, 297 (N.D.1996) ("We recognize a court must balance the burden created by a divorce when it is impossible to maintain two households at the predivorce standard of living."); *Wiege v. Wiege,* 518 N.W.2d 708, 712 (N.D.1994) ("The trial court's award of permanent support, combined with the rehabilitative support, *equitably* shares the overall reduction in the parties' separate standards of living and is not clearly erroneous.") (internal quotation marks omitted); *Wahlberg v. Wahlberg,* 479 N.W.2d 143, 145 (N.D.1992) ("Continuance of a standard of living is a

valid consideration in spousal support determinations, *e.g., Bagan v. Bagan,* 382 N.W.2d 645 (N.D.1986), as is balancing the burdens created by the separation when it is impossible to maintain two households at the pre-divorce standard, *e.g., Weir v. Weir,* 374 N.W.2d 858 (N.D.1985).'').

Sommer, 2001 ND 191, ¶ 10, 636 N.W.2d 423 (emphasis added).

Although, as in property division, equitable does not need to mean equal, equitable can mean equal. In *Glander v. Glander,* 1997 ND 192, 569 N.W.2d 262, our Court upheld an equalization of income between divorcing spouses. We noted that some jurisdictions reject equalization of income while others ''have approved indefinite spousal support that resulted in equalizing post-divorce income.'' *Id.* Our Court concluded that ''[w]hile arbitrary equalization of income between parting spouses would be questionable, we conclude the circumstances here justified it. In determining support, a court must 'balance the burden created by a divorce when it is impossible to maintain two households at the pre-divorce standard of living.' '' *Id.* at ¶ 18 (citations omitted).

In *Riehl v. Riehl,* 1999 ND 107, 595 N.W.2d 10, our Court stated ''[w]hile we have not endorsed the 'equalization of income between divorcing spouses,' (citation omitted) we conclude the period of spousal support in this case does not adequately address the burdens of the divorce.'' We reversed and remanded for the trial court to consider whether permanent spousal support would be equitable to offset the permanent economic disadvantage suffered by the wife in that case. *Id.*

I believe the trial court did not clearly err in equalizing the incomes through an award of spousal support under the facts and circumstances of this case. If Gerald wishes to decrease his spousal support payments upon his retirement, he may bring a motion for modification of the amount at that time. *See Sommer,* 2001 ND 191, 636 N.W.2d 423.

I respectfully dissent and would affirm the judgment of the trial court.

Following* In Re Marriage of Brown *and* NOTES *on page 454, please add the following to the first paragraph:

For a discussion of pensions, see, Gary A. Shulman & David I. Kelley, DIVIDING PENSIONS IN DIVORCE (2d. ed. 2004). Courts are willing to consider a pension in the dividing of marital property, even though a state statute may bar the pension's division as marital property. The court may use other non-exempt property to accommodate the asset. *See, e.g.,* Waln v. Waln, 694 N.W.2d 452 (Wis. App. 2005). The following assets often pose difficulties:

(1) Disability payments: West Virginia Supreme Court held that disability payments may be marital property subject to distribution if they were intended to be such when the disability policy was purchased. Conrad v. Conrad, 613 S.E.2d 772 (W. Va. 2005). Similarly, the Indiana Supreme Court held that only that portion of the Federal Employee's Liability Act benefits awarded to an injured railroad worker as compensation for lost

marital wages is marital property subject to division upon dissolution of the marriage. Beckley v. Beckley, 822 N.E.2d 158 (Ind. 2005).

(2) Goodwill: Goodwill may be classified as personal and enterprise, the latter marital property subject to division upon divorce, and the former a factor that may be considered with equitable factors used to divide assets at divorce. *In re* Marriage of Schneider, 214 Ill.2d 152, 291 Ill.Dec. 601, 824 N.E.2d 177 (2005).

Following **Mansell v. Mansell** *and the* **NOTE** *on page 463, please add the following:*

Courts are continuing the practice of requiring a military spouse to compensate a former spouse for any decrease in the non-military spouse's share of any military pension caused by the election by the military person to take disability payments. Compensation comes from other divisible assets. *See, e.g., In re* the Marriage of Lodeski, 107 P.3d 1097 (Colo. App. 2004); Whitfield v. Whitfield, 373 N.J.Super. 573, 862 A.2d 1187 (App.Div. 2004). Similarly, when an active duty soldier elected to take a "CSB/Redux Bonus" after fifteen years of military service, knowing it would reduce the military pension, the former non-electing spouse had a right to share in the bonus to the extent that the former spouse's award of the pension would be reduced. Boedeker v. Larson, 605 S.E.2d 764 (Va. Ct. App. 2004).

E. SUPPORT FOR CHILDREN

Prior to the **NOTES** *on* **Contribution to College Expenses** *please add at page 497:*

In re Barrett

Supreme Court of New Hampshire, 2004.
150 N.H. 520, 841 A.2d 74.

■ DALAINIS, J.

The respondent, John T. Coyne, appeals an order recommended by a Marital Master (*Harriet J. Fishman*, Esq.) and approved by the Portsmouth Family Division (*DeVries*, J.). We vacate and remand.

The record supports the following facts. Coyne and the petitioner, Susan C. Barrett, were divorced on August 22, 1996, in the Commonwealth of Pennsylvania. The parties agreed to share joint legal custody of their two daughters, Kathryn and Jacqueline, with Barrett having primary physical custody. Additionally, Coyne was ordered to pay child support.

Barrett and the children moved to New Hampshire in 1998. At approximately the same time, Coyne ceased communication with them, although he continued to pay child support. Kathryn attended Winnacunnet High School, a public secondary school in Hampton, during her freshman year. Kathryn had been diagnosed in 1997 with attention deficit disorder and she suffered emotional problems due to her estranged relationship with Coyne. As a result of both conditions, she failed her freshman year. Although Barrett met with the Winnacunnet administration, Kathryn was neither coded for special education nor provided with other assistance.

In order to help her daughter, Barrett decided to enroll her in private school. Kathryn took summer courses and qualified for acceptance as a sophomore at Tilton School (Tilton), a private secondary school. Despite the high cost of private school, Barrett believed that unless Kathryn attended private school she would continue to fail. When requested by Tilton to provide financial information, Coyne submitted the necessary forms without objection. Because of Coyne's and Barrett's financial status, Tilton did not give Kathryn significant financial aid.

Kathryn's grades improved upon her enrollment at Tilton and she passed both her sophomore and junior years. In 2002 Barrett suffered financial difficulties and asked Coyne to pay for Kathryn's tuition to enable her to attend Tilton in her senior year. Coyne refused Barrett's request.

Barrett filed a motion in the Portsmouth Family Division seeking an order that Coyne contribute financially towards Kathryn's senior year at Tilton. The trial court initially found, on October 2, 2002, that Coyne "[did] not have the ability to pay" any amount towards Kathryn's senior year at Tilton.

Barrett filed a motion for reconsideration, arguing that Coyne's ability to pay was greater than that presented to the court because Coyne had failed to include his current wife's income in his financial statements. The trial court reconsidered and ordered Coyne to pay $8,000 of Kathryn's school tuition.

On appeal, Coyne argues that the trial court erred in applying an "ability to pay" standard when ordering him to pay for Kathryn's private school tuition in addition to child support. We will uphold the trial court's decision unless it is unsupported by the evidence or tainted by an error of law. *In the Matter of Peirce and Peirce,* 146 N.H. 611, 613, 777 A.2d 874 (2001).

While we have considered the issue of college education expenses, *see In the Matter of Breault & Breault,* 149 N.H. 359, 821 A.2d 1118 (2003), the award of private secondary education expenses for a minor child is an issue of first impression for this court. Two statutes are relevant to our analysis: (1) RSA 458:17, I (1992), which provides that "the court shall make such ... decree in relation to the support, education, and custody of the children as shall be most conducive to their benefit and may order a reasonable provision for their support and education"; and (2) RSA chapter 458–C (Supp. 2002), the child support guidelines, adopted by the legislature "to establish a uniform system to be used in the determination of the amount of child support," RSA 458–C:1.

In cases of statutory interpretation, we are the final arbiter of the legislature's intent as expressed in the words of the statute considered as a whole. *In the Matter of Coderre & Coderre,* 148 N.H. 401, 403, 807 A.2d 1245 (2002). We interpret legislative intent from the statute as written, and, therefore, we will not consider what the legislature might have said or add words that the legislature did not include. *Id.* Furthermore, we interpret statutes in the context of the overall statutory scheme and not in isolation. *Id.*

There exists an inconsistency between RSA 458:17, I, and RSA chapter 458–C. RSA 458:17, I, on its face appears to authorize an award of education expenses in addition to an award for child support. RSA chapter 458–C, adopted after RSA 458:17, I, however, purports to allow for deviations from the child support guidelines only when "the application of the guidelines would be unjust or inappropriate," RSA 458–C:4, II, IV, because of "special circumstances," RSA 458–C:5, which include "ongoing extraordinary . . . education expenses," RSA 458–C:5, I(a).

We consider all statutes concerning the same subject matter in interpreting any one of them and, where reasonably possible, we construe statutes as consistent with each other. *Coderre,* 148 N.H. at 404, 807 A.2d 1245. When interpreting two statutes that deal with a similar subject matter, we construe them so that they do not contradict each other, and so that they lead to reasonable results and effectuate the legislative purpose of each statute. *Id.*

The purpose of RSA chapter 458–C is not only to ensure uniformity in determining the amount of child support, but also to ensure that both the custodial and non-custodial parents share in the support responsibility for their children, according to the relative percentage of each parent's income. *See* RSA 458–C:1; *see also* RSA 458–C:2, II, IX, XI; RSA 458–C:3, I, II, III.

Through a complex scheme of definitions and formulae, the legislature provided guidelines from which the trial court first determines a parent's total child support obligation. *See* RSA 458–C:2, II, XI; RSA 458–C:3. The legislature has also authorized the trial court to deviate from those guidelines when "the application of the guidelines would be unjust or inappropriate," RSA 458–C:4, II, IV, because of the existence of "special circumstances," RSA 458–C:5. Such "special circumstances" include, as noted above, "ongoing extraordinary . . . education expenses." RSA 458–C:5, I(a).

Under normal circumstances a trial court need not consider private secondary education expenses when determining a non-custodial parent's child support obligation because all children are entitled to a public education. Instead, it is only when the trial court finds that "special circumstances" exist that it may require an obligor parent to contribute to private or specialized education. RSA 458–C:5, I(a). So, while RSA 458:17, I, read separately from the rest of the child support scheme, on its face would appear to authorize an award of private secondary education expenses in addition to the amount awarded under the child support guidelines, such a deviation, absent "special circumstances," would be inconsistent with the child support guidelines. *See* RSA 458–C:5. Therefore, a trial court may deviate from the child support guidelines to account for private secondary education expenses only after a finding that "the application of the guidelines would be unjust or inappropriate," RSA 458–C:4, II, IV, because of "special circumstances," RSA 458–C:5.

While this is an issue of first impression in New Hampshire, other jurisdictions have addressed the parameters of "special circumstances" for the purpose of ordering a non-custodial parent to contribute towards the private education of a minor child. These jurisdictions focus upon two conditions: (1) a demonstrated "special need" of the child; and (2) the non-custodial parent's "ability to pay." *See Solomond v. Ball*, 22 Va.App. 385, 470 S.E.2d 157, 160 (1996); *In re Marriage of Stern*, 57 Wash.App. 707, 789 P.2d 807, 813 (1990); *In re Marriage of Aylesworth*, 106 Cal.App.3d 869, 165 Cal.Rptr. 389, 394 (1980). This approach is consistent with our own statute. *See* RSA 458–C:5.

Therefore, when making a finding that "special circumstances" exist that warrant a deviation from the child support guidelines so as to require a non-custodial parent to contribute toward private secondary education expenses, the trial court must find that both the child has a demonstrated "special need" and the non-custodial parent has "an ability to pay." Furthermore, when determining whether a demonstrated "special need" exists, the trial court may consider such factors as: (1) the child's attendance at private school prior to the separation and divorce; (2) the availability of satisfactory public education, including special education; (3) the child's academic performance; (4) the child's family and/or religious tradition; and (5) the child's particular emotional and/or physical needs. [Citations omitted.]

In this case the trial court required Coyne to contribute to the cost of Kathryn's private education without a finding of "special circumstances." We hold that this was error and remand for consideration of whether Kathryn's private education expenses constitute "special circumstances."

Additionally, Coyne argues that the trial court may not consider his current wife's income when determining whether to order him to contribute towards Kathryn's tuition. Coyne points to RSA 458–C:2, IV(b), which provides that when determining the gross income of a parent, that parent's spouse's income "shall not be considered as gross income to the parent unless the parent resigns from or refuses employment or is voluntarily unemployed or underemployed," and contends that, because neither condition is present in this case, such income may not, therefore, be considered. The circumstances in this case, however, deal, not with determining Coyne's gross income, but rather with determining whether to allow for a deviation from the child support guidelines. RSA 458–C:5, I(c) expressly allows the trial court to consider "[t]he economic consequences of the presence of stepparents." Therefore, upon remand the trial court may consider Coyne's current wife's income for the purpose of determining whether "special circumstances" exist so as to justify a deviation from the child support guidelines. *See* RSA 458–C:5, I(c).

Finally, we turn to Coyne's arguments that the trial court is precluded from awarding Barrett private secondary education expenses because she: (1) failed to pursue certain State and federal remedies; and (2) failed to inform Coyne of her decision to send Kathryn to private school, thus eliminating his ability to pursue those remedies.

Concerning the former argument, we hold that "the availability of a public education program and extensive federal and state guidelines regarding special education does not preclude a parent's decision to place a child in a private school." *Lee,* 728 A.2d at 156. Rather, in evaluating the placement of a child in private school, the court should determine whether "special circumstances" warrant such placement and may consider the "availability of satisfactory public education, including special education" in its analysis of "special needs."

As to the latter argument, Coyne points to RSA 186–C:16–b, I and II, under which there exist statutory periods within which to pursue certain "special education" remedies. Coyne contends that because Barrett failed to inform him of her decision to place Kathryn in private school, she eliminated his ability to pursue those remedies on Kathryn's behalf, since by the time he knew of such placement the statutory periods had expired. We begin by noting that Coyne and Barrett share joint legal custody of Kathryn. "Legal custody refers to the responsibility for making major decisions affecting the child's welfare," 59 Am. Jur. 2d *Parent and Child* § 26 (2002), and legal custodians are entitled to make the major decisions regarding the health, education and religious upbringing of the child, *Chandler v. Bishop,* 142 N.H. 404, 412, 702 A.2d 813 (1997). Thus, either Barrett or Coyne is entitled to bring a petition for "special education" on behalf of Kathryn, if they are unable to make a joint decision.

The trial court, in ruling against Coyne, found that Coyne "had knowledge of his daughter's attendance at [Tilton]" and did nothing to pursue "special education" on her behalf, thus defeating his argument that his opportunity to pursue such education was eliminated. We have not been provided with a record of the first trial court hearing on October 2, 2002. Absent such a record, we assume, for the purposes of appeal, that the evidence supported the trial court's findings, and we limit our review to legal errors apparent on the record available to us. *See Dombrowski v. Dombrowski,* 131 N.H. 654, 663, 559 A.2d 828 (1989).

Though the trial court found that Coyne had knowledge of Kathryn's attendance at Tilton, it did not specify whether that knowledge arose within the relevant statutory time period. It is clear from the limited record available to us that Coyne knew of Kathryn's attendance at Tilton because he filled out the forms to determine her financial aid. Though it is not clear from the record exactly when he filled out those forms, we infer from the trial court's ruling denying him relief that his knowledge must have arisen within the relevant statutory time period. Coyne does not argue that the lack of a record has prejudiced him. The trial court did not commit any legal error and Coyne has presented us with no basis to overturn its ruling.

Coyne also argues that his rights to due process and equal protection under the law were violated by the trial court's order. Because Coyne's constitutional arguments were not adequately briefed and argued, we decline to address them. *State v. Schultz,* 141 N.H. 101, 104, 677 A.2d 675 (1996).

Vacated and remanded.

■ BRODERICK, C.J., AND NADEAY AND DUGGAN, JJ., concurred; BROCK, C.J., retired, specially assigned under RSA 490:3, concurred.

NOTE

Resolving a split in the lower courts, the Ohio Supreme Court ruled that a court may order retroactive child support once paternity has been established, so long as the child files the petition within the time specified by the state statute of limitations, in this case five years after the child turns eighteen. Carnes v. Kemp, 104 Ohio St.3d 629, 821 N.E.2d 180 (2004). The New Hampshire Supreme Court ruled that the court may order interest on the arrearage too. *In re* Giacomini, 868 A.2d 283 (N.H. 2005). A useful tool in calculating child support may be found at: http://www.state.wv.us/wvsca/library/familylaw.htm.

After the Child Support Recovery Act of 1992, add at page 511:

DEADBEAT PARENT PUNISHMENT ACT

18 U.S.C. § 228(a)

228. Failure to pay legal child support obligations

(a) Offense.—Any person who—

(1) willfully fails to pay a support obligation with respect to a child who resides in another State, if such obligation has remained unpaid for a period longer than 1 year, or is greater than $5,000;

(2) travels in interstate or foreign commerce with the intent to evade a support obligation, if such obligation has remained unpaid for a period longer than 1 year, or is greater than $5,000; or

(3) willfully fails to pay a support obligation with respect to a child who resides in another State, if such obligation has remained unpaid for a period longer than 2 years, or is greater than $10,000; shall be punished as provided in subsection (c).

(b) Presumption.—The existence of a support obligation that was in effect for the time period charged in the indictment or information creates a rebuttable presumption that the obligor has the ability to pay the support obligation for that time period.

(c) Punishment.—The punishment for an offense under this section is—

(1) in the case of a first offense under subsection (a)(1), a fine under this title, imprisonment for not more than 6 months, or both; and

(2) in the case of an offense under paragraph (2) or (3) of subsection (a), or a second or subsequent offense under subsection (a)(1), a fine under this title, imprisonment for not more than 2 years, or both.

(d) Mandatory restitution.—Upon a conviction under this section, the court shall order restitution under section 3663A in an amount equal to the total unpaid support obligation as it exists at the time of sentencing.

F.   THE SCOPE OF ANTENUPTIAL CONTRACTING

Add the following case at the end of this section on page 547:

Adams v. Adams

Supreme Court of Georgia, 2004.
278 Ga. 521, 603 S.E.2d 273.

■ HUNSTEIN, JUSTICE.

Andy (Husband) and Kay (Wife) Adams were married in July 1994. Two days before their wedding, they executed an antenuptial agreement which provided, inter alia, that in the event of a separation, Wife would receive $10,000 for every year of marriage with a cap of $100,000. Wife also waived all claims to Husband's pre-marital property and all other claims she may have growing out of the marriage and its dissolution; agreed not to make a "continued lifestyle claim"; and agreed to forfeit her rights if she engaged in "unforgiven adultery." Both parties waived claims to separately titled property whether acquired prior to or during the marriage. At the time of the marriage, Husband's assets were valued at $4,526,708, and Wife's at $30,000.

In January 2003, Wife filed for divorce alleging adultery, cruel treatment, and an irretrievably broken marriage. She sought alimony and an equitable division of property. Husband answered, counterclaimed for divorce, and filed a motion to enforce the antenuptial agreement which the trial court granted. Husband then filed a motion for summary judgment in the divorce action. Wife failed to file a response and a divorce was granted. The trial court ordered Husband to pay to Wife a lump sum payment of $90,000 representing the agreed-upon $10,000 for each year of their marriage. Wife filed an application to appeal from the trial court's order that we granted to determine whether the antenuptial agreement is unconscionable as a matter of law and whether the trial court improperly limited the scope of the hearing on Husband's motion to enforce the antenuptial agreement. Finding no error, we affirm.

1.   In determining whether to enforce an antenuptial agreement in a divorce proceeding, a trial judge should consider whether: (1) the agreement was obtained through fraud, duress or mistake, or through misrepresentation or nondisclosure of material facts; (2) the agreement is unconscionable; and (3) the facts and circumstances have changed since the agreement was executed, so as to make its enforcement unfair and unreasonable. *Scherer v. Scherer,* 249 Ga. 635, 641(3), 292 S.E.2d 662 (1982). In this case, the trial court specifically found that the agreement was entered into without fraud, duress, mistake, coercion, or misrepresentation; it was reviewed by Wife; and Wife was advised of her right to and was given

sufficient opportunity to obtain independent legal review of the agreement before its execution. Wife does not challenge these findings. Instead, she alleges that the agreement is unconscionable when comparing the financial benefits she is entitled to receive under the agreement with Husband's financial status at the time of execution.

A review of the record and trial court's order upholding the agreement reveals that the trial court thoroughly evaluated the relevant considerations. At the time the agreement was executed, Wife successfully ran her own business and had $30,000 in assets while Husband owned several businesses and had a net worth of approximately $4.5 million. Both parties previously had been married and divorced. It was reasonable, therefore, for both Husband and Wife to anticipate the possibility of divorce, to seek to protect their individual assets, and to establish their respective property rights by contract in the event of divorce. See id. at 640(2), 292 S.E.2d 662 (antenuptial agreements permit persons " 'prior to marriage to anticipate the possibility of divorce and to establish their rights by contract in such an event' "). That the antenuptial agreement may have perpetuated the already existing disparity between the parties' estates does not in and of itself render the agreement unconscionable when, as here, there was full and fair disclosure of the assets of the parties prior to the execution of the agreement, and Wife entered into the agreement fully, voluntarily, and with full understanding of its terms after being offered the opportunity to consult with independent counsel. Accordingly, we find the agreement into which the parties entered was fair, both at the time it was executed and in light of subsequent events,[1] and we find no abuse of discretion by the trial court in enforcing the antenuptial agreement.

2. We reject Wife's contention that the trial court erred in excluding from the hearing on the motion to enforce the antenuptial agreement evidence of Husband's alleged infidelity during the marriage. While there may be rare circumstances where such evidence could be relevant to demonstrate unconscionability or changed circumstances under *Scherer,* supra, under the specific facts of this case, Wife's allegations were irrelevant to such determination.

Judgment affirmed.

All the Justices concur.

NOTE

In Alexander v. Alexander, 279 Ga. 116, 610 S.E.2d 48 (2005), the Supreme Court of Georgia upheld a trial court's refusal to uphold and antenuptial agreement when the husband had failed to disclose an investment account worth approximately $40,000.

---

1. At the time of divorce, the financial status of the parties remained substantially the same, with certain of Husband's real property holdings having increased in value and the value of certain businesses having decreased.

J. PROBLEMS OF ENFORCEMENT

At page 599, replace the statute with the following:

28 U.S.C.A. § 1738B

Full faith and credit for child support orders

(a) General rule.—The appropriate authorities of each State—

(1) shall enforce according to its terms a child support order made consistently with this section by a court of another State; and

(2) shall not seek or make a modification of such an order except in accordance with subsections (e), (f), and (i).

(b) Definitions.—In this section:

"child" means—

    (A) a person under 18 years of age; and

    (B) a person 18 or more years of age with respect to whom a child support order has been issued pursuant to the laws of a State.

"child's State" means the State in which a child resides.

"child's home State" means the State in which a child lived with a parent or a person acting as parent for at least 6 consecutive months immediately preceding the time of filing of a petition or comparable pleading for support and, if a child is less than 6 months old, the State in which the child lived from birth with any of them. A period of temporary absence of any of them is counted as part of the 6-month period.

"child support" means a payment of money, continuing support, or arrearages or the provision of a benefit (including payment of health insurance, child care, and educational expenses) for the support of a child.

"child support order"—

    (A) means a judgment, decree, or order of a court requiring the payment of child support in periodic amounts or in a lump sum; and

    (B) includes—

        (i) a permanent or temporary order; and

        (ii) an initial order or a modification of an order.

"contestant" means—

    (A) a person (including a parent) who—

        (i) claims a right to receive child support;

        (ii) is a party to a proceeding that may result in the issuance of a child support order; or

        (iii) is under a child support order; and

(B) a State or political subdivision of a State to which the right to obtain child support has been assigned.

"court" means a court or administrative agency of a State that is authorized by State law to establish the amount of child support payable by a contestant or make a modification of a child support order.

"modification" means a change in a child support order that affects the amount, scope, or duration of the order and modifies, replaces, supersedes, or otherwise is made subsequent to the child support order.

"State" means a State of the United States, the District of Columbia, the Commonwealth of Puerto Rico, the territories and possessions of the United States, and Indian country (as defined in section 1151 of title 18).

(c) Requirements of child support orders.—A child support order made by a court of a State is made consistently with this section if—

(1) a court that makes the order, pursuant to the laws of the State in which the court is located and subsections (e), (f), and (g)—

(A) has subject matter jurisdiction to hear the matter and enter such an order; and

(B) has personal jurisdiction over the contestants; and

(2) reasonable notice and opportunity to be heard is given to the contestants.

(d) Continuing jurisdiction.—A court of a State that has made a child support order consistently with this section has continuing, exclusive jurisdiction over the order if the State is the child's State or the residence of any individual contestant unless the court of another State, acting in accordance with subsections (e) and (f), has made a modification of the order.

(e) Authority to modify orders.—A court of a State may modify a child support order issued by a court of another State if—

(1) the court has jurisdiction to make such a child support order pursuant to subsection (i); and

(2)(A) the court of the other State no longer has continuing, exclusive jurisdiction of the child support order because that State no longer is the child's State or the residence of any individual contestant; or

(B) each individual contestant has filed written consent with the State of continuing, exclusive jurisdiction for a court of another State to modify the order and assume continuing, exclusive jurisdiction over the order.

(f) Recognition of child support orders.—If 1 or more child support orders have been issued with regard to an obligor and a child, a court shall apply the following rules in determining which order to recognize for purposes of continuing, exclusive jurisdiction and enforcement:

(1) If only 1 court has issued a child support order, the order of that court must be recognized.

(2) If 2 or more courts have issued child support orders for the same obligor and child, and only 1 of the courts would have continuing, exclusive jurisdiction under this section, the order of that court must be recognized.

(3) If 2 or more courts have issued child support orders for the same obligor and child, and more than 1 of the courts would have continuing, exclusive jurisdiction under this section, an order issued by a court in the current home State of the child must be recognized, but if an order has not been issued in the current home State of the child, the order most recently issued must be recognized.

(4) If 2 or more courts have issued child support orders for the same obligor and child, and none of the courts would have continuing, exclusive jurisdiction under this section, a court having jurisdiction over the parties shall issue a child support order, which must be recognized.

(5) The court that has issued an order recognized under this subsection is the court having continuing, exclusive jurisdiction under subsection (d).

(g) Enforcement of modified orders.—A court of a State that no longer has continuing, exclusive jurisdiction of a child support order may enforce the order with respect to nonmodifiable obligations and unsatisfied obligations that accrued before the date on which a modification of the order is made under subsections (e) and (f).

(h) Choice of law.—

(1) In general.—In a proceeding to establish, modify, or enforce a child support order, the forum State's law shall apply except as provided in paragraphs (2) and (3).

(2) Law of State of issuance of order.—In interpreting a child support order including the duration of current payments and other obligations of support, a court shall apply the law of the State of the court that issued the order.

(3) Period of limitation.—In an action to enforce arrears under a child support order, a court shall apply the statute of limitation of the forum State or the State of the court that issued the order, whichever statute provides the longer period of limitation.

(i) Registration for modification.—If there is no individual contestant or child residing in the issuing State, the party or support enforcement agency seeking to modify, or to modify and enforce, a child support order issued in another State shall register that order in a State with jurisdiction over the nonmovant for the purpose of modification.

CHAPTER VI

PARENT AND CHILD: LEGAL AND BIOLOGICAL RELATIONSHIPS

B. ESTABLISHING LEGAL PARENTAGE

Please replace NOTE on "What about maternity?" at page 661 with the following:

UNIFORM PARENTAGE ACT (2002)

[Reprinted with permission from the National Conference of Commissioners on Uniform State Laws.]

SECTION 201. ESTABLISHMENT OF PARENT–CHILD RELATIONSHIP.

(a) The mother-child relationship is established between a woman and a child by:

(1) the woman's having given birth to the child [, except as otherwise provided in [Article] 8];

(2) an adjudication of the woman's maternity; [or]

(3) adoption of the child by the woman [; or

(4) an adjudication confirming the woman as a parent of a child born to a gestational mother if the agreement was validated under [Article] 8 or is enforceable under other law].

(b) The father-child relationship is established between a man and a child by:

(1) an unrebutted presumption of the man's paternity of the child under Section 204;

(2) an effective acknowledgment of paternity by the man under [Article] 3, unless the acknowledgment has been rescinded or successfully challenged;

(3) an adjudication of the man's paternity;

(4) adoption of the child by the man; [or]

(5) the man's having consented to assisted reproduction by a woman under [Article] 7 which resulted in the birth of the child [; or

(6) an adjudication confirming the man as a parent of a child born to a gestational mother if the agreement was validated under [Article] 8 or is enforceable under other law].

SECTION 204. PRESUMPTION OF PATERNITY.

(a) A man is presumed to be the father of a child if:

(1) he and the mother of the child are married to each other and the child is born during the marriage;

(2) he and the mother of the child were married to each other and the child is born within 300 days after the marriage is terminated by death, annulment, declaration of invalidity, or divorce [, or after a decree of separation];

(3) before the birth of the child, he and the mother of the child married each other in apparent compliance with law, even if the attempted marriage is or could be declared invalid, and the child is born during the invalid marriage or within 300 days after its termination by death, annulment, declaration of invalidity, or divorce [, or after a decree of separation];

(4) after the birth of the child, he and the mother of the child married each other in apparent compliance with law, whether or not the marriage is or could be declared invalid, and he voluntarily asserted his paternity of the child, and:

(A) the assertion is in a record filed with [state agency maintaining birth records];

(B) he agreed to be and is named as the child's father on the child's birth certificate; or

(C) he promised in a record to support the child as his own; or

(5) for the first two years of the child's life, he resided in the same household with the child and openly held out the child as his own.

(b) A presumption of paternity established under this section may be rebutted only by an adjudication under [Article] 6.

At the end of **Little v. Streater,** *please add at page 671:*

G.P. v. State

Florida District Court of Appeals, 2003.
842 So.2d 1059.

■ STONE, J.

We reverse a declaratory judgment in which the trial court found that sections 63.087–088(5), Florida Statutes, relating to private adoptions under the Florida Adoption Act, were not unconstitutional. The Attorney General of Florida has intentionally failed to file a contesting brief and neither the attorney general nor the Palm Beach County State Attorney appeared at the hearing below.

Appellants are four women who have each executed a formal consent for adoption of their children and have authorized an intermediary to file a petition to terminate their parental rights. Because, in each case, the identity of the fathers is unknown, constructive notice is required under the challenged statutory provisions.

Appellants moved for declaratory relief, challenging sections 63.087 and 63.088(5) as violative of their right to privacy guaranteed under the

Fourteenth Amendment of the United States Constitution and Article I, § 23 of the Florida Constitution. Although the trial court agreed that the provisions violated Appellants' right to privacy, the court found that Appellants had failed to prove that the state did not have a compelling interest to invade their privacy or that the interest could be achieved through less intrusive means. The court did find that the statutes were unconstitutional as to the women whose pregnancy was a result of sexual battery.

Under the challenged statutes, Appellants would be forced to publish information relating to their sexual relations that may have led to the child's conception. Section 63.087(6)(f) provides, in relevant part:

(f) The petition must include:

1.   The minor's name, gender, date of birth, and place of birth. The petition must contain all names by which the minor is or has been known, excluding the minor's prospective adoptive name but including the minor's legal name at the time of the filing of the petition, to allow interested parties to the action, including parents, persons having legal custody of the minor, persons with custodial or visitation rights to the minor, and persons entitled to notice pursuant to the Uniform Child Custody Jurisdiction Act or the Indian Child Welfare Act, to identify their own interest in the action.

2.   If the petition is filed before the day the minor is 6 months old and if the identity or location of the father is unknown, each city in which the mother resided or traveled, in which conception may have occurred, during the 12 months before the minor's birth, including the county and state in which that city is located.

3.   Unless a consent to adoption or affidavit of nonpaternity executed by each person whose consent is required under s. 63.062 is attached to the petition, the name and the city of residence, including the county and state in which that city is located, of:

a.   The minor's mother;

b.   Any man who the mother reasonably believes may be the minor's father....

§ 63.087(6)(f)1–3, Fla. Stat. (2002).

Notice and service requirements are governed by section 63.088, Florida Statutes. Appellants challenge only subsection (5) of section 63.088, which states:

(5) LOCATION UNKNOWN OR IDENTITY UNKNOWN. This subsection only applies if, as to any person whose consent is required under s. 63.062 and who has not executed an affidavit of nonpaternity, the location or identity of the person is unknown and the inquiry under subsection (3) fails to identify the person or the diligent search under subsection (4) fails to locate the person. The unlocated or unidentified person must be served notice under subsection (2) by constructive service in the manner provided in chapter 49 in each

county identified in the petition, as provided in s. 63.087(6). The notice, in addition to all information required in the petition under s. 63.087(6) and chapter 49, must contain a physical description, including, but not limited to, age, race, hair and eye color, and approximate height and weight of the minor's mother and of any person the mother reasonably believes may be the father; the minor's date of birth, and any date and city, including the county and state in which the city is located, in which conception may have occurred. If any of the facts that must be included in the notice under this subsection are unknown and cannot be reasonably ascertained, the notice must so state.

§ 63.088(5), Fla. Stat.

Article I, section 23 of the Florida Constitution, recognizes a right to privacy in this state and provides: "[e]very natural person has the right to be let alone and free from governmental intrusion into the person's private life as otherwise provided herein." This right to privacy encompasses at least two different categories of interest. The first is "the individual interest in avoiding disclosure of personal matters[.]" *Rasmussen v. S. Fla. Blood Serv., Inc.*, 500 So.2d 533, 536 (Fla.1987)(quoting *Whalen v. Roe,* 429 U.S. 589, 599–600, 97 S.Ct. 869, 51 L.Ed.2d 64 (1977)). The second is "the interest in independence in making certain kinds of important decisions." *Id.* In deciding whether this constitutional right is impacted, the courts consider both the individual's subjective expectation and the values of privacy that our society seeks to foster. *Jackson v. State,* 833 So.2d 243 (Fla. 4th DCA 2002).

The concern as to sections 63.087 and 63.088(5) is that the offending provisions substantially interfere with both a woman's independence in choosing adoption as an alternative and with the right not to disclose the intimate personal information that is required when the father is unknown. We deem the invasion of both of these interests so patent in this instance as to not require our analysis of cases interpreting this constitutional provision. *See generally, Von Eiff v. Azicri,* 720 So.2d 510 (Fla.1998); *In re T.W.,* 551 So.2d 1186 (Fla.1989).

Having thus determined that the statutes violate a fundamental right to privacy, the burden of proof shifted to the state to justify the intrusion on the mothers' privacy. *See Von Eiff,* 720 So.2d at 514. The standard is one of strict scrutiny. The state has the burden of demonstrating that the challenged statutes serve a compelling state interest and that they accomplish the intended result, i.e., notice to fathers, through the use of the least intrusive means. *Id.; Fla. Bd. of Bar Examiners Re: Applicant,* 443 So.2d 71, 74 (Fla.1983)("The compelling state interest or strict scrutiny standard imposes a heavy burden of justification upon the state to show an important societal need and the use of the least intrusive means to achieve that goal.").

The legislature's intent in enacting the stringent notice provisions was to finalize private adoptions by ensuring that all possible avenues of affording parents their due process have been exhausted and to protect the child by ensuring that any future challenge to the adoption based on lack of notice would be unsuccessful.

The state has failed to demonstrate, however, how any compelling interest of either the putative father or the state outweighs the privacy rights of the mother and child in not being identified in such a personal, intimate, and intrusive manner.

We do not address the alternative proposals that have been raised by the appellants which are designed to ensure that notice is sufficient to protect the due process rights of the unknown fathers, such as by registration with a state or national database, or simply by a more narrowly tailored statute.

It is sufficient, here, given the state's effective waiver of interest, to simply recognize that the state failed to demonstrate a sufficiently compelling interest for such an invasion of privacy and that the interests sought to be achieved could not have been accomplished by less intrusive means. Strict scrutiny imposes a heavy burden on the state. *Fla. Bd. of Bar Examiners,* 443 So.2d at 74. Thus, the trial court erred in placing the burden on Appellants to prove the state did not have a compelling interest and that the means used were not the least intrusive.

We conclude that the state failed to meet its burden of proof in demonstrating the validity of the challenged provisions. The state has, in effect, conceded that the statutes cannot survive a strict scrutiny challenge. Accordingly, the order on appeal is reversed. We remand for further proceedings as governed by the remainder of the statute.

■ WARNER and HAZOURI, JJ., concur.

C.   PROCREATIVE DECISION MAKING: SPECIAL ISSUES OF THE NEW AND OLD TECHNOLOGIES

2.   ASSISTED CONCEPTION

Add the following to the paragraph on page 697:

UNIFORM PARENTAGE ACT (2002)

[Reprinted with permission from the National Conference of Commissioners on Uniform State Laws.]

SECTION 701.   SCOPE OF ARTICLE. This [article] does not apply to the birth of a child conceived by means of sexual intercourse [, or as the result of a gestational agreement as provided in [Article] 8].

SECTION 702.   PARENTAL STATUS OF DONOR. A donor is not a parent of a child conceived by means of assisted reproduction.

SECTION 703.   PATERNITY OF CHILD OF ASSISTED REPRODUCTION. A man who provides sperm for, or consents to, assisted reproduction by a woman as provided in Section 704 with the intent to be the parent of her child, is a parent of the resulting child.

SECTION 704.   CONSENT TO ASSISTED REPRODUCTION.

(a) Consent by a woman, and a man who intends to be a parent of a child born to the woman by assisted reproduction must be in a record signed by the woman and the man. This requirement does not apply to a donor.

(b) Failure a man to sign a consent required by subsection (a), before or after birth of the child, does not preclude a finding of paternity if the woman and the man, during the first two years of the child's life resided together in the same household with the child and openly held out the child as their own.

SECTION 705.   LIMITATION ON HUSBAND'S DISPUTE OF PATERNITY.

(a) Except as otherwise provided in subsection (b), the husband of a wife who gives birth to a child by means of assisted reproduction may not challenge his paternity of the child unless:

(1) within two years after learning of the birth of the child he commences a proceeding to adjudicate his paternity; and

(2) the court finds that he did not consent to the assisted reproduction, before or after birth of the child.

(b) A proceeding to adjudicate paternity may be maintained at any time if the court determines that:

(1) the husband did not provide sperm for, or before or after the birth of the child consent to, assisted reproduction by his wife;

(2) the husband and the mother of the child have not cohabited since the probable time of assisted reproduction; and

(3) the husband never openly held out the child as his own.

(c) The limitation provided in this section applies to a marriage declared invalid after assisted reproduction.

SECTION 706.   EFFECT OF DISSOLUTION OF MARRIAGE OR WITHDRAWAL OF CONSENT.

(a) If a marriage is dissolved before placement of eggs, sperm, or embryos, the former spouse is not a parent of the resulting child unless the former spouse consented in a record that if assisted reproduction were to occur after a divorce, the former spouse would be a parent of the child.

(b) The consent of a woman or a man to assisted reproduction may be withdrawn by that individual in a record at any time before placement of eggs, sperm, or embryos. An individual who withdraws consent under this section is not a parent of the resulting child.

SECTION 707. PARENTAL STATUS OF DECEASED INDIVIDUAL.

If an individual who consented in a record to be a parent by assisted reproduction dies before placement of eggs, sperm, or embryos, the deceased individual is not a parent of the resulting child unless the deceased spouse consented in a record that if assisted reproduction were to occur after death, the deceased individual would be a parent of the child.

Replace R.S. v. R.S. at page 701 with the following decision:

In re M.J.

Supreme Court of Illinois, 2003.
203 Ill.2d 526, 272 Ill.Dec. 329, 787 N.E.2d 144..

■ JUSTICE KILBRIDE delivered the opinion of the court.

Appellant, Alexis Mitchell, brought this action against appellee, Raymond Banary, her former paramour, seeking to establish paternity and to impose support obligations for twin boys conceived through artificial insemination by an anonymous donor. The circuit court of Cook County dismissed Alexis' suit. The appellate court affirmed. 325 Ill.App.3d 826, 259 Ill.Dec. 641, 759 N.E.2d 121. We allowed Alexis' petition for leave to appeal. 177 Ill.2d R. 315. We also granted the Lambda Legal Defense and Education Fund, Inc., leave to submit an *amicus curiae* brief in support of Alexis. See 155 Ill.2d R. 345. We now affirm in part, reverse in part, and hold that the Illinois Parentage Act does not bar common law claims for child support.

. . .

Alexis is a single woman who was 40 years old at the time of the filing of her complaint, and Raymond is a male who was 57 years old at the time of the filing of the complaint. Alexis and Raymond first met in 1986 and began an intimate relationship lasting 10 years. When they met, Raymond introduced himself to Alexis as "Jim Richardson" and told her that he was divorced.

During their 10–year relationship, the parties discussed marriage. Alexis and Raymond are of different races and, according to Alexis, Raymond told her that he would have to wait until retirement to marry because his community would not accept a mixed-race marriage. Raymond promised Alexis that upon his retirement, they would move to another community and be married.

The parties also discussed Alexis' desire to have children with Raymond. Despite their attempts to conceive, Alexis did not become pregnant, and it became apparent that Raymond could not father children. In 1991, Raymond suggested to Alexis that she become artificially inseminated by an anonymous donor as a means to have their child. Artificial insemination by a donor is also known as heterologous artificial insemination. Alexis claims that Raymond promised her that he would provide financial support for any child born by means of artificial insemination. However, Raymond's written consent to the procedure was never obtained. Alexis contends that Raymond orally consented to the procedure and that but for Raymond's promise to support the children, Alexis would not have completed the procedure.

According to Alexis, with Raymond's continuing consent and active encouragement, she attempted to become pregnant through artificial insemination. Raymond provided financial assistance for the insemination procedure; accompanied Alexis to the doctor's office for examinations;

injected Alexis with medication designed to enhance her fertility; and participated in selecting the donor so that the offspring would appear to be a product of their relationship.

On the fifth attempt, Alexis became pregnant and gave birth to twin boys in 1993. Raymond participated in selecting names for the children. After the births, Raymond acknowledged the children as his own. He also provided support for them in the form of monthly payments of cash and the purchase of food, clothing, furniture, toys, and play equipment. In her complaint, Alexis further describes many family vacations with Raymond to 10 different states and Mexico, and alleges that Raymond also paid for the children's medical, travel, and entertainment expenses.

In 1996, Alexis discovered that Raymond was not named Jim Richardson and that he was married. Upon discovering Raymond's true name and marital status, Alexis ended their relationship. Since 1996, Raymond has provided no financial support for the children.

Alexis filed a three-count complaint against Raymond seeking to establish paternity and impose a support obligation for the benefit of the twin boys. In the first two counts, Alexis sought to impose child support obligations by invoking common law theories of breach of an oral agreement and promissory estoppel. In the remaining count of her complaint, Alexis sought a declaration of paternity and establishment of child support pursuant to the Illinois Parentage Act (750 ILCS 40/1 *et seq.* (West 1998)).

Raymond filed a motion to dismiss, arguing that Alexis' common law claims, contained in counts I and II, were unenforceable under the provisions of the Frauds Act (740 ILCS 80/0.01 *et seq.* (West 1998)) and contravened Illinois public policy. Raymond also argued that all three counts should be dismissed pursuant to section 2–615 of the Code (735 ILCS 5/2–615 (West 1998)) because Alexis failed to set forth a legally recognized basis for the imposition of a father-child relationship or for child support under the Illinois Parentage Act (750 ILCS 40/1 *et seq.* (West 1998)).

The circuit court granted Raymond's motion and dismissed Alexis' complaint. The circuit court interpreted the Illinois Parentage Act as requiring that a husband consent in writing before he is treated in law as the natural father of a child conceived to his wife by means of artificial insemination. The circuit court commented that it would not be rational that unmarried couples would have fewer safeguards in such a matter. The circuit court therefore held that Alexis' common law theories were not actionable because the Illinois Parentage Act expressly requires written consent. The circuit court did not refer to the Frauds Act in its dismissal of the complaint.

Alexis appealed the circuit court's decision, and the appellate court majority determined that Alexis' common law theories for child support fail because the Illinois Parentage Act governs artificial insemination and requires that the "husband's consent must be in writing." The appellate court held that written consent is required before an unmarried man becomes legally obligated to support a child born as a result of artificial insemination. Based on its decision, the appellate court did not reach the issue concerning the Frauds Act.

. . .

In construing a statute, this court must give effect to the intent of the legislature. *Antunes v. Sookhakitch*, 146 Ill.2d 477, 484, 167 Ill.Dec. 981, 588 N.E.2d 1111 (1992). To ascertain legislative intent, we must examine the language of the entire statute and consider each part or section in connection with every other part or section. *Castaneda v. Illinois Human Rights Comm'n*, 132 Ill.2d 304, 318, 138 Ill.Dec. 270, 547 N.E.2d 437 (1989). Where the language is clear and unambiguous, we must apply the statute without resort to further aids of statutory construction. *Davis v. Toshiba Machine Co., America*, 186 Ill.2d 181, 184–85, 237 Ill.Dec. 769, 710 N.E.2d 399 (1999). With these principles in mind, we now turn to the interpretation of the Illinois Parentage Act.

In 1984, the General Assembly enacted the Illinois Parentage Act (750 ILCS 40/1 *et seq.* (West 1998)) "to define the legal relationships of a child born to a wife and husband requesting and consenting to * * * artificial insemination." Pub. Act 83–1026, eff. January 5, 1984. Section 3 of the Illinois Parentage Act provides:

> "(a) If, under the supervision of a licensed physician and with the consent of her husband, a wife is inseminated artificially with semen donated by a man not her husband, the husband shall be treated in law as if he were the natural father of a child thereby conceived. The husband's consent must be in writing executed and acknowledged by both the husband and wife. The physician who is to perform the technique shall certify their signatures and the date of the insemination, and file the husband's consent in the medical record where it shall be kept confidential and held by the patient's physician. However, the physician's failure to do so shall not affect the legal relationship between father and child. All papers and records pertaining to the insemination, whether part of the permanent medical record held by the physician or not, are subject to inspection only upon an order of the court for good cause shown.

> (b) The donor of the semen provided to a licensed physician for use in artificial insemination of a woman other than the donor's wife shall be treated in law as if he were not the natural father of a child thereby conceived." 750 ILCS 40/3(a) (West 1998).

Any child born as a result of artificial insemination is considered the legitimate child of the husband and wife consenting to the use of the technique. 750 ILCS 40/2 (West 1998). Our interpretation of the express language of this provision of the statute indicates that the primary purpose of the Illinois Parentage Act is to provide a legal mechanism for a husband and wife to obtain donor sperm for use in artificial insemination and to ensure that a child is considered the legitimate child of the husband and wife requesting and consenting to the artificial technique.

Section 3(b) of the Illinois Parentage Act also provides a statutory vehicle for women to obtain semen for artificial insemination without fear that the donor may claim paternity. 750 ILCS 40/3(b) (West 1998). Additionally, section 3(b) protects sperm donors from claims of paternity and liability for child support.

The parties dispute whether, under section 3(a) of the Illinois Parentage Act, the failure to provide written consent will preclude the establishment of a parent-child relationship and the imposition of a support obligation. This court has not conclusively interpreted the written-consent provision of the Act. We have, however, commented that the provision in the Act that "the husband's consent to the [artificial insemination] procedure 'must be in writing' *could be* considered a mandatory requirement for establishing a parent-child relationship pursuant to the statute." (Emphasis added.) *In re Marriage of Adams,* 133 Ill.2d 437, 444, 141 Ill.Dec. 448, 551 N.E.2d 635 (1990), citing *Andrews v. Foxworthy,* 71 Ill.2d 13, 21, 15 Ill.Dec. 648, 373 N.E.2d 1332 (1978) (the word "must" is generally construed in a mandatory sense.)

Whether a statutory provision is deemed mandatory or merely directory depends upon the intent of its drafters. *People v. Youngbey,* 82 Ill.2d 556, 562, 45 Ill.Dec. 938, 413 N.E.2d 416 (1980). An important aid in the determination of whether a provision is mandatory or directory is the form of the verb used in the statute. *Youngbey,* 82 Ill.2d at 562, 45 Ill.Dec. 938, 413 N.E.2d 416. If the provision merely directs a manner of conduct, it is directory. *Andrews,* 71 Ill.2d at 21, 15 Ill.Dec. 648, 373 N.E.2d 1332. If the conduct is, however, prescribed in order to safeguard one's rights, the statute is mandatory. *Andrews,* 71 Ill.2d at 21, 15 Ill.Dec. 648, 373 N.E.2d 1332.

The first sentence of section 3(a) provides for the establishment of a parent-child relationship by consent. The second sentence of section 3(a) unequivocally requires that the consent for establishment of a parent-child relationship be in writing. This provision is clearly designed to safeguard rights concerning parentage. In light of the purpose of the written-consent requirement, we must conclude that the written-consent provision of section 3(a) of the Illinois Parentage Act is mandatory. Thus, section 3(a) of the Illinois Parentage Act mandates that written consent be obtained before parental responsibility may be established. Consequently, the failure to provide or obtain written consent will preclude a claim for paternity and child support under the Illinois Parentage Act. Accordingly, the appellate court did not err in affirming the circuit court's dismissal of count III of Alexis' complaint.

We note that the language of the Illinois Parentage Act was largely adopted from section 5 of the Uniform Parentage Act (UPA) (Unif. Parentage Act § 5, 9B U.L.A. 377 (1973)), as approved by the National Conference of Commissioners on Uniform State Laws. The commentary to section 5 of the UPA states:

"This Act does not deal with the many complex and serious legal problems raised by the practice of artificial insemination. It was though [*sic*] useful, however, to single out and cover in this Act at least one fact situation that occurs frequently. Further consideration of other legal aspects of artificial insemination has been urged on the National Conference of Commissioners on Uniform State Laws and is recommended to state legislators." Unif. Parentage Act § 5, 9B U.L.A. 408, Comment (1973).

At the time the Illinois Parentage Act was enacted, the legislature intended to clarify the legal relationships among the parties involved in the artificial insemination procedure. See L. Smith, *The AID Child and In re Marriage of Adams: Ambiguities in the Illinois Parentage Act,* 21 Loy. U. Chi. L.J. 1173, 1192–93 (1990). However, as recognized by the commentary to section 5 of the UPA, the artificial insemination legislation "does not deal with the many complex and serious legal problems raised by the practice of artificial insemination." Unif. Parentage Act § 5, 9B U.L.A. 408, Comment (1973). Accordingly, the UPA comment urges that state legislators consider other legal aspects of artificial insemination.

In its current form, the Illinois Parentage Act fails to address the full spectrum of legal problems facing children born as a result of artificial insemination and other modern methods of assisted reproduction. The rapid evolution of assisted reproduction technology will continue to produce legal problems similar to those presented in this case. We urge the Illinois legislature to enact laws that are responsive to these problems in order to safeguard the interests of children born as a result of assisted reproductive technology.

The need for reform to the Illinois Parentage Act is clear where, as here, we are compelled to apply the statute, in its current form, to a complex legal situation that the legislature did not anticipate when it passed the Illinois Parentage Act nearly 20 years ago.

Based on our determination that written consent is a prerequisite for invoking the protections of the Illinois Parentage Act, we need not and do not make any determination with regard to whether the Illinois Parentage Act applies to unmarried persons. Section 3(a) of the Illinois Parentage Act is simply not satisfied in this case because written consent was lacking.

Our determination that Alexis may not maintain an action under the Illinois Parentage Act does not end our inquiry. We must now determine whether the Illinois Parentage Act precludes common law claims for child support. Two Illinois appellate court cases have addressed this issue. These cases are *In re Marriage of Adams,* 174 Ill.App.3d 595, 124 Ill.Dec. 184, 528 N.E.2d 1075 (1988), *rev'd on other grounds,* 133 Ill.2d 437, 141 Ill.Dec. 448, 551 N.E.2d 635 (1990), and *In re Marriage of Witbeck–Wildhagen,* 281 Ill.App.3d 502, 217 Ill.Dec. 329, 667 N.E.2d 122 (1996). Each case reached a different result based on its unique facts.

In *Adams,* the appellate court held that the Illinois Parentage Act does not bar the imposition of a support obligation under an estoppel or waiver theory and that the failure to execute a written consent did not bar further inquiry into the circumstances surrounding the decision to use artificial insemination. *Adams,* 174 Ill.App.3d at 610–11, 124 Ill.Dec. 184, 528 N.E.2d 1075. The appellate court affirmed the trial court's finding that there was "actual consent" by the husband to the insemination procedure, who twice attempted to have his vasectomy reversed, had knowledge of and paid for tests and medical bills, accepted joint responsibility for the child, and listed the child as a dependent on his federal income tax return. *Adams,* 174 Ill.App.3d at 613–15, 124 Ill.Dec. 184, 528 N.E.2d 1075. This court reversed and remanded the cause, on other grounds, holding that Florida law governed because the parties had resided in that state when the procedure was performed. *Adams,* 133 Ill.2d at 448, 141 Ill.Dec. 448, 551 N.E.2d 635. We did not, however, reach the issue of whether a cause of action for child support could be maintained under common law theories.

In *Witbeck-Wildhagen,* 281 Ill.App.3d 502, 217 Ill.Dec. 329, 667 N.E.2d 122, the husband made it clear that he did not consent to the procedure, and the wife acknowledged that he did not consent. Nonetheless, the wife petitioned to have the husband declared the legal father of her child and she sought child support. The appellate court upheld the trial court's finding that the husband did not consent to the insemination procedure since there was no evidence of the husband's consent, written or otherwise. *Witbeck-Wildhagen,* 281 Ill.App.3d at 506–07, 217 Ill.Dec. 329, 667 N.E.2d 122. The appellate court specifically stated that it was not deciding whether the failure to obtain written consent would be an absolute bar to the establishment of the father-child relationship where the conduct of the father otherwise demonstrated his consent. *Witbeck-Wildhagen,* 281 Ill. App.3d at 506–07, 217 Ill.Dec. 329, 667 N.E.2d 122. The appellate court recognized that this was not a case where the husband was "attempting to evade responsibility for his own actions in helping to conceive or encouraging the conception of a child." *Witbeck-Wildhagen,* 281 Ill.App.3d at 507, 217 Ill.Dec. 329, 667 N.E.2d 122.

Although the appellate court reached opposite conclusions in *Adams* and *Witbeck-Wildhagen,* a finding of the existence or nonexistence of consent was based on an examination of the specific facts in each case.

In interpreting the Illinois Parentage Act, this court has specifically noted that "[i]t may be the case that a support obligation will be found even in the absence of a parent-child relationship." *In re Marriage of Adams,* 133 Ill.2d 437, 445, 141 Ill.Dec. 448, 551 N.E.2d 635 (1990). In *Adams,* this court recognized its duty, in an action where the interests of a minor are at stake, to ensure that the rights of the child are adequately protected. *Adams,* 133 Ill.2d at 445, 141 Ill.Dec. 448, 551 N.E.2d 635, citing *Muscarello v. Peterson,* 20 Ill.2d 548, 170 N.E.2d 564 (1960). We also suggested that estoppel might be available to prove consent. *Adams,* 133 Ill.2d at 448, 141 Ill.Dec. 448, 551 N.E.2d 635.

Illinois has articulated its public policy recognizing the right of every child to the physical, mental, emotional, and monetary support of his or her parents. See 750 ILCS 45/1.1 (West 1998). Public policy considerations also seek to prevent children born as a result of assisted reproductive technology procedures from becoming public charges. See *Department of Public Aid ex rel. Cox v. Miller,* 146 Ill.2d 399, 411–12, 166 Ill.Dec. 922, 586 N.E.2d 1251 (1992) (concluding that the legislature intends to provide parental support for all minor children and commenting that "[l]egislative common sense dictates that if parents do not support their children, an already strained State welfare system must do so"). Illinois has a strong interest in protecting and promoting the welfare of its children. See *In re Marriage of Lappe,* 176 Ill.2d 414, 431, 223 Ill.Dec. 647, 680 N.E.2d 380 (1997). We believe that, consistently with this important public policy, cases involving assisted reproduction must be decided based on the particular circumstances presented.

In considering the reach of the Illinois Parentage Act, we note that the statute contains only three sections: (1) the title section; (2) a section declaring that children conceived as a result of artificial insemination are deemed the same as the naturally conceived legitimate child of the husband and wife; and (3) a section concerning consent procedures of the "husband," and protections for and against the sperm donor. In interpreting a statute, courts should not add requirements or impose limitations that are inconsistent with the plain meaning of the enactment. *Nottage v. Jeka,* 172 Ill.2d 386, 392, 217 Ill.Dec. 298, 667 N.E.2d 91 (1996). Our examination of these three sections of the Illinois Parentage Act finds nothing to prohibit common law actions to establish parental responsibility, and the state's public policy considerations support a finding in favor of allowing common law actions. Moreover, this court has a duty to ensure that the rights of children are adequately protected. *Adams,* 133 Ill.2d at 445, 141 Ill.Dec. 448, 551 N.E.2d 635.

We believe that if the legislature had intended to bar common law actions for child support, it would have clearly stated its intent, and we will not imply a legislative intent where none is expressed. See *Nottage,* 172 Ill.2d at 395, 217 Ill.Dec. 298, 667 N.E.2d 91. We therefore determine that the best interests of children and society are served by recognizing that parental responsibility may be imposed based on conduct evincing actual consent to the artificial insemination procedure.

The courts of other states have reached similar results and have assigned parental responsibility based on conduct evincing consent to the artificial insemination. See *Gursky v. Gursky,* 39 Misc.2d 1083, 242 N.Y.S.2d 406 (1963) (husband held liable for support of a child conceived by artificial insemination under either the basis of implied consent to support or the application of the doctrine of estoppel); *K.S. v. G.S.,* 182 N.J.Super. 102, 440 A.2d 64 (1981) (oral consent of husband was effective at the time pregnancy occurs unless established by clear and convincing evidence that consent has been revoked or rescinded); *In re Marriage of L.M.S.,* 105 Wis.2d 118, 122–23, 312 N.W.2d 853, 855 (App.1981) (sterile man who suggested to his wife that she become pregnant by another man and promised that he would acknowledge the child as his own has a legal obligation "to support the child for whose existence he is responsible"); *In re Baby Doe,* 291 S.C. 389, 353 S.E.2d 877 (1987) (husband's consent to artificial insemination may be express, or implied from conduct).

Here, Raymond's *alleged* conduct evinces a powerful case of actual consent. The allegations demonstrate a deliberate course of conduct with the precise goal of causing the birth of these children. In comparison, statutes and case law do not equivocate in imposing child support obligations for other children born out of wedlock. Moreover, a state may not discriminate against a child based on the marital status of the parties at the time of the child's birth. See *Miller,* 146 Ill.2d at 405, 166 Ill.Dec. 922, 586 N.E.2d 1251; *Gomez v. Perez,* 409 U.S. 535, 538, 93 S.Ct. 872, 875, 35 L.Ed.2d 56, 60 (1973); *Mills v. Habluetzel,* 456 U.S. 91, 92, 102 S.Ct. 1549, 1551, 71 L.Ed.2d 770, 773 (1982). Thus, if an unmarried man who biologically causes conception through sexual relations without the premeditated intent of birth is legally obligated to support a child, then the equivalent resulting birth of a child caused by the deliberate conduct of artificial insemination should receive the same treatment in the eyes of the law. Regardless of the method of conception, a child is born in need of support. Under the alleged facts of this case, to hold otherwise would deprive the children of financial support merely because of deception and a technical oversight. Simply put, we cannot accept Raymond's argument that these children and their mother must be left to fend for themselves.

Claims of parentage and support of children produced as a result of assisted reproductive technologies are unique and must be decided based on the particular facts in each case. We hold that the Illinois Parentage Act does not preclude Alexis' claims based on common law theories of oral contract or promissory estoppel. Accordingly, the circuit court erred in dismissing counts I and II of Alexis' complaint on this basis, and the appellate court erred in affirming that order. We make no determination on the merits of Alexis' claims, or Raymond's affirmative defenses, including the Frauds Act, since these claims and defenses must be developed in the circuit court.

Our holding is limited to the unique circumstances of this case. We do not address issues raised by the *amicus,* because these issues were not previously raised by the parties to this appeal. See *Burger v. Lutheran General Hospital,* 198 Ill.2d 21, 62, 259 Ill.Dec. 753, 759 N.E.2d 533 (2001).

For the foregoing reasons, we affirm that part of the appellate court judgment affirming the circuit court's dismissal of count III of Alexis' complaint, we reverse that part of the judgment of the appellate court affirming the dismissal of Alexis' claim for child support under counts I and II, and we remand the cause to the circuit court of Cook County for further proceedings not inconsistent with this opinion.

Judgments affirmed in part and reversed in part; cause remanded.

3. CONTRACTS TO BEAR A CHILD

Following the **NOTES** *on page 772, please add the following:*

Many of the decisions involving artificial insemination involve lesbians and the evolving arena of same-sex relationships. In seeking to determine parentage and attendant benefits and responsibilities, courts often borrow from existing cases involving opposite-sex parties. For example, in King v. S.B. (*In re* the Parentage of A.B.), 818 N.E.2d 126 (Ind. Ct. App. 2004), two women in a nine-year domestic relationship agreed that one would conceive a child through artificial insemination and after birth, both of the women would raise the child as parents. In holding that both women were parents, the court stressed that both women acted in good faith in deciding to co-parent and the biological parent cannot unilaterally abrogate the resulting parenting roles. Likewise, a Vermont family court applied a presumption of parenthood when the two lesbians shared a committed relationship and mutually agreed to bear a child. *Opposing Courts Decide Parentage of Child Born Via AI During Civil Union*, 31 Fam. L. Rep. (BNA) 1051 (Nov. 30, 2004). But a Virginia trial court refused to recognize any parentage claim made by the non-biological parent, a decision based in part on Virginia's refusal to recognize the civil union commitment made by the two women in Vermont. *Id.*

One decision involved two cohabiting women. One woman donated an ovum and it was fertilized with donated sperm, then the embryo was implanted in the other woman who carried it to term. Two years after the birth of the child the two woman petitioned the court to recognize them as co-custodians but the court rejected the petition as not being in the best interest of the child. The Ohio Court of Appeals reversed and held that the arrangement was in the best interest of the child but did not identify both women as parents. *In re* J.D.M., 2004 WL 2272063 (Ohio Ct. App.2004). Among gay men the process of becoming parents through donated sperm and a surrogate is expanding as well. *See* Sandra G. Boodman, *Fatherhood by a New Formula*, WASH. POST, Jan. 18, 2005, at F1.

Suggested Reading: **Ellen Waldman,** ***The Parent Trap: Uncovering the Myth of "Coerced Parenthood" in Frozen Embryo Disputes,*** **53 AM. U. L. REV. 1021–1062 (2004); Jane Muller–Patterson,** *Expanding the Definition of Parenthood: Why Equitable Estoppel as Used to Impose a Child Support Obligation on a Lesbian Domestic Partner Isn't Equitable,* **4 GEO. J. GENDER & L. 781–819 (2003).**

CHAPTER VII

RAISING CHILDREN: COMPETING INTERESTS OF PARENT, CHILD AND STATE

A. THE INTEREST IN ASSURING AN EDUCATION

The NOTE at page 817 refers to the constitutionality of school vouchers and should be amended to read that the Supreme Court of the United States, in a 5–4 decision, held that Cleveland's school voucher program is constitutional because it vests private individuals with genuine and independent choices. Zelman v. Simmons–Harris, 536 U.S. 639, 122 S.Ct. 2460, 153 L.Ed.2d 604 (2002).

D. RESPONDING TO CHILD ABUSE

The NOTE at page 867 makes reference to the South Carolina decision of Whitner v. State and this should be updated to refer to a more recent decision from the state's supreme court holding that a mother's use of cocaine during pregnancy was deemed the cause of her stillborn baby's death. State's highest court again allowed mother to be charged with the state's crime of "homicide by child abuse." South Carolina v. McKnight, 576 S.E.2d 168 (S.C.2003).

Please add to the NOTES following DeShaney v. Winnebago County DSS, the following at page 907:

Courts have continued their reluctance to provide any civil remedies to litigants. See, for example, Arbaugh v. Board of Education, 214 W. Va. 677, 591 S.E.2d 235 (2003), holding that West Virginia law does not give rise to a private civil cause of action for failure to report suspected child abuse under the state¿s reporting statute. The Minnesota Court of Appeals ruled that the state¿s Child Abuse Reporting Act did not grant to the non-custodial father a civil cause of action against the county after the mother¿s boyfriend killed his child. Radke v. County of Freeborn, 676 N.W.2d 295 (Minn. Ct. App. 2004). But the U.S. Court of Appeals for the Tenth Circuit Ruled that a state statute that promised a process by which a restraining order issued against an abusive spouse would be given vitality through careful and prompt consideration by law enforcement officials, provided a basis for a procedural due process claim against the local municipality. Gonzales v. City of Castle Rock, 366 F.3d 1093 (10th Cir. 2004). In a 7-2 decision on June 27, 2005, the Supreme Court rejected the argument and held that the city was not liable. Castle Rock, Colo. v. Gonzales, 2005 WL 1499788.

E. MEDICAL DECISION MAKING FOR AND BY CHILDREN

Following "Treatment for Children in Life Threatening Circumstances," please add at page 931, the holding from the Nebraska Supreme Court that a state law requiring a blood test for newborns does not violate a parent's right to free exercise of religion. Requiring the blood test was rationally related to the state's interest in preventing the spread of disease and is a neutral requirement of general applicability. Douglas County v. Anaya, *694 N.W.2d 601 (Neb. 2005).*

Please amend the California Family Code on page 969 to read as follows:

CALIFORNIA FAMILY CODE

§ 6910. Parent or guardian may authorize care provider to consent

The parent, guardian, or caregiver of a minor who is a relative of the minor and who may authorize medical care and dental care under Section 6550, may authorize in writing an adult into whose care a minor has been entrusted to consent to medical care or to dental care, or both, for the minor.

Following **In re L.H.R.** *in the* **NOTES** *beginning at page 973, please add the following case:*

Montalvo v. Borkovec

Court of Appeals of Wisconsin, 2002.
256 Wis.2d 472, 647 N.W.2d 413, appeal denied, 257 Wis.2d 118, 653 N.W.2d 890, cert. denied, 538 U.S. 907 (2003).

■ WEDEMEYER, P.J.

Nancy Montalvo, Brian Vila and Emanuel L. Vila (by his guardian ad litem, Timothy J. Aiken) appeal from judgments entered after the trial court dismissed their complaint against Dr. Brent W. Arnold, Dr. Jonathan H. Berkoff, St. Mary's Hospital of Milwaukee, the Wisconsin Patients Compensation Fund and Physicians Insurance Co. of Wisconsin. The complaint alleged that the defendants were negligent for failing to sufficiently inform Montalvo and Vila of the risk of disability to Emanuel following his premature birth by cesarean section.

Montalvo, Vila, and Emanuel raise ten arguments.[1] We address only those arguments necessary to the resolution of this case. Because under our current rules of pleading and procedure, substantive law, and public policy the plaintiffs' claims cannot be pursued, we affirm.

---

1. They argue: (1) Montalvo had a right to informed consent prior to the cesarean procedure; (2) the decision to use potentially harmful therapy is subject to informed consent; (3) Wisconsin abortion law does not apply to this situation; (4) with the exception of the drug/alcohol abuse provisions of ch. 48, expectant mothers have the absolute right to control the manner of delivery; (5) the concept of "viability" cannot mean preservation of life at any cost; (6) the lifelong ramifications of perinatal treatment decisions man-

On November 21, 1996, Montalvo entered St. Mary's Hospital in Milwaukee, Wisconsin, with pre-term labor symptoms. An ultrasound revealed that the baby was 23 and 3/7 weeks old, and weighed 679 grams. Attempts to interrupt her labor and delay the birth were unsuccessful. Prior to delivery of the child, the parents executed an informed consent agreement for a cesarean procedure.

Dr. Terre Borkovec performed the cesarean section. At birth, Emanuel was "handed off" to Dr. Arnold, a neonatologist, who successfully performed life-saving resuscitation measures.

On November 19, 1999, Montalvo filed a complaint against Borkovec and Arnold alleging that both physicians violated the informed consent statute, Wis. Stat. § 448.30, in performing the cesarean section. The complaint also alleged that Arnold, Berkoff, and St. Mary's Hospital were negligent for violating the same informed consent statute when they performed "life-saving measures" for Emanuel. The complaint alleged that because the physicians failed to advise the parents of "the risks or potential consequences of a child born at 23 or 24 weeks gestation and/or with a birth weight of less than 750 grams," consent was not informed and a variety of damages resulted.

Berkoff, Arnold, and St. Mary's Hospital moved to dismiss the claims contending that the complaint failed to state a claim upon which relief could be granted pursuant to Wis. Stat. § 802.06(2)(a)6. During a hearing on the motions, and prior to rendering a decision, the trial court ascertained that the plaintiffs were not alleging harm to Emanuel as the result of "extraordinary care measures" but were claiming that the decision to use "extraordinary care measures" should have been relegated to them as parents rather than left to the physicians. Lastly, the plaintiffs were not alleging that Emanuel was disabled by any actions taken by the physicians or St. Mary's Hospital.

The trial court dismissed the complaint ruling first that the only claim pled for a violation of the informed consent statute in performing the cesarean section was against Arnold. Because, however, he was only a bystander to the delivery, he was not required under the statute to provide informed consent because he did not perform the procedure. Second, the trial court ruled that Wisconsin law does not leave the resuscitation decision upon the birth of a child solely to the parents because of the community's interest in protecting children, and the physicians' commitment to preserving life. Montalvo now appeals.

A motion to dismiss a complaint for failure to state a claim upon which relief may be granted tests the legal sufficiency of the pleading. *Evans v. Cameron,* 121 Wis.2d 421, 426, 360 N.W.2d 25 (1985). As a question of law,

date that such decisions be made by the parents only after being fully informed of all the risks and alternatives; (7) federal funding statutes do not control Wisconsin informed consent law; (8) the Americans with Disabilities Act does not control this case; (9) there is no constitutional basis for federal or state government interference in the medical decision-making process; and (10) compelling parents to agree to surgeries or therapies whose benefit versus risk analysis is unclear puts an unfair burden on parents.

we review the trial court's decision independently, keeping in mind the value we accord the trial court's analysis. We must affirm a judgment dismissing a complaint for failure to state a claim if, upon review of the complaint, as liberally construed, it is quite clear that under no conditions can the plaintiff recover based upon the facts alleged and inferences reasonably drawn. *Bartley v. Thompson,* 198 Wis.2d 323, 332, 542 N.W.2d 227 (Ct.App.1995). With these rubrics of review in mind, we now examine the issues dispositive of this appeal.

The original defendants in this case were Drs. Borkovec, Arnold, Berkoff and St. Mary's Hospital. Borkovec, who performed the cesarean section, was voluntarily dismissed from the case. That left Arnold as the only target allegedly negligent for failure to obtain a properly informed consent for the performance of the cesarean section. Yet, it was undisputed that Arnold, although present when the cesarean section occurred, did not participate in the procedure. The trial court construed Wis. Stat. § 448.30 to provide that only the treating physician, here Borkovec, owed the responsibility of informed consent to the parents. Borkovec, however, was no longer a party to the action. The statute does not impose the duty of informed consent on non-treating physicians. Because Arnold neither participated nor assisted, he was not a treating physician with respect to the cesarean procedure, and did not have a duty to comply with the informed consent statute.

Thus, the trial court concluded that with respect to the cesarean procedure, no claim had been properly pleaded upon which relief could be granted. We know of no authority to the contrary. In this respect, the trial court did not err. On appeal, Montalvo has not contested this ruling. Consequently, the only claims remaining to be addressed by the trial court were the failure to properly obtain informed consent relating to resuscitation efforts by Arnold, Berkoff, and St. Mary's Hospital.

On the remaining informed consent issue relating to the resuscitation efforts, the essential question is whether the complaint states a legally cognizable claim against the remaining defendants. The trial court ruled it did not.

Our informed consent law requires a physician to disclose information necessary for a reasonable person to make an intelligent decision with respect to the choices of treatment or diagnosis. *Kuklinski v. Rodriguez,* 203 Wis.2d 324, 329, 552 N.W.2d 869 (Ct.App.1996). It is a right found in both the common law of this state and in statutory provisions. Wisconsin Stat. § 448.30 codified the duty-to-disclose law recognized by *Scaria v. St. Paul Fire & Marine Ins. Co.,* 68 Wis.2d 1, 13, 227 N.W.2d 647 (1975), and reads:

> **Information on alternate modes of treatment.** Any physician who treats a patient shall inform the patient about the availability of all alternate, viable medical modes of treatment and about the benefits and risks of these treatments. The physician's duty to inform the patient under this section does not require disclosure of:
>
> (1) Information beyond what a reasonably well-qualified physician in a similar medical classification would know.

(2) Detailed technical information that in all probability a patient would not understand.

(3) Risks apparent or known to the patient.

(4) Extremely remote possibilities that might falsely or detrimentally alarm the patient.

(5) Information in emergencies where failure to provide treatment would be more harmful to the patient than treatment.

(6) Information in cases where the patient is incapable of consenting.

The statute is basically divided into two parts: what information a treating physician is obligated to convey to a patient and what information he/she need not convey. The plain language of the statute places an obligation on a physician to provide information only about available and viable options of treatment.

In addressing the obligatory first part of the statute, our supreme court has declared: "[W]hat a physician must disclose is contingent upon what, under the circumstances of a given case, a reasonable person in the patient's position would need to know in order to make an intelligent and informed decision." *Johnson v. Kokemoor,* 199 Wis.2d 615, 639, 545 N.W.2d 495 (1996). Restricting the application of the obligation, we declared in *Mathias v. St. Catherine's Hospital, Inc.,* 212 Wis.2d 540, 569 N.W.2d 330 (Ct.App.1997): "The law in Wisconsin on informed consent is well settled. . . . the duty to advise a patient of the risks of treatment lies with the doctor. . . . The court was explicit in pointing out that the duty to obtain informed consent lay with the doctor, not the hospital." *Id.* at 548, 569 N.W.2d 330 (citations omitted). Thus, St. Mary's Hospital was not a proper defendant. We continue the analysis then only as the second claim applies to Arnold and Berkoff.

Doubtless, the doctrine of informed consent comes into play only when there is a need to make a choice of available, viable alternatives. In other words, there must be a choice that can be made. The process of decision-making necessarily implies assessing and selecting an available alternative. In the context of treatment required after the cesarean procedure was performed on Emanuel, there are two reasons why no available, viable alternative existed to give rise to the obligation to engage in the informed consent process.

First, requiring the informed consent process here presumes that a right to decide not to resuscitate the newly born child or to withhold life-sustaining medical care actually existed. This premise is faulty. In *Edna M.F. v. Eisenberg,* 210 Wis.2d 557, 568, 563 N.W.2d 485 (1997), our supreme court set forth the preconditions required for permitting the withholding or withdrawal of life-sustaining medical treatment. There, the appointed guardian of her incompetent sister, Edna, sought permission to direct the withholding of medical care from Edna even though she was not in a persistent vegetative state. *Id.* at 559–60, 563 N.W.2d 485. She claimed that Edna would not want to live in her condition, completely dependent on others for her care and existence, non-responsive and immobile. *Id.* at 560–

61, 563 N.W.2d 485. The court, in refusing to extend the right to refuse life-sustaining medical treatment beyond individuals in a persistent vegetative state, relied on the analysis of the United States Supreme Court in *Cruzan v. Director, Missouri Department of Health,* 497 U.S. 261, 110 S.Ct. 2841, 111 L.Ed.2d 224 (1990): "[W]e think a State may properly decline to make judgments about the 'quality' of life that a particular individual may enjoy, and simply assert an unqualified interest in the preservation of human life to be weighed against the constitutionally protected interests of the individual." *Edna M.F.,* 210 Wis.2d at 563, 563 N.W.2d 485 (quoting *Cruzan,* 497 U.S. at 282, 110 S.Ct. 2841, 111 L.Ed.2d 224).

The *Edna* court, in examining the sensitive issues before it and the need to balance the interests of the individual versus those of the state, was quick to appreciate the consequences of ultimate decisions made by third-party surrogates for those who cannot speak for themselves. It thus concluded that either withholding or withdrawing life-sustaining medical treatment is not in the best interests of any patient who is not in a persistent vegetative state. *Edna M.F.,* 210 Wis.2d at 566–68, 563 N.W.2d 485. Thus, in Wisconsin, in the absence of a persistent vegetative state, the right of a parent to withhold life-sustaining treatment from a child does not exist. It is not disputed here that there was no evidence that Emanuel was in "a persistent vegetative state." Accordingly, the alternative of withholding life-sustaining treatment did not exist.

The second reason why a viable alternative did not exist to trigger informed consent is the existence of the United States Child Abuse Protection and Treatment Act (CAPTA) of 1984, Pub.L. No. 98–457, 98 Stat. 1749 (codified at 42 U.S.C. § 5101 et seq.). Because Wisconsin has fulfilled the necessary obligations to receive federal funds under CAPTA, CAPTA and its regulations are fully applicable in this state. *Jeanine B. v. Thompson,* 967 F.Supp. 1104, 1111–12, 1118 (E.D.Wis.1997).

CAPTA was enacted to establish eligibility for states to obtain federal funding for the prevention of child abuse and to develop and implement a successful and comprehensive child and family protection strategy. Under CAPTA, states must have in place procedures for responding to child neglect. 42 U.S.C. § 5106(b)(4)(C). The Act includes a provision preventing "the withholding of medically indicated treatment from a disabled infant with a life-threatening condition." 45 C.F.R. § 1340.15(b)(1). In the regulations enacted under the statute, "withholding of medically indicated treatment" is defined as "the failure to respond to the infant's life-threatening conditions by providing treatment ... which, in the treating physician's ... reasonable medical judgment, will be most likely to be effective in ... correcting all such conditions...." 45 C.F.R. § 1340.15(b)(2). The regulations further include the "authority to initiate legal proceedings ... to prevent the withholding of medically indicated treatment from disabled infants with life-threatening conditions." 45 C.F.R. § 1340.15(c)(2)(iii). The implied choice of withholding treatment, proposed by the plaintiffs, is exactly what CAPTA prohibits.

It is noteworthy that in the complaint, plaintiffs did not allege that Emanuel was born with a known disability or that they would have chosen to withhold life-sustaining treatment. Instead, they allege that they were not given the statistics about the possible risks that he could develop a disability if he lived, and they should have been given the opportunity to withhold life-saving measures immediately after Emanuel's birth. Under the common law of Wisconsin and federal statutory law, however, Emanuel's parents did not have the right to withhold or withdraw immediate postnatal care from him. Thus, no viable alternative health treatment existed to trigger the informed consent process.[4]

We now examine the applicability of the second part of the informed consent statute; i.e., the six exception sections, providing conditions under which the treating physician is not obligated to inform the patient. Germane to our analysis is subsection (5) which renders unnecessary the disclosure of "information in emergencies where failure to provide treatment would be more harmful to the patient than treatment."

The complaint alleges that "attempts . . . to interrupt the preterm labor . . . [were] unsuccessful" resulting in Emanuel's premature birth by cesarean section, and that "upon Emanuel Vila's delivery, he was immediately handed off to defendant Brent Arnold, M.D. who initiated heroic and extraordinary life saving measures" on him. The allegations suggest that an emergency arose requiring an immediate response, which occurred. Montalvo does not suggest that all emergency actions should have ceased while Arnold explained possible options. Such an argument would be frivolous. Given the allegations of the complaint, it cannot be gainsaid that failure to provide treatment would have been more harmful than treatment.

Although Montalvo concedes that as parents they have "no right to terminate the child's life," they assert that if "there is a balance between giving therapies that help, but which may also seriously harm, the parents should be the final arbiters of that choice." In the exigent circumstances confronting the treating physician here, no "balance" existed as proposed by the parents. Failure to treat was tantamount to a death sentence. Under the pleaded circumstances, informed consent was not required.

. . .

In Wisconsin, the interest in preserving life is of paramount significance. In re *L.W.*, 167 Wis.2d 53, 90, 482 N.W.2d 60 (1992). As a result, there is a presumption that continued life is in the best interests of a patient. *Id.* at 86, 482 N.W.2d 60. In the absence of proof of a persistent vegetative state, our courts have never decided it is in the best interests of

---

4. In *Iafelice v. Zarafu*, 221 N.J.Super. 278, 534 A.2d 417 (1987), the New Jersey Appellate Division examined the exact same issue presented by this appeal and exclaimed:

> The mistaken premise of this appeal is that allowing the child to die untreated was a legally viable alternative . . . we find no support for the belief that a newborn child may be put to death through [allowing a natural delivery with no resuscitation efforts upon birth] on the mere expectation that she will, in some unquantified way, be a defective person. As the Supreme Court wrote in *Berman v. Allan*, 80 N.J. 421, 430, 404 A.2d 8 (1979), "It is life itself, that is jealously safeguarded, not life in a perfect state."

Id. at 418.

a patient to withhold or withdraw life-sustaining medical care. When appropriate circumstances are present, Wisconsin courts have not hesitated to dismiss complaints on public policy grounds, particularly where allowing recovery would place an unreasonable burden on physicians or where allowing recovery would provoke an exercise that has no sensible or just terminal point. *Rieck v. Medical Protective Co.,* 64 Wis.2d 514, 518–19, 219 N.W.2d 242 (1974).

The physicians involved in the resuscitation measures could be faced with a "damned if you do, damned if you don't" dilemma as demonstrated by the result of *Burks v. St. Joseph's Hospital,* 227 Wis.2d 811, 596 N.W.2d 391 (1999). In *Burks,* the physicians made a decision not to resuscitate based upon a judgment that a premature baby was not viable. *Id.* at 813, 596 N.W.2d 391. The baby died. *Id.* The parents brought a claim under the Emergency Medical Treatment and Active Labor Act (EMTALA) against the physician who determined that the infant was not viable and who did not resuscitate the child. *Id.* at 814, 596 N.W.2d 391. The claim was allowed because a hospital is required to provide emergency room patients with a medical screening examination including care to stabilize them. *Id.* at 817–18, 596 N.W.2d 391. If treating physicians can be sued for failing to resuscitate a baby they feel is not viable, and for resuscitating a viable baby such as Emanuel, they are placed in a continuing "damned" status. The public policy of Wisconsin does not tolerate such a "lose-lose" enigma.

If the parents' claim is allowed to proceed, courts will be required to decide which potential imperfections or disabilities are, as characterized in appellant's brief, "worse than death." They will have to determine which disability entitles a child to live and which disability allows a third-party surrogate to withhold or withdraw life-sustaining treatment with the intent to allow a disabled person to die. This determination could vary greatly based on the parents' beliefs. One set of parents may view a particular disability as "worse than death," while another set of parents would not. Such a process, not unreasonably, has kaleidoscopic, unending implications. The trial court did not err in reaching its conclusion based upon public policy reasons.

Judgments affirmed.

F.   A TORT ACTION FOR FAILURE TO PERFORM PARENTAL DUTIES?

In conjunction with Burnette v. Wahl *at page 974, please add* Newman v. Cole, *872 So.2d 138 (Ala. 2003), holding that there is an exception to the state's parental immunity doctrine for when it may be shown by clear and convincing evidence that a parent wilfully and intentionally caused the death of his or her child. There is another exception to the parental immunity doctrine for child sexual abuse.*

Newman v. Cole

Supreme Court of Alabama, 2003.
872 So.2d 138.

■ PER CURIAM.

In this wrongful-death action, Anna Belle Newman, the personal representative of the estate of the decedent, Clinton Patterson Cole ("Clinton"), sued Clinton's father, John Cole, and his stepmother, Tara Cole (sometimes referred to hereinafter collectively as "the Coles"), for allegedly causing Clinton's death. Newman's complaint asserted claims of negligence, wantonness, and willful and intentional conduct.

The Coles moved to dismiss the complaint based on the doctrine of parental immunity. That doctrine was judicially created in the case of *Hewellette v. George,* 68 Miss. 703, 9 So. 885 (Miss.1891), abrogated by *Glaskox v. Glaskox,* 614 So.2d 906 (Miss.1992), and was adopted by the this Court in *Owens v. Auto Mutual Indemnity Co.,* 235 Ala. 9, 177 So. 133 (Ala.1937). The present form of the doctrine in this State was most recently discussed by the Court of Civil Appeals:

> "Under Alabama law, '[t]he parental immunity doctrine prohibits all civil suits brought by unemancipated minor children against their parents for the torts of their parents.' *Mitchell v. Davis,* 598 So.2d 801, 803 (Ala.1992). Only one exception to this rule has emerged-when a child alleges sexual abuse by a parent, the parental immunity doctrine will not bar an action against the parent, although proof of the alleged conduct must be tested under a 'clear and convincing' standard. *Hurst v. Capitell,* 539 So.2d 264, 266 (Ala.1989)."

Hinson v. Holt, 776 So.2d 804, 811 (Ala.Civ.App.1998).

On July 3, 2002, the trial court granted the Coles' motion to dismiss the complaint. Newman appealed, arguing that this Court should abolish the doctrine, or, in the alternative, craft an exception to the doctrine that encompasses the facts alleged in this case.

Clinton was 16 years old at the time of his death, which occurred during an altercation with his father over Clinton's failure to perform household chores; Newman asserts that the altercation ended with the father's striking Clinton repeatedly in the chest and then holding him on the ground in a "choke hold" while Tara Cole sprayed him in the face with water from a garden hose. The father held Clinton on the ground for approximately 20 minutes; he let go of Clinton when a police officer arrived. Clinton was unconscious, and he was taken to a local hospital; he died the next day.

Although the facts in this case are tragic and compelling, the legal issue is clear-cut: Whether this Court should abolish the doctrine of parental immunity, or to what extent, if any, it should modify the application of the doctrine in light of the circumstances of this case. We hold that a further exception to the doctrine should be recognized where it is shown by clear and convincing evidence that a parent's willful and intentional injury caused the death of his or her child. Newman asserts that Alabama is the last state not to have entirely abrogated or significantly modified the doctrine. Newman's argument, supported by the briefs of amici curiae National Crime Victims Bar Association and Alabama Trial Lawyers Association, asserts that to apply the parental-immunity doctrine in the circumstances of this case is fundamentally unjust and contrary to long-settled principles of tort law. Newman and the amici support their argument by noting the large number of other states that have abrogated, or significantly modified, the doctrine. Newman argues that this Court should abrogate the doctrine entirely, or, alternatively, either craft an exception to the doctrine in the case of a parent who intentionally or willfully and wantonly injures his or her child, or craft an exception for a wrongful-death action in which a parent is accused of causing a child's death. Newman and the amici assert, without significant rebuttal from the Coles, that Alabama's application of the doctrine is the strictest imposition of parental immunity against minors in the United States.

The Coles, on the other hand, argue that the Legislature is the entity that should make any changes to the settled doctrine of parental immunity, and that abrogation of the doctrine would adversely impact families and give rise to unwarranted lawsuits by unemancipated minors against their parents.

Thus, the parties' arguments offer the Court three options: (1) we might simply decline to interfere with the doctrine, (2) we might abrogate the doctrine entirely, or (3) we might craft an exception to the doctrine, as we did in *Hurst v. Capitell,* 539 So.2d 264 (Ala.1989), to fit the circumstances of this case.

We discussed the history of the doctrine in this State, and the rationale for crafting an exception, in *Hurst:*

"The parental immunity doctrine had its genesis in the United States in *Hewellette v. George,* 68 Miss. 703, 9 So. 885 (1891), abrogated by *Glaskox v. Glaskox,* 614 So.2d 906 (Miss.1992), in which a minor daughter was precluded from suing her deceased mother's estate for damages resulting from mental suffering and injury to her character incurred during her confinement in an asylum for 11 days caused by her mother. The court gave this reason for its holding:

" 'The peace of society, and of the families composing society, and a sound public policy, designed to subserve the repose of families and the best interests of society, forbid to the minor child a right to appear in court in the assertion of a claim to civil redress for personal injuries suffered at the hands of the parent. The state, through its criminal laws, will give the minor child protection from parental violence and wrongdoing, and this is all the child can be heard to demand.'

"68 Miss. at 711, 9 So. at 887.

"The parental immunity doctrine was not based upon English common law, statutes, or previous cases; rather, it was judicially created by the Mississippi Supreme Court. In fact, even the *Hewellette* opinion recognized the limitation on the application of parental immunity to those cases involving unemancipated children.

" 'If . . . the relation of parent and child had been finally dissolved, insofar as that relationship imposed the duty upon the parent to protect and care for and control, and the child to aid and comfort and obey, *then it may be the child could successfully maintain an action against the parent for personal injuries*. But so long as the parent is under obligation to care for, guide, and control, and the child is under reciprocal obligation to aid and comfort and obey, no such action as this can be maintained.'

"*Id.*, 68 Miss. at 711, 9 So. at 887. (Emphasis added [in *Hurst*].)

"The first Alabama case addressing the issue of parental immunity, *Owens v. Auto Mut. Indemnity Co.*, 235 Ala. 9, 177 So. 133 (1937), quoted from a New Hampshire case that states a similar reason for the rule:

" 'It is declared in *Lloyd Dunlap v. Dunlap*, 84 N.H. 352, 150 A. 905, 71 A.L.R. 1055 [1930] that the ' ''disability of a child to sue the parent for an injury negligently inflicted by the latter upon the former while a minor *is not absolute, but is imposed for the protection of family control and harmony, and exists only where the suit, or the prospect of a suit, might disturb the family relations.*'' ' ''

"235 Ala. at 10, 177 So. at 134. (Emphasis added [in *Hurst*].)

"We reaffirmed the doctrine in *Hill v. Giordano*, 447 So.2d 164 (Ala.1984) (Jones, J., dissenting), based on the authority of *Owens*, supra, and held that 'any modification or abolition of the parental immunity doctrine should be left to the prerogative of the legislature.' 447 So.2d at 164. However, we also stated three months later in *Lloyd v. Service Corporation of Alabama, Inc.*, 453 So.2d 735 (Ala.1984):

" 'While the preferred method for modification of a rule of law is by legislative action, it is clearly within the power of the judiciary, and, at times, appropriate for the judiciary, to change an established rule of law. . . .

" ' . . . *[W]here a judicial creation has become outmoded or unjust in application, it is more often appropriate for the judicial body to act to modify the law.*'

"(Emphasis added [in *Hurst*].)

"*Because the doctrine was judicially created, it is not exclusively a legislative issue and it may be judicially qualified.* Since our decision in *Hill* to defer to the Legislature on this issue, the Legislature has declined to act in regard to the doctrine, while the incidents of sexual abuse involving children have continued to occur. To leave children who are victims of such wrongful, intentional, heinous acts without a right to redress those wrongs in a civil action is unconscionable, especially where the harm to the family fabric has already occurred through that abuse. Because we see no reason to adhere to the doctrine of parental immunity when the purpose for that immunity is no longer served, as in Melissa's case, we are today creating an exception to the doctrine, limited to sexual abuse cases only.

"In creating this exception for sexual abuse cases, we believe it is unnecessary to spell out a separate body of procedural and substantive rules to govern such cases. Traditional rules of tort law relating to intentional infliction of personal injury are generally sufficient for the governance of such claims and the defenses asserted thereto.

"In the interest of preserving the unqualified right of parents to reasonably discipline their children, we do deem it appropriate, however, to require that the proof of alleged sexually abusive conduct be tested under a 'clear and convincing' standard, as opposed to a mere 'substantial evidence' standard. Because we are restricting this exception to the general rule to cases involving 'sexual abuse,' and requiring a 'clear and convincing' standard of proof, we do not perceive of our recognition of this narrow exception as posing an undue risk of limiting the parents' legitimate role in the disciplining of their children."

539 So.2d at 265–66 (last emphasis added).

At this time, some 14 years after *Hurst* was decided, the Legislature has made no other modification to the doctrine. During that same time, we considered the doctrine once more in *Mitchell v. Davis,* 598 So.2d 801 (Ala.1992), holding that the doctrine of parental immunity applied to foster parents and recognizing the exception crafted in *Hurst.* As stated in *Hurst,* the doctrine was judicially created, and it is therefore subject to judicial modification. But this Court still attaches great importance to the underlying reason for the doctrine-to avoid unduly limiting the legitimate interest of parents in rearing and disciplining their children. In *Broadwell v. Holmes,* 871 S.W.2d 471 (Tenn.1994), the Supreme Court of Tennessee articulated well the importance of this interest:

"The parental right to govern the rearing of a child has been afforded protection under both the federal and state constitutions. This Court has stated, 'Tennessee's historically strong protection of parental rights and the reasoning of federal constitutional cases convince us that parental rights constitute a fundamental liberty interest under Article I, Section 8 of the Tennessee Constitution.' *Hawk v. Hawk,* 855 S.W.2d 573, 579 (Tenn.[1993]); see also *Davis v. Davis,* 842 S.W.2d 588, 601 (Tenn.1992)[,] *cert. denied,* 507 U.S. 911, 113 S.Ct. 1259, 122 L.Ed.2d 657 (1993); *Bellotti v. Baird,* 443 U.S. 622, 638, 99 S.Ct. 3035, 3045, 61 L.Ed.2d 797 (1979) (recognition of parents' right to be free of undue, adverse interference by state); *Quilloin v. Walcott,* 434 U.S. 246, 255, 98 S.Ct. 549, 554, 54 L.Ed.2d 511 (1978) (recognition that parent-child relationship is constitutionally protected); *Wisconsin v. Yoder,* 406 U.S. 205, 232, 92 S.Ct. 1526, 1541, 32 L.Ed.2d 15 (1972) (recognition of parents' primary role in child rearing as a 'fundamental interest' and 'an enduring American tradition'); *Prince v. Massachusetts,* 321 U.S. 158, 166, 64 S.Ct. 438, 442, 88 L.Ed. 645 (1944) (recognition that the custody, care and nurture of the child 'reside first in the parents, whose primary function and freedom include preparation for obligations the state can neither supply nor hinder'). The integrity of the family unit has found protection against arbitrary state interference in the Due Process Clause of the Fourteenth Amendment,

Cleveland Board of Education v. LaFleur, 414 U.S. 632, 639–40, 94 S.Ct. 791, 796–97, 39 L.Ed.2d 52 (1974); *Roe v. Wade,* 410 U.S. 113, 152–53, 93 S.Ct. 705, 726–27, 35 L.Ed.2d 147 (1973); *Meyer v. Nebraska,* 262 U.S. 390, 399, 43 S.Ct. 625, 626, 67 L.Ed. 1042 (1923); the equal protection clause of the Fourteenth Amendment, *Skinner v. Oklahoma,* 316 U.S. 535, 541, 62 S.Ct. 1110, 1113, 86 L.Ed. 1655 (1942); and the Ninth Amendment. [*Griswold*] *v. Connecticut,* 381 U.S. 479, 496, 85 S.Ct. 1678, 1688, 14 L.Ed.2d 510 (1965) (Goldberg, J., concurring).

"Courts have expressed a concern that without the imposition of parent-child immunity, juries would feel free to express their disapproval of what they consider to be unusual or inappropriate child rearing practices by awarding damages to children whose parents' conduct was only unconventional. See, e.g., *Pedigo v. Rowley,* 101 Idaho 201, 205, 610 P.2d 560, 564 (1980); *Holodook v. Spencer,* [36 N.Y.2d 35,] 364 N.Y.S.2d [859] at 869–71, 324 N.E.2d [338] at 345–46 (N.Y.1974). Courts also properly have found that parents whose '[p]hysical, mental or financial weakness [causes them] to provide what many a reasonable man would consider substandard maintenance, guidance, education and recreation for their children, and in many instances to provide a family home which is not reasonably safe as a place of abode,' should not be liable to the child for these 'unintended injuries.' *Chaffin v. Chaffin,* 239 Or. 374, 397 P.2d 771, 774 (1964) (*en banc*), *overruled by Heino v. Harper,* 306 Or. 347, 759 P.2d 253 (1988) (abolishing interspousal immunity); *accord Cannon v. Cannon,* 287 N.Y. 425, 40 N.E.2d 236, 237–38 (1942), *overruled by Gelbman v. Gelbman,* 23 N.Y.2d 434, 297 N.Y.S.2d 529, 245 N.E.2d 192, 193 (1969) (abolishing bar to intrafamily lawsuits), *but see Holodook v. Spencer,* 364 N.Y.S.2d at 865, 324 N.E.2d at 342 (negligent failure to supervise child not recognized as a tort). Such imposition of liability could effectively curtail the exercise of constitutionally guaranteed parental discretion in matters of child rearing. Consequently, it reasonably can be argued that parental immunity that relates to the right and duty to rear children implements a constitutional right. *See Hawk v. Hawk,* 855 S.W.2d at 579 (recognizing a fundamental constitutional right of parents to care for their children without unwarranted state intervention)."

871 S.W.2d at 475–76.

This Court has been equally loathe to interfere with the parent-child relationship:

" ' . . . So strong is the presumption, that "the care which is prompted by the parental instinct, and responded to by filial affection, is most valuable of all"; and so great is the reluctance of the court to separate a child of tender years from those who according to the ordinary laws of human nature, must feel the greatest affection for it, and take the deepest interest in its welfare-that the parental authority will not be interfered with, except in case of gross misconduct or where, from some other cause, the parent wants either the capacity or the means for the proper nurture and training of the child.' "

Ex parte Sullivan, 407 So.2d 559, 563 (Ala.1981) (quoting *Striplin v. Ware,* 36 Ala. 87, 89–90 (1860)). See also *R.J.D. v. Vaughan Clinic, P.C.,* 572 So.2d 1225, 1228 (Ala.1990).

Given the weight we assign to the sanctity of the parent-child relationship, we decline to follow the example of many of our sister states and wholly abrogate the doctrine of parental immunity. Further, we decline to consider any exception to the doctrine that would permit a claim by an injured child against a parent where the injury was not willful and intentional. In *Hurst* we held that the exception to the parental-immunity doctrine giving the injured child a right to redress was in response to "wrongful, intentional, heinous acts," 539 So.2d at 266, committed by the parent. Most recently, in *Mitchell,* supra, we held that the parental-immunity doctrine also protected foster parents as to any claim by a foster child based upon the foster parents' alleged negligence. As the court stated in *Broadwell:*

> "[T]he rights, responsibilities, and privileges of parents in relation to their children are so unique that the ordinary standards of care which regulate conduct between others are not applicable to conduct incident to the particular relationship of parent and child. That relationship includes responsibilities not owed by parents to any persons other than their children; these responsibilities are inseparable from the privileges that parents have in rearing their children which are not recognized in any other relationship."

871 S.W.2d at 475.

In view of this unique and special relationship, we note first that this opinion leaves the doctrine unchanged with respect to the protection afforded a parent from any claim by his or her child based upon unintentional conduct. Further, we consider only the specific circumstances of the case before us and apply our holding only to the situation where it can be shown by clear and convincing evidence that a parent's willful and intentional infliction of injury resulted in the death of his or her child.

As we noted in *Hurst,* supra, this Court declined to modify the doctrine in *Hill,* supra, a wrongful-death case in which the father's alleged negligence in piloting a plane resulted in the deaths of his two minor sons. However, the holding in *Hurst* makes clear that the rationale that supported *Hill,* i.e., deference to the Legislature, is no longer a dispositive basis for not modifying the judicially created doctrine. Accordingly, we cannot overlook the fact that the wrongful death of a child profoundly impacts the parent-child relationship. Plainly, the death of a child removes the parental interests the doctrine was intended to protect with respect to that child. Certainly, the parent's responsibilities to the child and the child's dependence upon the parent are terminated by the child's death. See, e.g., *Floyd v. Abercrombie,* 816 So.2d 1051 (Ala.Civ.App.2001) ; *Anderson v. Loper,* 689 So.2d 118 (Ala.Civ.App.1996)(discussing a parent's duties toward his or her unemancipated child). As Justice Jones, dissenting from the majority's opinion in *Hill*, aptly stated:

> "The purpose of the wrongful death statute [Ala.Code 1975, § 6–5–410] is to prevent homicide by wrongful act, omission, or negligence 'without respect to personal condition or disability of the person so protected.' *Breed v. Atlanta, B. & C.R.R.*, 241 Ala. 640, 642, 4 So.2d 315, 316 (1941). The parental immunity doctrine has its basis in domestic harmony. Isn't the commission of the tort, in and of itself, disruptive to domestic harmony?"

447 So.2d at 168.

In assessing the balance between the unique nature and critical importance of the parent-child relationship and the right of any victim for redress for a willful or intentional injury, we find the analysis of the Supreme Court of West Virginia instructive. In *Courtney v. Courtney*, 186 W.Va. 597, 413 S.E.2d 418 (1991), that court considered claims by a mother and her son against her ex-husband and the son's father for a number of intentional assaults. The court stated:

> "Courts have recognized that not every physical touching of a child will result in liability. Parents are able to discipline their children by administering reasonable physical punishment. However, when such punishment becomes excessive and results in substantial traumatic injury to the child, liability arises. Several courts have quoted this language from the California Supreme Court in *Emery v. Emery*, 45 Cal.2d 421, 429–30, 289 P.2d 218, 224 (1955):

> " 'Since the law imposes on the parent a duty to rear and discipline his child and confers the right to prescribe a course of reasonable conduct for its development, the parent has a wide discretion in the performance of his parental functions, but that discretion does not include the right wilfully to inflict personal injuries beyond the limits of reasonable parental discipline. No sound public policy would be subserved by extending it beyond those limits. While it may seem repugnant to allow a minor to sue his parent, we think it more repugnant to leave a minor child without redress for the damage he has suffered by reason of his parent's wilful or malicious misconduct. A child, like every other individual, has a right to freedom from such injury.'

> "See *Attwood v. Attwood's Estate*, 276 Ark. 230, 633 S.W.2d 366 (1982); *Rodebaugh v. Grand Trunk W.R.R. Co.*, 4 Mich.App. 559, 145 N.W.2d 401 (1966).

> "Thus, the general rule is that parental immunity is abrogated where the parent causes injury or death to his or her child from intentional or wilful conduct, but liability does not arise from reasonable corporal punishment for disciplinary purposes."

186 W.Va. at 607, 413 S.E.2d at 428.

Similarly, we recognize an exception to the doctrine of parental immunity in this State for a civil wrongful-death action by the personal representative of a decedent child against the child's parent where the parent willfully and intentionally inflicted the injury that caused the child's death. As in *Hurst,* supra, "in the interest of preserving the unqualified right of parents to reasonably discipline their children," 539 So.2d at 266, we require that the proof of the alleged willful and intentional nature of the injury that caused the child's death be tested under the clear-and-convincing-evidence standard rather than the substantial-evidence standard.

Accordingly, the judgment of the trial court is affirmed with respect to Newman's wrongful-death claims based on negligence and wantonness; the judgment is reversed with respect to Newman's wrongful-death claim based upon willful and intentional conduct, to the extent that claim implicates a willful and intentional injury, and the cause is remanded for further proceedings consistent with this opinion.

AFFIRMED IN PART; REVERSED IN PART; AND REMANDED.

■ JOHNSTONE and Woodall, JJ., concur; Houston and Harwood, JJ., concur in the result;

■ LYONS, J., concurs in the result in part and dissents in part; MOORE, C.J., and see, BROWN, and STUART, JJ., dissent.

[The concurring opinions, a concurring and partially dissenting opinion of LYONS J., and the dissenting opinions of BROWN, STUART and SEE have been omitted.]

■ MOORE, CHIEF JUSTICE (dissenting).

I must dissent from the per curiam opinion because this Court appears to have created a right in the estate of a minor child to maintain a wrongful-death action against his parent. Such a right does not exist under the law of this State, and the maintenance of a tort action by a minor child (or his estate) against a parent does not exist under the common law. This is a tragic case in which the wrongful death of a minor child cries out for redress. But it is the criminal law that has consistently been the source of punishment for any wrong committed by a parent against a child. One of the defendants in this case, John Cole, was found guilty of manslaughter by a jury in criminal court and faces the punishment prescribed by law for his actions.

With regard to the civil liability of a parent for wrongs committed against a minor child, the parental-immunity doctrine first recognized in *Owens v. Auto Mutual Indemnity Co.,* 235 Ala. 9, 177 So. 133 (Ala.1937), has been the precedent of this State. According to *Hurst v. Capitell,* 539 So.2d 264, 265 (Ala.1989): "The parental immunity doctrine had its genesis in the United States in *Hewellette v. George,* 68 Miss. 703, 9 So. 885 (1891)." But, in fact, a precursor to the doctrine appeared 36 years before *Hewellette* when the Supreme Court of Texas held:

" 'Honor thy father and mother' is a command not only of the decalogue, but of nature; and suits in which rights can be claimed only through the alleged turpitude of a parent, are not to be encouraged."

Stramler v. Coe, 15 Tex. 211, 214–15 (1855). According to a majority of legal commentators who have addressed the subject, *Hewellette* was the first statement in the United States of the doctrine of parental immunity. But such a position ignores *Stramler* and *Lander v. Seaver*, 32 Vt. 114 (1859),[1] which did not use the term "parental immunity," but which certainly described the principle. The principle clearly existed before 1891, even if the words "parental immunity" did not appear in a published opinion.

In 1984, in *Hill v. Giordano*, 447 So.2d 164 (Ala.1984), the Alabama Supreme Court specifically rejected an attempt to abolish or modify the parental-immunity doctrine that had existed in Alabama since 1937, stating that "any modification or abolition of the parental immunity doctrine should be left to the prerogative of the legislature." 447 So.2d at 164.

However, the per curiam opinion today rejects *Hill*, stating that " '[b]ecause the doctrine was judicially created, it is not exclusively a legislative issue and it may be judicially qualified,' " 872 So.2d at 142:

" '"While the preferred method for modification of a rule of law is by legislative action, it is clearly within the power of the judiciary, and, at times appropriate for the judiciary, to change an established rule of law. . . .

" ' " . . . [W]here a judicial creation has become outmoded or unjust in application it is more often appropriate for the judicial body to act to modify the law." ' "

872 So.2d at 142 (quoting *Hurst*, 539 So.2d at 266, quoting in turn *Lloyd v. Service Corp. of Alabama, Inc.*, 453 So.2d 735 (Ala.1984)).

But was the doctrine of parental immunity in fact a judicial creation? Even the per curiam opinion must recognize that for the past 65 years, *Owens* has been precedent in our law. The rule of precedent was stated clearly by Sir William Blackstone in his *Commentaries* on the common law:

"[I]t is an established rule to abide by former precedent, where the same points come again in litigation; as well to keep the scale of justice even and steady, and not liable to waiver with every new judge's opinion; as also because the law in that case being solemnly declared

---

1.   In *Lander* the Supreme Court of Vermont stated:

"The parent, unquestionably, is answerable only for malice or wicked motives or an evil heart in punishing his child. This great and to some extent irresponsible power of control and correction is invested in the parent by nature and necessity. It springs from the natural relation of parent and child. It is felt rather as a duty than a power. *From the intimacy and nature of the relation, and the necessary character of family government, the law suffers no intrusion upon the authority of the parent, and the privacy of domestic life,* unless in extreme cases of cruelty and injustice."

32 Vt. at 122. In "extreme cases of cruelty and injustice," the criminal law existed to address the problem.

and determined, what before was uncertain, and perhaps indifferent, has now become a permanent rule, which it is not in the breast of any subsequent judge to alter or vary from, according to his private sentiments: he being sworn to determine, not according to his own private judgment, but according to the known laws and customs of the land; not delegated to pronounce a new law, but to maintain and expound the old one."

1 Sir William Blackstone, *Commentaries* 69. The rule of precedent obviously has a valid purpose, i.e., to ensure the orderly rule of law by reliance upon former decisions, solemnly declared and determined. I would submit that the rule in *Owens* was solemnly declared and determined and that it reflected a fixed principle of the common law, i.e., that the common law did not sanction a tort action by a minor child against his parent,[2] and the doctrine of parental immunity was therefore not judicially created. However, the common law did permit exceptions to precedent when "the former determination is most evidently contrary to reason; much more if it be contrary to the divine law." 1 Blackstone, *Commentaries* 70. The rule espoused in *Owens* contradicts neither reason nor the divine law. Simply stated, the per curiam opinion has disregarded precedent in favor of its own private judgment and has judicially created an exception to the doctrine of parental immunity.

The entire rationale of the Court's opinion rests on the premise that the parental-immunity doctrine was judicially created; nevertheless, the Court cannot and does not explain why there is a complete void in the history of the common law of tort actions even being attempted by a minor against a parent. As the Rhode Island Supreme Court stated in 1925:

"That this [parental immunity] has been recognized as expressing the common law is evidenced by the fact that no case of the action of a minor child against his father for tort appears either in the English reports or in any state report down to 1891, although during that period numerous cases appear of criminal proceedings against parents for the abuse of their minor children in circumstances which would permit civil actions for damages if such right of action existed."

Matarese v. Matarese, 47 R.I. 131, 134, 131 A. 198, 199 (1925).

An even earlier court in Washington recognized this absence at common law of a tort action by a minor against his parent:

2. In a case dealing with a tort action brought by a child against a parent, the North Carolina Supreme Court stated:

"There is no authority at the common law for an action like the present; and while some may not regard the sources of the common law with reverence or with respect, yet, in its truest and most comprehensive sense, the common law is the richest heritage of the race. It is the embodiment of usage and general customs, common to all mankind; it is grounded in natural justice, and it is based upon rules of conduct which have been sanctioned by common consent and approved by the wisdom and experience of the ages."

Small v. Morrison, 185 N.C. 577, 586, 118 S.E. 12, 16 (1923) (action against father on behalf of infant child seeking recovery for injuries to infant allegedly caused by father's negligent operation of automobile).

"At common law it is well established that a minor child cannot sue a parent for a tort. It is said by Cooley on Torts, p. 276, under title of 'Wrongs to a Child': 'For an injury suffered by the child in that relation, no action will lie at the common law.' "

Roller v. Roller, 37 Wash. 242, 245, 79 P. 788, 789 (1905), disapproved as too broad in *Borst v. Borst,* 41 Wash.2d 642, 251 P.2d 149 (1952).

The history of the common law dictates that the immunity of a parent from a tort action by his minor child stems not from a judicially created doctrine, but from a well-reasoned and logical understanding that parents were afforded protection from civil actions by their minor children because of parental authority and a corresponding duty to care for, nurture, and administer discipline to those entrusted by God to their care. Parental authority to use force or restraint against a child in the exercise of discipline was recognized under the common law.

. . .

"[I]f it be once established that a child has a right to sue a parent for a tort, there is no practical line of demarkation which can be drawn, for the same principle which would allow the action in the case of a heinous crime, like the one involved in this case, would allow an action to be brought for any other tort. The principle permitting the action would be the same. The torts would be different only in degree. Hence all the disturbing confusion would be introduced which can be imagined under a system which would allow parents and children to be involved in litigation of this kind."*Roller,* 37 Wash. at 244, 79 P. at 789. Beyond the obvious point that this case involves tragic facts in that the father's discipline clearly involved excessive force, the per curiam opinion fails to explain the impetus for making another exception to this long-standing and rational rule.

Owens and the opinions of other states make clear that the principle of parental immunity is logical. The per curiam opinion clearly agrees that the principle is logical because the opinion only modifies the principle; it does not abolish it. Furthermore, the doctrine is not unjust, because the criminal law is available as redress for any acts by a parent that threaten the life or health of his or her child. Finally, other states have written extensively in the judicial opinions of their highest court as to the validity of the parental-immunity doctrine and have explained the multiple rationales behind the rule. See, e.g., *Roller,* supra; *Wick v. Wick,* 192 Wis. 260, 260–61, 212 N.W. 787, 787–88 (1927) (action by child against parents for injuries incurred in automobile accident), abrogated by *Goller v. White,* 20 Wis.2d 402, 122 N.W.2d 193 (1963); *Matarese,* supra. Because history and logic support the parental-immunity doctrine, I see no reason to modify the rule in this case. Therefore, I dissent.

CHAPTER VIII

VYING FOR CUSTODY

A. PARENT VERSUS PARENT

1. SOLE CUSTODY WITH VISITATION RIGHTS

The criteria of the Primary Caretaker Doctrine, announced in the West Virginia Supreme Court of Appeals case of Garska v. McCoy, *reproduced at page 984 of the case book, has been superseded by the following statutes:*

WEST VIRGINIA CODE (West 2002)

§ 48–9–206. Allocation of custodial responsibility

(a) Unless otherwise resolved by agreement of the parents under section 9–201 or unless manifestly harmful to the child, the court shall allocate custodial responsibility so that the proportion of custodial time the child spends with each parent approximates the proportion of time each parent spent performing caretaking functions for the child prior to the parents' separation or, if the parents never lived together, before the filing of the action, except to the extent required under section 9–209 or necessary to achieve any of the following objectives:

(1) To permit the child to have a relationship with each parent who has performed a reasonable share of parenting functions;

(2) To accommodate the firm and reasonable preferences of a child who is fourteen years of age or older, and with regard to a child under fourteen years of age, but sufficiently matured that he or she can intelligently express a voluntary preference for one parent, to give that preference such weight as circumstances warrant;

(3) To keep siblings together when the court finds that doing so is necessary to their welfare;

(4) To protect the child's welfare when, under an otherwise appropriate allocation, the child would be harmed because of a gross disparity in the quality of the emotional attachments between each parent and the child or in each parent's demonstrated ability or availability to meet a child's needs;

(5) To take into account any prior agreement of the parents that, under the circumstances as a whole including the reasonable expectations of the parents in the interest of the child, would be appropriate to consider;

(6) To avoid an allocation of custodial responsibility that would be extremely impractical or that would interfere substantially with the

child's need for stability in light of economic, physical or other circumstances, including the distance between the parents' residences, the cost and difficulty of transporting the child, the parents' and child's daily schedules, and the ability of the parents to cooperate in the arrangement;

(7) To apply the principles set forth in 9–403(d) of this article if one parent relocates or proposes to relocate at a distance that will impair the ability of a parent to exercise the amount of custodial responsibility that would otherwise be ordered under this section; and

(8) To consider the stage of a child's development.

(b) In determining the proportion of caretaking functions each parent previously performed for the child under subsection (a) of this section, the court shall not consider the divisions of functions arising from temporary arrangements after separation, whether those arrangements are consensual or by court order. The court may take into account information relating to the temporary arrangements in determining other issues under this section.

(c) If the court is unable to allocate custodial responsibility under subsection (a) of this section because the allocation under that subsection would be manifestly harmful to the child, or because there is no history of past performance of caretaking functions, as in the case of a newborn, or because the history does not establish a pattern of caretaking sufficiently dispositive of the issues of the case, the court shall allocate custodial responsibility based on the child's best interest, taking into account the factors in considerations that are set forth in this section and in section two hundred nine and 9–403(d) of this article and preserving to the extent possible this section's priority on the share of past caretaking functions each parent performed.

(d) In determining how to schedule the custodial time allocated to each parent, the court shall take account of the economic, physical and other practical circumstances such as those listed in subdivision (6), subsection (a) of this section.

§ 48–9–207. Allocation of significant decision-making responsibility

(a) Unless otherwise resolved by agreement of the parents under section 9–201, the court shall allocate responsibility for making significant life decisions on behalf of the child, including the child's education and health care, to one parent or to two parents jointly, in accordance with the child's best interest, in light of:

(1) The allocation of custodial responsibility under section 9–206 of this article;

(2) The level of each parent's participation in past decision-making on behalf of the child;

(3) The wishes of the parents;

(4) The level of ability and cooperation the parents have demonstrated in decision-making on behalf of the child;

(5) Prior agreements of the parties; and

(6) The existence of any limiting factors, as set forth in section 9–209 of this article.

(b) If each of the child's legal parents has been exercising a reasonable share of parenting functions for the child, the court shall presume that an allocation of decision-making responsibility to both parents jointly is in the child's best interests. The presumption is overcome if there is a history of domestic abuse, or by a showing that joint allocation of decision-making responsibility is not in the child's best interest.

(c) Unless otherwise provided or agreed by the parents, each parent who is exercising custodial responsibility shall be given sole responsibility for day-to-day decisions for the child, while the child is in that parent's care and control, including emergency decisions affecting the health and safety of the child.

NOTE

The present West Virginia approach reflects that of the A.L.I. Principles of Dissolution that were published in 2002 which replaced "custody" and "visitation" with "custodial responsibility". For readings about this and other suggested approaches see Katherine T. Bartlett, *U.S. Custody Law in the Context of the ALI Principles of the Law of Family Dissolutions*, 10 VA. J. OF SOC. POLICY AND THE LAW 5 (2002); Michael T. Flannery, *Is "Bird Nesting" in the Best Interest of Children?*, 57 S.M.U. L. REV. 295–352 (2004); Hung–En Liu, *Custody Decisions in Social and Cultural Contexts: In–Depth and Focus Group Interviews with Nineteen Judges in Taiwan*, 17 COLUM. J. ASIAN L. 225–305 (2004); and Elizabeth S. Scott, *Pluralism, Parental Preference and Child Custody*, 60 CAL. REV. 515 (1992). For an article specifically dealing with the new West Virginia law, John D. Athey, *The Ramifications of West Virginia's Codified Child Custody Law: A Departure from Garska v. McCoy*, 106 W. VA. L. REV. 389 (2004).

F. PROBLEMS OF ENFORCEMENT

4. ACROSS STATE LINES

Following **Friedrich v. Friedrich** *and prior to the International Child Abduction Remedies Act of 1988, please add at page 1166:*

Delvoye v. Lee

United States Court of Appeals, Third Circuit, 2003.
329 F.3d 330.

■ SCHWARZER, SENIOR DISTRICT JUDGE.

This is an appeal from an order of the district court denying Wim Delvoye's petition to return Baby S to Belgium under the *Hague Conven-*

tion on the Civil Aspects of International Child Abduction, Oct. 25, 1980; T.I.A.S. No. 11670, 19 I.L.M. 1501 (the "Convention"). The district court found and concluded that petitioner had failed to meet his burden of proving that Baby S was an habitual resident of Belgium and thus was wrongfully removed from that country. We affirm.

Petitioner and respondent met in New York early in 2000. Petitioner resided in Belgium but made several trips to visit respondent. On his visits to New York, a romantic relationship developed between them. In August 2000, respondent moved into petitioner's New York apartment. While continuing to live in Belgium, petitioner spent about a quarter of his time in New York. In September 2000, respondent learned that she was pregnant with petitioner's child. Respondent began prenatal care in New York, but because petitioner refused to pay the cost of delivery of the baby in the United States and Belgium offered free medical services, respondent agreed to have the baby in Belgium. In November 2000, she traveled to Belgium on a three-month tourist visa, bringing along only one or two suitcases. She left the rest of her belongings, including her non-maternity clothes, in the New York apartment. While in Belgium respondent lived out of her suitcases. When her visa expired she did not extend it. The baby was born on May 14, 2001. By then the relationship between the parties had deteriorated. After initially resisting, petitioner signed the consent form that enabled respondent to get an American passport for Baby S and agreed to respondent's return to the United States with Baby S in July 2001. Over the next two months, petitioner made several trips to the United States and the parties made several attempts to reconcile. When those efforts failed, petitioner filed this petition. Following an evidentiary hearing, the district court denied the petition. This appeal followed. Because the order is a final disposition of the petition, we have jurisdiction under 28 U.S.C. § 1291.

Article 3 of the Convention provides in relevant part:

The removal ... of a child is to be considered wrongful where—a) it is in breach of rights of custody attributed to a person ... either jointly or alone, under the law of the State in which the child was *habitually resident* immediately before the removal....

(Emphasis added.)

The determination of a person's habitual residence is a mixed question of fact and law. We review the district court's findings of historical and narrative facts for clear error, but exercise plenary review over the court's application of legal precepts to the facts. *Feder v. Evans–Feder,* 63 F.3d 217, 222 n. 9 (3d Cir.1995); *see also Mozes v. Mozes,* 239 F.3d 1067, 1073 (9th Cir.2001).

The issue before us is whether Baby S was "habitually resident" in Belgium at the time of his removal to the United States. In *Feder,* we defined the relevant concept:

[A] child's habitual residence is the place where he ... has been physically present for an amount of time sufficient for acclimatization and which has a "degree of settled purpose" from the child's perspective.... [A] determination of whether any particular place satisfies this standard must focus on the child and consists of an analysis of the child's circumstances in that place and the parents' present, shared intentions regarding their child's presence there.

63 F.3d at 224.

The district court held that petitioner had failed to meet his burden of proving that Baby S was an habitual resident of Belgium. It reasoned that a two-month-old infant, who is still nursing, has not been present long enough to have an acclimatization apart from his parents.

This case then presents the unique question of whether and when a very young infant acquires an habitual residence. It differs from the run of decisions under the Convention where the child is assumed to have an habitual residence initially and the controversy is over a change of that residence. No decisions have squarely addressed the issue before us. The leading treatise on the Convention provides some general guidance:

There is general agreement on a theoretical level that because of the factual basis of the concept there is no place for habitual residence of dependence. However, in practice it is often not possible to make a distinction between the habitual residence of a child and that of its custodian. Where a child is very young it would, under ordinary circumstances, be very difficult for him ... to have the capability or intention to acquire a separate habitual residence.

Paul Beaumont & Peter McEleavy, *The Hague Convention on International Child Abduction* 91 (1999). An English court has said: "The habitual residence of the child is where it last had a settled home which was in essence where the matrimonial home was." *Dickson v. Dickson,* 1990 SCLR 692. And an Australian court has stated: "A young child cannot acquire habitual residence in isolation from those who care for him. While 'A' lived with both parents, he shared their common habitual residence or lack of it." *Re F* (1991) 1 F.L.R. 548, 551.

Where a matrimonial home exists, i.e., where both parents share a settled intent to reside, determining the habitual residence of an infant presents no particular problem, it simply calls for application of the analysis under the Convention with which courts have become familiar. Where the parents' relationship has broken down, however, as in this case, the character of the problem changes. Of course, the mere fact that conflict has developed between the parents does not *ipso facto* disestablish a child's habitual residence, once it has come into existence. But where the conflict is contemporaneous with the birth of the child, no habitual residence may ever come into existence.

That is not to say that the infant's habitual residence automatically becomes that of his mother. In *Nunez-Escudero v. Tice–Menley,* 58 F.3d 374 (8th Cir.1995), Nunez-Escudero and Tice–Menley married in Mexico in August 1992. A child was born there in July 1993. In September, Tice–

Menley left Mexico with her two-month-old infant and returned to the United States. Nunez–Escudero filed a petition under the Convention alleging that his son had been wrongfully removed. The district court denied the petition on the ground that return of the child would subject him to a grave risk of harm. The court of appeals reversed and remanded. The mother contended that the court should affirm, notwithstanding the erroneous grave risk of harm determination, on the ground that the infant was not an habitual resident of Mexico. The court rejected the argument and remanded for a determination of the child's habitual residence, stating.

> To say that the child's habitual residence derived from his mother would be inconsistent with the Convention, for it would reward an abducting parent and create an impermissible presumption that the child's habitual residence is where the mother happens to be.

58 F.3d at 379.

The instant case differs from *Nunez-Escudero*. Because the petitioner and respondent had married in Mexico and lived there together for nearly a year before the child was born, a basis existed for finding the child's habitual residence to be in Mexico. Here, in contrast, the district court found that respondent, at petitioner's urging, had traveled to Belgium to avoid the cost of the birth of the child and intended to live there only temporarily. She retained her ties to New York, not having taken her non-maternity clothes, holding only a three-month visa and living out of the two suitcases she brought with her. Thus, there is lacking the requisite "degree of common purpose" to habitually reside in Belgium. As explained in *Re Bates*,

> There must be a degree of settled purpose.... All that is necessary is that the purpose of living where one does has a sufficient degree of continuity to be properly described as settled.

No. CA 122–89, High Court of Justice, Family Div'l Ct. Royal Courts of Justice, United Kingdom (1989), quoted in *Feder*, 63 F.3d at 223.

Because petitioner and respondent lacked the "shared intentions regarding their child's presence [in Belgium]," *Feder*, 63 F.3d at 224, Baby S did not become an habitual resident there. Even if petitioner intended that he become an habitual resident, respondent evidenced no such intention. Addressing the status of a newborn child, one Scottish commentator said:

> [A] newborn child born in the country where his ... parents have their habitual residence could normally be regarded as habitually resident in that country. Where a child is born while his ... mother is temporarily present in a country other than that of her habitual residence it does seem, however, that the child will normally have no habitual residence until living in a country on a footing of some stability.

Dr. E.M. Clive, "The Concept of Habitual Residence," *The Juridical Review part 3*, 138, 146 (1997).

Based on the district court's factual findings, which have not been challenged, we conclude that petitioner failed to prove that Baby S was habitually resident in Belgium.

We affirm the district court's order.

CHAPTER IX

PARENTAL RIGHTS TERMINATION AND ADOPTION

A. SEVERING PARENTAL RIGHTS INVOLUNTARILY

2. JUSTIFYING PEREMPTORY INTERVENTION

Following the California Family Code provisions at page 1196, please add:

In re K.A.W.

Supreme Court of Missouri, En Banc, 2004.
133 S.W.3d 1.

■ RICHARD B. TEITELMAN, JUDGE.

K.A.W. and K.A.W. (twins) are minor children born to T.W. ("Mother"). Mother's parental rights were terminated on December 11, 2002, pursuant to section 211.447, and she appeals. Mother argues that the trial court's findings with respect to sections 211.447.4(2), (3) and (6) and 211.447.6 were insufficient. She also contends that the trial court erred because it failed to make required findings.

This case was transferred to this Court prior to disposition by the court of appeals because of this Court's desire to resolve this case forthwith in accordance with the admonition of section 453.011.1 that cases involving termination of parental rights and adoption be given priority.

The judgment is reversed, and the cause is remanded. If further proceedings include the termination of Mother's parental rights, the trial court is directed to consider and make findings on each of the statutorily required subdivisions or factors for all grounds for termination of parental rights on which the trial court bases its decision.

When Mother was pregnant with the twins she was already raising three other young children on her own while trying to hold a job. Overwhelmed, she struggled with the question of whether it was best to place her twins up for adoption. Eventually, Mother decided that she should place them up for adoption because, as she later testified, she wanted them "to have a better life."

The twin girls were born in June 2000, approximately three months premature. They required a two-month hospital stay. Although Mother had decided to place her twins for adoption, she did not abandon them. Rather, she visited the twins in the hospital daily and continued caring for them, holding, feeding and talking to them. Mother expressed breastmilk for their best care rather than allowing them to be fed formula. She took a special class to learn more about how to care for her premature twins. When the twins were released from the hospital, Mother woke hourly to feed and administer medicine to them, while still maintaining her obligations to her other children and her job.

While caring for her children, Mother carefully tried to investigate prospective families that might be suitable for the twins. She obtained the help of adoption professionals and attorneys. She expressed interest in an "open adoption" so that she could maintain contact with the twins and continue to support them. Mother was told she would need to look beyond Missouri, which does not allow "open adoption."[3]

An adoption facilitator presented a prospective family from California. Mother visited the couple for 10 days to be sure they were fit. Later, Mother became convinced that the California couple was not as good a placement as she originally believed (among other things, they were becoming reluctant to maintain contact), so when she was in California for a visit, she retained the twins in her custody and began to seek another placement. Mother was advised that a British couple was still interested in adopting her babies. Mother had previously investigated the couple and believed them to be excellent candidates. The husband was an attorney, and the couple supported doing an open adoption. The British couple came to California, and the twins, Mother and the couple traveled a circuitous route from California to Arkansas by car. Mother was counseled by a British social worker and three attorneys that she should complete the adoption there because open adoption was not permitted in Missouri. Mother was advised to claim that she was an Arkansas resident. She refused, but she did provide an Arkansas address that belonged to a relative. An Arkansas judge approved the adoption.

Eventually, British officials determined that the British couple was unfit. The twins were taken into the custody of a British children's services agency. The Arkansas court entered an order setting aside the adoption decree for lack of jurisdiction because none of the parties were Arkansas residents. The twins were returned to Missouri, where they were placed in the custody of the Missouri division of family services (DFS).

When Mother learned that the second adoption effort had failed, she decided that adoption was not the appropriate option, and she resolved to rear the babies herself and rally the support of her family so that she could do it well.[4]

---

3. Subsequent media reports that Mother sold her twins on the internet were investigated by the state and revealed to be completely false. There was some evidence that Mother accepted small gifts, including earrings, but no gift was worth more than $100 and nothing in the record supports the media suggestions that Mother was attempting to sell the twins.

4. Mother twice failed in her efforts to find a suitable placement for her twins, yet this is not uncommon. The difficulty in finding safe permanent homes for children is illustrated by data that children in the custody of Missouri DFS are moved from placement to placement an average of over three times per child. Citizens for Missouri's Children, Children's Trust Fund, *KIDS COUNT in Missouri 2002 Data Book*, 36 (2003).

The record indicates that, once DFS gained jurisdiction of the twins, Mother's equivocation ceased other than a few week period shortly after DFS took jurisdiction, when she considered allowing the foster parents to adopt the children but ultimately rejected that alternative and strove to gain back custody of the twins instead. After DFS gained jurisdiction of the twins, there is no evidence that any of Mother's conduct would indicate a likelihood of future problems. Instead, all of the evidence indicates that Mother remedied every potential problem noted by DFS. She complied fully with DFS's entire parenting plan, which had as its ostensible goal reunification:

- The plan required Mother to take parenting classes. Mother took parenting classes, and her instructor testified that Mother was the most involved and participatory member of the class.

- The plan required Mother to visit the twins regularly. Mother visited the twins as often as the court would allow and fought for the right to visit more frequently.

- The plan required Mother to provide financial support for the twins. Mother did so and frequently paid in advance.

- Mother was required to undergo a psychological examination, and she did so willingly. On her own initiative, she also obtained counseling.

- She submitted to drug screenings (which she passed) although there was no allegation of drug use.

A DFS worker later testified that Mother complied with everything that had been asked of her including every element of the plan. Nevertheless, the juvenile officer filed a petition to terminate Mother's parental rights. The petition alleged that termination was warranted according to sections 211.447.4(2), (3) and (6) and that termination was in the twins' best interests.

The trial court conducted a hearing and issued "Findings, Conclusions and Judgment Terminating Parental Rights." The trial court's findings incorporated its earlier "Findings and Judgment of Disposition" and "Permanency Planning Order." The trial court terminated Mother's parental rights under subdivisions (2), (3) and (6) of section 211.447.4, ruling:

> 15. ... "Mother" has abused and neglected "The Twins". Section 211.447.4(2), RSMo.
>
> (a) "Mother" has committed severe and recurrent acts of emotional abuse toward "The Twins." Section 211.447.4(2)(c), RSMo. These acts include the multiple, unstable, inappropriate, temporary placements including, but not limited to, placements in California, Arkansas, and Great Britain within a span of a few months during the first months of "The Twins" lives....

16. ... [T]he conditions which caused this Court to assume jurisdiction over "The Twins" or conditions of a potentially harmful nature continue to exist and will not be remedied at an early date to permit return of "The Twins" in the near future to the custody of "Mother", and under all the circumstances, continuation of any relationship between the "Mother" and "The Twins" greatly diminishes the prospects of "The Twins" for early integration into a stable and permanent home. Section 211.447.4(3), RSMo. These conditions include, but are not limited to, the multiple placements of "The Twins" during the first months of their lives and the resulting instability; "Mother's" continued stress and being overwhelmed with the reality of The Twins; the continued indecisiveness of "Mother" in dealing with "The Twins"; and the lack of family support for "Mother" in caring for the needs of "The Twins." Additionally, further movement of "The Twins" from the stability of their environment since April 18, 2001, would be harmful to "The Twins" in light of the Reactive Detachment [sic] Disorder in Partial Remission, a major mental disorder, suffered by "The Twins" as a result of the multiple placements and resulting instability....

17. ... "Mother" is unfit to be a party to the parent-child relationship with "The Twins" because of her consistent pattern of emotional abuse and, additionally, because of specific conditions directly relating to her relationship with "The Twins", all of which are of a duration and nature rendering "Mother" unable for the reasonably foreseeable future to care appropriately for the ongoing physical, mental and emotional needs of "The Twins". Section 211.447.4(6), RSMo. These considerations include, but are not limited to, "Mother's" continued indecisiveness in dealing with the lives of "The Twins" and their welfare; and the lack of family support for "Mother" in caring for health and welfare of "The Twins". ...

. . .

19. ... [T]here are no emotional ties between "The Twins" and "Mother". This is a direct result of the actions of "Mother" in her multiple placements of "The Twins" and resulting instability and emotional harm suffered by "The Twins". Section 211.447.6(1), RSMo.

20. ... "The Twins" are not bonded with "Mother". This is a direct result of the deliberate acts of "Mother", who knew or should have known said acts would subject "The Twins" to a substantial and real risk of physical and mental harm. Section 211.447.6(7), RSMo.

. . .

22. The multiple placements and instability of "Mother" have caused emotional harm to "The Twins", and these actions by "Mother" continue to affect "The Twins" to this day, and "Mother" is unwilling or unable to provide "The Twins" with the stability necessary for their overall welfare.

23. Termination of the parental rights of "Mother" is necessary to serve the best interests of "The Twins", in light of all the evidence, and . . . the evidence supporting termination of the parental rights of "Mother" is clear, cogent and convincing. Section 211.447.5, RSMo.

. . .

25. This Court has considered all subsections of Section 211.447.4 and Section 211.447.6, RSMo, and except as expressly provided herein, finds the subsections irrelevant because there was inadequate evidence of their applicability presented during the evidentiary hearing.

. . .

27. The parental rights of "Mother" . . . with "The Twins" . . . shall be, and hereby are, terminated.

Mother appeals, arguing that the trial court's findings with respect to sections 211.447.4(2), (3) and (6) and 211.447.6 were insufficient. She also contends that the trial court erred because it failed to make required findings.

"Courts typically terminate parental rights under a 'parental fault' standard, in which the court focuses on the behavior of the parent or parents, a 'best interests of the child' standard, in which the court focuses on the effect of termination of parental rights on the child, or a combination of both." 2 Am Jur 2d *Adoption* sec. 134 (2003). Missouri, through section 211.447, terminates parental rights under a combination of both standards. Additionally, section 211.443 provides that Missouri uses a rule of construction for section 211.447, that it:

[S]hall be construed so as to promote the best interests and welfare of the child as determined by the juvenile court in consideration of the following:

(1) The recognition and protection of the constitutional rights of all parties in the proceedings;

(2) The recognition and protection of the birth family relationship when possible and appropriate; and

(3) The entitlement of every child to a permanent and stable home.

. . .

An essential part of any determination whether to terminate parental rights is whether, considered at the time of the termination and looking to the future, the child would be harmed by a continued relationship with the parent. A prospective analysis is required to determine whether grounds exist and what is in the best interests of the child for the reasonably foreseeable future. Obviously, it is difficult to predict the future. Section 211.447 provides for detailed consideration of the parent's past conduct as well as the parent's conduct following the trial court's assumption of jurisdiction as good evidence of future behavior. *In the Interest of M.E.W.*, 729 S.W.2d 194, 196 (Mo. banc 1987) (court needs to consider existing conditions, which may have arisen or were discovered after it assumed jurisdiction); *In the Interest of C.L.W.*, 115 S.W.3d 354, 356 (Mo.App.2003) (court must look at totality of parent's conduct both prior to and after filing of termination petition); *In the Interest of S.H.*, 915 S.W.2d 399, 404–5 (Mo.App.1996) (past patterns provide vital clues to present and future conduct). However, it is insufficient merely to point to past acts, note that they resulted in abuse or neglect and then terminate parental rights. *In the Interest of C.L.W.*, 115 S.W.3d at 356. Past behavior can support grounds for termination, but only if it is convincingly linked to predicted future behavior. There must be some explicit consideration of whether the past acts provide an indication of the likelihood of future harm. *In the Interest of L.G.*, 764 S.W.2d 89, 95 (Mo. banc 1989) (state met its burden by proving likely harm to child would occur in future). "A judge may properly be guided by evidence demonstrating reason to believe that a parent will correct a condition or weakness that currently disables the parent from serving his or her child's best interests." 2 Am Jur 2d *Adoption* sec. 135 (2003).

Courts have required that abuse or neglect sufficient to support termination under section 211.447.4(2) be based on conduct at the time of termination, not just at the time jurisdiction was initially taken. *In the Interest of B.C.K. and K.S.P.*, 103 S.W.3d at 328; *In the Interest of T.A.S.*, 32 S.W.3d 804, 812 (Mo.App.2000) (*T.A.S. I*). Similarly, courts have required that a failure to rectify sufficient to support termination under section 211.447.4(3) be based on a determination that conditions of a potentially harmful nature continued to exist as of the termination, rather than a mere finding that conditions that led to the assumption of jurisdiction still persisted. *In the Interest of T.A.S.*, 62 S.W.3d 650, 656–7 (Mo.App. 2001) (*T.A.S. II*). Section 211.447.4(6) explicitly requires analysis of the "reasonably foreseeable future." *In the Interest of C.W. and S.J.W.*, 64 S.W.3d 321, 325 (Mo.App.2001). Findings supporting earlier determinations are not irrelevant, but they must be updated to address the extent to which they describe the time of the termination and the potential for future harm. *T.A.S. I* at 812; *T.A.S. II* at 656–7. To that end, a trial court cannot support a termination by merely incorporating earlier findings supporting its assumption of jurisdiction or some other earlier disposition.

. . .

Another essential part of any determination whether to terminate parental rights is whether the cited conduct of the parent has had or will have a detrimental impact upon the child. *In the Interest of P.C., B.M., and C.M.*, 62 S.W.3d 600, 604 (Mo.App.2001) (the trial court must hear some evidence describing what impact the questioned conduct has had on the children). Poor conduct or character flaws are not relevant unless they could actually result in future harm to the child. For example, sections 211.447.4(2)(a) and 211.447.4(3)(c) provide that the parent's mental condition is a factor supporting termination only if it "renders the parent unable to knowingly provide the child the necessary care, custody and control."

Another essential part of any determination whether to terminate parental rights is whether the cited acts or conditions of the parent, and their accompanying impact upon the child, are severe enough to constitute abuse or neglect. *In the Interest of P.C., B.M., and C.M.*, 62 S.W.3d at 604 (parent's acts may have been inappropriate but were not severe enough to support termination). Some parental conduct will harm a child without constituting abuse or neglect. *In the Interest of B.C.K. and K.S.P.*, 103 S.W.3d at 328. It is essential that the trial court determine whether the parent's acts are of sufficient severity.

For some types of parenting problems, the required level of severity the court must find is specified by the statute. For example, sections 211.447.4(2)(b) and 211.447.4(3)(d) provide that chemical dependency is of sufficient severity to support termination if it "prevents the parent from consistently providing the necessary care, custody and control over the child and which cannot be treated so as to enable the parent to consistently provide such care, custody and control." For another example, not every criminal act committed by the parent is severe enough to be abuse or neglect. Section 211.447.4(4) provides that it will be a grounds for termination of parental rights if the "parent has been found guilty or pled guilty to a felony violation of chapter 566, RSMo [sexual offenses], when the child or any child in the family was a victim, or a violation of section 568.020, RSMo [incest], when the child or any child in the family was a victim." Section 211.447.6(6) provides for consideration of the "conviction of the parent of a felony offense that the court finds is of such a nature that the child will be deprived of a stable home for a period of years . . . ." These sections provide guidance as to how severe a parent's criminal conduct must be to constitute abuse.[7]

Isolated abusive acts or conditions may not support termination when considered individually, but if they form a consistent pattern, are recurrent or are repeated, they can, when considered in combination, rise to the level of abuse and support termination. Sec. 211.447.4(2)(c), (2)(d), (3), (6).

. . .

The trial court found that Mother's acts included "multiple, unstable, inappropriate, temporary placements including, but not limited to, placements in California, Arkansas, and Great Britain within a span of a few months during the first months of 'The Twins' lives."

There is no dispute that Mother twice attempted to place her twins for adoption. However, the record does not contain evidence that the first placement in California was unstable or inappropriate. The "placements in . . . Arkansas and Great Britain" refer to the single attempted adoption of

---

7. Although it was not explicitly relied upon by the trial court in the termination of parental rights, Mother pleaded guilty to welfare fraud because she provided false information and failed to provide required information to the state. Considering the severity of the crimes described in subdivisions 211.447.4(4) and 211.447.6(6), welfare fraud of this nature is not abuse, and the trial court correctly declined to include it as supporting termination.

the twins in Arkansas by the couple from Great Britain and, thus, constitute but one placement.

The two attempts at placement of the twins for adoption may have been mistakes, and may even have harmed the twins, but no reported Missouri case has ever held that placing a child up for adoption more than once rises to the level of abuse, and there is no reason to consider it abuse in this case. Mother's two attempts at placing her twins for adoption are not an indication of potential future harm to the twins, especially without evidence that she would try to again place the twins for adoption if she regains custody of them. There is no evidence in the record that Mother intends to do anything other than regain permanent custody of her twins.

The trial court erred in concluding that these placements support findings that Mother committed "severe and recurrent acts of emotional abuse" and that Mother created "conditions of a potentially harmful nature [that] continue to exist and will not be remedied at an early date." There is no evidence that the placements were abusive or that they indicate a likelihood of future harm. Therefore, they do not constitute evidence that "instantly tilts the scales in favor of termination." *T.A.S. II* at 655.

. . .

Mother's mental state cannot constitute abuse unless it rises to the level described by sections 211.447.4(2)(a) and (3)(c): "[a] mental condition which is shown by competent evidence either to be permanent or such that there is no reasonable likelihood that the condition can be reversed and which renders the parent unable to knowingly provide the child the necessary care, custody and control."[8] *In the Interest of C.L.W.,* 115 S.W.3d at 360–1 (Prewitt, J., dissenting); Mark Hardin and Robert Lancour, *Early Termination of Parental Rights: Developing Appropriate Statutory Grounds,* 14 (1996) (more required than just presence of mental or emotional disability—incapacity must be so severe that parent is incapable of providing minimally acceptable care).

It is hard to imagine a single working mother of five children living in poverty without enormous stress. Feeling overwhelmed in this context is not an indication of emotional instability, nor is it child abuse; rather, it is normal. DFS hired an expert to evaluate Mother's mental ability to care for her children. The expert found that Mother's "difficulties in parenting are not substantially different from those of many other single parents caring

---

8. "Before the court can use mental incapacity as the basis for terminating a parent's rights, it must find that the mental defect or disability renders the parent unable to provide for the needs and well-being of his or her children. ... It is sufficient to show that the parent's emotional problems are so severe as to prevent the maintenance of any meaningful relationship with his or her children. In such cases, it is often necessary to provide expert testimony that the parent's emotional instability is not likely to improve in the future. ... In order to prevail in a termination proceeding based on mental incapacity, the petition should present sufficient evidence of the adverse effects which the parent's incapacity has on the well-being of the child. Absent such a showing, most courts will be reluctant to order termination on this ground alone." 32 Am Jur Proof of Facts 3d *Parental Rights* sec. 5 (2003).

for large families . . ., she appears to be an adequate parent, and there is no evidence that her parental rights should be terminated.''

Sections 211.447.4(2)(a) and 211.447.4(3)(c) provide that a mental or emotional condition must be analyzed in three prongs to make an adequate finding: (1) documentation—whether the condition is supported by competent evidence; (2) duration—whether the condition is permanent or such that there is no reasonable likelihood that it can be reversed; and (3) severity of effect—whether the condition is so severe as to render the parent unable to knowingly provide the child necessary care, custody and control.

Considering each of these three prongs, the problems cited by the trial court (stress, feeling overwhelmed and indecisiveness) do not support termination of parental rights. The expert evidence as to Mother's mental state did not constitute competent evidence that these problems were abnormal. These problems were situational and not necessarily permanent; therefore, the importance of the parenting or reunification plan and the services provided by DFS to Mother. There is evidence that Mother complied with the plan and that the services helped. The trial court's use of the word "continued" is without any support in the record. Even if there was reason to believe that these problems "continued," there is no evidence in the record that such a combination of problems ever caused abuse or would cause future harm. The only evidence on this question was provided by the DFS expert who concluded that these reactions were expectable and not a potential cause of future harm.

Therefore, these findings do not support the termination of Mother's parental rights.

The trial court found that the twins suffered from "Reactive Detachment Disorder in Partial Remission, a major mental disorder, suffered by 'The Twins' as a result of the multiple placements and resulting instability." This opinion was rendered by only one of the several physicians who evaluated the twins—Dr. Luby. Dr. Luby actually diagnosed the twins with Reactive *Attachment* Disorder in Partial Remission. The trial court also omitted a modifier used by Dr. Luby: "moderate" (Dr. Luby testified that the condition can be severe, moderate or mild). Dr. Luby asked to be allowed to see the twins interact with Mother, but the request was denied—significantly undermining the reliability of the diagnosis. The two experts who evaluated the twins in the presence of Mother did not agree with Dr. Luby's diagnosis.

Furthermore, Dr. Luby acknowledged that she did not document any of the standard diagnostic criteria for Reactive Attachment Disorder. Even DFS showed little confidence in Dr. Luby's assessment. DFS did not arrange for treatment and did not inform the foster parents of the diagnosis. Moreover, despite the diagnosis, even Dr. Luby acknowledged that she could see no harm in placing the twins back with Mother.

The two psychologists who evaluated the twins *and witnessed their interaction with Mother* strongly disagreed with Dr. Luby's diagnosis. Dr.

Dean Rosen, a clinical psychologist, found that the twins were comfortable with Mother, paying little or no attention to others when their mother was in the room. He observed no signs of Reactive Attachment Disorder. Dr. Rosen found a "good indication there was a bond with [their] mother" and that Mother demonstrated appropriate parenting skills. Dr. Rosen testified that there would be no harm in returning the twins to their mother.

Dr. Daniel Cuneo, a clinical psychologist, was also allowed to observe the twins with their mother. He concluded that the twins showed no signs of Reactive Attachment Disorder. He found that the twins played with and appropriately modeled their mother's behavior, that the children were comfortable and that Mother set limits for the twins while showing affection toward them. Dr. Cuneo observed that the twins showed affection for their mother. He also found no reason to expect the twins to be harmed by being returned to their mother.

A primary focus of a proceeding to terminate parental rights is the relationship between the parent and the child. The findings of experts who have had the opportunity to observe and evaluate that relationship should be given great weight.

The trial court's finding that the twins suffer from "Reactive Detachment [sic] Disorder in Partial Remission, a major mental disorder" that would be worsened by their being placed in Mother's custody, is not supported by clear, cogent and convincing evidence. The evidence only supports a conclusion that the twins may have been emotionally harmed by having been placed multiple times, but that such harm has been ameliorated and that the continuation of Mother's parental rights does not pose a threat of future harm. Therefore, this finding does not support a termination of Mother's parental rights.

Section 211.447.4(2) provides for termination of parental rights if:

The child has been abused or neglected. In determining whether to terminate parental rights pursuant to this subdivision, the court shall consider and make findings on the following conditions or acts of the parent:

(a) A mental condition which is shown by competent evidence either to be permanent or such that there is no reasonable likelihood that the condition can be reversed and which renders the parent unable to knowingly provide the child the necessary care, custody and control;

(b) Chemical dependency which prevents the parent from consistently providing the necessary care, custody and control of the child and which cannot be treated so as to enable the parent to consistently provide such care, custody and control;

(c) A severe act or recurrent acts of physical, emotional or sexual abuse toward the child or any child in the family by the parent, including an act of incest, or by another under circumstances that indicate that the parent knew or should have known that such acts were being committed toward the child or any child in the family; or

(d) Repeated or continuous failure by the parent, although physically or financially able, to provide the child with adequate food, clothing, shelter, or education as defined by law, or other care and control necessary for the child's physical, mental, or emotional health and development;

The trial court concluded that it had considered all applicable subdivisions or factors and omitted those it determined to be irrelevant or supported by inadequate evidence of applicability. Section 211.447 does not provide the trial court with such discretion. *In the Interest of L.G.,* 764 S.W.2d 89, 94 (Mo. banc 1989). "The court is required to make specific findings on *each* of these four factors [or subdivisions]. If a factor is not relevant to the case, the court should state why the given factor is not relevant." *T.A.S. I* at 810 (emphasis in original); *In the Interest of B.C.K. and K.S.P.,* 103 S.W.3d at 327 (trial court must consider and make findings on four factors). "Strict and literal compliance with the statutory requirements is necessary in termination of parental rights cases." *T.A.S. I.* "Statutory mandates to make findings may not be overlooked on appeal." *In re A.P.,* 988 S.W.2d 59, 62 (Mo.App.1999). Section 211.447.4(2) provides that the trial court "shall consider and make findings" on all four factors, (a) through (d). Yet, the trial court only considered factor (c).

As to factor (c), the trial court's finding that Mother "has committed severe and recurrent acts of emotional abuse toward 'The Twins'" by placing the twins with two families within a span of a few months is not sufficient, as discussed above.

As to factors (a), (b) and (d), the evidence indicates that, rather than being irrelevant or unsupported, many of the omitted findings would have supported Mother's claims. There is no question that Mother has neither a mental condition nor chemical dependency that would preclude her from having custody of her children. Therefore, factors (a) and (b) favor Mother. Factor (d) also strongly favors Mother, in that she has continuously (even when the children were in DFS custody and foster care) provided the twins with monetary and emotional support.

Therefore, the trial court's findings as to section 211.447.4(2) are either absent or insufficient, and the trial court's reliance upon section 211.447.4(2) as grounds for termination is error.

. . .

Section 211.447.4(6) provides for termination of parental rights if:

The parent is unfit to be a party to the parent and child relationship because of a consistent pattern of committing a specific abuse, including but not limited to, abuses as defined in section 455.010, RSMo, child abuse or drug abuse before the child or of specific conditions directly relating to the parent and child relationship either of which are determined by the court to be of a duration or nature that renders the parent unable, for the reasonably foreseeable future, to care appropriately for the ongoing physical, mental or emotional needs of the child. It is presumed that a parent is unfit to be a party to the parent-child relationship upon a showing that within a three-year period immediately prior to the termination adjudication, the parent's parental rights to one or more other children were involuntarily terminated pursuant to subsection 2 or 3 of this section or subdivisions (1), (2), (3) or (4) of subsection 4 of this section or similar laws of other states.

The trial court found that Mother had abused the twins in such a way as to satisfy both prongs of section 211.447.4(6)—finding both a "consistent pattern of committing a specific abuse" and "specific conditions directly relating to the parent and child relationship." Both prongs must be (and were) accompanied by a finding that they will "be of a duration or nature that renders the parent unable, for the reasonably foreseeable future, to care appropriately for the ongoing physical, mental or emotional needs of the child." *In the Interest of C.W. and S.J.W.*, 64 S.W.3d at 325.

Subdivision (6) describes findings that the parent continues to have parenting problems that endanger the child coupled with an inability to remedy those problems within the reasonably foreseeable future. *See* Roya R. Hough, *Juvenile Law: A Year in Review*, 63 Mo. L.Rev. 459, 465–66 (1998) (focus in broad language of subdivision (6) is on "kid time"— whether "from the child's perspective, the amount of time necessary for the parent to overcome the barriers to reunification is unreasonable, as measured by the child's need for permanency at the earliest possible date"). Past abuse alone cannot be a basis for terminating parental rights under subdivision (6). Instead, the abuse must be of such a duration and nature that the trial court determines that the parent will not remedy the problem and so it renders the parent unfit for the reasonably foreseeable future. *In the Interest of P.C., B.M., and C.M.*, 62 S.W.3d at 606.

In support of termination under this subdivision, the trial court cited:

> ... "Mother's" continued stress and being overwhelmed with the reality of "The Twins"; "Mother's" continued indecisiveness in dealing with the lives of "The Twins" and their welfare; and the lack of family support for "Mother" in caring for health and welfare of "The Twins".

As discussed above, these findings are insufficient to support termination, even in combination. They are particularly inappropriate for section 211.447.4(6). They do not describe a parent that continues to have parenting problems that endanger a child coupled with an inability to remedy those problems within the reasonably foreseeable future. They are specific past acts or conditions and the record indicates that all of them ended by the time of the termination proceedings. Regardless of the past, section 211.447.4(6) "requires the trial court to determine that the parent is *currently* unfit ... to be a party to the parent and child relationship." *T.A.S. I* at 815 (emphasis added). Such a determination must be supported by findings as to acts or conditions that persist at the time of termination. *Id.*

Therefore, the trial court's findings as to section 211.447.4(6) are insufficient, and the trial court's reliance upon section 211.447.4(6) as grounds for termination is error.

Mother's parental rights were terminated because of little more than her efforts to find an adoptive family for her twins. There is not substantial evidence in the record that Mother did so for personal gain, and the evidence is that she consistently sought to protect her twins by finding a good adoptive family that would allow her to retain contact with the twins. This cannot, without more, provide grounds for termination of parental rights.

Countless psychological and child development studies have shown that children—especially infants and young children under the age of five—who are needlessly separated from their familiar parent suffer resulting deficits in their emotional and intellectual development. Joseph Goldstein, Albert J. Solnit, Sonja Goldstein and Anna Freud, *The Best Interests of the Child: The Least Detrimental Alternative,* 20 (1996). The complex and vital parent-child interactions necessary for healthy child development "thrive in the protective enclave of family life under guardianship by parents who are autonomous." *Id.* at 90. "When family integrity is broken or weakened by state intrusion, [the child's] needs are thwarted.... The effect on the child's developmental progress is likely to be detrimental." *Id.* Accordingly, courts should follow an approach of cautious restraint in intruding on the family relationship—an approach that recognizes that parents are generally entitled to raise their children as they think best, free from state interference, and that favors the minimum amount of state intervention necessary consistent with the best interests of the child. Parental rights should be terminated only when it is clearly necessary to ensure safe and permanent homes for children. Donald N. Duquette and Mark Hardin, *Adoption 2002: The President's Initiative on Adoption and Foster Care, Guidelines for Public Policy and State Legislative Governing Permanence for Children,* VI–1 (1999). "A parent's interest in retaining custody of his children is both legally cognizable and substantial, and may not be overridden in the absence of persuasive evidence that the children's well-being requires that custody be placed elsewhere." 59 Am Jur 2d *Parent and Child* sec. 36 (2003).

Many of the findings necessary to support a termination of Mother's parental rights as to the twins are absent from the trial court's ruling. The findings actually provided by the trial court are insufficient to support termination.

The judgment is reversed and the cause is remanded. If further proceedings include the termination of Mother's parental rights, the trial court is directed to consider and make findings on each of the statutorily required subdivisions or factors for all grounds for termination of parental rights on which the trial court bases its decision.[9]

---

9. As the judgment is reversed and the cause is remanded, Mother's other claims of error need not be reviewed. Because the case is remanded for further proceedings on all

■ WHITE, C.J., WOLFF and STITH, JJ., concur. PRICE, J., dissents in separate opinion filed.

■ BENTON and LIMBAUGH, JJ., concur in opinion of PRICE, J.

■ WILLIAM RAY PRICE, JR., JUDGE, dissenting.

. . .

In termination of parental rights cases, appellate courts should defer to the trial court's ability to judge the credibility of witnesses and should sustain the judgment unless there is no substantial evidence to support it, it is contrary to the evidence, or it erroneously declares or applies the law. *In the Interest of M.E.W.,* 729 S.W.2d 194, 195–96 (Mo. banc 1987). Appellate courts also should review conflicting evidence in the light most favorable to the judgment of the trial court. *Id.* at 196. "Clear, cogent and convincing" evidence is required to support the trial court's finding that a ground for termination of parental rights exists, and appellate courts must take that into account when reviewing whether "substantial evidence" supports the trial court's judgment. *See* sec. 211.447.5.

Appellate courts should recognize that the trial court occupies a "superior position" from which to "judge the credibility of witnesses and their character, sincerity, and other intangibles that might not be completely shown in the cold record." *Young v. Young,* 59 S.W.3d 23, 29 (Mo.App. 2001). In considering witness testimony, "[a] trial court is free to believe or disbelieve all, part, or none" of a witness's testimony. *Id.*

The trial court found that Mother engaged in a "consistent pattern of emotional abuse" of the twins. *See* sec. 211.447.4(6). Mother's pattern of behavior toward the twins supports this finding, particularly her failure to consider their well-being when making decisions about their care and in her repeated placement and subsequent withdrawal of the twins for adoption.[4]

The trial court also found that Mother's pattern of abuse was "of a duration or nature that renders [her] unable, for the reasonably foreseeable future, to care appropriately for the ongoing physical, mental, or emotional needs" of the twins. Sec. 211.447.4(6). The following evidence in the record is substantial and clearly, cogently, and convincingly supports these findings. *See M.E.W.,* 729 S.W.2d at 195–96; sec. 211.447.5.

---

three grounds for termination, the issue of whether the termination was in the twins' best interests is not reached.

4. Since the twins returned to the United States on April 18, 2001, they have been in the custody of their foster parents. The foster parents have an adopted son who is approximately nine months older than the twins. The son was placed with the foster parents prior to the twins' arrival and has remained in the parents' custody since that initial placement. The foster parents' adop-

tion of the twins was approved at the circuit court level, but Mother moved to stay that adoption pending the resolution of this appeal.

Mother's court-ordered visits and child support obligations to the twins concluded on June 23, 2002, by order of the trial court. The twins turned two years old three days after that last visit. They are nearly four years old now.

The record reveals that when Mother was pregnant, her doctor prescribed a medication for her to prevent premature labor. Mother quit taking the medicine of her own accord, and she later told a psychologist that she stopped taking the medicine because "she was tired of being pregnant." The twins were born at 28 weeks, or approximately three months prematurely, and they weighed slightly more than two pounds each. Mother had similarly stopped taking this medication in a previous pregnancy because "she didn't like to be on medication," and that child was also premature.

The twins' pediatrician testified that, after their release from the hospital, Mother missed their first appointment and three weeks elapsed between their release and first visit to him. He described the twins at that time as having "numerous medical problems" and said this initial visit for the twins after their departure from the hospital was "very important."[5] As a result of missed appointments, the doctor sent a letter to DFS stating that "[n]ot showing up for routine medical visits for the twins is not acceptable care."

Mother testified she first considered adoption because the twins' father told her no man would want her with three children, much less five of them. A disturbing statement in its own right, it prefaced Mother's chain of decisions predicated on her own desires that demonstrated her "unfit to be a party to the parent and child relationship." Sec. 211.447.4(6).

Mother first attempted to place the twins with R.A. and V.A., a married couple residing in California. She admitted placing the twins with them "because they were well off financially." Mother acknowledged that she was aware of V.A.'s criminal record before placing the twins with them. After leaving the twins in the custody of R.A. and V.A., Mother surreptitiously removed the twins from their home a month and a half later because she heard a rumor "they were strapped for money or they were filing for bankruptcy" and because when Mother called them, V.A. "acted nonchalant."[6] She told R.A. and V.A. she was taking them out for a visit, when in fact she took them to a hotel where A.K. and J.K., a married couple residing in the United Kingdom, met her two days later.

After driving from California to Arkansas with A.K. and J.K., Mother transferred custody of the twins to them. A child abuse investigator from DFS testified that Mother said she had placed her children with A.K. and J.K. because they were going to allow her to come to the United Kingdom

---

5. The pediatrician testified that Mother had repeatedly missed visits with him for her other children. With her oldest son, J.G., who has a heart problem, Mother missed at least six appointments, and she missed at least four appointments with the twins' sister, N.W.

6. Mother testified that she called or talked to V.A. "practically every day" when the twins were in R.A. and V.A.'s custody, which was from approximately October 19 through November 29, 2001. Mother stated V.A. made her feel like she "was being a pest" and V.A. "act[ed] nonchalant, like why was [Mother] calling her" one day when Mother called. Mother cited this conversation and reports of their financial problems as the only reasons she withdrew the children from R.A. and V.A.'s custody.

every year on the twins' birthday, which would be a good experience for her, and that she thought they would pay her airfare for those annual visits.

Mother's first objection to A.K. and J.K. having custody of the twins occurred approximately on January 16, 2001, as a response to media reports that she had sold the twins over the Internet.[7] British authorities rendered the placement with A.K. and J.K. short-term by taking custody of the twins on January 18, 2001, approximately two and a half weeks after their arrival in the United Kingdom, based on allegations of A.K.'s and J.K.'s unfitness.[8]

Both placements of the twins, with R.A. and V.A. and with A.K. and J.K., were illegal under Missouri law. The transfer of custody from Mother to both couples violated section 453.110, the purpose of which is "to prohibit the indiscriminate transfer of children" and to prevent parents from passing them on "like chattel to a new owner." *In re Baby Girl* 64, 850 S.W.2d 64, 68 (Mo. banc 1993).

Mother also admitted that she gave a false address to the Arkansas court to effect the twins' placement with A.K. and J.K. Mother told a psychologist that she knew she was required to be an Arkansas resident to ensure the twins' adoption there, so she used an aunt's Arkansas address instead of her own. Relying on her falsified information, the probate court of Pulaski County, Arkansas, entered an adoption decree for the twins on December 22, 2000. After learning that none of the parties was an Arkansas resident at the time the adoption decree was entered, the Arkansas court entered an order on March 6, 2001, to set aside that decree for lack of jurisdiction.

. . .

The majority cites, in its conclusion, studies showing that children needlessly separated from their parents suffer resulting deficits in their emotional and intellectual development. This point is undisputed. Even Mother, despite her initial testimony that she had never considered the emotional impact on the twins of her consistent pattern of placing and removing them and that she was the victim in this case, admitted subsequently that the twins were harmed by the multiple placements.

The majority also relies on authority that a child's developmental progress can be hampered by state intrusion. The majority ignores, howev-

---

7. As Mother put it, "January 16th is when my life was on the news." She expressed no concern as to any effect this media exposure may have had on the twins.

8. During the summer of 2001, Mother resumed her attempts to place the twins for adoption. She requested a meeting with the twins' foster parents in July to speak with them about adopting the twins. By the end of August, however, she had changed her mind again and withdrawn her offer to consent to adoption.

Even though she had previously declined to attempt to place the twins with her family and her mother had indicated earlier she did not want the twins, in April 2002 Mother testified that she would be amenable to letting her mother adopt the twins because then she could stay with them at her mother's.

er, that since the twins were released from the hospital in August 2000, they have been in Mother's sole care, custody, and control for 52 days. The absence of the twins from her custody was not her choice after DFS removed them upon their return from the United Kingdom, but the failed placements were direct consequences of her decisions and actions accomplished without mention of concern for the twins' well-being. The majority ignores that Mother voluntarily succumbed the custody of the twins to others—both times purportedly permanently—and that the state intervened only after the second placement was deemed unfit by foreign authorities acting on behalf of the twins' welfare. Any compromise in her family's integrity was accomplished directly as a result of Mother's decisions made without consideration of the twins' well-being.

The reality of this case is that the twins were born on June 26, 2000, and have been in the custody of foster parents since April 18, 2001, where they also have an adopted sibling. The testimony revealed that the twins need a stable environment and special attention to their emotional and physical needs, and Mother has never exhibited any ability to provide that for them.

When the trial court has received conflicting evidence, as in the instant case, the role of this Court is to "review the facts in the light most favorable to the trial court's judgment." *M.E.W.*, 729 S.W.2d at 196. In its review, the Court should "give due regard to the trial court's opportunity to judge the credibility of witnesses and sustain the decree unless there is no substantial evidence to support it, it is contrary to the evidence or it erroneously declares or applies the law." *Id.* at 195–96. "As long as the record contains credible evidence upon which the trial court could have formulated its beliefs," an appellate court should not "substitute its judgment for that of the trial court." *Patton v. Patton,* 973 S.W.2d 139, 145 (Mo.App.1998).

The standard of review precludes this Court from searching the record for facts that could have supported a contrary judgment from the trial court. Unfortunately, that is exactly what the majority has chosen to do. Perhaps more unfortunately, the majority has chosen to sacrifice the best interests and welfare of two innocent children in favor of a parent who has demonstrated, time and again, her inability to make appropriate decisions concerning their care. In doing so, the majority deviates from the dictate of section 211.443, which requires courts to interpret the termination of parental rights statutes "so as to promote the best interests and welfare of the child."

Substantial clear, cogent, and convincing evidence supports the trial court's finding that termination of Mother's parental rights was justified pursuant to section 211.447.4(6) and that termination was in the twins' best interests. I would affirm the judgment.

Please add to the* NOTES *following Santosky v. Kramer at page 1194 the following:

The Illinois Supreme Court, in a decision that addresses the complicated procedures involved in termination, has ruled that a clear and convincing standard is used during the phase of a termination proceeding to overcome the parental presumption. But then the court may use a preponderance of the evidence standard to decide to terminate the parent's rights in the child and freeing the child for adoption. People v. Brenda T. (*In re D.T.*), 212 Ill.2d 347, 289 Ill.Dec. 11, 818 N.E.2d 1214 (2004).

*In reference to parental termination of incarcerated parents and **Matter of Gregory B.** at page 1197, please note that the Florida Supreme Court has ruled that the time for which a parent is expected to be incarcerated in the future should be the test for termination. In other words, will the future incarceration of the parent constitute a substantial portion of the child's future minority, or whether the time the parent has been incarcerated to date has been a substantial portion of the child's life.* **B.C. v. Florida Dep't of Children & Families, 887 So.2d 1046 (Fla. 2004).**

At the end of the section add at page 1219.

NOTE

A majority of the states have enacted some form of "Safe Haven" statute. The practical effect is to allow parents to leave their unwanted newborns at certain locations without fear of criminal prosecution. While the number is not believed to be large, this "legalized abandonment" process was designed to deal with the significant number of babies who were abandoned (sometimes in garbage cans or toilets), some of whom were found only when dead. For a three part article describing the laws and how they might be meeting their goals, see Annette R. Appell, Safe Havens to Abandon Babies, in 5(4) ADOPTION QUARTERLY 59 (2002); 6(1) ADOPTION QUARTERLY 61 (2002); and 6(2) ADOPTION QUARTERLY 67 (2002). The following Florida provision is an example of such a "Safe Haven" law.

FLORIDA STATUTES ANNOTATED (West 2002 and 2005 Supp.)

383.50. Treatment of abandoned newborn infant

(1) As used in this section, the term "newborn infant" means a child that a licensed physician reasonably believes to be approximately 3 days old or younger at the time the child is left at a hospital, emergency medical services station, or fire station.

(2) There is a presumption that the parent who leaves the newborn infant in accordance with this section intended to leave the newborn infant and consented to termination of parental rights.

(3) Each emergency medical services station or fire station staffed with full-time firefighters, emergency medical technicians, or paramedics shall accept any newborn infant left with a firefighter, emergency medical technician, or paramedic. The firefighter, emergency medical technician, or paramedic shall consider these actions as implied consent to and shall:

(a) Provide emergency medical services to the newborn infant to the extent he or she is trained to provide those services, and

(b) Arrange for the immediate transportation of the newborn infant to the nearest hospital having emergency services.

A licensee as defined in § 401.23, a fire department, or an employee or agent of a licensee or fire department may treat and transport a newborn infant pursuant to this section. If a newborn infant is placed in the physical custody of an employee or agent of a licensee or fire department, such placement shall be considered implied consent for treatment and transport. A licensee, a fire department, or an employee or agent of a licensee or fire department is immune from criminal or civil liability for acting in good faith pursuant to this section. Nothing in this subsection limits liability for negligence.

(4) Each hospital of this state subject to s. 395.1041 shall, and any other hospital may, admit and provide all necessary emergency services and care, as defined in § 395.002(10), to any newborn infant left with the hospital in accordance with this section. The hospital or any of its licensed health care professionals shall consider these actions as implied consent for treatment, and a hospital accepting physical custody of a newborn infant has implied consent to perform all necessary emergency services and care. The hospital or any of its licensed health care professionals is immune from criminal or civil liability for acting in good faith in accordance with this section. Nothing in this subsection limits liability for negligence.

(5) Except where there is actual or suspected child abuse or neglect, any parent who leaves a newborn infant with a firefighter, emergency medical technician, or paramedic at a fire station or emergency medical services station, or brings a newborn infant to an emergency room of a hospital and expresses an intent to leave the newborn infant and not return, has the absolute right to remain anonymous and to leave at any time and may not be pursued or followed unless the parent seeks to reclaim the newborn infant.

(6) A parent of a newborn infant left at a hospital, emergency medical services station, or fire station under this section may claim his or her newborn infant up until the court enters a judgment terminating his or her parental rights. A claim to the newborn infant must be made to the entity having physical or legal custody of the newborn infant or to the circuit court before whom proceedings involving the newborn infant are pending.

(7) Upon admitting a newborn infant under this section, the hospital shall immediately contact a local licensed child-placing agency or alternatively contact the statewide central abuse hotline for the name of a licensed child-placing agency for purposes of transferring physical custody of the newborn infant. The hospital shall notify the licensed child-placing agency that a newborn infant has been left with the hospital and approximately when the licensed child-placing agency can take physical custody of the child. In cases where there is actual or suspected child abuse or neglect, the hospital or any of its licensed health care professionals shall report the

actual or suspected child abuse or neglect in accordance with §§ 39.201 and 395.1023 in lieu of contacting a licensed child-placing agency.

(8) Any newborn infant admitted to a hospital in accordance with this section is presumed eligible for coverage under Medicaid, subject to federal rules.

(9) A newborn infant left at a hospital, emergency medical services station, or fire station in accordance with this section shall not be deemed abandoned and subject to reporting and investigation requirements under § 39.201 unless there is actual or suspected child abuse or until the department takes physical custody of the child.

(10) A criminal investigation shall not be initiated solely because a newborn infant is left at a hospital under this section unless there is actual or suspected child abuse or neglect.

383.51. Confidentiality; identification of parent leaving newborn infant at hospital, emergency medical services station, or fire station

The identity of a parent who leaves a newborn infant at a hospital, emergency medical services station, or fire station in accordance with § 383.50 is confidential and exempt from the provisions of § 119.07(1) and § 24(a), Art. I of the State Constitution. The identity of a parent leaving a child shall be disclosed to a person claiming to be a parent of the newborn infant. This section is subject to the Open Government Sunset Review Act of 1995 in accordance with § 119.15, and shall stand repealed on October 2, 2007, unless reviewed and saved from repeal through reenactment by the Legislature.

B. ADOPTION

2. BALANCING THE RIGHTS OF THE PARTIES

At "Sexual Orientation", page 1232, please note that the American Academy of Pediatrics has endorsed adoption by same-sex couples (see http://www.aap.org/policy/020008.html.), and add the following decision:

Lofton v. Secretary of Department of Children and Family Services

United States Court of Appeals, Eleventh Circuit, 2004.
358 F.3d 804, cert. denied 125 S.Ct. 869 (2005).

■ BIRCH, CIRCUIT JUDGE.

In this appeal, we decide the states' rights issue of whether Florida Statute § 63.042(3), which prevents adoption by practicing homosexuals, is constitutional as enacted by the Florida legislature and as subsequently enforced. The district court granted summary judgment to Florida over an equal protection and due process challenge by homosexual persons desiring to adopt. We AFFIRM.

Since 1977, Florida's adoption law has contained a codified prohibition on adoption by any "homosexual" person. 1977 Fla. Laws, ch. 77–140, § 1, Fla. Stat. § 63.042(3) (2002).[2] For purposes of this statute, Florida courts have defined the term "homosexual" as being "limited to applicants who are known to engage in current, voluntary homosexual activity," thus drawing "a distinction between homosexual orientation and homosexual activity." *Fla. Dep't of Health & Rehab. Servs. v. Cox,* 627 So.2d 1210, 1215 (Fla.Dist.Ct.App.1993), *aff'd in relevant part,* 656 So.2d 902, 903 (Fla.1995). During the past twelve years, several legislative bills have attempted to repeal the statute, and three separate legal challenges to it have been filed in the Florida courts. To date, no attempt to overturn the provision has succeeded. We now consider the most recent challenge to the statute.

Six plaintiffs-appellants bring this case. The first, Steven Lofton, is a registered pediatric nurse who has raised from infancy three Florida foster children, each of whom tested positive for HIV at birth. By all accounts, Lofton's efforts in caring for these children have been exemplary, and his story has been chronicled in dozens of news stories and editorials as well as on national television. We confine our discussion of that story to those facts relevant to the legal issues before us and properly before us in the record. John Doe, also named as a plaintiff-appellant in this litigation, was born on 29 April 1991. Testing positive at birth for HIV and cocaine, Doe immediately entered the Florida foster care system. Shortly thereafter, Children's Home Society, a private agency, placed Doe in foster care with Lofton, who has extensive experience treating HIV patients. At eighteen months, Doe sero-reverted and has since tested HIV negative. In September of 1994, Lofton filed an application to adopt Doe but refused to answer the application's inquiry about his sexual preference and also failed to disclose Roger Croteau, his cohabitating partner, as a member of his household. After Lofton refused requests from the Department of Children and Families ("DCF") to supply the missing information, his application was rejected pursuant to the homosexual adoption provision.... Two years later, in light of the length of Doe's stay in Lofton's household, DCF offered Lofton the compromise of becoming Doe's legal guardian. This arrangement would have allowed Doe to leave the foster care system and DCF supervision. However, because it would have cost Lofton over $300 a month in lost foster care subsidies and would have jeopardized Doe's Medicaid coverage, Lofton declined the guardianship option unless it was an interim stage toward adoption. Under Florida law, DCF could not accommodate this condition, and the present litigation ensued.

Plaintiff-appellant Douglas E. Houghton, Jr., is a clinical nurse specialist and legal guardian of plaintiff-appellant John Roe, who is eleven years old. Houghton has been Roe's caretaker since 1996 when Roe's biological father, suffering from alcohol abuse and frequent unemployment, voluntarily left Roe, then four years old, with Houghton. That same year,

---

2. Fla. Stat. § 63.042(3) provides: "No person eligible to adopt under this statute   may adopt if that person is a homosexual."

Houghton was appointed co-guardian of Roe along with one Robert Obeso (who otherwise has no involvement in this case). After Roe's biological father consented to termination of his parental rights, Houghton attempted to adopt Roe. Because of Houghton's homosexuality, however, he did not receive a favorable preliminary home study evaluation, which precluded him from filing the necessary adoption petition in state circuit court. Fla. Stat. §§ 63.092(3), 63.112(2)(b).

Plaintiff-appellants Wayne Larue Smith and Daniel Skahen, an attorney and real estate broker residing together in Key West, became licensed DCF foster parents after completing a requisite ten-week course in January of 2000. Since then, they have cared for three foster children, none of whom has been available for adoption. On 1 May 2000, Smith and Skahen submitted applications with DCF to serve as adoptive parents. On their adoption applications, both Smith and Skahen indicated that they are homosexuals. On 15 May 2000, they received notices from DCF stating that their applications had been denied because of their homosexuality.

Appellants filed suit in the United States District Court for the Southern District of Florida and named as defendants Kathleen A. Kearney and Charles Auslander in their respective official capacities as DCF Secretary and DCF District Administrator for Dade and Monroe Counties. Their complaint alleged that the statute violates appellants' fundamental rights and the principles of equal protection. Jointly, appellants asked the district court to declare Fla. Stat. § 63.042(3) unconstitutional and to enjoin its enforcement. Appellants also sought class certification on behalf of two purported classes: all similarly situated adults and all similarly situated children. The district court denied the request for class certification and granted summary judgment in favor of the state on all counts, thereby upholding the statute. It is from this judgment that appellants now appeal.

Appellants assert three constitutional arguments on appeal. First, appellants argue that the statute violates Lofton, Houghton, Doe, and Roe's rights to familial privacy, intimate association, and family integrity under the Due Process Clause of the Fourteenth Amendment. Second, appellants argue that the Supreme Court's recent decision in *Lawrence v. Texas*, 539 U.S. 558, 123 S.Ct. 2472, 156 L.Ed.2d 508 (2003), recognized a fundamental right to private sexual intimacy and that the Florida statute, by disallowing adoption by individuals who engage in homosexual activity, impermissibly burdens the exercise of this right. Third, appellants allege that, by categorically prohibiting only homosexual persons from adopting children, the statute violates the Equal Protection Clause of the Fourteenth Amendment. Each of these challenges raises questions of first impression in this circuit.

We review a summary judgment decision *de novo* and apply the same legal standard used by the district court. *Nat'l Parks Conservation Ass'n v. Norton*, 324 F.3d 1229, 1236 (11th Cir.2003). In conducting our review, we view all evidence and factual inferences in the light most favorable to the nonmoving party. *Id.* Summary judgment is proper where "there is no genuine issue as to any material fact" and "the moving party is entitled to a judgment as a matter of law." Fed.R.Civ.P. 56(c). However, "the mere existence of *some* alleged factual dispute between the parties will not defeat an otherwise properly supported motion for summary judgment." *Anderson v. Liberty Lobby, Inc.,* 477 U.S. 242, 247–48, 106 S.Ct. 2505, 2510, 91 L.Ed.2d 202 (1986). Only factual disputes that are material under the substantive law governing the case will preclude entry of summary judgment. *Id.*

Appellants' challenge cannot be viewed apart from the context in which it arises. Under Florida law, "adoption is not a right; it is a statutory privilege." *Cox,* 627 So.2d at 1216. Unlike biological parentage, which precedes and transcends formal recognition by the state, adoption is wholly a creature of the state. *Cf. Smith v. Org. of Foster Families for Equal. & Reform,* 431 U.S. 816, 845, 97 S.Ct. 2094, 2110, 53 L.Ed.2d 14 (1977) (noting that, unlike the natural family, which has "its origins entirely apart from the power of the State," the foster parent-child relationship "has its source in state law and contractual arrangements"); *Lindley v. Sullivan,* 889 F.2d 124, 131 (7th Cir.1989) ("Because of its statutory basis, adoption differs from natural procreation in a most important and striking way.").

In formulating its adoption policies and procedures, the State of Florida acts in the protective and provisional role of *in loco parentis* for those children who, because of various circumstances, have become wards of the state. Thus, adoption law is unlike criminal law, for example, where the paramount substantive concern is not intruding on individuals' liberty interests, *see, e.g., Lawrence,* 539 U.S. 558, 123 S.Ct. 2472, 156 L.Ed.2d 508; *Roe v. Wade,* 410 U.S. 113, 93 S.Ct. 705, 35 L.Ed.2d 147 (1973), and the paramount procedural imperative is ensuring due process and fairness, *see, e.g., Strickland v. Washington,* 466 U.S. 668, 104 S.Ct. 2052, 80 L.Ed.2d 674 (1984); *Miranda v. Arizona,* 384 U.S. 436, 86 S.Ct. 1602, 16 L.Ed.2d 694 (1966); *Gideon v. Wainwright,* 372 U.S. 335, 83 S.Ct. 792, 9 L.Ed.2d 799 (1963). Adoption is also distinct from such contexts as government-benefit eligibility schemes or access to a public forum, where equality of treatment is the primary concern. By contrast, in the adoption context, the state's overriding interest is the best interests of the children whom it is seeking to place with adoptive families. *In re Adoption of H.Y.T.,* 458 So.2d 1127, 1128 (Fla.1984) (noting that, in Florida adoption proceedings, "the court's primary duty is to serve the best interests of the child—the object of the proceeding"). Florida, acting *parens patriae* for children who have lost their natural parents, bears the high duty of determining what adoptive home environments will best serve all aspects of the child's growth and development.

Because of the primacy of the welfare of the child, the state can make classifications for adoption purposes that would be constitutionally suspect in many other arenas. For example, Florida law requires that, in order to adopt any child other than a special needs child, an individual's primary residence and place of employment must be located in Florida. Fla. Stat. § 63.185. In screening adoption applicants, Florida considers such factors as physical and mental health, income and financial status, duration of marriage, housing, and neighborhood, among others. Fla. Admin. Code Ann. r. 65C–16.005(3) (2003). Similarly, Florida gives preference to candidates who demonstrate a commitment to "value, respect, appreciate, and educate the child regarding his or her racial and ethnic heritage." *Id.* Moreover, prospective adoptive parents are required to sign an affidavit of good moral character. *Id.* Many of these preferences and requirements, if employed outside the adoption arena, would be unlikely to withstand constitutional scrutiny. *See, e.g., Troxel v. Granville,* 530 U.S. 57, 68, 120 S.Ct. 2054, 2061, 147 L.Ed.2d 49 (2000) (recognizing that, absent neglect or abuse, the state may not "inject itself into the private realm of the family to further question the ability of that parent to make the best decisions concerning the rearing of that parent's children"); . . .

The decision to adopt a child is not a private one, but a public act. *Cox,* 627 So.2d at 1216. At a minimum, would-be adoptive parents are asking the state to confer official recognition—and, consequently, the highest level of constitutional insulation from subsequent state interference, *see Troxel,* 530 U.S. at 65, 120 S.Ct. at 2060—on a relationship where there exists no natural filial bond. In many cases, they also are asking the state to entrust into their permanent care a child for whom the state is currently serving as *in loco parentis.* In doing so, these prospective adoptive parents are electing to open their homes and their private lives to close scrutiny by the state. Florida's adoption application requires information on a variety of private matters, including an applicant's physical and psychiatric medical history, previous marriages, arrest record, financial status, and educational history. In this regard, Florida's adoption scheme is like any "complex social welfare system that necessarily deals with the intimacies of family life." *Bowen v. Gilliard,* 483 U.S. 587, 602, 107 S.Ct. 3008, 3017–18, 97 L.Ed.2d 485 (1987) (quoting *Califano v. Jobst,* 434 U.S. 47, 55 n. 11, 98 S.Ct. 95, 100 n. 11, 54 L.Ed.2d 228 (1977)). Accordingly, such intrusions into private family matters are on a different constitutional plane than those that "seek[ ] to foist orthodoxy on the unwilling by banning or criminally prosecuting" nonconformity. *Califano,* 434 U.S. at 55 n. 11, 98 S.Ct. at 100 n. 11; *cf. Lindley,* 889 F.2d at 131 (declining to find a privacy interest in adopting a child because state law "requires adopters to submit their personal lives to intensive scrutiny before the adoption may be approved").

In short, a person who seeks to adopt is asking the state to conduct an examination into his or her background and to make a determination as to the best interests of a child in need of adoption. In doing so, the state's overriding interest is not providing individuals the opportunity to become parents, but rather identifying those individuals whom it deems most capable of parenting adoptive children and providing them with a secure family environment. Indicative of the strength of the state's interest—indeed duty—in this context is the fact that appellants have not cited to us, nor have we found, a single precedent in which the Supreme Court or one of our sister circuits has sustained a constitutional challenge to an adoption scheme or practice by any individual other than a natural parent, and even many challenges by natural parents have failed. *See, e.g., Lehr v. Robertson,*

463 U.S. 248, 103 S.Ct. 2985, 77 L.Ed.2d 614 (1983); *Quilloin v. Walcott,* 434 U.S. 246, 98 S.Ct. 549, 54 L.Ed.2d 511 (1978). Of course, despite their highly sensitive nature, adoption schemes are by no means immune from constitutional scrutiny, and we now consider the constitutionality of the Florida statute. *See, e.g., Caban v. Mohammed,* 441 U.S. 380, 99 S.Ct. 1760, 60 L.Ed.2d 297 (1979) (invalidating on equal protection grounds a state law permitting unwed mothers, but not unwed fathers, to block adoption of their child simply by withholding consent).

Neither party disputes that there is no fundamental right to adopt, nor any fundamental right to be adopted.... Both parties likewise agree that adoption is a privilege created by statute and not by common law. Because there is no fundamental right to adopt or to be adopted, it follows that there can be no fundamental right to apply for adoption.

Nevertheless, appellants argue that, by prohibiting homosexual adoption, the state is refusing to recognize and protect constitutionally protected parent-child relationships between Lofton and Doe and between Houghton and Roe. Noting that the Supreme Court has identified "the interest of parents in the care, custody, and control of their children" as "perhaps the oldest of the fundamental liberty interests recognized by this Court," *Troxel,* 530 U.S. at 65, 120 S.Ct. at 2060, appellants argue that they are entitled to a similar constitutional liberty interest because they share deeply loving emotional bonds that are as close as those between a natural parent and child. They further contend that this liberty interest is significantly burdened by the Florida statute, which prevents them from obtaining permanency in their relationships and creates uncertainty about the future integrity of their families. Only by being given the opportunity to adopt, appellants assert, will they be able to protect their alleged right to "family integrity."

Although the text of the Constitution contains no reference to familial or parental rights, Supreme Court precedent has long recognized that "the Due Process Clause of the Fourteenth Amendment protects the fundamental right of parents to make decisions concerning the care, custody, and control of their children." *Id.* at 66, 120 S.Ct. at 2060. A corollary to this right is the "private realm of family life which the state cannot enter that has been afforded both substantive and procedural protection." *Smith v. Org. of Foster Families for Equal. & Reform,* 431 U.S. 816, 842, 97 S.Ct. 2094, 2108, 53 L.Ed.2d 14 (1977) (internal citation and quotation marks omitted). Historically, the Court's family and parental-rights holdings have involved biological families. *See, e.g., Troxel,* 530 U.S. 57, 120 S.Ct. 2054, 147 L.Ed.2d 49 (2000); *Wisconsin v. Yoder,* 406 U.S. 205, 92 S.Ct. 1526, 32 L.Ed.2d 15 (1972); *Stanley v. Illinois,* 405 U.S. 645, 92 S.Ct. 1208, 31 L.Ed.2d 551 (1972); *Pierce v. Soc'y of Sisters,* 268 U.S. 510, 45 S.Ct. 571, 69 L.Ed. 1070 (1925); *Meyer v. Nebraska,* 262 U.S. 390, 43 S.Ct. 625, 67 L.Ed. 1042 (1923). The Court itself has noted that "the usual understanding of 'family' implies biological relationships, and most decisions treating the relation between parent and child have stressed this element." *Smith,* 431 U.S. at 843, 97 S.Ct. at 2109. Appellants, however, seize on a few lines of *dicta* from *Smith,* in which the Court acknowledged that "biological relationships are not [the] exclusive determination of the existence of a family," *id.,* and noted that "[a]doption, for instance, is recognized as the legal equivalent of biological parenthood," *id.* at 844 n. 51, 97 S.Ct. at 2109 & n. 51. Extrapolating from *Smith,* appellants argue that parental and familial rights should be extended to individuals such as foster parents and legal guardians and that the touchstone of this liberty interest is not biological ties or official legal recognition, but the emotional bond that develops between and among individuals as a result of shared daily life.

We do not read *Smith* so broadly. In *Smith,* the Court considered whether the appellee foster families possessed a constitutional liberty interest in "the integrity of their family unit" such that the state could not disrupt the families without procedural due process. *Id.* at 842, 97 S. Ct at 2108. Although the Court found it unnecessary to resolve that question, Justice Brennan, writing for the majority, did note that the importance of familial relationships stems not merely from blood relationships, but also from "the emotional attachments that derive from the intimacy of daily association." *Id.* at 844, 97 S.Ct. at 2109. The *Smith* Court went on, however, to discuss the "important distinctions between the foster family and the natural family," particularly the fact that foster families have their genesis in state law. *Id.* at 845, 97 S.Ct. at 2110. The Court stressed that the parameters of whatever potential liberty interest such families might possess would be defined by state law and the justifiable expectations it created. *Id.* at 845–46, 97 S.Ct. at 2110. The Court found that the expectations created by New York law—which accorded only limited recognition to foster families—supported only "the most limited constitutional 'liberty' in the foster family." *Id.* at 846, 97 S.Ct. at 2110. Basing its holding on other grounds, the Court concluded that the procedures provided under New York law were "adequate to protect whatever liberty interest appellees may have." *Id.* at 856, 97 S.Ct. at 2115.

In *Drummond v. Fulton County Dep't of Family & Children's Servs.,* the former Fifth Circuit construed *Smith's dicta* in considering due process and equal protection claims brought by white foster parents challenging Georgia's refusal to permit them to adopt their mixed-race foster child, whom they had parented for two years. 563 F.2d 1200, 1206 (5th Cir.1977) (en banc), *cert. denied,* 437 U.S. 910, 98 S.Ct. 3103, 57 L.Ed.2d 1141 (1978). Arguing that theirs was a "psychological family," the foster parents advanced a theory identical to that of present appellants:

> Plaintiffs maintain that during the period Timmy lived with them mutual feelings of love and dependence developed which are analogous to those found in most biological families. By so characterizing their home situation they seek to come within the protection which courts have afforded to the family unit. They assert that their relationship to Timmy is part of the familial right to privacy which is a protected interest under the Fourteenth Amendment. As the "psychological parents" of Timmy, they claim entitlement to the parental rights referred to in numerous decisions.

Id. at 1206 (internal citation omitted). Relying on *Smith,* the *Drummond* court rejected plaintiffs' argument. Examining state law to determine the extent of plaintiffs' constitutional interests, the court found that "[t]here is no basis in the Georgia law, which creates the foster relationship, for a justifiable expectation that the relationship will be left undisturbed." *Id.* at 1207. The *Drummond* court stated:

> The very fact that the relationship before us is a creature of state law, as well as the fact that it has never been recognized as equivalent to either the natural family or the adoptive family by any court, demonstrates that it is not a protected liberty interest, but an interest limited by the very laws which create it.

Id.; accord Mullins, 57 F.3d at 794 (holding that biological grandparents possessed no liberty interest in adopting two of their grandchildren who were available for adoption); *Procopio v. Johnson,* 994 F.2d 325, 329 (7th Cir.1993) (relying on *Smith* and holding that "[n]otwithstanding the preference that state law grants to foster families seeking to adopt their foster children, this priority does not rise to the level of an entitlement or expectancy").

Neither *Smith* nor *Drummond,* however, categorically foreclosed the possibility that, under exceptional circumstances, a foster family could possess some degree of constitutional protection if state law created a "justifiable expectation" of family unit permanency. *Drummond,* 563 F.2d at 1207. Here, we find that under Florida law neither a foster parent nor a legal guardian could have a justifiable expectation of a permanent relationship with his or her child free from state oversight or intervention. Under Florida law, foster care is designed to be a short-term arrangement while the state attempts to find a permanent adoptive home. For instance, Florida law permits foster care as a "permanency option" only for children at least fourteen years of age, Fla. Stat. § 39.623(1), and DCF may remove a foster child anytime that it believes it to be in the child's best interests, *id.* § 409.165(3)(f). Similarly, legal guardians in Florida are subject to ongoing judicial oversight, including the duty to file annual guardianship reports and annual review by the appointing court, *id.* §§ 744.361–372, and can be removed for a wide variety of reasons, *id.* § 744.474 (permitting removal of a guardian for such causes as incapacity, illness, substance abuse, conviction of a felony, failure to file annual guardianship reports, and failure to fulfill guardianship education requirements). In both cases, the state is not interfering with natural family units that exist independent of its power, but is regulating ones created by it. Lofton and Houghton entered into relationships to be a foster parent and legal guardian, respectively, with an implicit understanding that these relationships would not be immune from state oversight and would be permitted to continue only upon state approval. The emotional connections between Lofton and his foster child and between Houghton and his ward originate in arrangements that have been subject to state oversight from the outset. We conclude that Lofton, Doe, Houghton, and Roe could have no justifiable expectation of permanency in their relationships. Nor could Lofton and Houghton have developed expectations that they would be allowed to adopt, in light of the adoption provision itself.

Even if Florida law did create an expectation of permanency, appellants misconstrue the nature of the liberty interest that it would confer upon them. The resulting liberty interest at most would provide *procedural* due process protection in the event the state were to attempt to remove Doe or Roe. *See Smith,* 431 U.S. at 845, 97 S.Ct. at 2110 (considering whether foster families' asserted liberty interest in remaining intact warranted greater procedural safeguards than were currently provided under New York law); *Drummond,* 563 F.2d at 1204 (considering, if foster family possesses constitutional rights, "how much procedural protection is required in order to safeguard them?"). Such a procedural right does not translate, however, into a substantive right to be free from state inference. Nor does it create an affirmative right to be accorded official recognition as "parent" and "child." *Cf. Harris v. McRae,* 448 U.S. 297, 100 S.Ct. 2671, 65 L.Ed.2d 784 (1980) (holding that the government's refusal to subsidize the exercise of a constitutional right does not constitute a violation of that right); *Webster v. Reprod. Health Servs.,* 492 U.S. 490, 109 S.Ct. 3040, 106 L.Ed.2d 410 (1989) (same); *Mullins,* 57 F.3d at 794 ("A negative right to be free of governmental interference in an already existing familial relationship does not translate into an affirmative right to create an entirely new family unit out of whole cloth."). In sum, Florida's statute by itself poses no threat to whatever hypothetical constitutional protection foster families and guardian-ward relationships may possess.

We conclude that appellants' right-to-family-integrity argument fails to state a claim. There is no precedent for appellants' novel proposition that long-term foster care arrangements and guardianships are entitled to constitutional protection akin to that accorded to natural and adoptive families. Moreover, we decline appellants' invitation to recognize a new fundamental right to family integrity for groups of individuals who have formed deeply loving and interdependent relationships. Under appellants' theory, any collection of individuals living together and enjoying strong emotional bonds could claim a right to legal recognition of their family unit, and every removal of a child from a long-term foster care placement—or simply the state's failure to give long-term foster parents the opportunity to adopt—would give rise to a constitutional claim. Such an expansion of the venerable right of parental control would well exceed our judicial mandate as a lower federal court. *See Collins v. City of Harker Heights,* 503 U.S. 115, 125, 112 S.Ct. 1061, 1068, 117 L.Ed.2d 261 (1992) (noting that the doctrine of judicial restraint requires even the Supreme Court to exercise "the utmost care" whenever asked to break new ground in the field of fundamental rights).

Laws that burden the exercise of a fundamental right require strict scrutiny and are sustained only if narrowly tailored to further a compelling government interest. *See, e.g., Zablocki v. Redhail,* 434 U.S. 374, 388, 98 S.Ct. 673, 682, 54 L.Ed.2d 618 (1978); *Shapiro v. Thompson,* 394 U.S. 618, 634, 89 S.Ct. 1322, 1331, 22 L.Ed.2d 600 (1969). Appellants argue that the

Supreme Court's recent decision in *Lawrence v. Texas,* 539 U.S. 558, 123 S.Ct. 2472, 156 L.Ed.2d 508 (2003), which struck down Texas's sodomy statute, identified a hitherto unarticulated fundamental right to private sexual intimacy. They contend that the Florida statute, by disallowing adoption to any individual who chooses to engage in homosexual conduct, impermissibly burdens the exercise of this right.

We begin with the threshold question of whether *Lawrence* identified a new fundamental right to private sexual intimacy. *Lawrence*'s holding was that substantive due process does not permit a state to impose a criminal prohibition on private consensual homosexual conduct. The effect of this holding was to establish a greater respect than previously existed in the law for the right of consenting adults to engage in private sexual conduct. ___ U.S. at ___, 123 S.Ct. at 2478. Nowhere, however, did the Court characterize this right as "fundamental." *Cf. id.* at ___, 123 S.Ct. at 2488 (Scalia, J., dissenting) (observing that "nowhere does the Court's opinion declare that homosexual sodomy is a 'fundamental right' under the Due Process Clause"). Nor did the Court locate this right directly in the Constitution, but instead treated it as the by-product of several different constitutional principles and liberty interests.

We are particularly hesitant to infer a new fundamental liberty interest from an opinion whose language and reasoning are inconsistent with standard fundamental-rights analysis. The Court has noted that it must "exercise the utmost care whenever [it is] asked to break new ground" in the field of fundamental rights, *Washington v. Glucksberg,* 521 U.S. 702, 720, 117 S.Ct. 2258, 2268, 138 L.Ed.2d 772 (1997) (citation omitted), which is precisely what the *Lawrence* petitioners and their *amici curiae* had asked the Court to do. That the Court declined the invitation is apparent from the absence of the "two primary features" of fundamental-rights analysis in its opinion. *Glucksberg,* 521 U.S. at 720, 117 S.Ct. at 2268. First, the *Lawrence* opinion contains virtually no inquiry into the question of whether the petitioners' asserted right is one of "those fundamental rights and liberties which are, objectively, deeply rooted in this Nation's history and tradition and implicit in the concept of ordered liberty, such that neither liberty nor justice would exist if they were sacrificed." *Id.* at 720–21, 117 S.Ct. at 2268 (internal citations and quotation marks omitted). Second, the opinion notably never provides the " 'careful description' of the asserted fundamental liberty interest" that is to accompany fundamental-rights analysis. *Id.* at 721, 117 S.Ct. at 2268 (citation omitted); *see also Reno v. Flores,* 507 U.S. 292, 302, 113 S.Ct. 1439, 1447, 123 L.Ed.2d 1 (1993) (" 'Substantive due process' analysis must begin with a careful description of the asserted right...."). Rather, the constitutional liberty interests on which the Court relied were invoked, not with "careful description," but with sweeping generality. *See, e.g., Lawrence,* 539 U.S. 558, 123 S.Ct. at 2475 ("Liberty protects the person from unwarranted government intrusions into a dwelling or other private places."); *id.* ("The instant case involves liberty of the person both in its spatial and more transcendent dimensions."); *id.* at ___, 123 S.Ct. at 2484 ("[T]here is a realm of personal liberty which the government may not enter.") (citation omitted). Most significant, however, is the fact that the *Lawrence* Court never applied strict scrutiny, the proper standard when fundamental rights are implicated, but instead invalidated the Texas statute on rational-basis grounds, holding that it "furthers no legitimate state interest which can justify its intrusion into the personal and private life of the individual." *Id.* at ___, 123 S.Ct. at 2484; *see also id.* at ___, 123 S.Ct. at 2488 (Scalia, J., dissenting) (observing that the majority opinion did not "subject the Texas law to the standard of review that would be appropriate (strict scrutiny) if homosexual sodomy *were* a 'fundamental right' ").

We conclude that it is a strained and ultimately incorrect reading of *Lawrence* to interpret it to announce a new fundamental right. Accordingly, we need not resolve the second prong of appellants' fundamental-rights argument: whether exclusion from the statutory privilege of adoption because of appellants' sexual conduct creates an impermissible burden on the exercise of their asserted right to private sexual intimacy. *Cf. Lyng v. Castillo,* 477 U.S. 635, 638, 106 S.Ct. 2727, 2729, 91 L.Ed.2d 527 (1986) (only classifications that " 'directly and substantially' interfere" with a fundamental right constitute an impermissible "burden") (citation omitted).

Moreover, the holding of *Lawrence* does not control the present case. Apart from the shared homosexuality component, there are marked differences in the facts of the two cases. The Court itself stressed the limited factual situation it was addressing in *Lawrence*:

> The present case does not involve minors. It does not involve persons who might be injured or coerced or who are situated in relationships where consent might not easily be refused. It does not involve public conduct or prostitution. It does not involve whether the government must give formal recognition to any relationship that homosexual persons seek to enter. The case does involve two adults who, with full and mutual consent from each other, engaged in sexual practices common to a homosexual lifestyle.

Lawrence, 539 U.S. at ___, 123 S.Ct. at 2484. Here, the involved actors are not only consenting adults, but minors as well. The relevant state action is not criminal prohibition, but grant of a statutory privilege. And the asserted liberty interest is not the negative right to engage in private conduct without facing criminal sanctions, but the affirmative right to receive official and public recognition. Hence, we conclude that the *Lawrence* decision cannot be extrapolated to create a right to adopt for homosexual persons.

The Equal Protection Clause of the Fourteenth Amendment proclaims that "[n]o State shall ... deny to any person within its jurisdiction the equal protection of laws." U.S. Const. amend. XIV, § 1. The central mandate of the equal protection guarantee is that "[t]he sovereign may not draw distinctions between individuals based solely on differences that are irrelevant to a legitimate governmental objective." *Lehr v. Robertson,* 463 U.S. 248, 265, 103 S.Ct. 2985, 2995, 77 L.Ed.2d 614 (1983). Equal protection, however, does not forbid legislative classifications. *Nordlinger v.*

Hahn, 505 U.S. 1, 10, 112 S.Ct. 2326, 2331, 120 L.Ed.2d 1 (1992). "It simply keeps governmental decisionmakers from treating differently persons who are in all relevant respects alike." *Id.* Unless the challenged classification burdens a fundamental right or targets a suspect class, the Equal Protection Clause requires only that the classification be rationally related to a legitimate state interest. *Romer v. Evans,* 517 U.S. 620, 631, 116 S.Ct. 1620, 1627, 134 L.Ed.2d 855 (1996). As we have explained, Florida's statute burdens no fundamental rights. Moreover, all of our sister circuits that have considered the question have declined to treat homosexuals as a suspect class. Because the present case involves neither a fundamental right nor a suspect class, we review the Florida statute under the rational-basis standard.

Rational-basis review, "a paradigm of judicial restraint," does not provide "a license for courts to judge the wisdom, fairness, or logic of legislative choices." *F.C.C. v. Beach Communications, Inc.,* 508 U.S. 307, 313–14, 113 S.Ct. 2096, 2101, 124 L.Ed.2d 211 (1993) (citation omitted). The question is simply whether the challenged legislation is rationally related to a legitimate state interest. *Heller v. Doe,* 509 U.S. 312, 320, 113 S.Ct. 2637, 2642, 125 L.Ed.2d 257 (1993). Under this deferential standard, a legislative classification "is accorded a strong presumption of validity," *id.* at 319, 113 S.Ct. at 2642, and "must be upheld against equal protection challenge if there is any reasonably conceivable state of facts that could provide a rational basis for the classification," *id.* at 320, 113 S.Ct. at 2642 (citation omitted). This holds true "even if the law seems unwise or works to the disadvantage of a particular group, or if the rationale for it seems tenuous." *Romer,* 517 U.S. at 632, 116 S.Ct. at 1627. Moreover, a state has "no obligation to produce evidence to sustain the rationality of a statutory classification." *Heller,* 509 U.S. at 320, 113 S.Ct. at 2643. Rather, "the burden is on the one attacking the legislative arrangement to negative every conceivable basis which might support it, whether or not the basis has a foundation in the record." *Id.* at 320–21, 113 S.Ct. at 2643 (citation omitted).

Cognizant of the narrow parameters of our review, we now analyze the challenged Florida law. Florida contends that the statute is only one aspect of its broader adoption policy, which is designed to create adoptive homes that resemble the nuclear family as closely as possible. Florida argues that the statute is rationally related to Florida's interest in furthering the best interests of adopted children by placing them in families with married mothers and fathers. Such homes, Florida asserts, provide the stability that marriage affords and the presence of both male and female authority figures, which it considers critical to optimal childhood development and socialization. In particular, Florida emphasizes a vital role that dual-gender parenting plays in shaping sexual and gender identity and in providing heterosexual role modeling. Florida argues that disallowing adoption into homosexual households, which are necessarily motherless or fatherless and lack the stability that comes with marriage, is a rational means of furthering Florida's interest in promoting adoption by marital families.

Florida clearly has a legitimate interest in encouraging a stable and nurturing environment for the education and socialization of its adopted children. *See, e.g., Palmore v. Sidoti*, 466 U.S. 429, 433, 104 S.Ct. 1879, 1882, 80 L.Ed.2d 421 (1984) ("The State, of course, has a duty of the highest order to protect the interests of minor children, particularly those of tender years."); *Stanley*, 405 U.S. at 652, 92 S.Ct. at 1213 (noting that "protect [ing] the moral, emotional, mental, and physical welfare of the minor" is a "legitimate interest[ ], well within the power of the State to implement") (internal quotation marks omitted). It is chiefly from parental figures that children learn about the world and their place in it, and the formative influence of parents extends well beyond the years spent under their roof, shaping their children's psychology, character, and personality for years to come. In time, children grow up to become full members of society, which they in turn influence, whether for good or ill. The adage that "the hand that rocks the cradle rules the world" hardly overstates the ripple effect that parents have on the public good by virtue of their role in raising their children. It is hard to conceive an interest more legitimate and more paramount for the state than promoting an optimal social structure for educating, socializing, and preparing its future citizens to become productive participants in civil society—particularly when those future citizens are displaced children for whom the state is standing *in loco parentis*.

More importantly for present purposes, the state has a legitimate interest in encouraging this optimal family structure by seeking to place adoptive children in homes that have both a mother and father. Florida argues that its preference for adoptive marital families is based on the premise that the marital family structure is more stable than other household arrangements and that children benefit from the presence of both a father and mother in the home. Given that appellants have offered no competent evidence to the contrary, we find this premise to be one of those "unprovable assumptions" that nevertheless can provide a legitimate basis for legislative action. *Paris Adult Theatre I v. Slaton*, 413 U.S. 49, 62–63, 93 S.Ct. 2628, 2638, 37 L.Ed.2d 446 (1973). Although social theorists from Plato to Simone de Beauvoir have proposed alternative child-rearing arrangements, none has proven as enduring as the marital family struc-ture, nor has the accumulated wisdom of several millennia of human experience discovered a superior model. *See, e.g.,* Plato, *The Republic*, Bk. V, 459d–461e; Simone de Beauvoir, *The Second Sex* (H.M. Parshley trans., Vintage Books 1989) (1949). Against this "sum of experience," it is rational for Florida to conclude that it is in the best interests of adoptive children, many of whom come from troubled and unstable backgrounds, to be placed in a home anchored by both a father and a mother. *Paris Adult Theatre I*, 413 U.S. at 63, 93 S.Ct. at 2638.

Appellants offer little to dispute whether Florida's preference for marital adoptive families is a legitimate state interest. Instead, they main-tain that the statute is not rationally related to this interest. Arguing that the statute is both overinclusive and underinclusive, appellants contend that the real motivation behind the statute cannot be the best interest of adoptive children.

In evaluating this argument, we note from the outset that "it is entirely irrelevant for constitutional purposes whether the conceived reason for the challenged distinction actually motivated the legislature." *Beach Communications,* 508 U.S. at 315, 113 S.Ct. at 2102; *see also City of Renton v. Playtime Theatres, Inc.,* 475 U.S. 41, 48, 106 S.Ct. 925, 929, 89 L.Ed.2d 29 (1986) ("It is a familiar principle of constitutional law that this Court will not strike down an otherwise constitutional statute on the basis of an alleged illicit legislative motive.") (citation omitted). Instead, the question before us is whether the Florida legislature *could* have reasonably believed that prohibiting adoption into homosexual environments would further its interest in placing adoptive children in homes that will provide them with optimal developmental conditions. *See Panama City Med. Diagnostic Ltd. v. Williams,* 13 F.3d 1541, 1545 (11th Cir.1994) ("The task is to determine if any set of facts may be reasonably conceived of to justify the legislation."). Unless appellants' evidence, which we view on summary judgment review in the light most favorable to appellants, can negate every plausible rational connection between the statute and Florida's interest in the welfare of its children, we are compelled to uphold the statute. *See Vance v. Bradley,* 440 U.S. 93, 111, 99 S.Ct. 939, 949, 59 L.Ed.2d 171 (1979) ("In an equal protection case of this type, however, those challenging the legislative judgment must convince the court that the legislative facts on which the classification is apparently based could not reasonably be conceived to be true by the governmental decisionmaker."). We turn now to appellants' specific arguments. Appellants note that Florida law permits adoption by unmarried individuals and that, among children coming out the Florida foster care system, 25% of adoptions are to parents who are currently single. Their argument is that homosexual persons are similarly situated to unmarried persons with regard to Florida's asserted interest in promoting married-couple adoption. According to appellants, this disparate treatment lacks a rational basis and, therefore, disproves any rational connection between the statute and Florida's asserted interest in promoting adoption into married homes. Citing *City of Cleburne v. Cleburne Living Ctr., Inc.,* 473 U.S. 432, 105 S.Ct. 3249, 87 L.Ed.2d 313 (1985), appellants argue that the state has not satisfied *Cleburne*'s threshold requirement that it demonstrate that homosexuals pose a unique threat to children that others similarly situated in relevant respects do not.[18]

---

18. Appellants also point to the fact that, in addition to single parents, substance abusers and perpetrators of domestic violence are not *categorically* excluded from adopting under Florida law. Appellants, however, have offered no evidence that such individuals are in reality ever permitted to adopt in Florida and actually have stipulated to the contrary. Appellants stipulated pre-trial that "[p]ersons with substance abuse problems are excluded from adopting children in Florida if it is determined that the abuse threatens the child." R4–124 at 4. Likewise, appellants stipulated that Florida law categorically excludes from adopting children those convicted of certain crimes of domestic violence. *See id.* Moreover, Florida law bars foster care and adoptive placement by DCF

1. In any case in which a record check reveals a felony conviction for child abuse, abandonment, or neglect; for spousal abuse;

We find appellants' reading of *Cleburne* to be an unwarranted interpretation. In *Cleburne*, the Supreme Court invalidated under the rational-basis test a municipal zoning ordinance requiring a group home for the mentally retarded to obtain a special use permit. *Id.* at 435, 105 S.Ct. at 3252. The municipality argued that it had a legitimate interest in (1) protecting the residents of the home from a nearby flood plain, (2) limiting potential liability for acts of residents of the home, (3) maintaining low-density land uses in the neighborhood, (4) reducing congestion in neighborhood streets, and (5) avoiding fire hazards. *Id.* at 449–50, 105 S.Ct. at 3259–60. The Court, however, found that the municipality failed to distinguish how these concerns applied particularly to mentally retarded residents of the home and not to a number of other persons who could freely occupy the identical structure without a permit, such as boarding houses, fraternity houses, and nursing homes. *Id.* The Court concluded that the purported justifications for the ordinance made no sense in light of how it treated other groups similarly situated. *Id.* at 450, 105 S.Ct. at 3260. Appellants have overstated *Cleburne*'s holding by asserting that it places a burden on the State of Florida to show that homosexuals pose a greater threat than other unmarried adults who are allowed to adopt. The *Cleburne* Court reasserted the unremarkable principle that, when a statute imposes a classification on a particular group, its failure to impose the same classification on "other groups similarly situated in relevant respects" can be probative of a lack of a rational basis. *Bd. of Trustees of the Univ. of Alabama v. Garrett*, 531 U.S. 356, 366 n. 4, 121 S.Ct. 955, 963 n. 4, 148 L.Ed.2d 866 (2001) (explaining *Cleburne*'s rationale); *see also Nordlinger*, 505 U.S. at 10, 112 S.Ct. at 2331 (noting that disparate treatment is permissible unless differently treated classes "are in *all* relevant respects alike") (emphasis added).

This case is distinguishable from *Cleburne*. The Florida legislature could rationally conclude that homosexuals and heterosexual singles are not "similarly situated in relevant respects." It is not irrational to think that heterosexual singles have a markedly greater probability of eventually establishing a married household and, thus, providing their adopted children with a stable, dual-gender parenting environment. Moreover, as the state noted, the legislature could rationally act on the theory that heterosexual singles, even if they never marry, are better positioned than homosexual individuals to provide adopted children with education and guidance relative to their sexual development throughout pubescence and adolescence.[19] In a previous challenge to Florida's statute, a Florida appellate court observed:

---

for a crime against children, including child pornography, or for a crime involving violence, including rape, sexual assault, or homicide but not including other physical assault or battery, if the department finds that a court of competent jurisdiction has determined that the felony was committed at any time; and

2. In any case in which a record check reveals a felony conviction for physical assault, battery, or a drug-related offense, if the department finds that a court of competent jurisdiction has determined that the felony was committed within the past 5 years.

Fla. Stat. § 435.045(1)(a).

19. The New Hampshire Supreme Court, in considering the constitutionality of

[W]hatever causes a person to become a homosexual, it is clear that the state cannot know the sexual preferences that a child will exhibit as an adult. Statistically, the state does know that a very high percentage of children available for adoption will develop heterosexual preferences. As a result, those children will need education and guidance after puberty concerning relationships with the opposite sex. In our society, we expect that parents will provide this education to teenagers in the home. These subjects are often very embarrassing for teenagers and some aspects of the education are accomplished by the parents telling stories about their own adolescence and explaining their own experiences with the opposite sex. It is in the best interests of a child if his or her parents can personally relate to the child's problems and assist the child in the difficult transition to heterosexual adulthood. Given that adopted children tend to have some developmental problems arising from adoption or from their experiences prior to adoption, it is perhaps more important for adopted children than other children to have a stable heterosexual household during puberty and the teenage years.

Cox, 627 So.2d at 1220. "It could be that the assumptions underlying these rationales are erroneous, but the very fact that they are arguable is sufficient, on rational-basis review, to immunize the legislative choice from constitutional challenge." *Heller,* 509 U.S. at 333, 113 S.Ct. at 2649–50 (citation and internal punctuation marks omitted). Although the influence of environmental factors in forming patterns of sexual behavior and the importance of heterosexual role models are matters of ongoing debate, they ultimately involve empirical disputes not readily amenable to judicial resolution—as well as policy judgments best exercised in the legislative arena. For our present purposes, it is sufficient that these considerations provide a reasonably conceivable rationale for Florida to preclude all homosexuals, but not all heterosexual singles, from adopting.

The possibility, raised by appellants, that some homosexual households, including those of appellants, would provide a better environment than would some heterosexual single-parent households does not alter our analysis. The Supreme Court repeatedly has instructed that neither the fact that a classification may be overinclusive or underinclusive nor the fact that a generalization underlying a classification is subject to exceptions renders the classification irrational. "[C]ourts are compelled under rational-basis review to accept a legislature's generalizations even when there is an imperfect fit between means and ends." *Id.* at 321, 113 S.Ct. at 2643. We conclude that there are plausible rational reasons for the disparate treatment of homosexuals and heterosexual singles under Florida adoption

a similar prohibition on homosexual adoption, concluded that the prohibition was rationally related to the state's desire "to provide appropriate role models for children" in the development of their sexual and gender identities. *In re Op. of the Justices,* 129 N.H. 290, 530 A.2d 21, 25 (1987). That court noted that "the source of sexual orientation is still inadequately understood and is thought to be a combination of genetic and environmental influences. Given the reasonable possibility of environmental influences, we believe that the legislature can rationally act on the theory that a role model can influence the child's developing sexual identity." *Id.* (citation omitted).

law and that, to the extent that the classification may be imperfect, that imperfection does not rise to the level of a constitutional infraction.

Appellants make much of the fact that Florida has over three thousand children who are currently in foster care and, consequently, have not been placed with permanent adoptive families. According to appellants, because excluding homosexuals from the pool of prospective adoptive parents will not create more eligible married couples to reduce the backlog, it is impossible for the legislature to believe that the statute advances the state's interest in placing children with married couples.

We do not agree that the statute does not further the state's interest in promoting nuclear-family adoption because it may delay the adoption of some children. Appellants misconstrue Florida's interest, which is not simply to place children in a permanent home as quickly as possible, but, when placing them, to do so in an optimal home, i.e., one in which there is a heterosexual couple or the potential for one. According to appellants' logic, every restriction on adoptive-parent candidates, such as income, in-state residency, and criminal record—none of which creates more available married couples—are likewise constitutionally suspect as long as Florida has a backlog of unadopted foster children. The best interests of children, however, are not automatically served by adoption into *any* available home merely because it is permanent. Moreover, the legislature could rationally act on the theory that not placing adoptees in homosexual households increases the probability that these children eventually will be placed with married-couple families, thus furthering the state's goal of optimal placement. Therefore, we conclude that Florida's current foster care backlog does not render the statute irrational.

c. Foster Care and Legal Guardianship

Noting that Florida law permits homosexuals to become foster parents and permanent guardians, appellants contend that this fact demonstrates that Florida must not truly believe that placement in a homosexual household is not in a child's best interests.[21] We do not find that the fact that Florida has permitted homosexual foster homes and guardianships defeats the rational relationship between the statute and the state's asserted interest. We have not located and appellants have not cited any precedent indicating that a disparity between a law and its enforcement is a relevant consideration on rational-basis review, which only asks whether the legislature could have reasonably thought that the challenged law would further a legitimate state interest. Thus, to the extent that foster care and guardianship placements with homosexuals are the handiwork of Florida's executive branch, they are irrelevant to the question of the *legislative* rationale for Florida's adoption scheme.[22] To the extent that

---

21. Aside from their own situations, appellants have offered no competent evidence as to the extent of homosexual foster homes and guardianships in Florida. Florida asserts, and appellants do not dispute, that in discovery it was able to locate only one known homosexual foster parent, aside from present parties, in all of Dade and Monroe Counties.

22. For similar reasons, we find inapposite appellants' proffer of the deposition testi-

these placements are the product of an intentional legislative choice to treat foster care and guardianships differently than adoption, the distinction is not an irrational one. Indeed, it bears a rational relationship to Florida's interest in promoting the nuclear-family model of adoption since foster care and guardianship have neither the permanence nor the societal, cultural, and legal significance as does adoptive parenthood, which is the legal equivalent of natural parenthood. Fla. Stat. § 63.032(2).

Foster care and legal guardianship are designed to address a different situation than permanent adoption, and "the legislature must be allowed leeway to approach a perceived problem incrementally." *Beach Communications,* 508 U.S. at 316, 113 S.Ct. at 2102. The fact that "[t]he legislature may select one phase of one field and apply a remedy there, neglecting the others," does not render the legislative solution invalid. *Id.* (citation omitted); *Heller,* 509 U.S. at 321, 113 S.Ct. at 2643 ("The problems of government are practical ones and may justify, if they do not require, rough accommodations—illogical, it may be, and unscientific.") (citation omitted). We conclude that the rationality of the statute is not defeated by the fact that Florida permits homosexual persons to serve as foster parents and legal guardians.

Appellants cite recent social science research and the opinion of mental health professionals and child welfare organizations as evidence that there is no child welfare basis for excluding homosexuals from adopting. They argue that the cited studies show that the parenting skills of homosexual parents are at least equivalent to those of heterosexual parents and that children raised by homosexual parents suffer no adverse outcomes. Appellants also point to the policies and practices of numerous adoption agencies that permit homosexual persons to adopt.

In considering appellants' argument, we must ask not whether the latest in social science research and professional opinion *support* the decision of the Florida legislature, but whether that evidence is so well established and so far beyond dispute that it would be irrational for the Florida legislature to believe that the interests of its children are best served by not permitting homosexual adoption. Also, we must credit any conceivable rational reason that the legislature might have for choosing not to alter its statutory scheme in response to this recent social science research. We must assume, for example, that the legislature might be aware of the critiques of the studies cited by appellants—critiques that have highlighted significant flaws in the studies' methodologies and conclusions, such as the use of small, self-selected samples; reliance on self-report instruments; politically driven hypotheses; and the use of unrepresentative study populations consisting of disproportionately affluent, educated parents. Alternatively, the legislature might consider and credit other studies

mony of DCF personnel acknowledging that they were personally unaware of any harms to children caused by having homosexual parents. Even if these statements of personal opinion can be charged to DCF (whose official position throughout this litigation has been to the contrary), they are irrelevant to the question of whether the Florida *legislature* could have had a rational basis for enacting the statute.

that have found that children raised in homosexual households fare differently on a number of measures, doing worse on some of them, than children raised in similarly situated heterosexual households. Or the legislature might consider, and even credit, the research cited by appellants, but find it premature to rely on a very recent and still developing body of research, particularly in light of the absence of longitudinal studies following child subjects into adulthood and of studies of adopted, rather than natural, children of homosexual parents.

We do not find any of these possible legislative responses to be irrational. Openly homosexual households represent a very recent phenomenon, and sufficient time has not yet passed to permit any scientific study of how children raised in those households fare as adults. Scientific attempts to study homosexual parenting in general are still in their nascent stages and so far have yielded inconclusive and conflicting results. Thus, it is hardly surprising that the question of the effects of homosexual parenting on childhood development is one on which even experts of good faith reasonably disagree. Given this state of affairs, it is not irrational for the Florida legislature to credit one side of the debate over the other. Nor is it irrational for the legislature to proceed with deliberate caution before placing adoptive children in an alternative, but unproven, family structure that has not yet been conclusively demonstrated to be equivalent to the marital family structure that has established a proven track record spanning centuries. Accordingly, we conclude that appellants' proffered social science evidence does not disprove the rational basis of the Florida statute.

Finally, we disagree with appellants' contention that *Romer* requires us to strike down the Florida statute. In *Romer,* the Supreme Court invalidated Amendment 2 to the Colorado state constitution, which prohibited all legislative, executive, or judicial action designed to protect homosexual persons from discrimination. 517 U.S. 620, 624, 116 S.Ct. 1620, 1623, 134 L.Ed.2d 855 (1996). The constitutional defect in Amendment 2 was the disjunction between the "[s]weeping and comprehensive" classification it imposed on homosexuals and the state's asserted bases for the classification—respect for freedom of association and conservation of resources to fight race and gender discrimination. *Id.* at 627, 116 S.Ct. at 1625. The Court concluded that the Amendment's "sheer breadth is so discontinuous with the reasons offered for it that the amendment seems inexplicable by anything but animus toward the class it affects." *Id.* at 632, 116 S.Ct. at 1627.

Unlike Colorado's Amendment 2, Florida's statute is not so "[s]weeping and comprehensive" as to render Florida's rationales for the statute "inexplicable by anything but animus" toward its homosexual residents. Amendment 2 deprived homosexual persons of "protections against exclusion from an almost limitless number of transactions and endeavors that constitute ordinary civic life in a free society." *Id.* at 631, 116 S.Ct. at 1627. In contrast to this "broad and undifferentiated disability," the Florida classification is limited to the narrow and discrete context of access to the statutory privilege of adoption and, more importantly, has a plausible connection with the state's asserted interest. *Id.* at 632, 116 S.Ct. at 1627. Moreover, not only is the effect of Florida's classification dramatically smaller, but the classification itself is narrower. Whereas Amendment 2's classification encompassed both conduct *and* status, *id.* at 624, 116 S.Ct. at 1623 (quoting the text of Amendment 2, which covered "homosexual, lesbian or bisexual orientation, conduct, practices or relationships"), Florida's adoption prohibition is limited to conduct, *see Cox,* 627 So.2d at 1215. Thus, we conclude that *Romer's* unique factual situation and narrow holding are inapposite to this case.

We exercise great caution when asked to take sides in an ongoing public policy debate, such as the current one over the compatibility of homosexual conduct with the duties of adoptive parenthood. *See Reno,* 507 U.S. at 315, 113 S.Ct. at 1454; *Schall v. Martin,* 467 U.S. 253, 281, 104 S.Ct. 2403, 2419, 81 L.Ed.2d 207 (1984). The State of Florida has made the determination that it is not in the best interests of its displaced children to be adopted by individuals who "engage in current, voluntary homosexual activity," *Cox,* 627 So.2d at 1215, and we have found nothing in the Constitution that forbids this policy judgment. Thus, any argument that the Florida legislature was misguided in its decision is one of legislative policy, not constitutional law. The legislature is the proper forum for this debate, and we do not sit as a superlegislature "to award by judicial decree what was not achievable by political consensus." *Thomasson v. Perry,* 80 F.3d 915, 923 (4th Cir.1996).

The judgment of the district court is AFFIRMED.

CALIFORNIA FAMILY CODE (West 2004, Cum. Supp. 2005)

9000. Petition for adoption; caption; contents; guardianship petition; order of adoption

(a) A stepparent desiring to adopt a child of the stepparent's spouse may for that purpose file a petition in the county in which the petitioner resides.

(b) A domestic partner, as defined in Section 297, desiring to adopt a child of his or her domestic partner may for that purpose file a petition in the county in which the petitioner resides.

(c) The caption of the adoption petition shall contain the names of the petitioners, but not the child's name. The petition shall state the child's sex and date of birth and the name the child had before adoption.

(d) If the child is the subject of a guardianship petition, the adoption petition shall so state and shall include the caption and docket number or have attached a copy of the letters of the guardianship or temporary guardianship. The petitioners shall notify the court of any petition for guardianship or temporary guardianship filed after the adoption petition. The guardianship proceeding shall be consolidated with the adoption proceeding.

(e) The order of adoption shall contain the child's adopted name, but not the name the child had before adoption.

(f) If the petitioner has entered into a postadoption contact agreement with the birth parent as set forth in Section 8616.5, the agreement, signed by the participating parties, shall be attached to and filed with the petition for adoption.

(g) For the purposes of this chapter, stepparent adoption includes adoption by a domestic partner, as defined in Section 297.

8. EQUITABLE ADOPTION

Please add the following decision prior to the article by John Jeffries at page 1316:

In re Estate of Ford

California Supreme Court, 2004.
32 Cal.4th 160, 8 Cal.Rptr.3d 541, 82 P.3d 747.

■ WERDEGAR, J.

Terrold Bean claims the right to inherit the intestate estate of Arthur Patrick Ford as Ford's equitably adopted son. The superior court denied the claim, and the Court of Appeal affirmed the denial, for lack of clear and convincing evidence that Ford intended to adopt Bean. After reviewing California case law on equitable adoption, we conclude that no equitable adoption is shown unless the parties' conduct and statements clearly and convincingly demonstrate an intent to adopt. We will therefore affirm the judgment of the Court of Appeal.

Born in 1953, Bean was declared a ward of the court and placed in the home of Ford and his wife, Kathleen Ford, as a foster child in 1955. Bean never knew his natural father, whose identity is uncertain, and he was declared free of his mother's control in 1958, at the age of four. Bean lived continuously with Mr. and Mrs. Ford and their natural daughter, Mary Catherine, for about 18 years, until Mrs. Ford's death in 1973, then with Ford and Mary Catherine for another two years, until 1975.

During part of the time Bean lived with the Fords, they cared for other foster children and received a county stipend for doing so. Although the Fords stopped taking in foster children after Mrs. Ford became ill with cancer, they retained custody of Bean. The last two other foster children left the home around the time of Mrs. Ford's death, but Bean, who at 18 years of age could have left, stayed with Ford and Mary Catherine.

Bean knew the Fords were not his natural parents, but as a child he called them "Mommy" and "Daddy," and later "Mom" and "Dad." Joan Malpassi, Mary Catherine's friend since childhood and later administrator of Ford's estate, testified that Bean's relationship with Mary Catherine was "as two siblings" and that the Fords treated Bean "more like Mary rather than a foster son, like a real son was my observation." Mary Catherine later listed Bean as her brother on a life insurance application.

Bean remained involved with Ford and Mary Catherine even after leaving the Ford home and marrying. Ford loaned Bean money to help furnish his new household and later forgave the unpaid part of the debt when Bean's marriage was dissolved. Bean visited Ford and Mary Catherine several times per year both during his marriage and after his divorce. When Ford suffered a disabling stroke in 1989, Mary Catherine conferred with Bean and Malpassi over Ford's care; Ford was placed in a board and care facility where Bean continued to visit him regularly until his death in 2000.

Mary Catherine died in 1999. Bean and Malpassi arranged her funeral. Bean petitioned for Malpassi to be appointed Ford's conservator, and with Malpassi's agreement Bean obtained a power of attorney to take care of Ford's affairs pending establishment of the conservatorship. Bean also administered Mary Catherine's estate, which was distributed to the Ford conservatorship. When a decision was needed as to whether Ford should receive medical life support, Malpassi consulted with Bean in deciding he should. When Ford died, Bean and Malpassi arranged the funeral.

The Fords never petitioned to adopt Bean. Mrs. Ford told Barbara Carter, a family friend, that "they wanted to adopt Terry," but she was "under the impression that she could not put in for adoption while he was in the home." She worried that if Bean was removed during the adoption process he might be put in "a foster home that wasn't safe."

Ford's nearest relatives at the time of his death were the two children of his predeceased brother, nephew John J. Ford III and niece Veronica Newbeck. Neither had had any contact with Ford for about 15 years before his death, and neither attended his funeral. John J. Ford III filed a petition to determine entitlement to distribution (Prob.Code, § 11700), listing both himself and Newbeck as heirs. Bean filed a statement of interest claiming entitlement to Ford's entire estate under Probate Code sections 6454 (foster child heirship) and 6455 (equitable adoption) as well as sections 6402, subdivision (a) and 6450.

After trial, the superior court ruled against Bean. Probate Code section 6454's requirement of a legal barrier to adoption was unmet, since the Fords could have adopted Bean after his mother's parental rights were terminated in 1958. The doctrine of equitable adoption, the trial court found, was inapplicable because "there is no evidence that [Ford] ever told [Bean] or anyone else that he wanted to adopt him nor publicly told anyone that [Bean] was his adopted son." There was thus no clear and convincing evidence of "an intent to adopt."

Bean appealed only on the equitable adoption issue. The Court of Appeal affirmed, agreeing with the trial court that equitable adoption must be proven by clear and convincing evidence. Moreover, the reviewing court held, any error by the trial court in this respect would be harmless because the evidence did not support equitable adoption on any standard of proof "for the same reasons articulated by the trial court."

We granted Bean's petition for review.

Chapter 2 of part 2 of division 6 of the Probate Code, sections 6450 to 6455, defines the parent-child relationship for purposes of intestate succession. Section 6450, subdivision (b) provides that such a relationship exists between adopting parents and the adopted child. Section 6453, subdivision (a) provides that the relationship exists between a child and a presumptive parent under the Uniform Parentage Act. Section 6454 delineates the circumstances in which a foster parent or stepparent is deemed a parent for the purpose of succession, requiring both a personal relationship beginning during the child's minority and enduring for the child's and parent's joint lifetimes, and a legal barrier but for which the foster parent or stepparent would have adopted the child. (See generally *Estate of Joseph* (1998) 17 Cal.4th 203, 208–212, 70 Cal.Rptr.2d 619, 949 P.2d 472.) Finally, section 6455 provides in full: "Nothing in this chapter affects or limits application of the judicial doctrine of equitable adoption for the benefit of the child or the child's issue." We therefore look to decisional law, rather than statute, for guidance on the equitable adoption doctrine's proper scope and application.

In its essence, the doctrine of equitable adoption allows a person who was accepted and treated as a natural or adopted child, and as to whom adoption typically was promised or contemplated but never performed, to share in inheritance of the foster parents' property. "The parents of a child turn him over to foster parents who agree to care for him as if he were their own child. Perhaps they also agree to adopt him. They do care for him, support him, educate him, and treat him in all respects as if he were their child, but they never adopt him. Upon their death he seeks to inherit their property on the theory that he should be treated as if he had been adopted. Many courts would honor his claim, at least under some circumstances, characterizing the case as one of equitable adoption, or adoption by estoppel, or virtual adoption, or specific enforcement of a contract to adopt." (Clark, The Law of Domestic Relations in the United States (2d ed.1988) § 20.9, p. 925.) The doctrine is widely applied to allow inheritance from the adoptive parent: at least 27 jurisdictions have so applied the doctrine, while only 10 have declined to recognize it in that context. (Annot., Modern Status of Law as to Equitable Adoption or Adoption by Estoppel (1980) 97 A.L.R.3d 347, § 3.)[2]

A California court first recognized the doctrine, albeit in the atypical context of inheritance *through* the adoptive parent, in *Estate of Grace* (1948) 88 Cal.App.2d 956, 200 P.2d 189. A California couple had taken custody of and raised a Texas girl, Edna Grace, having recorded in Texas a statement that they " 'hereby adopt' " the child, who was to be their heir and " 'a member of our family, with all the rights and privileges as if born to us.' " (*Id.* at p. 957, 200 P.2d 189.) Although Texas adoption law at that time did not recognize inheritance from an adoptive grandparent through an adoptive parent (*id.* at pp. 959–960, 200 P.2d 189), the California court upheld Grace's daughter's entitlement to inherit from her adoptive grand-

---

2. In California, at least, adoption itself is "purely statutory in origin and nature." (*Estate of Radovich* (1957) 48 Cal.2d 116, 128, 308 P.2d 14 (dis. opn. of Schauer, J.).) The effect of an equitable adoption finding, therefore, is limited to the child's inheritance rights and does not in other respects equate the child's rights with those of a statutorily adopted child.

parents as a matter of contract.[3] The parents had offered to adopt Grace and make her a full member of their family, and "[t]he child, by living with them as a member of the family, accepted the offer," creating a contract concluded and performed in California. (*Estate of Grace, supra,* at p. 962, 200 P.2d 189.) Quoting from a treatise, the appellate court noted that " 'the courts, in their effort to protect and promote the welfare of the child, have given effect to a contract to adopt, where it has been fully performed on the part of the child, although it was invalid under the laws where it was made.' " (*Id.* at p. 963, 200 P.2d 189).

This court decided its only case relating to equitable adoption nine years later. (*Estate of Radovich, supra,* 48 Cal.2d 116, 308 P.2d 14.) The question before us was not whether the child could inherit as an equitable adoptee—a final superior court decree established that he could—but the child's status, for purposes of inheritance taxation, as either the decedent's adopted child or a stranger in blood to the decedent. (*Id.* at pp. 118–119, 308 P.2d 14.) The majority took the former view, but its opinion rested on the in rem character of the superior court's probate decree and did not address the contours of the equitable adoption doctrine. (*Id.* at pp. 119–124, 308 P.2d 14.)

Justice Schauer's dissenting opinion, however, addressed the equitable adoption doctrine at some length, concluding the child took solely by virtue of an unperformed contract of adoption and thus as a stranger in blood. (*Estate of Radovich, supra,* 48 Cal.2d at pp. 129–135, 308 P.2d 14 (dis. opn. of Schauer, J.).) Citing sister-state authority, Justice Schauer explained: "When the child takes property in such a case it is as a purchaser by virtue of the contract [citation] and by way of damages or specific performance [citations].... The child shares in the estate of the deceased foster parent *as though* his own child but not as such. In order to do justice and equity, as far as possible, to one who, though having filled the place of a natural born child, through inadvertence or fault has not been legally adopted, the court enforces a contract under which the child is entitled to property, declaring that as a consideration on the part of the foster parents a portion of their property will pass on their death to the child." (*Id.* at p. 130, 308 P.2d 14.)

Although expressed in a dissenting opinion, Justice Schauer's explanation of the doctrine has been widely cited and relied upon by the Courts of Appeal. *Estate of Rivolo* (1961) 194 Cal.App.2d 773, 15 Cal.Rptr. 268 presented the issue in the straightforward context of intestate succession from the adoptive parent. The child was an eight-year-old orphan when the foster parents took her in and "told [her] that she would live with them and be their little girl," an arrangement she said pleased her. (*Id.* at p. 775, 15 Cal.Rptr. 268.) The foster parents took the child to the courthouse, where they took out letters of guardianship but told the child she was being

---

3. Much more recently, the Court of Appeal held an equitably adopted child was not "issue" of the adoptive parent as that term was used in a grandparent's will. (*Es-* *tate of Furia* (2002) 103 Cal.App.4th 1, 126 Cal.Rptr.2d 384.) We have no occasion here to decide whether that decision and *Estate of Grace* conflict or which is correct if they do.

adopted. Thereafter they referred to her as their adopted daughter. As a child, the daughter helped them in their business, and even after her marriage they remained "exceedingly close." (*Id.* at p. 776, 15 Cal.Rptr. 268.)

Citing *Estate of Radovich, supra,* 48 Cal.2d 116, 308 P.2d 14, the *Rivolo* court held it "well established that equity will specifically enforce an oral contract to adopt" and found that the record "establishes the existence of a contract of adoption and respondent's part performance thereof by clear, convincing and unequivocal evidence. It is uncontroverted that the respondent was at all times regarded and treated as the adopted daughter of the Rivolos; that they told her and others on numerous occasions that she was legally adopted and would be their sole heir." (*Estate of Rivolo, supra,* 194 Cal.App.2d at p. 777, 15 Cal.Rptr. 268.) "[U]nder the circumstances, equity demands recognition of her lifelong status as an adopted child of Frank Rivolo and her inheritance rights [citations]." (*Id.* at p. 778, 15 Cal.Rptr. 268.)

Estate of Wilson (1980) 111 Cal.App.3d 242, 168 Cal.Rptr. 533 also presented the question of intestate succession from the adoptive parent. The child, born in a home for unwed mothers, was placed with foster parents who petitioned to adopt him. The adoption petition was dismissed, however, because the natural mother's consent could not be obtained; although the court record refers to an "abandonment petition ... to be filed," the foster parents did not pursue that remedy and apparently made no further efforts to adopt. They nonetheless told the child he was adopted and treated him in all respects as their son; their relationship remained warm and familial until the deaths of both parents. (*Id.* at pp. 248–249, 168 Cal.Rptr. 533.) Following both *Estate of Rivolo* and *Estate of Radovich,* the appellate court regarded the issue as one of "the right of an equitably adopted child to inherit by virtue of contract" (*Estate of Wilson, supra,* at p. 247, 168 Cal.Rptr. 533) and found substantial evidence "that, according to the above-noted authority, the Wilsons and Keith had entered into a contract of adoption which was faithfully adhered to by them" (*id.* at p. 249, 168 Cal.Rptr. 533).

In *Estate of Bauer* (1980) 111 Cal.App.3d 554, 168 Cal.Rptr. 743, an inheritance tax case, the court found insufficient evidence of equitable adoption—the child did not live with the asserted parents either as a minor or for any extended time as an adult, and did not assume "any duties normally associated with a parent-child relationship" (*id.* at p. 559, 168 Cal.Rptr. 743)—but aptly summarized the doctrine as it had developed in California: "[E]quitable adoption requires some form of agreement to adopt, coupled with subsequent objective conduct indicating mutual recognition of an adoptive parent and child relationship to such an extent that in equity and good conscience an adoption should be deemed to have taken place." (*Id.* at p. 560, 168 Cal.Rptr. 743.)

In *Mingo v. Heckler* (9th Cir.1984) 745 F.2d 537, the federal court expanded on *Bauer's* agreement-plus-conduct analysis, distilling from the California decisions factors tending to show mutual recognition of a parent and child relationship: "[T]he adoptee lived with the adoptive parent for a number of years; the adoptee assumed the adoptive parent's surname; the adoptive parent told the adoptee that he or she was adopted; the adoptive parent publicly acknowledged the adoptee as his or her child; the adoptee considered and conducted himself or herself as a natural child; the adoptee worked or performed services for the adoptive parent; and the adoptive parent attempted legally to adopt or obtained guardianship papers for the child. Because the factors are merely examples of the type of conduct demonstrating an adoptive parent and child relationship, the claimant need not demonstrate that she satisfies every factor." (*Id.* at p. 539.) The court held that the child, who had lived with her grandmother and the grandmother's cohabitant from infancy, was entitled to Social Security benefits as the cohabitant's equitably adopted child. (*Id.* at pp. 538–540.)

As reflected in this summary, California decisions have explained equitable adoption as the specific enforcement of a contract to adopt. Yet it has long been clear that the doctrine, even in California, rested less on ordinary rules of contract law than on considerations of fairness and intent for, as Justice Schauer put it, the child "should have been" adopted and would have been but for the decedent's "inadvertence or fault." (*Estate of Radovich, supra,* 48 Cal.2d at pp. 134, 130, 308 P.2d 14 (dis. opn. of Schauer, J.), italics omitted.) In the earliest case, *Estate of Grace,* the court quoted a New Mexico case explaining why specific performance was an unrealistic description of equitable adoption: " 'A specific performance of a contract to adopt is impossible after the death of the parties who gave the promise. Equity was driven to the fiction that there had been an adoption. That fiction being indulged, the case was not one of specific performance.' " (*Estate of Grace, supra,* 88 Cal.App.2d at pp. 964–965, 200 P.2d 189, quoting *Wooley v. Shell Petroleum Corporation* (1935) 39 N.M. 256, 45 P.2d 927, 931–932.) In both *Estate of Rivolo, supra,* 194 Cal.App.2d 773, 15 Cal.Rptr. 268, and *Estate of Wilson, supra,* 111 Cal.App.3d 242, 168 Cal.Rptr. 533, moreover, the contracts purportedly being enforced were made between foster parents and their minor charges, yet neither court addressed the children's capacity to contract, suggesting, again, that the contract served mainly as evidence of the parties' intent, rather than as an enforceable legal basis for transmission of property.

Bean urges that equitable adoption be viewed not as specific enforcement of a contract to adopt, but as application of an equitable, restitutionary remedy he has identified as quasi-contract or, as his counsel emphasized at oral argument, as an application of equitable estoppel principles. While we have found no decisions articulating a quasi-contract theory, courts in several states have, instead of or in addition to the contract rationale, analyzed equitable adoption as arising from "a broader and vaguer equitable principle of estoppel." (Clark, The Law of Domestic Relations in the United States, *supra,* at p. 926.) Bean argues Mr. Ford's conduct toward him during their long and close relationship estops Ford's estate or heirs at law from denying his status as an equitably adopted child.

For several reasons, we conclude the California law of equitable adoption, which has rested on contract principles, does not recognize an estoppel arising merely from the existence of a familial relationship between the decedent and the claimant. The law of intestate succession is intended to carry out " 'the intent a decedent without a will is most likely to have had.' " (*Estate of Griswold* (2001) 25 Cal.4th 904, 912, 108 Cal.Rptr.2d 165, 24 P.3d 1191.) The existence of a mutually affectionate relationship, without any direct expression by the decedent of an intent to adopt the child or to have him or her treated as a legally adopted child, sheds little light on the decedent's likely intent regarding distribution of property. While a person with whom the decedent had a close, caring and enduring relationship may often be seen as more deserving of inheritance than the heir or heirs at law, whose personal relationships with the decedent may have been, as they were here, attenuated, equitable adoption in California is neither a means of compensating the child for services rendered to the parent nor a device to avoid the unjust enrichment of other, more distant relatives who will succeed to the estate under the intestacy statutes. Absent proof of an intent to adopt, we must follow the statutory law of intestate succession.

In addition, a rule looking to the parties' overall relationship in order to do equity in a given case, rather than to particular expressions of intent to adopt, would necessarily be a vague and subjective one, inconsistently applied, in an area of law where "consistent, bright-line rules" (*Estate of Furia, supra,* 103 Cal.App.4th at p. 6, 126 Cal.Rptr.2d 384) are greatly needed. Such a broad scope for equitable adoption would leave open to competing claims the estate of *any* foster parent or stepparent who treats a foster child or stepchild lovingly and on an equal basis with his or her natural or legally adopted children. A broad doctrine of equitable adoption would also render section 6454, in practice, a virtual nullity, since children meeting the familial-relationship criteria of that statute would necessarily be equitable adoptees as well.

While a California equitable adoption claimant need not prove all the elements of an enforceable contract to adopt, therefore, we conclude the claimant must demonstrate the existence of some direct expression, on the decedent's part, of an intent to adopt the claimant. This intent may be shown, of course, by proof of an unperformed express agreement or promise to adopt. But it may also be demonstrated by proof of other acts or statements directly showing that the decedent intended the child to be, or to be treated as, a legally adopted child, such as an invalid or unconsummated attempt to adopt, the decedent's statement of his or her intent to adopt the child, or the decedent's representation to the claimant or to the community at large that the claimant was the decedent's natural or legally adopted child. (See, e.g., *Estate of Rivolo, supra,* 194 Cal.App.2d at p. 775, 15 Cal.Rptr. 268 [parents who orally promised child she would "be their little girl" later told her and others they had adopted her]; *Estate of Wilson, supra,* 111 Cal.App.3d at p. 248, 168 Cal.Rptr. 533 [petition to adopt filed but dismissed for lack of natural mother's consent]; *Estate of Reid* (1978)

80 Cal.App.3d 185, 188, 145 Cal.Rptr. 451 [written agreement with adult child].)

Thus, in California the doctrine of equitable adoption is a relatively narrow one, applying only to those who " 'though having filled the place of a natural born child, through inadvertence or fault [have] not been legally adopted,' [where] *the evidence establishes an intent to adopt.*" (*Estate of Furia, supra,* 103 Cal.App.4th at p. 5, 126 Cal.Rptr.2d 384, italics added.) In addition to a statement or act by the decedent unequivocally evincing the decedent's intent to adopt, the claimant must show the decedent acted consistently with that intent by forming with the claimant a close and enduring familial relationship.[6] That is, in addition to a contract or other direct evidence of the intent to adopt, the evidence must show "objective conduct indicating mutual recognition of an adoptive parent and child relationship to such an extent that in equity and good conscience an adoption should be deemed to have taken place." (*Estate of Bauer, supra,* 111 Cal.App.3d at p. 560, 168 Cal.Rptr. 743.)

Bean also contends the lower courts erred in applying a standard of clear and convincing proof to the equitable adoption question. We disagree. Most courts that have considered the question require at least clear and convincing evidence in order to prove an equitable adoption. (See Clark, The Law of Domestic Relations in the United States, *supra,* at p. 927; Rein, *supra,* 37 Vand. L.Rev. at p. 780.) Several good reasons support the rule.

First, the claimant in an equitable adoption case is seeking inheritance outside the ordinary statutory course of intestate succession and without the formalities required by the adoption statutes. As the claim's "strength lies in inherent justice" (*Wooley v. Shell Petroleum Corporation, supra,* 45 P.2d at p. 932), the need in justice for this "extraordinary equitable intervention" (Rein, *supra,* 37 Vand. L.Rev. at p. 785) should appear clearly and unequivocally from the facts.

Second, the claim involves a relationship with persons who have died and who can, therefore, no longer testify to their intent. As with an alleged contract to make a will (see *Crail v. Blakely* (1973) 8 Cal.3d 744, 750, fn. 3, 106 Cal.Rptr. 187, 505 P.2d 1027), the law, in order to guard against fraudulent claims, should require more than a bare preponderance of evidence. Where "the lips of the alleged adopter have been sealed by death ... proof of the facts essential to invoke the intervention of equity should be clear, unequivocal and convincing." (*Cavanaugh v. Davis* (1951) 149 Tex. 573, 235 S.W.2d 972, 978.)

Finally, too relaxed a standard could create the danger that "a person could not help out a needy child without having a de facto adoption foisted upon him after death." (Rein, *supra,* 37 Vand. L.Rev. at p. 782.) As pointed out in an early Missouri decision, if the evidentiary burden is lowered too far, "then couples, childless or not, will be reluctant to take into their

---

6. A close familial relationship sufficient to support the decedent's intent to adopt must persist up to, or at least not be repudiated by the decedent before, the decedent's death.

homes orphan children, and for the welfare of such children, as well as for other reasons, the rule should be kept and observed. No one, after he or she has passed on, should be adjudged to have adopted a child unless the evidence is clear, cogent, and convincing. . . ." (*Benjamin v. Cronan* (1936) 338 Mo. 1177, 93 S.W.2d 975, 981.)

Evidence Code section 115 provides that the burden of proof in civil cases is a preponderance of the evidence "[e]xcept as otherwise provided by law." The law providing for a higher standard of proof may include decisional law. (*Weiner v. Fleischman* (1991) 54 Cal.3d 476, 483, 286 Cal.Rptr. 40, 816 P.2d 892.) Persuaded by the reasoning of sister-state decisions and commentary, we hold that in order to take as an equitably adopted child from the alleged adoptive parent's intestate estate, the claimant must prove the decedent's intent to adopt by clear and convincing evidence.

Although the evidence showed the Fords and Bean enjoyed a close and enduring familial relationship, evidence was totally lacking that the Fords ever made an attempt to adopt Bean or promised or stated their intent to do so; they neither held Bean out to the world as their natural or adopted child (Bean, for example, did not take the Ford name) nor represented to Bean that he was their child. Mrs. Ford's single statement to Barbara Carter was not clear and convincing evidence that Mr. Ford intended Bean to be, or be treated as, his adopted son. Substantial evidence thus supported the trial court, which heard the testimony live and could best assess its credibility and strength, in its finding that intent to adopt, and therefore Bean's claim of equitable adoption, was unproven. The judgment of the Court of Appeal is affirmed.

■ WE CONCUR: GEORGE, C.J., KENNARD, BAXTER, CHIN, BROWN, and MORENO, JJ.

9.   THE QUEST FOR BIOLOGICAL IDENTITY

Replace the existing case at page 1320 with the following:

In re Adoption of S.J.D.

Supreme Court of Iowa, 2002.
641 N.W.2d 794.

■ LAVORATO, CHIEF JUSTICE.

Steven J. Drahozal appeals from a district court ruling denying his request to unseal his adoption records so that he can learn the identity of his biological parents. He contends he has established the statutory requirement of good cause to unseal such records. He also contends that our statutory provisions requiring sealing of adoption records violate his right to free speech under the Federal and Iowa Constitutions. Because we conclude Steven has failed to establish such good cause and that the challenged statutes do not violate his right to free speech, we affirm.

Steven was born in Iowa City on June 27, 1971. John and Sharon Drahozal took custody of Steven on July 2, 1971, and the Drahozals' legal adoption of Steven was finalized in August 1972.

In February 2000, Steven filed a petition to unseal records pertaining to his adoption. *See* Iowa Code § 600.16A(2)(b) (1999). He alleged that good cause existed to open the records and that denial of his access to the records would violate his constitutional rights to privacy and equal protection. He also filed an "affidavit consenting to release of identifying information." *See* Iowa Code § 600.16A(3)(b). No adverse party responded to the petition.

In March, Steven filed an amended petition, adding an allegation that denial of his access to the records would violate his right to free speech. He also filed a "request for judicial notice of adjudicative facts," asking the court to take judicial notice of several treatises written by adoption experts. He submitted excerpts from these treatises following a hearing later in March.

Steven, his wife, Allison, and his adoptive parents testified at the hearing. His adoptive parents testified they were not opposed to Steven's search for his biological parents. Steven testified he wanted to obtain information from his adoption records and find his biological parents. His reasons for wanting to find them were to (1) satisfy his curiosity, that is, to see if someone else looks like him, or if he has siblings; (2) thank them for what they did; and (3) obtain medical information.

Steven's desire to obtain medical information stems from his own mental condition. At age 15, Steven was hospitalized because of a severe depression. He suffers from manic depression and takes Prozac to treat the illness. Steven testified he wanted to know if the manic depression is hereditary, and if so, to find out whether his biological family may be undergoing more effective treatment than what he receives. He admitted, however, that the treatment he presently receives is effective. Additionally, Steven expressed concerns about the health of his two biological children from a previous marriage.

Steven has obtained some information about his biological parents from the adoption agency that handled the adoption. For example, he learned (1) his biological maternal grandfather suffered from diabetes; (2) his biological parents' height, weight, and age at the time of Steven's birth; and (3) his ethnic heritage—German and Irish.

Following the hearing, the district court denied Steven's request, and Steven appealed.

Steven raises two issues on appeal. He challenges the district court's interpretation of the applicable statute. Specifically, he contends the district court erred when it ruled that the failure of Steven's biological parents to file a waiver of confidentiality pursuant to Iowa Code section 600.16A(2)(b)(1) is dispositive of good cause.

Steven also contends that denial of his request to unseal his adoption records violates his right to free speech. He contends that the freedom of speech guaranteed under the Federal Constitution and Iowa Constitution encompasses the right to receive information, including private information such as adoption records.

To the extent Steven raises questions of statutory interpretation, our review is for correction of errors at law. *State v. Ceron,* 573 N.W.2d 587, 589 (Iowa 1997). Because this is an adoption-related equitable proceeding, our review of the factual issues is de novo. *In re Adoption of Moriarty,* 260 Iowa 1279, 1285, 152 N.W.2d 218, 221 (1967).

We review constitutional issues de novo. *State v. Simpson,* 587 N.W.2d 770, 771 (Iowa 1998). Because statutes are cloaked with a strong presumption of constitutionality, a party challenging a statute as unconstitutional carries a heavy burden of rebutting this presumption. *In re Morrow,* 616 N.W.2d 544, 547 (Iowa 2000). In this regard, the challenger must negate every reasonable basis upon which the statute could be upheld as constitutional. *Id.* The challenger must also show beyond a reasonable doubt that a statute violates the constitution. *Johnston v. Veterans' Plaza Auth.,* 535 N.W.2d 131, 132 (Iowa 1995). If a statute is susceptible to more than one construction, one of which is constitutional and the other not, we are obliged to adopt the construction which will uphold it. *Santi v. Santi,* 633 N.W.2d 312, 316 (Iowa 2001).

Iowa Code section 600.16A(2)(b) provides in relevant part:

> All papers and records pertaining to ... an adoption shall not be open to inspection and the identity of the biological parents of an adopted person shall not be revealed except ... [t]he court, *for good cause,* shall order the opening of the permanent adoption record of the court for the adopted person who is an adult and reveal the names of either or both of the biological parents *following consideration of ... the following:*
>
> (1) A biological parent *may* file an affidavit requesting that the court reveal or not reveal the parent's identity. *The court shall consider any such affidavit in determining whether there is good cause to order opening of the records....*

Iowa Code § 600.16A(2)(b) (emphasis added).

In its ruling, the district court explained that it could open sealed adoption records

> upon showing that good cause exists, and both the adult adoptee and the terminated biological parents have indicated by affidavit that they desire to have the records opened. [Iowa Code] § 600.16A(2)(b)(1).

The court concluded that because the biological parents had not filed such an affidavit, the court had no authority to open the records under section 600.16A(2)(b)(1).

Additionally, the court concluded that Steven had not presented competent medical evidence to show the information was necessary to save the life of, or prevent irreparable physical or mental harm to, the adoptee or the adoptee's offspring. *See* Iowa Code § 600.16A(2)(d) (providing that the court "may, upon competent medical evidence, open termination or adoption records if opening is shown to be necessary to save the life of or prevent irreparable physical or mental harm to an adopted person or the person's offspring"). Even with this showing, the court noted that it would still be required to "make every reasonable effort to prevent" the revelation of identifying information to the adoptee. *See id.* (providing that even with the showing necessary to open the records, the court "shall make every reasonable effort to prevent the identity of the biological parents from becoming revealed under this paragraph to the adopted person").

Steven contends the district court erred in concluding that the failure of the biological parents to file an affidavit waiving confidentiality is dispositive of "good cause." We disagree with Steven's characterization of the district court's ruling, but we agree that the court erred in its interpretation of the statute.

The court did not rule that the failure of the biological parents to file a waiver of confidentiality was dispositive of good cause. Rather, the court ruled that the adult adoptee must show (1) good cause exists *and* (2) the adult adoptee and the biological parents have filed an affidavit waiving confidentiality. Nevertheless, this interpretation of the statute is erroneous.

The statute does not *require* a biological parent to file an affidavit requesting that the court reveal or not reveal the parent's identity. Rather, the statute states that a biological parent "may" file such an affidavit. Iowa Code § 600.16A(2)(b)(1). By using the word "may," the legislature signaled its intention to place the decision about whether to file an affidavit to reveal or not reveal the biological parent's identity squarely in the discretion of that parent. *Compare* Iowa Code § 4.1(30)(c) ("may" confers a power), *with id.* § 4.1(30)(a) ("shall" imposes a duty), *and id.* § 4.1(30)(b) ("must" states a requirement).

In addition, the statute directs the court to "consider" an affidavit filed by the biological parents in determining whether good cause exists to unseal the adoption records. Iowa Code § 600.16A(2)(b)(1); *see Webster's Third New International Dictionary* 483 (1993) (defining "consider" as "to reflect on; think about with a degree of care or caution"). While the existence of an affidavit might influence the district court's decision in one way or another, that fact should only be one part of the "good cause" determination, *not* a separate requirement, as the district court suggested. A determination of "good cause" should not rest on the existence of an affidavit filed by the biological parents. That brings us to two questions we must answer: what constitutes "good cause" to unseal adoption records, and whether Steven has shown the requisite "good cause."

V. Good Cause

A. Background. Our statute is silent on what constitutes "good cause" to unseal adoption records. We think some background would be helpful in understanding the concept of "good cause" in the context of unsealing adoption records.

Because English common law did not recognize the practice of adoption, adoption in this country is purely statutory. Jason Kuhns, Note, *The Sealed Adoption Records Controversy: Breaking Down the Walls of Secrecy,* 24 Golden Gate U.L.Rev. 259, 260 (Spring 1994) [hereinafter Kuhns]. In 1851, the Massachusetts Legislature passed the first general adoption law. *Id.* The early adoption statutes did not bar access to adoption records. *Id.* at 260–61.

A 1916 New York statute was among the first statutes to bar access to adoption records. *Id.* at 261. However, only the public—not the actual parties to the adoption—were barred from access to such records. *Id.*

The following year, Minnesota became the first state to enact a law closing adoption files from inspection by adult adoptees, their birth parents, and the general public. *Id.* By the end of the 1940s, most states had similar statutes. *Id.* Most provided that sealed adoption records could be opened only by court order. Melissa Arndt, Comment, *Severed Roots: The Sealed Adoption Records Controversy,* 6 N. Ill. U.L.Rev. 103, 105 (Winter 1986).

Iowa adopted a similar statute in 1941. 1941 Iowa Acts ch. 294, § 1 (codified at Iowa Code § 600.9 (1946)). It provided:

The complete record in adoption proceedings, after filing with the clerk of the court, shall be sealed by said clerk, and the record shall not thereafter be opened except on order of the court.

Iowa Code § 600.9 (1946).

Confidentiality has been and continues to be the touchstone for these adoption statutes. As one court noted,

[t]his confidentiality serves several purposes. It shields the adopted child from possibly disturbing facts surrounding his or her birth and parentage, it permits the adoptive parents to develop a close relationship with the child free from interference or distraction, and it provides the natural parents with an anonymity that they may consider vital. The State's interest in fostering an orderly and supervised system of adoptions is closely tied to these interests of the parties involved.

Linda F.M. v. Dep't of Health, 52 N.Y.2d 236, 437 N.Y.S.2d 283, 418 N.E.2d 1302, 1303 (1981) (citations omitted).

In the 1970s, in response to challenges from adoptees to the practice of sealing adoption records, states began to amend their adoption laws allowing adoptees access to their adoption records if they could show "special circumstances" or "good cause." Brett S. Silverman, *The Winds of Change in Adoption Laws: Should Adoptees Have Access to Adoption Records?,* 39 Fam. & Conciliation Courts Rev. 85, 85 (Jan.2001).

B. Purpose underlying the good cause exception. The "good cause" provision has been described as "an escape valve from the generally impenetrable nature of adoption records [that] permits individual judicial treatment where circumstances and justice so require." *Application of Hayden,* 106 Misc.2d 849, 435 N.Y.S.2d 541, 542 (N.Y.Sup.Ct.1981). The legislature has determined that this escape valve is to be used in "situations where the stringent confidentiality requirements may lead to harmful and untenuous results in a particular case." *Id.*

1. The adoptee's burden and the court's function. To establish good cause, the adoptee must show a compelling need for the identifying information. *Bradey v. Children's Bureau of South Carolina,* 275 S.C. 622, 274 S.E.2d 418, 421 (1981). And what constitutes a compelling need depends upon the circumstances of each case. *Id.*

The court's function regarding "good cause" is to determine whether such cause exists and the extent of disclosure that is appropriate based on the facts of each case. *Linda F.M.,* 437 N.Y.S.2d 283, 418 N.E.2d at 1304.

2. What courts have said constitutes good cause and does not constitute good cause. Good cause in the context of a request to unseal adoption records rests "upon an appropriate showing of psychological trauma or medical need." *Hayden,* 435 N.Y.S.2d at 542 (petitioner's allegation that her fear she may be a "DES Baby," which caused strain in her psychological makeup and concern for her medical well-being, justified a full hearing on the merits of her petition to unseal adoption records); *see also Juman v. Louise Wise Servs.,* 159 Misc.2d 314, 608 N.Y.S.2d 612, 617–18 (N.Y.Sup.Ct.1994) (holding that adopted child's schizophrenia was good cause for disclosure of information about the child's biological parents "that goes beyond the scope of medical histories"). Such cause, however, must rest on more than mere curiosity. *Linda F.M.,* 437 N.Y.S.2d 283, 418 N.E.2d at 1304.

Given the high burden the good cause requirement places on an adoptee, it is not surprising that an adoptee's attempt to secure identifying information has failed in a number of cases. *See, e.g., Aimone v. Finley,* 113 Ill.App.3d 507, 69 Ill.Dec. 433, 447 N.E.2d 868, 870 (1983) (expectation of possibility that an adopted person may inherit from her natural parents is not sufficient cause to open sealed adoption files); *In re Adoption of Baby S.,* 308 N.J.Super. 207, 705 A.2d 822, 823, 825 (1997) (natural mother who wanted to identify and locate the child she gave up for adoption, speak to him, tell him she is his biological mother, and perhaps leave her estate to him in her will, failed to show good cause for unsealing of records); *Backes v. Catholic Family & Cmty. Servs.,* 210 N.J.Super. 186, 509 A.2d 283, 293 (1985) (adult adoptee with "no psychological problem of a pathological nature," and who did not need additional medical information for the treatment of his child failed to show "good cause" required for unsealing adoption records); *Application of Romano,* 109 Misc.2d 99, 438 N.Y.S.2d 967, 971 (1981) (failure to show "good cause" where petition contained no affidavit to attest to the validity of adoptee's claim of psychological need to learn "where his 'natural roots' lie with respect to race, nationality, religion, culture and heredity").

C. Analysis. Earlier we mentioned the interests that confidentiality in adoption statues are meant to serve. These interests include those of the adoptee, whether a minor or adult, the adopting parents, the biological parents, and the state. We think section 600.16A is the legislature's attempt to balance those interests. The balance has been struck heavily in favor of keeping adoption records sealed.

Yet, in two instances, the legislature has left open a window of opportunity for unsealing adoption records. One instance involves the good cause exception. However, we think the bar is high as far as proving this exception. Proof of this appears in Iowa Code section 600.16A(2)(d), which pertinently provides:

> The juvenile court or court may, upon competent medical evidence, open termination or adoption records if opening is shown to be necessary to save the life of or prevent irreparable physical or mental harm to an adopted person or the person's offspring. The juvenile court or court shall make every reasonable effort to prevent the identity of the biological parents from becoming revealed under this paragraph to the adopted person. The juvenile court may, however, permit revelation of the identity of the biological parents to medical personnel attending the adopted person or the person's offspring. These medical personnel shall make every reasonable effort to prevent the identity of the biological parents from becoming revealed to the adopted person.

Iowa Code § 600.16A(2)(d). Thus, the court may order the adoption record unsealed only if competent medical evidence shows such action is necessary to save the life of or prevent irreparable physical or mental harm to an adopted person or the person's offspring. Additionally, even if medical need dictates opening the records, the legislature has taken pains to insure as reasonably as possible that *identifying* information will not be revealed in the process.

Finally, to underscore how important the legislature believes it is to preserve the privacy of the biological parents and prevent revelation of their identities, the legislature has made it a criminal offense to reveal such information contrary to the terms of the statute. *See* Iowa Code § 600.16A(5) ("Any person, other than the adopting parents or the adopted person, who discloses information in violation of this section, is guilty of a simple misdemeanor.").

The other instance in which the legislature has allowed inroads into the confidentiality of adoption records is found in Iowa Code section 600.16A(3). That provision provides for revealing identifying information regarding biological parents and *adult* adopted children if both the adult adopted child and a biological parent have placed in the adoption record written consent to reveal their identities. Either party, however, may withdraw that consent at any time by placing a written withdrawal of consent in the adoption record. *See* Iowa Code § 600.16A(3).

Under our statute, we think good cause to invade the privacy of biological parents by revealing their identities without their consent should include no less than a showing of a medical need to save the life of or prevent irreparable physical or mental harm to an adult adopted person requesting the identifying information. This showing should be made upon competent medical evidence. This of course is the same standard found in section 600.16A(2)(d), earlier mentioned, and comports with the standard for good cause adopted by most courts. We see no reason why the standard for good cause should be any less onerous than the section 600.16A(2)(d) standard when a biological parent has not consented to a revelation of his or her identity.

As mentioned, section 600.16A(2)(b)(1) allows the court to consider a biological parent's consent to reveal his or her identity in determining good cause. However, because the facts here do not show that either biological parent has filed an affidavit requesting that the court reveal their identities, we make no determination regarding how that additional factor should affect a good cause showing.

Steven has argued forcibly that scholars and authorities in the area of adoption now view the process of adoption in a light different from what the view was when the present statute was enacted. While some may agree that "changed attitudes may warrant a new look at the purpose and effect of this law by the legislature," it is not our function "to redraft or to interpret laws differently" from what the legislature intended "solely to reflect current values or lifestyles." *Hayden,* 435 N.Y.S.2d at 542. We agree with the court in *Hayden* that "[i]t is best left to the legislature to distinguish the changing mores from shifting moods in society." *Id.*

The record before us falls far short of meeting the high standard we feel the legislature has set for a showing of good cause to reveal the identifying information Steven seeks. He testified that he wants to find his biological parents to (1) satisfy his curiosity, (2) thank them for what they did, and (3) obtain medical information. Steven's wife testified that he became more restless when he started to get involved in his research and questioning about his biological family. Clearly, Steven's "curiosity" and "restlessness" are not a sufficient showing of good cause.

The record does reflect that Steven has been treated for a mental illness, manic depression. However, he presented no medical evidence to link the disorder to his status as an adopted child. It also appears from the record that the disorder, while it may be hereditary, has no other relation to his status as an adoptee. Moreover, he expressed more of a curiosity over whether the condition is hereditary than any particular medical reason for wanting to know. Finally, the record is clear that Steven has been able to function in society, in spite of his mental condition and in spite of his stated "curiosity" and "distraction" over finding his biological parents. He has graduated from law school, and apparently fulfills his duties as a husband and father without significant problems.

In short, Steven has failed to show a compelling need for the identifying information. His proof falls far short of establishing by competent medical evidence that he needs the identifying information to save his life or to prevent irreparable physical or mental harm to himself—the minimum showing necessary to meet the high standard set by the legislature for the good cause requirement.

That brings us to the last issue Steven raises: whether the statute violates what he claims is his constitutional right to receive information, including private information such as adoption records.

Steven contends that denying him—an adult adoptee—the right to see his adoption records violates his freedom of speech under the First Amendment of the Federal Constitution and article I, section 7 of the Iowa Constitution. In support of his contention, he argues that freedom of speech under these constitutional provisions encompass the right to receive information, including private information such as adoption records.

The First Amendment of the Federal Constitution prohibits Congress from making any law abridging free speech. This prohibition applies to the states through the Fourteenth Amendment. *Cantwell v. Connecticut*, 310 U.S. 296, 303, 60 S.Ct. 900, 903, 84 L.Ed. 1213, 1217–18 (1940). The Iowa Constitution also protects free speech and imposes the "same restrictions on the regulation of speech as does the Federal Constitution." *State v. Milner*, 571 N.W.2d 7, 12 (Iowa 1997).

To date "[n]o federal or state court has accepted" this constitutional challenge. Kuhns, 24 Golden Gate U.L. Rev at 268. As Kuhns explains,

> [a]lthough recognizing that adoptees have a general right to privacy and to receive information, the courts have rejected the argument that adoptees have a fundamental right to learn the identities of their biological parents. The courts maintain that no constitutional or personal right is unconditional and absolute to the exclusion of the rights of all other individuals. The right to privacy and to information asserted by adoptees directly conflicts with the right to privacy of birth parents to be left alone. Due to these conflicting interests, the sealed records statutes are upheld because they bear a rational relationship to the permissible state objective of protecting the integrity of the adoption process. Although the adoptee may no longer need the state's protection upon reaching adulthood, courts state that the birth parents' interest in confidentiality may actually become stronger.

Id. at 268–69 (footnotes omitted); *accord In re Roger B.*, 84 Ill.2d 323, 49 Ill.Dec. 731, 418 N.E.2d 751, 757 (1981); *Mills v. Atlantic City Dep't of Vital Statistics*, 148 N.J.Super. 302, 372 A.2d 646, 650–52 (1977). We agree with this analysis and adopt it. We conclude therefore that Steven has not established beyond a reasonable doubt that our statutory provisions regarding sealing of adoption records violate free speech under the Federal or Iowa Constitutions.

Although the district court erred in its interpretation of Iowa Code section 600.16A(2)(b)(1), we conclude the court did not err in denying Steven's request to unseal his adoption records. We conclude based on the record before us that Steven has failed to show good cause to unseal these records. Additionally, we reject his claim that our adoption statutes requiring sealing of adoption records violate his freedom of speech under either the Federal or Iowa Constitutions. For these reasons, we affirm.

†